Britain, Europe and the World 1871–1971

Second Edition

David Arnold
SENIOR HISTORY MASTER, STOWE SCHOOL

Edward Arnold

© **David Arnold** 1973

First published 1966
by Edward Arnold (Publishers) Ltd.,
25 Hill Street,
London W1X 8LL

Reprinted 1967, 1969, 1970, 1971
Second Edition 1973

ISBN: 0 7131 1776 1

Cover photographs by:
Camera Press
Radio Times Hulton Picture Library

Printed in Great Britain by
Richard Clay (The Chaucer Press), Ltd, Bungay, Suffolk

Preface

This book is intended as a practical manual of instruction – a simple introduction to something complicated.

The first edition, which appeared in 1966, broke away from the convention of writing history as a continuous narrative. Whereas a book on British History, for example, might have only one chapter on the years between the wars, combining all aspects of the history of those years, I preferred to write a large number of separate chapters, an average of five pages long, each explaining one topic. In that edition, which covered 1870–1955, there were seventy-five such chapters. In this, which deals with 1871–1971, there are ninety, and each one may be read in isolation. But they are grouped together in ten sections, one on 'The East' for example, and another on 'International Affairs, 1918–1945', so that the book forms a coherent whole.

The decision to include British, European, and World History all in one volume seemed justified on two grounds: it helped to show how they were connected, and it was convenient to have them all in one book for anyone studying one of the 'O' level syllabuses which demand both British History and also either European or World History. The 'O' level candidate was, of course, particularly in mind while writing this book. But the first edition has also been used successfully by both CSE and 'A' level candidates. This is because it is possible to regard it as a guide book with two functions: first to provide an introduction to a problem or topic, and second, to help the reader find his way around the period and order his thoughts on why things happened the way they did.

The maps and diagrams are deliberately simple and illustrate specific points made in the text. The appendices provide information to which the reader is likely to want easy access. There are cross-references when something mentioned at one point is dealt with more fully elsewhere. And as well as a General Index there is an Index of Persons which includes brief biographical notes.

It remains only to thank my wife, who again typed the manuscript, and to whom I owe for that and much besides an incalculable debt of gratitude.

D. J. A.

Stowe, 1973.

iii

Contents

List of Maps

List of Diagrams

Section I   The Old World

1   THE WORLD IN 1871

IN 1871 Europe was the centre of the world. Its climate and its natural resources had over the centuries made possible technical developments far in advance of the rest of the world. The climate was harsh enough to stimulate men to adapt natural resources to their own purposes, and mild enough for survival to be possible. The natural resources were remarkably rich, and by 1871, four or five hundred years after the European peoples made contact with other parts of the world, it seemed as if they might soon control the whole world. But just as the Europeans acquired the technical skill and industrial power to subjugate the rest of the world they turned their skills and their power against each other. The people of other parts of the world gained the opportunity to throw off or avoid European control because Europe weakened itself by plunging into the protracted civil war of 1914–45.

The nature of Europe

Geographically there is no obvious justification for giving the Western end of the Asian land-mass the name of Europe, and Europe has never been united politically. Indeed, until the upheaval of the French Revolution and the Napoleonic Wars it was divided into hundreds of independent and semi-independent states. Such unity as Europe had derived from the consciousness of a common cultural inheritance, a common history, and a common religion. And even in this very general way Europe had for centuries been divided into three broad linguistic, cultural, and religious groups: the Germanic Protestant North, the Latin Roman Catholic South, and the Slav Orthodox East.

By 1871, however, the divisions which increasingly mattered in Europe were neither these broad cultural divisions nor necessarily the established political divisions, but rather the divisions based on a consciousness of nationality—a consciousness of belonging to a racial, linguistic, or historical group which felt itself to be a nation, and either was, or intended to become, a separate united independent state.

Nationalism was not a new force in Europe. It was the natural outcome of the difficulties of communications and administration which had resulted in the overthrow of the international Roman

Empire and had caused Europe to develop as a collection of small
independent states. Throughout the Middle Ages Nationalism
can be seen asserting itself against the claims of international
Christianity. And by the nineteenth century Nationalism had
become a powerful emotional force, with Europeans more and
more conscious of their differences rather than their similarities,
and European history had become the story of nations jealous
of each other's power, developing separately, carefully maintaining
their independence, but combining temporarily and fighting to
prevent each other from getting too powerful.

The European Nations

Eastern Europe had long been dominated by two large, inefficient, centralised, and autocratically ruled Empires. To the
North was Russia, stretching away into Asia, and further South
the crumbling Ottoman Empire of the Turks reached into three
continents.

In Central Europe were two more great Empires. In the South-
East the Hapsburg territories were now known as the Dual
Monarchy of Austria–Hungary. And in the North a new German
Empire had just been formed in January 1871 in the fit of Nationa-
list fervour stimulated among Germans by their victory over
France in the Franco–Prussian War of 1870–71. In both of these
Empires a parliamentary constitution gave a broader base to
government than in Russia or the Ottoman Empire, but in both
rule was through ministers responsible to the monarch—not to
parliament.

The political structure of Western Europe was far more complicated than that of Central and Eastern Europe. But most
West European states were monarchies with parliamentary constitutions based on a limited franchise. The two great powers
among them were Great Britain, a parliamentary monarchy in
which real power lay with the aristocracy and the middle class,
and France, which had had a succession of different constitutions
during the past century, and where a constituent assembly was
now drawing up a republican constitution for a Third Republic.

Industrialisation and Liberalism

In 1870 the difference between the system of government pre-
valent in Eastern Europe and that which was becoming increasingly
usual in the West was clear. In the East, and to a lesser extent the
South, where a peasant economy persisted, political power remained in the hands of the landed aristocracy. But in the North-

West, where society was being transformed by industrialisation, the old traditional political systems were giving place to parliamentary democracy.

Many factors influence a country's constitutional development, but economic factors are always important, and in the Europe of the 1870s a close connection can be seen between industrial and constitutional development. Russia, which was producing less than a million tons of coal a year, was still ruled by an autocratic system. Germany, which was producing nearly thirty million tons of coal a year, had weak representative institutions. Britain, which was producing well over a hundred million tons of coal a year, had a parliamentary system which gave very considerable power to the elected representatives of the middle class.

What was happening in North-West Europe was that industrialisation was producing a large middle class, owning factories and machinery, employing labour, and demanding political power to match its economic power. This class appealed to the political philosophy of Liberalism to justify its demands, and industrialisation produced not only parliamentary constitutions based on a middle-class franchise but also Liberal governments committed to removing restrictions to industrial development.

Another effect of industrialisation was to make those countries which became heavily industrialised less self-sufficient, for they could only get the raw materials and food they needed by selling manufactured goods, and thus they depended on international trade. The Liberal therefore advocated international Free Trade, which would stimulate more trade and more industrialisation and make the peoples of the world increasingly interdependent. And he would welcome this interdependence, for he saw it as a means of extending and increasing the benefits which would come from trade. Thus the natural tendency of Liberalism was to break down national barriers and produce an international society united by a common interest in expanding industrial output.

Liberalism, Nationalism, and Socialism

The ultimately internationalist nature of Liberalism brought it into conflict with Nationalism, for the Nationalist was concerned not with the progress of the whole human race, which the Liberal believed would be furthered by Free Trade, but rather with strengthening his own country. The Nationalist, in order to allow his own country's industry to develop without foreign competition, would impose duties on goods from other countries and so restrict the free flow of trade. Thus industrialisation was helping to harden national divisions at the same time as it made nations more dependent on each other.

In the conflict with Nationalism Liberalism inevitably lost, for Nationalism was a far more powerful emotional force, and by the 1880s Liberalism was already on the decline in Western Europe. On the one hand it was giving way before a revival of conservative authoritarianism—now in alliance with Nationalism. On the other hand it was being superseded by Socialism.

Socialism, like Liberalism, was a product of industrialisation, for industrialisation produced not only a Liberal middle class but also a town-dwelling working class which eventually sought both economic and political power and appealed to Socialism to justify its demands. Socialism was far more obviously internationalist than Liberalism, for it involved the idea that class was more important than nationality and that wage-earners of all nationalities should unite against all capitalists. And fear of international Socialism did even more than distrust of Liberalism to stimulate a return to conservative authoritarianism and Nationalism towards the end of the nineteenth century.

The spread of European influence

Europe was developing into an industrial society. This led to a search for raw materials, food, and markets. And this in turn brought Europeans increasingly into contact with the rest of the world. By 1871 European influence was already widespread. Europeans had settled in North and South America and in Australia and New Zealand, and although they were only established in Africa in the extreme North and South and at the outlets of rivers they were soon going to divide almost the whole continent between them. They controlled much of Asia, and their technical achievements were even enabling them to force the ancient civilisations of China and Japan to open their doors to European trade.

The areas of independence

There were very few areas of the world which never came under European control before the second World War. The Turks always retained their independence, though they lost most of their Empire to the Europeans, and the only part which had not come under European control by 1919 was the desert area of central Arabia and the independent sheikdom of the Yemen. Persia was always technically independent despite the Anglo-Russian *entente* of 1907 (p. 83). Afghanistan kept its independence as a buffer state between Russia and Britain's Indian Empire, and Siam kept its independence as a buffer state between French Indo-China and the Indian Empire. Liberia, which had been founded by Americans in the nineteenth century as a home for freed slaves, was the only African state never to come under European control. China was saved from partition by the quarrels of the Europeans among themselves. And although the Russians penetrated Manchuria early in the twentieth century, they were kept out of Korea by the Japanese, who also drove them from Manchuria. The Japanese themselves countered the threat of colonisation from Europe by efficient imitation of European techniques.

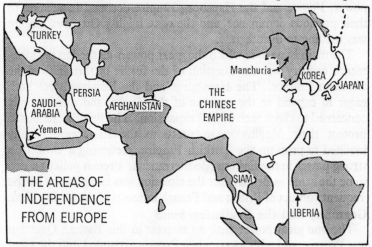

The end of European history

Industrialisation, which was transforming Europe from a rural to an urban society and stimulating the new forces of Liberalism and Socialism and the old force of Nationalism, was also opening up the rest of the world. At the same time it was providing the technical accomplishments which would make both material progress and mass destruction easier; and during the next century the Europeans were to take advantage of both of these opportunities. But the effect of European industrialisation which in the long run was probably most important was the stimulus it gave to the rest of the world. When the Europeans opened up the rest of the world they were letting loose forces they could not control. And in less than a century Europe would have become of secondary importance in the world, and European history meaningless outside the context of developments in the wider world.

2   BISMARCK'S EUROPE

The great powers and the Eastern Question

IN the century between 1815 and 1914 most disputes between the great powers of Europe were settled by negotiation. Even the wars were of a limited nature rather than great struggles to the death such as happened before 1815 and after 1914.

The great powers in 1815 were France, the Hapsburg Empire, Russia, Great Britain, Prussia, and, in a sense, the Ottoman Empire. In the next half-century Great Britain and Prussia increased in strength, Russia remained a source of vast untapped power, France and the Hapsburg Empire declined in relation to their previous dominance, and the once mighty Ottoman Empire was tending to disintegrate.

The main issue over which the great powers clashed in the nineteenth century was the question of the future of the lands of the Ottoman Empire. The Hapsburgs and the Russians were both eager to expand at the expense of the Turks, and were equally concerned to check each other's expansion. The British, anxious to protect their Mediterranean route to the East, were usually inclined to prop up the Turkish Empire, preferring a weak to a strong power in the Eastern Mediterranean. French policy tended to be the same as British, but the situation was complicated by the requent conflict of British and French interests in the Middle East.

Germany and the *Dreikaiserbund*

The one great power with no interest in this Eastern Question was Prussia, and after 1871, when Prussia expanded into the German Empire and became the dominant power in Europe, this meant that the power which stood at the centre of European diplomacy was the only one with no direct interest in the most important issue of European international relations. In practice Germany could not avoid entanglement in Balkan affairs, and for the next twenty years Balkan affairs perpetually disrupted the careful plans of Otto von Bismarck, the German Chancellor.

Bismarck's main aim in Europe after 1871 was to maintain peace and stability while he concentrated on the internal affairs of Germany. He believed in maintaining a powerful army, and although he never used it throughout his term as Chancellor, its mere existence lent force to his diplomacy. But he also saw that a powerful army would be insufficient against a combination of several other great powers, and he drew the conclusion that it was necessary to 'try to be *à trois* in a world governed by five powers'.

Friendship with France was impossible because the German Empire had just annexed Alsace and Lorraine. A permanent understanding with Britain was impossible because Britain maintained a policy of isolation. So if Bismarck was to keep Germany in a group of three it was essential to have the friendship of Austria-Hungary and Russia, and in 1873 he managed to negotiate the Three Emperors' League, or *Dreikaiserbund*, in which Alexander II of Russia, Franz Josef of Austria-Hungary, and Wilhelm I of Germany agreed to stand together against republicanism and to consult each other about military matters and the Balkans.

The Eastern crisis of 1875-8

Soon afterwards the Eastern Question was raised again as the result of the nationalism of the Balkan peoples. In 1875 the subject peoples living in the provinces of Bosnia and Herzegovina rebelled, the revolt spread across the Balkans and led to the wholesale slaughter of Bulgars by the Turks, and there arose a serious danger that the Russians would intervene to support their fellow Slavs. After a number of diplomatic moves by the great powers in an unsuccessful attempt to persuade the Turks to reform and avoid Russian intervention, the Russians declared war on the Ottoman Empire in the spring of 1877 and invaded.

As the Russian forces approached the Straits at the beginning of 1878 the British government moved its fleet to Constantinople and thus dissuaded the Russians from pressing their advantage any further. Even so, the Treaty of San Stefano, signed between the Russians and the Turks in March 1878, destroyed the control of the Turks over most of their European territories by providing for the establishment of a big new state of Bulgaria.

The Hapsburgs disliked this, for it seemed that this new state would be virtually a Russian dependency. The British similarly disliked it, especially as Bulgaria's Southern boundary was on the Aegean Sea, and Disraeli therefore demanded an international congress. Bismarck, anxious to avoid conflict between Austria-Hungary and Russia, offered his services as an 'honest broker' and presided over the conference which met in Berlin in June.

The Congress of Berlin, 1878

The Congress of Berlin was the last important readjustment of the Balkans in the nineteenth century, and the negotiations before and during the Congress produced three important territorial changes in the East Mediterranean area:

(1) The big new state of Bulgaria was divided in three. The Nor-

thern part continued as Bulgaria. A smaller area, known as Eastern Roumelia, remained in the Ottoman Empire to give the Sultan a defensible Northern frontier along the Balkan mountains, but it was to be ruled as an autonomous state by a Christian governor. The large Southern area, including Macedonia, was returned to full Ottoman control.

(2) Austria–Hungary was allowed to occupy Bosnia, Herzegovina, and the *sanjak*, or district, of Novibazar, though all this remained technically part of the Ottoman Empire.

(3) Great Britain gained control of Cyprus as a base from which to counter any future Russian threat.

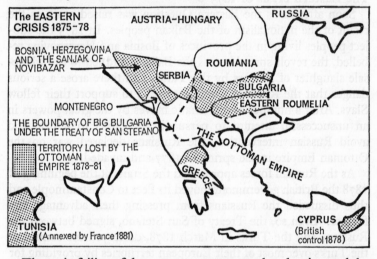

The EASTERN CRISIS 1875-78

AUSTRIA-HUNGARY RUSSIA

BOSNIA, HERZEGOVINA AND THE SANJAK OF NOVIBAZAR

SERBIA ROUMANIA

BULGARIA

EASTERN ROUMELIA

MONTENEGRO

THE BOUNDARY OF BIG BULGARIA UNDER THE TREATY OF SAN STEFANO

TERRITORY LOST BY THE OTTOMAN EMPIRE 1878-81

THE OTTOMAN EMPIRE

GREECE

TUNISIA (Annexed by France 1881)

CYPRUS (British control 1878)

The main failing of these arrangements was that they ignored the importance of the Nationalist feelings of the peoples of these areas. The arrangements for Eastern Roumelia were overthrown seven years later. The return of Macedonia to the Turks eventually produced the Balkan Wars (pp. 101–3). The transfer of Bosnia and Herzegovina to Austrian control led to a major international crisis in 1908–9 (p. 86) and eventually to a world war in 1914. And the British were still using force to deal with the problems of Greek and Turkish Nationalism in Cyprus in the mid-twentieth century.

All this has led to suggestions that San Stefano was a more satisfactory settlement of the Eastern Question than the Congress of Berlin. But whatever merits San Stefano may seem in retrospect to have had it was at the time entirely unacceptable to the great powers. And although the Congress did not provide a permanent solution to the Eastern Question it did at least postpone trouble.

The Austro-German Alliance of 1879

One inevitable effect of the Congress of Berlin was to cause bad relations between Russia and the other two powers of the *Dreikaiserbund*. For while Austria–Hungary had acquired control of Bosnia and Herzegovina Russia had suffered a diplomatic defeat, and moreover this was largely because Bismarck, seeing that support of Russia would involve offending Britain as well as Austria, had chosen to support Austria rather than Russia.

The consequence was the break-up of the *Dreikaiserbund*, and the natural sequel to this in 1879 was a military treaty between Germany and Austria–Hungary which took the form of a defensive alliance directed against Russia. But this does not mean that Bismarck had abandoned his policy of keeping Austria–Hungary and Russia together. On the contrary, the main value of the alliance to him was that it helped to ensure peace in Eastern Europe by placing him in a position to exercise a restraining influence over Austria–Hungary while at the same time dissuading Russia from attacking Austria–Hungary.

The *Dreikaiserbund* of 1881

The Russians soon realised the disadvantages of their position of diplomatic isolation, and when they made overtures for the renewal of the *Dreikaiserbund* Bismarck made every effort to persuade Austria–Hungary to agree and by 1881 succeeded. A new agreement between the three Emperors provided for benevolent neutrality in the event of any attack by a fourth power.

The Triple Alliance of 1882

At the same time Bismarck usually tried to avoid quarrelling with the other great powers. He respected Britain's sensitivity as a naval power by refraining from building a fleet, and her sensitivity as a colonial power by avoiding colonial conflict. He also tried to divert the French away from the problem of Alsace and Lorraine by encouraging their colonial ambitions in Africa.

It was his secret encouragement which in 1881 led the French to seize Tunisia, and thus in 1882 indirectly produced the Triple Alliance of Germany, Austria–Hungary, and Italy (p. 95), for it was the Italians' resentment of the French seizure of Tunisia which led them to seek allies against France.

However, the *Dreikaiserbund* rather than the Triple Alliance remained the cornerstone of Bismarck's policy.

Eastern Roumelia, 1885

In 1885 the *Dreikaiserbund* broke down again. One of its clauses

had been an agreement to recognise the preponderant influence of
Russia in Bulgaria. But Bulgaria had declined to become a mere
Russian satellite, so in 1885 when Eastern Roumelia declared its
union with Bulgaria Russia wanted to prevent the union. However, Britain and Austria–Hungary, constant in their opposition to
Russia's wishes, also reversed their policies towards Bulgaria and
supported the union. Bismarck, as in 1878, was unwilling to offend
both Austria–Hungary and Britain for the sake of Russia, and since
he did not give the Russians any support they had to accept the
expansion of Bulgaria.

It was clear that there could not be any hope for co-operation
between Austria–Hungary and Russia in the Balkans, and this
made Alexander III determined to withdraw from the *Dreikaiserbund* when it came up for renewal in 1887.

The Reinsurance Treaty, 1887

But Alexander III was still anxious to remain friendly with
Germany, so the Russians once again made friendly overtures to
Germany, just as they had after the humiliations of the Congress
of Berlin and the Austro–German Alliance of 1879. And this
time their advances resulted in a Russo–German treaty commonly
known as the Reinsurance Treaty, which was signed in 1887 to
last three years. Each of the parties promised to remain neutral in
the event of the other going to war unless Russia attacked Austria
or Germany attacked France, and the treaty also included a promise of German diplomatic support for Russia over Bulgaria. But
within six weeks of being signed the Reinsurance Treaty virtually
broke down, for the Russians demanded the expulsion of the new
anti-Russian King Ferdinand of Bulgaria and Bismarck failed to
give the support he had promised.

For nearly twenty years he had been trying to ensure stability
in Europe by maintaining friendly relations with both Austria–
Hungary and Russia and by preventing any clash between them.
Events in the Balkans had made this difficult and sometimes impossible, and indeed it is doubtful whether Bismarck could have
succeeded in re-negotiating the Reinsurance Treaty in 1890 even
if he had not been dismissed (p. 13). But at least he would not
have abandoned the attempt to keep Russia's friendship. His successors made precisely that mistake, and in 1914 it was German
encouragement of a clash between Austria–Hungary and Russia in
the Balkans—a direct reversal of Bismarck's policy—which precipitated the first World War.

3   THE GERMAN EMPIRE

The constitution

THE GERMAN EMPIRE was proclaimed in the Hall of Mirrors at Versailles in January 1871 after victory in the Franco-Prussian War of 1870. In form it was a federation of twenty-five German states. In practice it was an extension of Prussian power over the other German states. Prussia was larger in area and population than the rest of the German Empire put together. Berlin, the capital of Prussia, was the capital of the Empire. King Wilhelm I of Prussia was German Emperor, or *Kaiser*, with complete control over the appointment of his Chancellor, the chief minister of Germany, and as Emperor he was also Commander-in-Chief of the army and navy. The Chancellor exercised executive power, controlled foreign policy, initiated legislation, decided the appointments of other members of the government and of senior administrative officials, and was answerable for his actions only to the Kaiser.

There was an Imperial parliament, the *Reichstag*, which was elected by universal manhood suffrage, and a majority vote of the *Reichstag* was needed for the passage of new legislation. But legislation could not be initiated in the *Reichstag*, which had no control over the Chancellor, who could, and often did, remain in office without a majority of *Reichstag* deputies supporting him.

There was also a federal council, the *Bundesrat*, in which the representatives of the various states had to vote in accordance with the instructions of their monarchs. The constitution could not be altered if as many as 14 out of the 58 members of the *Bundesrat* voted against the proposal, and thus the Kaiser, who as king of Prussia appointed 17 representatives, was able to block any constitutional change.

The unification of Germany

Bismarck, who had been Minister-President of Prussia since 1862, was the first Chancellor of the German Empire. He wanted to build a prosperous, stable, and united Germany, and therefore arranged for a unified railway system, a unified postal and telegraph service, one Imperial coinage, and a common code of civil and criminal law throughout the Empire. He established one national army and one national administrative service—though in practice both of these were under Prussian control. And he also aimed, in this case unsuccessfully, at the effective assimilation within the Empire of the main minority groups: the Poles in the

East, the Danes in the North, and the French in Alsace-Lorraine.

The Kulturkampf

One of the main obstacles to the power of the State seemed to Bismarck to be the power of the Roman Catholic Church, for in 1864, in a *Syllabus of Modern Errors*, Pope Pius IX had condemned civil marriage and secular education, and in 1870 he proclaimed the doctrine of the infallibility of the Pope on matters of faith and morals.

In 1872 Bismarck began an attack on the Roman Catholic Church with a decree expelling the Jesuits from Germany, and in a series of laws over the next six years, the May Laws, severe limitations were placed on the Roman Catholic Church in Prussia and state control was imposed on education and over the marriage laws. The powerful National Liberal Party, whose political philosophy of Liberalism had also been condemned in the *Syllabus of Errors*, supported Bismarck in this conflict, which its members regarded as a *Kulturkampf*—a struggle for civilisation.

In 1878, however, Leo XIII, a far more moderate man than Pius IX, became Pope, and Bismarck, who was by now more concerned with plans for the imposition of protective tariffs and for the suppression of Socialism, took the opportunity to abandon the *Kulturkampf* and seek the support of the Catholic Centre Party to which he had so far been bitterly opposed.

Protection

One reason Bismarck wanted to impose import duties was in order to provide the federal government with increased revenue and make it less dependent on its income from the member states of the Empire. But he particularly wanted a tariff on iron and steel in order to protect this comparatively new German industry from foreign competition in the home market, and thus enable it to grow. Its growth was important not only for general economic reasons but also so that Germany should not be dependent on imports for vital war materials. He also particularly wanted a tariff on grain in order to prevent the decline of German agriculture, which could not hope to compete on even terms with cheap imports from America and Russia. He felt this was important partly because he saw agriculture as the basis of traditional conservatism on which the future social and political well-being of Germany would depend, and partly because he felt that it was vital that Germany should be able to feed herself in time of war without needing to rely on imports.

Bismarck was assured of the support of the conservative element in the *Reichstag* representing the landowning class, but the National Liberals, on whose support he had relied through most of the seventies, were a Free Trade party, and thus he was only able to get the legislation imposing Protection through the *Reichstag* in 1879 by getting additional support from the Catholic Centre Party.

Socialism

He also needed Catholic support against the Socialists, whose success in winning nearly half a million votes in the elections of 1877 had seriously disturbed him, and he was successful in getting it because Socialism was another of the errors condemned by Pius IX in the *Syllabus* of 1864.

Bismarck approached the problem of destroying Socialism in two ways. When two attempts were made to assassinate the Emperor in the summer of 1878 he seized the opportunity, even though neither attempt had been made by a Socialist, to persuade the *Reichstag* to pass an anti-Socialist law banning Socialist organisations and publications. Then, while suppressing the Socialists, he promoted social reform legislation aimed at undermining Socialism by stealing some of the more obviously popular aspects of the programme. Thus a state system of insurance against sickness was introduced in 1883, followed by insurance against accidents in 1884, and in 1889 old age pensions were started—twenty years before they were introduced in Britain. Neither method of destroying Socialism was successful. Support for the Social Democrats increased, even though the party was illegal, and in 1890 when the anti-Socialist law lapsed the Socialists won a million and a half votes and 35 seats in the *Reichstag*.

The fall of Bismarck

The problem of how to deal with the Socialists together with the issue of relations with Russia helped to bring about the dismissal of Bismarck, who had survived as Chancellor throughout the reign of Wilhelm I and through the brief ninety-nine day reign of Friedrich III in 1888, but only lasted for two years under the young Emperor Wilhelm II. Both the anti-Socialist law and the Reinsurance Treaty with Russia (p. 10) were due to expire in 1890. Bismarck wanted to make the anti-Socialist law permanent and try to negotiate an extension of the Reinsurance Treaty. Wilhelm II was prepared to let both lapse. The clash of personalities between the elderly obstinate Chancellor and the young arrogant Emperor made

things worse. Wilhelm was determined not to leave everything to
Bismarck as his grandfather had done, and matters came to a head
when the Emperor instructed Bismarck to draw up an order
restricting the Chancellor's powers. Bismarck refused to do so and
resigned.

Germany under Wilhelm II

Wilhelm was determined that in future he would himself maintain control of German affairs, and none of his four peace-time
Chancellors, Caprivi (1890–4), Hohenlohe (1894–1900), Bülow
(1900–9), and Bethmann-Hollweg (1909–17), was at all outstanding.

His foreign policy was disastrous (pp. 84–88), and at home the
autocratic position he was trying to establish was being eroded
from both right and left. His popularity with the army leaders
declined, largely as the result of his support for the navy, until in
1908 they insisted that he should limit his personal influence and
power. His attempt to kill Socialism with kindness was so unsuccessful that in 1912, in the last general election before the first
World War, the Social Democrats won over four million votes and
110 seats—nearly a third of the total—making them the largest
party in the Reichstag.

Meanwhile the industrial, military, and naval strength of Germany was increasing rapidly. Whereas in 1880 Germany had only
been producing half as much steel as Great Britain, by 1914 she
was producing more than twice as much. This was partly due to a
new process developed by a Welshman called Gilchrist Thomas,
which enabled the German steel industry to use the phosphoric
iron ores of Lorraine, which had been annexed from France in
1871. But it was also the result of deliberate government policy—
not merely Protection, which was introduced in 1879, the same
year as the Gilchrist Thomas process was perfected, but also subsidies, which the government paid to steel manufacturers enabling
them to sell large quantities of steel to Britain at an uneconomic
price. Although in the short run this meant that the German tax-
payer was subsidising the British ship-building industry, in the
long run it meant that the German steel industry was being built
up at the expense of the British and in many ways became more
efficient. Indeed, the German fleet, though far smaller than the
Royal Navy, was ship for ship, gun for gun, and shell for shell
more effective than the British fleet, which as a matter of policy
was built from British steel and armed with British explosives.

The policy of conscripting all young men for two years service in the armed forces, and the rapid growth of population from just over forty millions in 1871 to nearly sixty-eight millions by 1914 ensured the existence of an exceptionally large army and consequently a large home market for armaments firms such as Krupps and Thyssens. These firms were then able to build up an extensive export trade, so that Germany had a massive armaments capacity when war broke out in 1914.

Military dictatorship and collapse

In a country with as strong a military tradition as Germany it was natural that the military leaders should have political influence, and one effect of the war was to transfer control of the country from the civilians to the army. After August 1916 when General Ludendorff became First Quartermaster-General he virtually ruled Germany. Nominally the Kaiser, as Commander-in-Chief, and Hindenburg, as Chief of the General Staff, were both his superiors. But in practice Ludendorff was a dictator, making political as well as military decisions, and the next two Chancellors after Bethmann-Hollweg, who resigned in July 1917, merely acted as spokesmen for him. He voluntarily brought his own dictatorship to an end late in September 1918 when he decided that the war was lost and that it was necessary to establish constitutional government and ask for an armistice.

Two days later Prince Max von Baden became Chancellor and formed a government which was responsible to the *Reichstag*. But this experiment at constitutional monarchy lasted less than six weeks. The German armies were defeated and knew it. The urban population was starving and in a revolutionary mood. And the Allies were unwilling to negotiate with the Kaiser. The Social Democrats were now an important political force both because of their numbers in the *Reichstag* and their support in the towns, but they were divided. The mass of the party, known as the Majority Socialists, had supported the war, and their leaders, such as Karl Ebert, had taken office under Prince Max. But two splinter groups which had opposed the war led a revolution in early November. Government broke down, and on 9th November 1918 the Kaiser abdicated and Prince Max handed over the Chancellorship to Ebert. The Majority Socialists were left to salvage what they could of Imperial Germany from foreign enemies and from their own revolutionary comrades.

O VER the centuries the Hapsburg family had built up a large Empire in Eastern Europe, and in the second half of the nineteenth century it was ruled by the Emperor Franz Josef, who had come to the throne in 1848 at the age of eighteen. It included eleven different racial groups. In the North were four Slav peoples: Czechs, Slovaks, Poles, and Ruthenians. In a strip across the middle lived four non-Slav races: Germans, Italians, Magyars, and Roumanians. And in the South were three more Slav peoples: Slovenes, Croats, and Serbs.

The Dual Monarchy

After 1867 the Empire was known as the Dual Monarchy of Austria-Hungary, with one half ruled by a German, or Austrian,

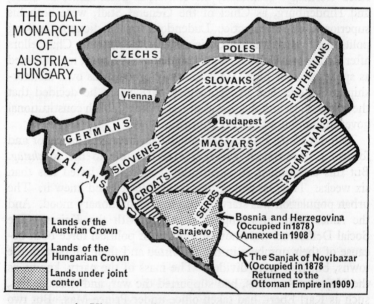

THE DUAL
MONARCHY
OF
AUSTRIA-
HUNGARY

CZECHS   POLES

SLOVAKS   RUTHENIANS

Vienna

GERMANS   Budapest

ITALIANS   SLOVENES   MAGYARS   ROUMANIANS

CROATS

SERBS

Sarajevo

Lands of the
Austrian Crown

Lands of the
Hungarian Crown

Lands under joint
control

Bosnia and Herzegovina
(Occupied in 1878)
(Annexed in 1908)

The Sanjak of Novibazar
(Occupied in 1878
Returned to the
Ottoman Empire in 1909)

government in Vienna, and the other half ruled by a Magyar, or Hungarian, government in Budapest. The two separate states were connected by the person of the Emperor who ruled Hungary as its king and retained autocratic power in both halves of his Empire. For all internal purposes the two countries were separate, but the Dual Monarchy had a common war department, foreign office, and finance ministry, to which Austria contributed 70% and Hungary 30% of the money needed for the army and foreign affairs.

Austria

The Austrian half of the Dual Monarchy was the more advanced and progressive part of the Empire, both economically and constitutionally. Although power remained in the hands of the German-speaking aristocracy, equality of languages and nationalities was recognised, and Count Eduard von Taaffe, who was Prime Minister from 1879–93, encouraged progress for the non-German peoples.

In 1907 universal manhood suffrage was introduced and parliament was given supreme power, subject to the Emperor's right to overrule it. But in practice nationalist conflict between Czechs and Germans made government impossible without perpetual intervention by the Emperor. Moreover, parliament had no control at all over so important an issue as going to war, and in 1914 it was adjourned in March and was still not sitting when the war began in July.

Hungary

The Magyars were far more repressive than the Germans in their treatment of subject peoples. While von Taaffe was pursuing a liberal policy in Austria, Koloman Tisza, who was Prime Minister of Hungary from 1875–90, deprived the subject peoples of the right of using their own languages in schools or administration. The franchise was limited to those with a high property qualification, and the elections to the Budapest parliament were public and organised in such a way as to restrict the representation of the subject peoples, who by the twentieth century were increasingly anxious for Home Rule or even independence.

Disintegration

The South-Eastern tracts of the Empire had been won in previous centuries from the Ottoman Turks, and the Hapsburgs still sometimes hoped for further expansion into the Balkans. At one time the subject peoples of the Turks in the Balkans would have welcomed Austrian expansion, but during the nineteenth century they had come increasingly to want independence and had no wish to exchange a Turkish master for an Austrian one. If they looked for a champion at all it was to the great Orthodox Slav nation of Russia that they looked rather than to Catholic Germanic Austria. And the Austrian occupation of Bosnia and Herzegovina in 1878 and annexation thirty years later (p. 86) was bitterly resented.

In the years just before the first World War the likelihood of any further Austrian expansion was declining. It was as much as the Hapsburgs could do to hold their ramshackle Empire together, and they only managed to do so because the various opposition groups were so disunited. Indeed, there seemed more likelihood of Serb expansion at the expense of Austria-Hungary than of Hapsburg expansion at the expense of the Serbs, and it was this danger which caused Austria-Hungary to attack Serbia in 1914. The fact that Russia was not prepared to let Austria-Hungary destroy Serbia precipitated the first World War, and under the pressure of that war Austria-Hungary disintegrated.

In 1914 Hapsburg armies suffered defeat at the hands of both Serbs and Russians, and as a result the Germans virtually took control of Austria-Hungary. The Hapsburg dynasty survived under German patronage for four more years, but the subject peoples could not be relied on to fight and were deserting in their thousands even before the death of Franz Josef in November 1916. Franz Josef's successor, the Emperor Karl, was never able to establish effective control over the Empire. Desertions increased on such a scale that contingents were formed from the subject peoples to fight for the Allies on both Eastern and Western fronts. At the end of October 1918 all the peoples of the Empire proclaimed their independence. Even the Austrians and Magyars broke away from the dynasty, and in November Karl renounced any claim to authority over them and then went into exile.

Austria between the wars

Austria was now a small weak republic whose complete economic collapse was only prevented in 1923 by loans arranged by the League of Nations. The obvious solution to Austria's difficulties, union with Germany, was forbidden by the peace treaties, and in 1931 even her wish for a customs union with Germany was frustrated by French pressure.

The two main political parties were the left-wing Social Democrats, who were strong in the towns and particularly Vienna, where a third of the population lived, and the right-wing Christian Socials, a conservative authoritarian party which was supported by the mass of the Catholic peasantry in the countryside. At first government was by a coalition, but from 1922 the Christian Socials ruled on their own. However, the depression produced the rise of a third party, the Austrian Nazis, who became increasingly vigorous after Hitler came to power in Germany in January 1933. Dr. Dollfüss, the Christian Social Chancellor, had no wish to see Austria absorbed by Nazi Germany, and to avoid it he followed in Hitler's footsteps, but used Hitler's methods against the Nazis. In March he suspended parliamentary government, and later in the same year he had the opposition parties dissolved.

Then in February 1934 the Social Democrats were suppressed in four days fighting in Vienna, and in March Dollfüss placed Austria under the protection of Mussolini's Italy. In the short run this policy was successful, though Dollfüss did not live to see it. When he was assassinated by the Austrian Nazis in July 1934 Hitler was dissuaded from seizing Austria by Mussolini's prompt transfer of troops to the Italian frontier. But in the long run Dollfüss's policy was a failure. He had destroyed the Social Democrats, the most reliably anti-Nazi element in Austria, and Mussolini proved unreliable. In 1936 Mussolini became friendly with Hitler, and in March 1938, when Hitler annexed Austria, Mussolini valued Hitler's friendship more highly than the independence of Austria and did not even protest.

Hungary between the wars

Hungary, like Austria, suffered heavy territorial losses at the end of the first World War, and, again like Austria, the small state which remained was economically weak. Politically she was far more unstable. The democratic republic formed in November 1918 lasted until March 1919 when a Communist, Béla Kun, established a Soviet Republic. That in turn only lasted until July 1919, when a Roumanian army suppressed Béla Kun's government and for three months occupied Budapest. The old ruling class then returned to power, the great landowners got their land back, and in March 1920 Hungary became a monarchy again. But her neighbours, Czechoslovakia, Roumania, and Jugoslavia, would not tolerate a Hapsburg on the Hungarian throne. So although Hungary retained much the same constitution as before he war, ultimate power rested with a Regent, Admiral Horthy, and Hungary became that oft-remarked incongruity, a kingdom without a king ruled by an admiral without a navy.

Horthy ruled Hungary effectively in a traditional conservative manner during the twenties, but in the thirties, partly as the result of the economic depression and partly because of a revival of expansionist ambitions, a Hungarian Nazi Party, the National Unity Party, became increasingly influential. In September 1938 and again in March 1939 Hitler provided Hungary with land taken from Czechoslovakia, and Hungary came more and more under German influence. In the second World War as in the first her fortunes were tied to those of Germany, and in 1944 as in 1918 Hungary only escaped German control by suffering military defeat alongside her German patrons.

5 IMPERIAL RUSSIA

The last of the Romanovs

THE HALF-CENTURY of Russian history before the revolutions of 1917 is the story of how the Romanov dynasty tried to deal with changing circumstances by repression, reforms, and concessions. The repression increased unrest. The reforms created new problems. The concessions were insufficient.

Alexander II (1855–81): The early years of the reign of Alexander II, the 'Tsar-Liberator', had seen a considerable move in the direction of progress and reform. Above all, the serfs had been freed in 1861 and a system of local government by elected local assemblies, or *zemstva,* had been established in 1864. But nothing was done to limit the autocratic power of the monarch, and the later years of Alexander's reign also saw the development of an anarchist revolutionary movement. After numerous attempts to kill him he was eventually assassinated in 1881—on the same day that he signed a decree promising a number of liberal reforms.

Alexander III (1881–94): His son, Alexander III, imposed a policy of rigorous repression on Russia. The powers and size of the secret police were increased. In many areas officials were appointed with the power to arrest and fine without trial. The press and the universities were carefully controlled. The franchise for elections to *zemstva* was limited. Contact with Western Europe was restricted. And at the same time an attempt was made to Russify the non-Russian peoples of the Empire, who numbered more than half the total population, and to bring all peoples of the Empire within the Orthodox Church. The non-Russian peoples were forbidden to use their own languages and customs. Moslems, Roman Catholics, Protestants, and Jews were all persecuted, and at the beginning of the reign the government encouraged widespread massacres, or *pogroms,* of Jews.

Nicholas II (1894–1917): When Nicholas II succeeded his father there were widespread hopes that he would bring an age of Liberalism and reform, but these hopes were rapidly dashed, for right at the beginning of his reign he declared to delegates of the *zemstva* that he would maintain the autocratic principle as firmly as his father and that the idea that the *zemstva* should take any part in national affairs was a 'senseless dream'.

Industrialisation

Meanwhile, however, the industrialisation of Russia had already begun, and in the long run this was to produce pressures for social and constitutional change which the Tsarist autocracy would be unable to withstand. In 1885 a railway linking Moscow with the newly colonised areas of South-East Asia was begun, and in 1891 construction had started on the Trans-Siberian Railway, which, when it was completed in 1902, stretched 5,542 miles from St. Petersburg to Vladivostock. Moreover, by the beginning of Nicholas II's reign the Russian iron industry, which had been virtually non-existent a few years earlier, was producing well over a million tons of pig iron a year.

This industrial development was encouraged by Count Witte, who was Minister of Finance from 1893, the year before Nicholas came to the throne, until 1903. Witte believed in a centralised planned economy and thought that the autocratic system of government in Russia should make it possible to organise the economy far more efficiently than could the parliamentary democracies of Western Europe, which were committed to a free economy. He imposed a high tariff on imported manufactured goods, thus protecting the growing industries of Russia from foreign competition, and at the same time he used compulsion to ensure that large quantities of wheat were exported. These measures gave Russia a favourable balance of payments and enabled him to put Russia on the gold standard in 1896 and thus attract foreign investment in Russian industrial development. Foreign investment made possible such a rapid growth of Russian heavy industry that between 1894 and 1914 Russian production of pig iron quadrupled, reaching just over five million tons a year.

Inevitably Witte's policies caused hardship, and in 1896, the year he put Russia on the gold standard, there were widespread strikes. In general the government's answer to unrest was repression, but there was some attempt to ameliorate the situation, and in 1897, for example, the working day in factories was officially limited to eleven hours.

The 1905 Revolution

Meanwhile, especially as the result of the building of the Trans-Siberian Railway, Russia was extending her influence in the Far East. The acquisition of the lease of Port Arthur in 1898, the occupation of Manchuria at the time of the Boxer Rising (p. 318), and the subsequent attempt to extend Russian influence into Korea led in February 1904 to the Russo-Japanese War. The war led to a rise in prices, wages did not keep pace with prices, and industrial

unrest spread rapidly. On Sunday 22nd January 1905 a crowd
of St. Petersburg workers and their families, many of them from
the great *Putilov* armaments works, went to the Winter Palace led
by an Orthodox priest, Father Gapon, to present a petition to the
Tsar. Although the demonstration was a peaceful one the troops
at the palace shot down several hundred of the demonstrators.

The immediate outcome was a great extension of disaffection.
There were widespread strikes and a wave of terrorism in which
the Tsar's uncle, the Grand Duke Sergei, was assassinated in
February 1905. And as the year passed the government found itself
faced with increasing opposition from several directions. The aristocratic and middle-class Liberals wanted constitutional government. The peasants wanted to own the land they worked. Many
industrial workers were eager for a thoroughgoing revolution.
And the non-Russian nationalities of the Western and Baltic provinces, of the Caucasus, and of Central Asia wanted independence
or self-government for their national groups.

Faced with increasing disaffection Nicholas II considered establishing martial law. But he could not be sure of the loyalty of the
armed forces. The morale of the army, which had been defeated
by the Japanese at Mukden in March, and of the navy, which had
suffered an even more crushing defeat at Tsushima in May, was
very low. And in June the crew of one of the cruisers of the Black
Sea fleet, the *Potemkin*, mutinied.

The October Manifesto and the constitution

In October Nicholas at last decided to make concessions to the
growing opposition, and on the 30th he issued a manifesto in which
he promised to establish human rights, such as freedom of speech,
and to allow the election of a consultative assembly, a *duma*, whose
agreement would be needed for the pasage of any law. Many of
the aristocratic and middle-class Liberals were satisfied by this,
and soon afterwards many peasants were conciliated by the government's cancellation of the debts they still owed on the lands they
had acquired at the time of the emancipation of the serfs. The
industrial working class remained bitterly dissatisfied, and their
dissatisfaction found expression in December when a general
strike was proclaimed. But the October Manifesto had destroyed
the impetus of the revolutionary movement, and the government
was able to suppress the strikers.

The promised constitution took effect in May 1906. Although it
asserted that the Tsar was still 'the supreme autocratic power',

provision was made for the election of a *duma* by virtually universal manhood suffrage on a system of direct voting, and legislation, and any alteration to the constitution, needed the consent of the *duma*.

The *dumas*

In the first *duma*, which met the same month, the Constitutional Democrats, usually known as the *Kadets* from the pronunciation of the initial letters of their name, were the largest party. Under their influence the *duma* promptly demanded further social and constitutional reforms, but these demands were quite unacceptable to the Tsar, and in July he dissolved the *duma*.

A second *duma* was elected and met in March 1907. This time both the Socialist Revolutionaries, known as the *Essaires* from the initials of their party name, and the Social Democrats took part. The *Essaires*, who derived most of their support from the peasants, and the Social Democrats, who derived most of theirs from the urban industrial workers, had mostly boycotted the elections to the first *duma* because they were dissatisfied with the constitution, and although between them they won less than a fifth of the seats in the second *duma*, their presence helped to make it even less acceptable to the Tsar than the first, and in July he dissolved it.

The Tsar's government then altered the constitution without the *duma's* consent, and in particular drastically reduced the representation of the peasants, the industrial workers, and the non-Russian peoples. When a third *duma* was elected later in the year the largest single group was a moderate Conservative party whose members were known as the *Octobrists* because they had been satisfied with the October Manifesto of 1905. The more extreme Conservative parties also increased in size, and the number of *Essaires*, Social Democrats, and even *Kadets*, was greatly reduced. Understandably, this *duma* was more willing than the previous ones to co-operate with the Tsarist government, and it ran its full five-year term till 1912, when a fourth and similar *duma* was elected.

Despite the ineffectiveness of the third and fourth *dumas* the pre-war period saw land reforms, reforms of justice and local government, and a great extension of education all instituted by the Tsarist government. To many middle-class Liberals there seemed every prospect that these reforms and the rapid industrial progress which was accompanying them would be followed by further constitutional development.

War and the March Revolution

When war began in 1914 the Liberals hoped that the government's dependence on the people for the effective waging of war would produce rapid constitutional advance, but the Tsar believed he could rely on the loyalty of the mass of the peasants to win the war; and once the *duma* had voted war credits he adjourned it.

But against Germany, as against Japan a decade earlier, war brought defeat, and defeat brought political upheaval. In the military crisis of August 1915, as the German forces swept into Russia, the Tsar made the mistake of taking command of the Russian armies. This was bad enough in itself. What was worse was that the Tsarina, an unbalanced neurotic woman, was left in control of the government. And she was under the influence of a dissolute Siberian peasant, Gregory Rasputin, who had a reputation as a miracle worker and seemed to have a unique ability to help the sickly Crown Prince Alexei. Rasputin's only political importance was that he took care to ensure the appointment of weak and incompetent ministers who would not interfere with his personal debauchery. But this was enough to ensure the grotesque mismanagement of Russia's affairs during the critical war years.

Further military disasters and rapid inflation in 1916 produced a revolutionary atmosphere. In November the *duma* was recalled and openly condemned the government, and in December a group of noblemen and *duma* leaders murdered Rasputin. The *duma* now hoped for the peaceful establishment of genuine constitutional monarchy, but things had gone too far. The industrial workers wanted food, the peasants wanted land, and both wanted an end to the war.

On 8th March 1917 strikes and bread riots broke out in Petrograd, as St. Petersburg had been called since the beginning of the war, and within a week the Russian constitution was transformed. The troops called out against the rioters mutinied. The *duma* established a provisional government with one of the *Kadet* leaders, Prince Lvov, as Prime Minister. The *Essaires* and Social Democrats in Petrograd established a Workers' and Soldiers' Council, or *soviet*. And on the 15th the Tsar abdicated.

Apparently the provisional government was now in control of the country, but it lacked widespread authority, for the *duma* to which it was responsible had been elected on a very limited franchise, and already on 14th March the Soviet had issued orders to the units of the garrison to elect unit *soviets* and to obey the orders of the provisional government only when they did not conflict with its own orders. One revolution was virtually over. Another was beginning.

6 THE THIRD REPUBLIC

IN 1875 the French Assembly which had been elected in the crisis of February 1871 with an overwhelming Monarchist majority adopted a republican constitution because it could not agree about who should be king. Within another decade the way in which the constitution worked was well established. France had a President, Senate, and Chamber of Deputies, roughly corresponding to the British monarch, Lords, and Commons. The President was elected for a seven-year term by the National Assembly—that is, by the two houses in joint session. The three hundred senators held office for nine years, and every three years a third of them came up for election by local electoral colleges. The six hundred members of the Chamber of Deputies were elected by universal male suffrage in a general election held regularly every four years.

The instability of parliamentary government

There seemed no obvious reason why this constitution should last any longer than any of the systems of government of the preceding century. Surprisingly, it lasted sixty-five years, despite the fact that it did not give France stable government.

In the early years the members of the Chamber of Deputies were loosely grouped into Radicals on the Left, Opportunists in the Centre, and Monarchists on the Right. An obviously right-wing politician would probably be a Roman Catholic, would want the monarchy restored, and would vote in favour of expenditure on the army and the colonies. An obviously left-wing politician would staunchly uphold the Republican constitution, proclaim a belief in individual liberty, and be anti-militarist, anti-colonial, and anti-clerical. But there was no general agreement among either Left or Right even on these issues. Thus the great Radical leader Clemenceau always believed in the need for a strong army, and many Radicals were Roman Catholics. This meant that individuals aligned in different ways depending on the particular issue under consideration, and that it was impossible to form a united party with an overall majority on every issue. The effect of this, together with the fact that the Chamber of Deputies could only be dissolved at the end of its four-year term, thus enabling deputies to overthrow a government without having to face a general election, was that it could often be very difficult for the President to find a Prime Minister capable of maintaining a majority for any length of time, and thus the average duration of a French

25

government up to the first World War was less than ten months.

1885–93. The years of Boulanger and Panama

During the first decade of its existence the Third Republic had
generally been ruled by the Opportunists of the Centre, who had an
essentially practical approach to government. But in 1885 there
was widespread discontent with the weakness of French governments and the obvious corruption in French politics. There had
been little development of local government and even minor local
matters were decided in Paris. Often the only way people could
influence local affairs was through their deputy in Paris, and this
resulted in widespread bribery. So the election of 1885 produced
a revival of the Right, who gained a third of the seats in the
Chamber.

This meant that the Opportunists now had to rely on Radical
support to keep any government in office. One effect of this
increase of Radical influence was an extension of anti-clerical
legislation, and from 1886 onwards members of religious orders
were forbidden to teach in state schools. One effect of the increased influence of Clemenceau, with his great interest in military
efficiency, was the appointment as Minister of War of General
Boulanger.

The Boulanger crisis: But the appointment of Boulanger re-
bounded against the Radicals. He gained great personal support as
the result of his institution of some genuine reforms, his remarkable capacity for publicising himself, and his outspoken attacks
on the parliamentary system, with which so many people were
already disillusioned. Support for him increased after his dismissal in 1887, and developed so much that in 1888, when he won
a by-election in Paris with an overwhelming majority, it seemed
that with the Paris mob behind him he could seize dictatorial
power. He failed to seize his opportunity, and thereafter support
for him rapidly declined. Two months later, faced with the prospect of a trial for conspiracy against the state, he fled the country.
The Third Republic had survived the first major threat to its
existence through no obvious merit of its own.

The Panama scandal: Soon it was shaken by another crisis which
brought politicians and the parliamentary system into even greater
discredit. In 1891 it was revealed that a French company engaged in building the Panama Canal had bribed more than a
hundred deputies in order to get money from the state to help it
out of financial difficulties. This would probably have been the
end of the Third Republic if Boulanger had still been a force in

French politics. As it was, two governments fell in quick succession and a stimulus was given on the one hand to extreme Nationalism and anti-Semitism, for both foreigners and Jews had been involved in the Panama scandal, and on the other to Socialism. The Opportunists and Radicals now tended to draw away from each other, and while the Opportunists moved towards the Right, the Radicals drew closer to the Socialists, who became a significant political force for the first time in the elections of 1893, winning 49 seats.

The Dreyfus Case

However, the elections of 1893 gave a clear victory to the Opportunists, who were now usually known as Progressists—for no good reason, since they were in fact increasingly conservative in attitude—and for the next six years they usually dominated the governments of France. During these years French political differences were intensified by *L'Affaire Dreyfus*.

In 1894 Captain Alfred Dreyfus, the only Jewish officer on the French General Staff, was accused of selling military secrets to the Germans. He was court-martialled, found guilty, and sentenced to life imprisonment. But the leakages of information continued and in 1897 Colonel Picquart, the head of the Intelligence Service, concluded that the real criminal was an officer named Esterhazy. Picquart was told to keep quiet and was posted abroad, but before going he informed a friend and the information reached Clemenceau, who had lost his seat in the Assembly as the result of being involved in the Panama scandal and was now running a newspaper called *L'Aurore*.

Clemenceau agitated for the trial of Esterhazy and a court-martial took place, but on 9th January 1898 Esterhazy was acquitted and Picquart was dismissed from the army. Four days later, on 13th January, the affair became a national issue when a letter by the novelist Emile Zola appeared in *L'Aurore* under the headline *J'Accuse* asserting that the trials of both Dreyfus and Esterhazy had been rigged. France was now divided into Dreyfusards on the Left, who claimed to be fighting for the principles of individual liberty and justice, and anti-Dreyfusards on the Right, who declared that the honour of the nation and of the army was more important than abstract principles.

All the governments of this period were either unwilling or too weak to reopen the case and give Dreyfus a fair trial, and some took refuge in asserting the existence of documents which established Dreyfus' guilt. But then Colonel Henri, Picquart's successor as head of the Intelligence Service, was shown to have forged the documents. He confessed and committed suicide.

In the summer of 1899 a new government was formed under Waldeck–Rousseau, who promised a retrial of Dreyfus. In August, when Dreyfus was court-martialled again, his defence counsel was assassinated and the outcome of the trial was another miscarriage of justice: Dreyfus was found 'guilty with extenuating circumstances', and his sentence was reduced to ten years. Both Dreyfusards and anti-Dreyfusards were indignant, and once again there was a danger that the Republic would be overthrown. But Waldeck–Rousseau got the President to pardon Dreyfus, and although it was not until 1906 that Dreyfus was finally cleared and reinstated, feeling died down after 1899.

'No enemies on the left.' 1899–1911

Although Waldeck–Rousseau was himself a Progressist the government he formed was predominantly Radical. He remained in office for three years until in 1902, just after the Republican *bloc* which he led had been successful in the general election, ill-health caused him to resign. The *bloc* was held together for several more years by anti-clericalism and anti-militarism, both of which had been revived by the Dreyfus case. The anti-clericalism resulted in the compulsory dissolution of numerous religious orders, the closing of church schools, and the breaking off in 1904 of diplomatic relations with the Papacy, and it culminated in 1905 in a law disestablishing the Roman Catholic Church. The anti-militarism resulted in cuts in expenditure on the army and navy, and in 1905 produced a reduction of compulsory military service from three to two years.

The Republican *bloc*, whose slogan was 'No enemies on the Left', was eventually broken not by its right-wing enemies but by its inability to avoid having enemies on the Left. In the twentieth century Syndicalism (p. 181) became popular among French workers and a prolonged strike wave began in 1906. Clemenceau, Prime Minister for the first time from October 1906 to July 1909, repeatedly felt obliged to use troops against the strikers, and when his successor, Briand, who had begun his career as a Socialist, failed to find any solution other than force the Republican *bloc* fell to pieces.

The pre-war years, 1911–14

French political life was even more unstable than usual in the three years before the first World War, and seven different governments held office. However, a law passed in August 1913 reintroducing three years military service had the effect of welding the Republican *bloc* together again, and it fought and won the general election of May 1914 on a promise to repeal the three years law. In the event it never kept its promise, for in less than three months France was at war with Germany.

The war, 1914-18

The resources of the Third Republic were strained to the limit in the first World War. The French army was heavily defeated and driven back in the early weeks, but it made an astonishing recovery and checked the Germans at the Marne. During 1915 and 1916 France bore the brunt of the fighting on the Western front, and by 1917 her army was exhausted. Military defeats produced mutinies in the army, the news of the Russian Revolution set off a wave of strikes by French workers, and some ministers began to consider accepting peace terms.

But the parliamentary system proved itself adaptable to the changed conditions of total war, and at the end of 1917 Clemenceau became Prime Minister for the second time with a policy of waging war to the limit and was granted virtually dictatorial powers. A year later the war was over and France was victorious.

The survival of the Third Republic

The Third Republic had survived the storms of the Boulanger crisis, the Panama scandal, and the Dreyfus case. It had also survived protracted struggles with the Roman Catholic Church and with the Syndicalist movement in the trade unions. Now it had even survived a war with Germany. In the past its position had always seemed precarious, and it often appeared that it only survived because its enemies were divided and the possible alternatives were even less popular. Now its prestige was immeasurably strengthened by victory and by the recovery of Alsace–Lorraine. It was inconceivable that any other constitutional system should replace it.

But while the Third Republic as a system of government had been strengthened France herself had been seriously weakened. She had lost a million and a half men, and the rich industrial area of the North-East had been devastated. Germany, although defeated, was potentially far more powerful, and the possibility of her future military revival formed a serious threat to French security.

7 GLADSTONE AND DISRAELI

THE United Kingdom of Great Britain and Ireland was governed in the middle of the nineteenth century by a group of ministers known as the cabinet, who depended for their continuance in office on the support of an elected parliament. The members of parliament were, like the majority of those who elected them, from either the upper or middle class, and traditionally they were grouped into two large parties, the Whigs and the Tories, both led by members of the landed aristocracy.

The Tories, who were increasingly associated with the political philosophy of Conservatism and who traditionally derived their support from the naturally conservative landed gentry, had split in 1846 when their leader, Sir Robert Peel, offended the landed gentry by repealing the Corn Laws which protected British agriculture from foreign competition.

The Whigs, who were increasingly associated with the political philosophy of Liberalism, traditionally derived much of their support from the propertied middle class. The combination of the growth of the middle class with the split in the Tory Party enabled the Whigs to dominate most governments in the middle years of the nineteenth century.

Although most leaders of both parties were aristocrats it was possible for middle-class men of outstanding ability to rise to the top. W. E. Gladstone, the son of a rich Liverpool merchant who had made his fortune out of the slave trade, entered parliament as a Tory in 1832, was given cabinet office in 1843 by Peel, whom he followed into opposition in 1846, and by 1868 was the leader of a combination of Whigs, Peelites, and Radical reformers which by then was known as the Liberal Party. Benjamin Disraeli, the son of a distinguished Jewish scholar who had immigrated to England, entered parliament in 1837, also as a Tory, and in 1846 led the Tory rebellion against Peel over the repeal of the Corn Laws. He soon realised that a party representing the landed gentry alone could not possibly survive, and during the mid-century years of Whig dominance he laboriously recreated the Tory Party, seeking support from all those groups which had cause to dislike Liberalism.

After 1852 Disraeli and Gladstone alternated as Chancellor of the Exchequer, and in 1867 when Disraeli was Chancellor of the Exchequer for the third time he steered through the Commons a Bill which had the effect of enfranchising the urban working class.

Then in 1868 at the age of sixty-three he became Prime Minister, and thereafter he and Gladstone alternated as Prime Minister—Disraeli from February to December 1868, Gladstone from 1868 till 1874, Disraeli again from 1874 till 1880, and Gladstone again from 1880 till 1885. Until Disraeli's death in 1881 British politics had the appearance very largely of a struggle between these two men and the attitudes and interests they represented.

Liberal reform

Gladstone's first ministry was notable for a series of Liberal reforms which broke down the barriers of privilege and opened the way for individual advancement. The class barrier which limited entry into the Civil Service to those with family influence was broken in 1870 by opening entry to the Civil Service to public competition. The religious barrier restricting entry to Oxford and Cambridge to members of the Church of England was destroyed in 1871. And in the same year the barrier of wealth restricting advancement in the army was weakened by the abolition of the practice of purchasing commissions and promotion. A measure which affected a far wider range of people was the Education Act of 1870 (p. 363) which ensured that there should be elementary schools throughout the country.

These reforms also tended to promote efficiency. The quality of the Civil Service, the academic standards of Oxford and Cambridge, and the efficiency of the army were all improved; and the Education Act also helped to increase national efficiency, for the extension of education is one of the essentials for the effective development of an industrial economy.

Gladstone, as a Liberal, believed that societies worked best and that individuals had the greatest chance of happiness when governments interfered as little as possible. Sometimes the government had to interfere to ensure efficiency, and thus in 1871 a Trade Union Act tidied up the legislation affecting trade unions, in 1873 a Judicature Act thoroughly reorganised the country's very muddled legal system, and throughout the period of Gladstone's first ministry Edward Cardwell, the War Secretary, carried out a thorough-going reform of the organisation of infantry regiments, the system of recruitment, and the army's command structure. But in general Gladstone's main object was to reduce government intervention and expenditure, and to encourage the development of a free society, with the minimum restrictions on individual liberty.

Social reform and Conservatism

Disraeli was fundamentally opposed to this attitude. He saw Liberalism as the excuse of a grasping and irresponsible capitalist class for building private fortunes at the expense of an exploited working class, from whom arose 'a wail of intolerable serfage'. He saw that the breaches made by the Liberals in the barriers of privilege were of little value to a working class living in poverty and squalor, and he preferred practical social reforms. Thus 1875, the year after Disraeli returned to power, saw a Public Health Act, which provided for the appointment of Medical Officers of Health to fight infectious diseases and ensure good sewage maintenance, an Artisans' Dwellings Act, which gave the town councils of larger towns the power to pull down slums and build new houses in their place, and a Sale of Food and Drugs Act, which took steps to protect the public from goods harmful to health.

Disraeli's Conservatism, in fact, was not merely a belief that men should treasure the institutions and assets they inherited from the past, but also a conviction that men should build for the future in a practical fashion rather than relying on any particular ideology, such as Liberalism. He valued the monarchy and hoped to establish an alliance between the aristocracy and the working class against the middle-class Liberals. This accounts for the 1867 Reform Act and also for his repeal of Gladstone's Trade Union Act of 1871 which had left the unions virtually powerless. In 1875 Disraeli replaced it with a Conspiracy and Protection of Property Act, making it legal for a union to take any action which would be legal if done by an individual and also permitting peaceful picketing, thus assisting the development of trade unions and helping to defend the working class from middle-class exploitation.

Foreign policy

The difference of attitude between Gladstone and Disraeli is also apparent in the field of foreign policy. Gladstone's belief in Liberty went hand in hand with a belief that men could only be truly free if they lived in accordance with the moral law, and he applied this principle to the conduct of international affairs as well as to national affairs and private life. His belief in the sanctity of treaties led him at the beginning of the Franco–Prussian War in 1870 to make it clear that Britain would uphold the neutrality of Belgium, which had been guaranteed in 1839, and in the same year he condemned the unilateral Russian renunciation of treaty clauses which excluded Russian warships from the Black Sea. A belief in self-determination led him in 1871 to demand a plebiscite when the new German Empire annexed the provinces of Alsace and Lorraine from France. And his belief in arbitration led him in 1872 to pay to the U.S.A. the grossly inflated sum of £3,250,000 as compensation for the damage done in the American Civil War by a British-built ship, the *Alabama*, saying that it was as 'dust in the balance compared with the moral value of the example set'.

Disraeli, who regarded Gladstone's moralising as dishonest cant, was motivated primarily by a determination to maintain the interests and prestige of his country. The difference between the two men's attitudes was particularly marked during the Eastern crisis of 1875-8 (p. 7). Disraeli as Prime Minister was concerned to prevent any extension of Russian influence in the Balkans and to avoid war, and he regarded as irresponsible Gladstone's expressions of moral indignation against the Turkish slaughter of their Bulgarian subjects and his demand that the Turks should be cleared 'bag and baggage from the province they have desolated and profaned': on the one hand it provided the Russians with a justification for intervention; on the other it inflamed British public opinion against the Turks, so that it would be very difficult for Disraeli to take firm action to check Russian intervention.

In the event Disraeli and his Foreign Secretary, Lord Salisbury, conducted their foreign policy during the Eastern crisis with strength and subtlety and emerged from the Congress of Berlin with their aims achieved and their personal prestige enhanced.

While Disraeli gained a reputation for strength from his foreign dealings Gladstone gained a reputation for weakness. His failure to get the plebiscite he demanded in Alsace and Lorraine, his acceptance of the Russian renunciation of the Black Sea clauses once Russia accepted the principle of the sanctity of treaties, and his acceptance of the *Alabama* arbitration, all seemed to indicate weakness. But Gladstone could act firmly when he believed that firm action was both possible and justified. He had demonstrated this over the issue of Belgian neutrality in 1870. He was to demonstrate it again in 1885 when the Russians crossed the border of Afghanistan at Penjdeh, for by indicating that Britain was prepared to fight he dissuaded the Russians from advancing farther.

Imperialism

The difference between Gladstone and Disraeli is similarly apparent in their attitudes to Empire. Disraeli saw the Empire as the means by which England would 'command the respect of the world'. Gladstone saw it as a denial of the Liberal principle that all men should be free.

Disraeli's main concern was India. To secure Britain's communications with India he took the opportunity in 1875 of buying a seven-sixteenths share in the Suez Canal. To encourage the loyalty of the Indians to the monarchy he had Queen Victoria made 'Empress of India' in 1876. And in order to prevent any Russian advance towards India British forces invaded Afghanistan in 1878 and established a British mission at Kabul, the capital. He had comparatively little interest in Africa. But in 1877 when the Transvaal republic was threatened by the Zulus British officials in South Africa annexed it, and then at the beginning of 1879 they sent an expedition against the Zulus. Moreover, the failure of the Egyptian government in 1876 to pay its debts to British and French bondholders resulted in 1878 in Disraeli joining the French in establishing Anglo–French Dual Control over Egypt's finance.

These extension of British influence in South Africa, Afghanistan, and Egypt all had unfortunate repercussions. The force sent against the Zulus was slaughtered at Isandhlwana in January 1879, so that a further large force had to be sent to destroy the Zulu power. The members of the British mission at Kabul were massacred in September 1879, so that a further campaign was needed to establish Britain's position in Afghanistan. And in 1881 there was an Egyptian Nationalist rising against Dual Control.

To Gladstone these events seemed the natural sequel to Disraeli's Imperialism, and the disasters of Isandhlwana and Kabul lent force to his attacks on Imperialism in the Midlothian campaigns of 1879 and 1880 (p. 36). His own policy was one of disentanglement, so Britain withdrew from Afghanistan in 1880 and from the Transvaal in 1881. But in Egypt Gladstone felt he had a responsibility to the British bondholders. Instead of withdrawing he eventually in 1882 sent the fleet and an army, destroyed the power of the Egyptian Nationalists, and established a British Agent and Consul-General as the virtual ruler of Egypt. Ironically, this one imperial venture of Gladstone's constituted a more significant extension of British influence than all that Disraeli had accomplished.

Ireland

One of the most important issues in British politics in the period of the struggle between Gladstone and Disraeli was the Irish question. Gladstone, who declared just before becoming Prime Minister in 1868 that his mission was 'to pacify Ireland', did something to mollify the religious sentiments of the Roman Catholic Irish by disestablishing the Anglican Church there in 1869, and in 1870 he gave the Irish peasantry some protection from unscrupulous landlords by means of an Irish Land Act. This Act quietened agricultural unrest for a few years, but the agricultural depression which set in in 1875, and particularly the competition of cheap corn from America, intensified the problem again.

Disraeli, despite his protectionist attitude in 1846, made no attempt to protect Irish agriculture from American competition, and by 1880, when Gladstone returned to power, many Irish M.P.s, led by Charles Stuart Parnell, were deliberately obstructing the work of the Commons, and the Irish Land League, formed in 1879, was taking direct action in Ireland.

A further attempt to solve the problem by a combination of reform and firmness proved unsuccessful. A new Land Act passed in August 1881 did nothing to reduce the growing demand for Home Rule. A Coercion Act of March 1881 increased unrest. And two of Gladstone's reforms which were not particularly concerned with Ireland—the Ballot Act of 1872 (p. 360) and the Franchise Act of 1884 (p. 361)—immensely strengthened the position of the Irish by making possible the development of a powerful Irish Nationalist Party in the House of Commons.

At the end of 1885 Gladstone accepted that his own solution could not work and that Home Rule was the only solution to Ireland's problems. This decision split the Liberal Party and helped to bring to an end the long years of Liberal dominance in British politics. And when the Liberal Party, which Gladstone had split, lost its dominant position, the Conservative Party, which Disraeli had re-created, took that position over.

The legacy of Gladstone and Disraeli

Gladstone and Disraeli share the distinction of having ruled Britain at a time when her relative importance in the world was probably greater than ever before or since. Each of them had a considerable impact both on his own party and on the country, and their influence could still be felt long afterwards—though possibly not in ways which their contemporaries would have anticipated. The most durable feature of the policies of Gladstone, the great Liberal reformer, was the new attitude to international relations which he pioneered. The most lasting legacy of Disraeli, the flamboyant Imperialist, was an attitude to social reform which served as a model to Tory leaders in the mid-twentieth century.

Section II   Great Britain, 1871–1915

8   BRITAIN IN OUTLINE, 1868–1915

THE PERIOD when Gladstone and Disraeli dominated British politics saw a considerable movement away from an oligarchical system of government, with power in the hands of a small minority of the population, to a more democratic system in which most men had the right to vote for their representatives in parliament. One early effect of the extension of the franchise seemed to be a tendency for whichever party was in power to be defeated in general elections—no doubt because the faults of a government are more easily discerned than those of the opposition. Thus Disraeli's Conservative government was defeated in 1868, Gladstone's Liberal government was defeated in 1874, and Disraeli was again defeated in 1880.

Liberal dissension
In 1875, the year after his first government had come to an end with electoral defeat at the hands of the Conservatives, Gladstone announced his retirement from active politics. This announcement tended to open up the latent divisions in the Liberal Party. The Irish members were breaking away, the Radical and Whig elements were increasingly at odds, and besides these there were many, like Gladstone himself, who could not be grouped clearly with either the Whigs or the Radicals.

However, Gladstone did not stay in retirement long. Disraeli's policy over the Eastern crisis of 1875–8 stirred him to vigorous opposition. He went on to campaign for election as member of parliament for the Midlothian constituency, and after the Liberal victory in the general election of 1880 he was so obviously the dominant figure in the party that he again formed a government.

His second ministry was less successful than his first. The Irish issue took a disproportionate amount of the time and energy of the government. The cabinet was torn by dissension between the Whigs and the Radicals, and the dissension came to a head in June 1885 when seventy-six Liberals failed to vote in a division over a clause in the Budget. The government was defeated and Gladstone resigned.

Salisbury's caretaker government

The Marquess of Salisbury, who had been Disraeli's Foreign Secretary, was now faced with the difficult task of forming a Conservative government to rule with a minority in the House of Commons. He could not have an immediate election, as the Franchise Act of 1884 and the Redistribution Act of 1885 (pp. 360-1) had made it necessary to draw up new electoral rolls which would not be ready for some months. He could have declined to take office, and would have been well advised to do so, for Gladstone's government was already unpopular, and it would scarcely have become more popular if Gladstone had been obliged to carry on after a defeat in the Commons and with a divided party. But Salisbury made the mistake of accepting office, and in the six months before the general election the pendulum of public opinion had time to swing back towards the Liberals again.

Because of its weak position in the House of Commons the Conservative government was unable to do much, but it did end coercion in Ireland (p. 63), and its leaders entered into negotiations with Parnell, the leader of the Irish Nationalists.

The election of December 1885

There were three other important developments during this period:

(1) In September Joseph Chamberlain, without the authorisation of the other Liberal Party leaders, began campaigning for the election with a radical programme of reform of local government, education, and rural conditions.

(2) In December, two days before the election, Parnell, thinking that he was more likely to get support for Irish Home Rule from the Conservatives than the Liberals, told his supporters in England to vote Conservative.

(3) Meanwhile Gladstone had decided, without making his change of mind public, that Ireland should be given Home Rule.

In England the election was a victory for the Liberals, largely because of Joseph Chamberlain's 'unauthorised programme' of social reform. Even though Parnell's instructions to his supporters in England probably swung approximately 30 seats to the Conservatives the Liberals still won 86 seats more than the Conservatives. But in Ireland the Irish Nationalists had won 86 seats, and since they were allied with the Conservatives the sides in the Commons were exactly evenly balanced and Salisbury remained in office.

Gladstone's third ministry and Home Rule

When the news of Gladstone's conversion to Home Rule leaked out Parnell inevitably changed sides, and in February 1886 the government was defeated, and Salisbury resigned. The defection of the 86 Irish Nationalists from the Conservatives gave Gladstone a majority of 172, so when he formed his third ministry he did not need to hold a general election. But his party was even more divided than before. Many of the Whig leaders refused to join the cabinet, and although Chamberlain joined he resigned the following month because of his opposition to the Irish Home Rule Bill which Gladstone put before the cabinet. When the Bill came before the Commons 93 Liberals from both extremes of the party voted against it, and it was defeated by 343 votes to 313.

The election of July 1886

Instead of resigning Gladstone asked for a dissolution and fought a general election on the issue of Home Rule. He was heavily defeated. The Conservatives won 316 seats—40 more than the combined forces of the Liberals and Irish Nationalists, who now inevitably voted together. The Whigs and Radicals who had rebelled against Gladstone for the sake of maintaining the union of Great Britain and Ireland won 78 seats and, as Liberal Unionists, held the balance in the House of Commons.

The new pattern of politics

Thus the political alignments in the Commons had completely changed. After the election of December 1885 the balance between the two main parties had been held by the Irish Nationalists. But after the election of July 1886 the Irish Nationalists were committed to an alliance with the Liberals, and the balance between these two parties and the Conservatives was held by the Liberal Unionists. On the Irish question the Liberal Unionists could be relied on to vote with the Conservatives, but it was by no means obvious that they would vote with them on other issues, nor even that the Whig and Radical elements would vote the same way.

As it happens the alliance between the Conservatives and the Liberal Unionists did become permanent, for the Irish Question remained an important issue in British politics for another thirty-five years. But in July 1886 Lord Salisbury was so unsure of his position in parliament that he offered the premiership to Hartington, the Whig leader of the Liberal Unionists. Although Hartington refused Salisbury's offer, and although he and the other Liberal Unionists would not join Salisbury's government, they did agree to support it; and this co-operation between the Conservatives and the Liberal Unionists resulted in nearly twenty years of Conservative dominance.

Salisbury's second ministry

When Salisbury formed his second government in August 1886 he was to be Prime Minister for thirteen of the next sixteen years. The first six of these years came to an end after a general election in July 1892, which resulted in the combination of Liberal and Irish Nationalists having a majority of forty over the Conservatives and Liberal Unionists. When parliament reassembled in August a vote of confidence in Lord Salisbury was defeated, he resigned, and Gladstone formed his fourth and last ministry.

The Liberal interlude

Inevitably, since Gladstone took office in order to settle the Irish Question, and since the government depended on Irish support for survival in the Commons, Irish Home Rule was the main issue. In September 1893 the second Home Rule Bill was passed by the Commons, only to be rejected a week later by the Lords. The government now had either to accept defeat by the Lords or else fight a general election on the issue of reform of the House of Lords. Against the advice of Gladstone it accepted defeat. Six months later, at the age of 84, Gladstone resigned and was succeeded by his Foreign Secretary, Lord Rosebery, whose government lasted only fifteen months. It achieved little, for most of its controversial measures were defeated by the Lords, and in June 1895 Lord Rosebery resigned.

Salisbury's third ministry

Lord Salisbury now formed his third government. This time the Liberal Unionists agreed to join the Conservatives in office, and the two parties combined as the Unionist Party until 1922, by which time Ireland had gained her independence and the pattern of British politics had again completely changed.

In July 1895 the Unionists fought a general election and won a majority of 152. During the next few years the government's popularity declined so much that by October 1900 its majority had been reduced by by-election defeats to 124. A year earlier Great Britain had gone to war against the South African Boer republics, and now, when it seemed that the war was almost won, the government decided to make capital out of the patriotic fervour aroused by the war and fought a general election, even though it was under no constitutional obligation to do so for nearly two more years.

In this 'Khaki Election' of 1900 the government regained a few seats and continued in office with a majority of 134. The Boer War dragged on for another year and a half until May 1902, and a few weeks later Salisbury, whose third ministry had lasted for seven years, gave up the premiership to his nephew, A. J. Balfour.

Balfour's ministry

Balfour remained in office for nearly three and a half years in circumstances which became increasingly more difficult (pp. 52–3). At last, in December 1905, he resigned, and the Liberal leader, now Sir Henry Campbell-Bannerman, formed a government, asked for an immediate dissolution, and fought a general election. The Liberal Party won an overwhelming victory with a majority of 84 over all other parties, and with the further support of the Irish Nationalists and the members who later formed the Labour Party they had a majority of 356 over the Unionists. The twenty years of Conservative domination were to be followed by nearly ten years of Liberal rule.

Liberal rule, 1905–15

Campbell-Bannerman remained as Prime Minister for just over two years until in April 1908, when he was dying, he handed over to his Chancellor of the Exchequer, H. H. Asquith. By this time the government's position was being made increasingly difficult by the House of Lords, where the Unionists were using their majority to wreck the government's legislative programme. This precipitated a major constitutional crisis which was only resolved after two general elections, in January and December 1910, by a limitation of the powers of the Lords (p. 73).

The Liberals emerged from the election of December 1910 with 272 seats—exactly the same number as the Unionists. But with the support of the Irish Nationalists and of the Labour members they had an effective majority of 126 and were able to remain in office throughout the years leading up to the first World War.

When the war began the Conservatives, the Irish Nationalists, and most of the Labour Party declared their willingness to support the government, so the Liberals remained in power, though Lord Kitchener, who was known to have Conservative sympathies, was included in the cabinet as Secretary for War. But there was no quick victory, circumstances and attitudes underwent rapid changes, and in May 1915 Asquith gave in to Conservative pressure to form a coalition.

9　THE DECAY OF LIBERALISM

DURING the half-century after the Great Reform Act of 1832 Great Britain was ruled by Liberal governments for rather more than twice as long as by Conservative governments. But in 1885 the pattern of English politics changed. For the next twenty years, apart from six months in 1886 and three years from the summer of 1892 to the summer of 1895, the Conservatives were in office. Then in January 1906 the Liberals won a general election with an overwhelming majority, remained in power for ten years until a coalition was formed in the middle of the first World War, and after the coalition split in 1922 they not only never won an election but were never even the second largest party in the house.

The nature of Liberalism

The fundamental reason for this collapse is that by the twentieth century Liberalism was an out-worn creed. The nineteenth-century Liberal Party was a coalition of various groups—principally the Whig aristocrats, with a belief in constitutional monarchy dating from the Glorious Revolution of 1689, and the middle-class Liberals, who believed that society works best when men are free.

The Liberal believed in Free Trade. That is he believed that the natural law of supply and demand would produce the most prosperous economy, and therefore anything which restricted the operation of the law of supply and demand, such as tariffs to protect home industries from foreign competition, was wrong.

He also believed in freedom for all men to speak, worship, and even be ruled as they wished. Therefore he believed in religious toleration at home and opposed the subjugation of native peoples overseas.

Finally, he believed in *laissez-faire*, or leaving things alone. This meant giving industrialists freedom to run their industries as efficiently or as incompetently as they liked. Liberals pointed out that the efficient would prosper.

It was during the period that British governments were committed to these ideas that Britain rose to be the most powerful nation in the world. While a Free Trade country with a domestic policy of *laissez-faire* Britain achieved industrial pre-eminence as 'the workshop of the world'. While proclaiming a belief in Liberty, Britain achieved moral pre-eminence. But all three of these beliefs carried the seeds of disaster, both for Britain and for the Liberal Party, if they were taken to their logical conclusion.

Laissez-faire or social reform?

Laissez-faire allowed men the freedom to become rich and powerful, and inevitably also allowed freedom for others to be exploited and get poorer. Consequently many Liberals saw the need for the state to intervene to restrict liberty in the interest of the mass of the people; and much of the legislation of the Liberal governments in the years just before the first World War was of this sort. The Workmen's Compensation Act of 1906 was illiberal, for it encroached on the liberty of employers by compelling them to pay compensation for industrial accidents and diseases. The Old Age Pensions Act of 1908 was illiberal, for it restricted the freedom of men to do as they wished with their own money, and was based on the principle that the rich should be taxed not just to provide revenue but in order that their money might be redistributed to the poor. The National Insurance Act of 1911 was even more illiberal, for it compelled all employees earning less than £160 a year to pay an insurance contribution of 4*d.* a week.

Not all Liberals found it easy to accept this change from Liberalism to state intervention, and consequently the party came to be divided into *laissez-faire* Liberals and social reformers.

Freedom or Imperialism?

A belief in freedom and minority rights, carried to its logical conclusion, would mean leaving India to the Indians and South Africa to the Boers, and it might even entail leaving Persia to the Russians (p. 82). Many Liberals saw the disintegrating effect of such a policy on the British Empire and possibly on Great Britain herself. They believed in the need for continuity in foreign and colonial policy when governments changed. Some split from their fellow-Liberals in 1886 by voting against Home Rule for Ireland, and as Liberal Unionists they were gradually assimilated by the Conservative Party. Others who remained in the Liberal Party came to be known as Liberal Imperialists. Those who adhered to the old Liberal principles were dubbed Little Englanders.

Free Trade or Protection?

The double division into *laissez-faire* Liberals and social reformers and into Liberal Imperialists and Little Englanders existed at the end of the nineteenth century. But all Liberals were united in their belief in Free Trade. In 1903–5, when Joseph Chamberlain was campaigning to put up protective tariffs (p. 52), all Liberals rallied to oppose him. In 1923, when Stanley Baldwin fought an election on the issue of Protection (p. 207), the bitterly divided

Liberals reunited to defend Free Trade.

But by the end of the twenties even Free Trade was out of date. Many British goods were expensive by comparison with those of newly industrialised countries where labour was cheap, and consequently many British firms not only found it difficult to sell their goods abroad but even found that they could not compete with some foreign goods on the home market. Consequently, British manufacturers demanded Protection. By 1931 half the Liberal M.P.s supporting the National government (p. 174) were prepared to accept the imposition of tariffs, and the last prop of Liberalism had been knocked away.

The Newcastle programme

The divisions over the fundamental issues of social reform, Imperialism, and later even Free Trade were not the only factors which caused the decline of the Liberal Party. One of the strengths of Liberalism was its championship of minorities, but the championship of minority causes tends to alienate support as well as gathering it, and consequently the Liberal Party came to depend increasingly on the various minority groups which it championed, and in particular on the 'Celtic fringe'—the Welsh, the Scots, and the Irish.

In 1891 the Liberals in conference at Newcastle adopted what came to be called the 'Newcastle programme' in a bid to rally minority support to them. This included:

(1) Irish Home Rule, which would ensure the support of the Irish Nationalist Party;

(2) church disestablishment for Wales and Scotland, which would satisfy the large body of non-conformist voters;

(3) legislation to permit local authorities to forbid the sale of alcoholic drinks in their area—a striking illustration of the confusion of Liberal thought, and another offering to Welsh non-conformity;

(4) reform of the land laws, which would attract rural voters;

(5) legislation to make employers liable for industrial accidents, which would attract the trade unionists, who had not yet transferred their support to the Labour movement.

This programme was a burden rather than an asset to the Liberals, for it failed to provide genuine unity, and it committed them in a way that restricted their freedom of action in the future.

The challenge from Labour

The rise of the Labour Party also hastened the decline of the Liberals, especially as the Liberal and Labour Parties were not so much opponents as rivals for leadership of the left. In 1906 the Liberals won an overall majority in the Commons of sixty-four. But the Labour Party had already begun its bid to take over from them, and for nearly forty years the left-wing vote was so divided that neither left-wing party ever won an overall majority, even though their combined vote was often greater than that for the Conservatives. In the twenty years from 1910 to 1930 there were, apart from the Coupon Election of 1918 (p. 172) which was won by the war-time coalition, six general elections. Those of 1922 and 1924 brought the Conservatives to power with clear majorities. But the two elections of 1910 which confirmed Asquith's Liberal government in office only enabled it to command a majority in the Commons by relying on Irish Nationalist and Labour support. And the elections of 1923 and 1929, which brought Labour governments to power, made those governments dependent on Liberal support.

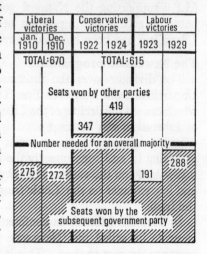

Liberal divisions

Against this background of ideological difference, dependence on minority groups, and the threat from the Labour Party, the Liberal leaders planned their policies, argued, intrigued, and eventually tore their party in pieces.

The division over Irish Home Rule was the first serious blow to Liberal unity, and resulted in twenty years of Conservative, or Unionist, dominance in politics. Then the Liberals had one last decade in power. But Liberalism was too weak a force to be able to repair successfully the damage done by the war-time split between Asquith and Lloyd George.

After the war many Liberal voters turned to the Conservative and Labour Parties. Some Liberal cabinet ministers did as well: in 1924 Lord Haldane became a member of the first Labour government, and later in the year Churchill took office as a Conservative.

10   CONSERVATISM, 1885–1905

Salisbury, Balfour, and Chamberlain

DURING the twenty years of Conservative predominance between 1885 and 1905 Lord Salisbury headed three governments. During his first ministry, from June 1885 to February 1886, he lacked a majority in the House of Commons and could therefore do little. During his second and third ministries (1886–92 and 1895–1902) he was in a position of strength in the Commons, but still did little. Salisbury's disinclination to take action was an essential part of his Conservatism. He felt it to be the task of the government to administer the country and to conserve its institutions and laws rather than change them. It was also an essential part of his own nature. Even in foreign policy, which interested him more than domestic affairs, he tended to await developments rather than plan ahead.

His nephew, A. J. Balfour, who succeeded him as Prime Minister from 1902 until 1905, was far more active, but the legislation introduced during his one short ministry was inadequate to cope with the problems of the early twentieth century.

The man who stands out as the dominant political figure of these decades is their Liberal Unionist ally, Joseph Chamberlain. He was a radical reformer at home and an imperialist abroad; and he seems to have been virtually Deputy Prime Minister in the years 1895–1903 when he was Colonial Secretary. He was a vigorous man who took the initiative in many spheres, but even his achievements, when measured against his aims, are remarkably few.

Ireland

The issue which held the Conservatives and Liberal Unionists together was that of Ireland. During Salisbury's first ministry, while Chamberlain was still a Liberal, the Conservatives were the allies of the Irish Nationalists. They ended coercion, passed the first Land Purchase Act, thus helping Irish peasants to buy their land, and entered into secret negotiations about Home Rule with Parnell. But as soon as Gladstone's conversion to Home Rule became public the Conservative leaders changed their attitude. In 1886 they combined with the Liberal rebels to defeat the first Home Rule Bill, and then Salisbury took office again committed to maintaining the union of Great Britain and Ireland.

At the beginning of Salisbury's second ministry his government's intransigence led to increased unrest in Ireland. Early in

1887 the government replied with a new Crimes Act, and for three years Balfour, as Chief Secretary for Ireland, imposed a rigorous policy of coercion. By 1890 he was successful enough to be able to relax the Crimes Act, and he even gained some popularity by measures such as the second Land Purchase Act of 1891.

While in opposition from 1892-5 the Conservatives were able to kill the second Home Rule Bill of 1893 by using their majority in the House of Lords. During Salisbury's third ministry nothing was done to improve the position of the Irish peasants, but in 1903, during Balfour's ministry, a Land Purchase Act on a far larger scale than before provided for state loans to enable the peasants to buy their land. But this was no final solution to the problems of a country which wanted to rule itself.

Foreign policy

In the sphere of foreign affairs these were the years of 'splendid isolation' (p. 74). Salisbury, who was Foreign Secretary as well as Prime Minister most of the while, helped to secure Britain's position in Egypt against French ambitions by means of the Mediterranean Agreement with Italy in 1887 (p. 95), by 1890 reached agreement with Germany and Portugal about the partition of Africa, negotiated several agreements with France about spheres of influence in Africa, and in 1898 unsuccessfully tried to reach agreement with Russia about the Far East.

Salisbury was less immediately responsible for later developments in foreign policy while he was still Foreign Secretary. It was Joseph Chamberlain who took the initiative in approaching Germany with suggestions for alliance in 1898, 1899, and 1901; and the war against the Boer republics from 1899 to 1902 arose out of South African affairs, which were Chamberlain's responsibility. Although Salisbury was still Prime Minister when the Japanese Alliance of 1902 was negotiated, it was Lord Lansdowne, who had taken over from him as Foreign Secretary, who negotiated it, and it was also Lansdowne who negotiated the Anglo-French *entente* of 1904 during Balfour's premiership.

Imperial affairs

It is generally assumed that the greatest achievement of the Conservative governments between 1885 and 1905 lay in the development of the Empire. But in fact the central government exercised comparatively little influence over imperial developments. Canada and Newfoundland, Cape Colony and Natal, New Zealand and the Australian colonies ruled themselves. The only direct contribution to their development by the British government lay in the Commonwealth of Australia Act of 1900 which sanctioned the decision of the Australian colonies to combine in a federation. Even in Egypt and India, for which the British government had a more direct responsibility, progress during this period was not the work of the British government at home but in Egypt of Sir Evelyn Baring, British Agent and Consul-General 1882–1907, and in India primarily of Lord Curzon, Viceroy 1898–1905.

The security of the whole Empire did, of course, depend on Britain's strength and on Salisbury's and Lansdowne's diplomacy. And there was some extension of territory on the government's initiative. Upper Burma was annexed during Salisbury's first ministry, and during his second ministry protectorates were established over Nyasaland and Zanzibar. While Chamberlain was Colonial Secretary protectorates were established over Ashanti and Northern Nigeria, the Sudan was reconquered, and in 1902 at the end of the Boer War the Transvaal and the Orange Free State were annexed. Moreover, an impetus was given to imperial developments in Africa by Chamberlain's work at the Colonial Office. But the real work of extending British influence in Africa was done not by the government but by the chartered companies, such as the Royal Niger Company and the British East Africa Company, and by individual adventurers, such as Cecil Rhodes.

Defence

During Salisbury's third ministry the inefficiency of the army was revealed by the Boer War, and the obsolescence of the Royal Navy was made clear by Germany's naval building programme.

Neither Salisbury's nor Balfour's government achieved any rea reform of the army, but the navy fared better. In 1905, to meet the changed international situation after the *entente cordiale* of 1904 (p. 80) and the defeat of Russia in the Far East by Japan (p. 82) the fleet was based on ports nearer home, and plans were also made for building a new type of battlecruiser and a new type of battleship, the *Dreadnought*, which was armed entirely with large guns and could easily out-shoot any other warship.

Social reform

The legislation for social reform during these years of Conservative domination was negligible. The social unrest during Salisbury's second ministry, of which the London Dock Strike of 1889 (p. 181) was a symptom, resulted in one measure of reform. A Factory Act of 1891 forbad employing children under twelve in factories, limited the hours of work for women, and gave local authorities the power to insist on sanitary conditions in factories.

During Salisbury's third ministry Joseph Chamberlain was responsible for the Workmen's Compensation Act of 1897, which provided that workers in some industries should be compensated by their employers for industrial accidents.

In 1905, the last year of Balfour's ministry, the Unemployed Workmen Act permitted the establishment of committees to help the unemployed find work, and it also permitted the committees to give to unemployed men money raised by voluntary subscription.

Local government

The reform of local government was the principal measure of domestic reform in these years. In 1888 the Local Government Act divided England and Wales into sixty-two administrative counties, with county councils elected by the ratepayers and responsible for matters such as roads, bridges, police, and public health. It was at this time that the County of London was established, and at the same time many large towns were made county boroughs— independent of the counties in which they were situated, and responsible for their own administration.

During the following years the new London County Council came increasingly under the control of 'progressive' councillors, who were very largely Liberals, so in 1899 Lord Salisbury's London Government Act limited the power of the L.C.C. by sub-dividing London outside the city into twenty-eight Metropolitan Boroughs.

Education

Since 1870 there had been provision for nation-wide elementary education (p. 363), and since 1880 it had been compulsory from the age of five till ten. In 1891 the Conservatives passed an Act to make all elementary education free.

In 1889 a Technical Instruction Act made technical education the responsibility of the new local government authorities, and soon the local authorities who controlled technical education, the School Boards controlling much of elementary education, and the old endowed grammar schools were all doing something to further the growth of secondary education. So in 1899 the government set up a Board of Education to co-ordinate the different aspects of the work of education, and in the same year the school-leaving age was raised to twelve.

A further advance was made by Balfour's Education Act of

1902. The old School Boards were abolished. Elementary and secondary education joined technical education as the responsibility of local government authorities. And all elementary education was to be paid for out of the general rates paid by householders.

Joseph Chamberlain

Apart from the few measures of social reform, and apart from the reorganisation of local government and education, the twenty years from 1885 to 1905 were years of stagnation in domestic affairs; and the history of these two decades is also, in a sense, the story of the failure of Joseph Chamberlain.

The policy of maintaining the union of Great Britain and Ireland, to which he sacrificed the Liberal Party in 1886, bedevilled English politics for the next thirty-five years until Ireland at last gained her independence.

The German alliance which he advocated was spurned by Germany, and during the next half-century the British Empire fought two wars against her.

The new era of social reform which his 'unauthorised programme' of 1885 (p. 37) had seemed to herald in, had to wait for twenty years until Chamberlain was himself in opposition to come to fruition. The tragedy here is that Chamberlain could have used his influence after the alliance of the Liberal Unionists and Conservatives in 1895 to give the new Unionist coalition its own brand of radicalism. But he turned down the Chancellorship of the Exchequer and the chance of promoting social reform.

He chose instead to be Colonial Secretary because he wanted to mould the future shape of the Empire. He envisaged a federal Empire with a central Imperial parliament, no internal tariff barriers, and a centralised system of defence. And thus the sphere of imperial affairs, where Chamberlain is usually thought to have been most successful, saw his greatest failure. For the Empire developed into a Commonwealth of independent nations, each of which put up its own tariff barriers and was responsible for all its own affairs, including defence.

The last episode in his career was his campaign for Protection (p. 52). Again he failed, for England remained a Free Trade country until his son, Neville Chamberlain, introduced Protection in 1931 (p. 212). But the immediate political effect of his campaign was vast. In 1886 he had helped to split the Liberal Party over the issue of Ireland. In 1903-5 his Protection campaign divided the Unionists and contributed much to the overwhelming Liberal victory in the election of January 1906.

11   CONSERVATIVE COLLAPSE, 1906

IN the election of January 1906 the Liberals won 377 seats, the Unionists 157, the Irish Nationalists 83, and those who later formed the Labour Party 53. It was natural that there should have been a swing of the pendulum of political opinion back to the Liberals, for it was now ten years since the country had had a Liberal government, and twenty since it had had an effective one. But this swing of allegiance was on an unprecedented scale.

Party differences

The Unionist and Liberal Parties of 1906 were very different from the Conservative–Tory and Liberal–Whig Parties of the middle of the nineteenth century, both of which had been led primarily by the aristocracy. In 1886 the Whig aristocracy had left the Liberals over the issue of Home Rule (p. 186), and as a result there was by the twentieth century a genuine social difference between the parties.

Unionist leadership was aristocratic, the Unionists dominated the House of Lords, and Unionist cabinets were to some extent a family affair. The brothers Arthur and Gerald Balfour both held cabinet office under their uncle, the third Marquess of Salisbury, and in 1903 Arthur Balfour, now Prime Minister himself, brought into the cabinet to join them their cousin, the fourth Marquess of Salisbury, who had recently succeeded his father to the title.

The Liberal leaders, on the other hand, included the young Welsh solicitor Lloyd George, from a Carmarthenshire village, and the Scottish trade unionist John Burns, who had played a leading part in the London Dock Strike of 1889 (p. 181).

The social difference went hand in hand with fundamentally different political attitudes. Some men wish to conserve the society they live in and distrust change. Others, who are less satisfied with their society, wish to reform and change it. This difference of attitude can cut across class divisions, but on the whole the more prosperous element of society saw little need for change and supported the Unionists, while the less satisfied elements, who wanted the government to legislate to improve society, supported the Liberals, and some of the most discontented, who wanted change on a revolutionary scale, voted for the new Labour Party.

Lack of social reform

Much discontent with the Unionists came from their failure to legislate. England was an outstandingly prosperous country, yet it had been calculated that more than a quarter of the population lived below the poverty line—hungry, ill-housed, under-clothed, unhealthy. Even the standard of living of the artisan class was being depressed in the early years of the twentieth century, for while prices rose their wages did not. The social reform of the previous twenty years had been woefully inadequate, and the working class therefore voted for the Liberals who offered social reform, against the Unionists who had neglected it.

The Taff Vale Case

Particularly violent ill-feeling against the Unionists was aroused by their failure to legislate to protect the Trade Unions after the judgment of the House of Lords in the Taff Vale Case (p. 182) had made the right to strike worthless. In the long run the rise of the Labour Party, which was greatly helped by the Taff Vale Case, harmed the Liberals more than the Conservatives, but in 1906 it was the Unionists who suffered. The Labour Party was not yet a serious rival to the Liberals, and its leaders had reached a secret agreement with the Liberals about co-operation in the election.

'Chinese slavery'

Another issue which aroused anger against the Unionists was the importation into the Transvaal of 47,000 Chinese coolies to work in the mines (p. 270). Balfour had given permission for this. They were legally bound to their employers, were not allowed to bring their wives and children, and were kept in compounds whose conditions horrified the British electorate. The working class was especially appalled at the apparent assumption that the well-being of the coolies was unimportant so long as their labour remained a useful commodity to the mine-owners. A cry was raised against 'Chinese slavery', and this was one of the main issues on which the Liberals attacked the Unionists in their election campaign.

The non-conformist vote

The Unionists were unpopular with the non-conformists not so much because of what they had failed to do during the previous twenty years as because of what they had done recently:

The Education Act of 1902 (p. 48): One effect of the Education Act was that the running cost of voluntary schools would be paid for out of the general rates so long as the school building was provided. This was bitterly resented by non-conformists, who objected to having to subsidise Anglican and even Roman Catholic schools. Lloyd George attacked this aspect of the Bill in the Commons, many non-conformists tried to make it unworkable, and passions were still raging furiously at the time of the election.

The Licensing Act of 1904: The Licensing Act, which arranged that the liquor trade should provide compensation for public house licensees who were refused permission to renew their licences, was regarded by non-conformists as condoning the evil of drink.

The legacy of the Boer War

Moreover, by 1906 the patriotic fervour of the time of the Boer War had died down. Many people now felt that the war should never have been started, and the government was also blamed for mismanaging it and for what Campbell-Bannerman called the 'methods of barbarism' used in its last phase (p. 269).

People also remembered the 'Khaki election' (pp. 39–40) in the middle of the Boer War, and many felt that they had been tricked into returning to power a government which claimed to have won a war which it did not in fact win for another year and a half.

Foreign policy

Even the Unionists' foreign policy was criticised. The Anglo-Japanese alliance of 1902 (p. 77) was disliked by many who saw it as an abandonment of 'splendid isolation', and the *entente cordiale* (p. 80) was criticised by those who disliked the French and re-garded France as Britain's natural enemy.

Protection

But the issue which damaged the position of the Unionists most was that of Protection. Joseph Chamberlain believed that it was necessary to abandon Britain's traditional policy of Free Trade, and in its place he offered Protection and Imperial Preference. He wanted to protect British agriculture and industry from competition by placing duties on foreign foodstuffs and manufactured goods. He wished at the same time to forge the Empire into an economic unit by giving considerable exemption from duty to goods from within the Empire.

These proposals harmed the Unionists in three ways:
(1) It became clear to the electorate that the Unionist leaders were divided. In May 1902, on the same day that Balfour had declared his intention to remove the duty on corn which had been imposed as a temporary measure to help pay for the Boer War, Chamberlain made a speech proclaiming the need for further duties. Until September 1903 the divided cabinet held together, but then there was a drastic cabinet reshuffle in which Chamberlain went out of office. For the next two years Chamberlain campaigned for

Protection, while Balfour, who realised that open adoption of Protection would lose votes and that open opposition to Chamberlain would split the party, neither disowned his policy nor acted in accordance with it.

(2) While Protection divided the Unionists it helped to unite the Liberals. Balfour resigned in December 1905 instead of asking for a dissolution because he thought that the Liberal leaders were so divided that Campbell-Bannerman might have difficulty in forming a cabinet, and public opinion might then swing back to the Unionists. But Campbell-Bannerman had few difficulties in forming his cabinet, and this was largely because Protection had driven the Liberal leaders together in defence of Free Trade.

(3) Above all the idea of Protection was itself unpopular. The electorate was not ready for so drastic a reversal of Britain's traditional policy, and to many Protection just looked like a clever way of taxing food. Balfour had never openly disowned Protection, so the electorate, faced with a choice between the united Liberals, who promised to keep food prices low, and the divided Unionists, many of whom were openly recommending a tax on food, tended to vote Liberal.

The Irish question

Even the Irish question was unable to save the Unionists. The Irish Land Purchase Act of 1903 did nothing to destroy the demand for Home Rule in Ireland, where, except in the Protestant North-East, the mass of the country as usual voted Irish Nationalist. In England the Irish Question was temporarily unimportant, for the Liberal leaders had dropped Home Rule from their programme, and the election was fought on other issues.

Liberal victory

The working class voted against the Unionists because of the Taff Vale Case and 'Chinese slavery', and most of them voted for the Liberals, who promised social reform and low food prices. The non-conformists voted against the Unionists because of the Education Act and the Licensing Act. Most of the Irish voted against them, as they always did. And memories of the Boer War and the 'Khaki election' and doubts about foreign policy all contributed to the Unionists' unpopularity. The only chance they had of winning the election lay in Liberal disunity, and in resigning when he did Balfour gambled intelligently. But the principle of Free Trade had united the Liberals, and they swept into power.

12   FROM EMPIRE TO
         COMMONWEALTH

IN 1876 the title 'Empress of India' was conferred by Act of
Parliament on Queen Victoria. Technically the imperial title
related only to India, but in practice all the lands whose peoples
owed allegiance to the Crown or were under its protection were
referred to as 'the British Empire'. Just three-quarters of a
century later another Queen came to the throne. But Queen
Elizabeth II was never an Empress. Instead she was 'Head of the
Commonwealth', for the Empire had given place to something
which Lord Rosebery had described as long ago as 1884 as 'the
British Commonwealth of Nations'.

The Imperial dilemma

Some time in the late nineteenth century a decision had to be
made about the future of the Empire. It could either become more
close-knit, with an Imperial federal constitution comparable with
that of the U.S.A., whereby each state controls its domestic
affairs but matters of general concern are dealt with by a central
federal government, or it could move in the other direction
towards decentralisation and possibly eventual disintegration.

For some time the problem was not faced nor even fully realised.
But the idea of the importance and unity of the Empire was emphasised at the first Colonial Conference, which was held in London in 1887 when the prime ministers of all the self-governing
colonies gathered together for the celebration of Queen Victoria's
Golden Jubilee—the fiftieth anniversary of her accession to the
throne.

Ten years later, when Queen Victoria's Diamond Jubilee was
celebrated in another burst of Imperial pageantry and the prime
ministers of the self-governing colonies again came to London,
Joseph Chamberlain, the Colonial Secretary, seized the opportunity of the third Colonial Conference to propose the establishment of a federal Empire with each colony running its own internal
affairs, but with a central federal parliament controlling defence
and economic policy. Only New Zealand and Tasmania supported the proposal, and Canada led the opposition to it.

Most of the self-governing colonies disliked the idea of a federal
parliament because they were so much smaller than Great Britain
that they would inevitably have been dominated by her. They
were unwilling to co-operate in a centralised defence policy be-

cause, once again, Britain's size and position in the world would
have entailed their subordination. And they had no wish for Empire Free Trade because one of their main reasons for imposing
protective tariffs was to keep out British manufactured goods,
which tended to stifle the development of their own industries.

Some people would no doubt argue that it could never have
worked anyway. Communications would have been largely by sea
over vast distances, and it would eventually have been necessary
to face the problem of building a multi-racial Empire in a world
where racial prejudice was still strong. Others would argue that
it was better that it should not happen, and that Britain's greatest
contribution to the world has been the formation of a voluntary
association of nations bound together by common traditions and
interests. Some may feel that a great opportunity was lost.

Imperial co-operation

But although the self-governing colonies were not prepared to
form a federal parliament they had a considerable sense of common interest with Britain. They would not accept central control
of defence, but some of 'the Dominions' agreed to contribute
towards the costs of the Royal Navy, and during the Boer War
(pp. 268–9) Canada, Australia and New Zealand sent units to
fight in South Africa. They rejected the idea of Empire Free
Trade, but they did indicate that they were prepared to trade on
preferential terms with other countries of the Commonwealth,
and Canada took the lead by offering a preferential tariff to
Great Britain.

Independence in foreign affairs

In the first quarter of the twentieth century two other Dominions were formed, the Union of South Africa in 1910, and the
Irish Free State in 1921. In both of these the majority of the
inhabitants were not of British descent, they had fought against
British control, and they did not have the close attachment to
Great Britain characteristic of Australians and New Zealanders.
Understandably they wanted complete independence from Britain
not only in domestic affairs but also in their relations with other
countries.

The first World War moved the Empire in the same direction.
Before 1914 the dependence of the Dominions on the Royal
Navy for their defence had tied them to Britain's foreign policy,
and Britain's declaration of war had automatically involved them
as well. This had been willingly accepted at the time, but some

of the Dominions later felt dissatisfied with this obvious subordination to Britain. Participation in the war had increased their national consciousness, and by the end of the war Canada and South Africa, which were noticeably more self-assertive than Australia and New Zealand, were demanding equality in foreign policy as much as in other matters.

Therefore in 1919 each of the Prime Ministers of the Dominions attended the Peace Conference in his own right and signed the peace treaties separately, and in 1920 all the Dominions, and India as well, became full members of the League of Nations.

In 1922 at the time of the Chanak crisis (p. 309) the question of the independence of the Dominions came up in a more crucial form, for although Australia and New Zealand were immediately willing to give assistance when Lloyd George asked for it, Canada, South Africa, and the Irish Free State were not prepared to be involved in a dispute which they felt to be no concern of theirs.

The Statute of Westminster, 1931

It was largely this question of external affairs which resulted in 1926 in a demand for clarification of the position of a Dominion.

At the Imperial Conference of 1926 the Canadians, South Africans, and Irish demanded that the king's representatives in their countries, the Governors-General, should represent only the monarch and not the British government, and that Dominion status should be defined. Both demands were accepted, and Lord Balfour devised a formula which the Conference adopted that Britain and the Dominions were 'equal in status, in no way subordinate to one another in any aspect of their domestic or external affairs, though united by common allegiance to the Crown'.

Legally the British government still had various powers over the Dominions, for the Imperial Conference was only a friendly discussion, and its decisions had no legal force. Constitutionally, however, the position was quite clear: Britain could not enforce her legal rights. Nevertheless, Canada, South Africa, and the Irish Free State demanded that the declaration of 1926 should be made legally binding. So in 1931 the Statute of Westminster was enacted by the British parliament, abolishing all legal limitations on the Dominions governments.

Equality in the thirties

The equality of status was demonstrated in the following year when a conference met not in London but Ottawa, and representatives of Britain and the Dominions bargained with each other on equal terms about tariffs and signed bi-lateral treaties arranging for preferential trade terms.

The independence of the Dominions and their differing attitudes towards Britain were demonstrated at the outbreak of war in September 1939. Australia and New Zealand, which had never formally adopted the Statue of Westminster, regarded themselves as constitutionally bound to go to war when their king did, and their governments did not declare war on Germany but merely asked their parliaments to confirm the fact that they were at war. Canada delayed declaring war for a week in order to make it clear that she was acting independently. In South Africa the cabinet was divided over the war issue, and war was only declared after a change of government. And Eire, as the Irish Free State was now called, proclaimed her neutrality and remained neutral throughout the war.

The Commonwealth after two World Wars

In the decade after the second World War the two most important aspects of the history of the British Commonwealth were the opening of its door to non-white peoples of the Empire and the demonstration that the door was also open for any independent Commonwealth country to leave if it wished.

When India and Pakistan gained their independence in 1947 they both remained in the Commonwealth, as did Ceylon in 1948. And most of the countries of the old Empire which gained their independence in the second half of the twentieth century also remained in the Commonwealth.

On the other hand Burma left the Commonwealth when it became independent in 1948; Eire also left in 1948; and South Africa, which had been a Dominion for half a century, left in 1961.

Before long it seemed possible that the Commonwealth might disintegrate. Conflicts between Commonwealth members, such as India and Pakistan, revealed the weakness of Commonwealth links. And then the British government's mishandling of the Rhodesian declaration of independence in 1965 (p. 377) strained the Commonwealth almost to breaking point. To some people the Commonwealth looked like nothing more than a myth for giving Britain an illusion of still being a great power.

But many of the newly emerging countries valued the Commonwealth for the practical advantages of membership, and in 1971 it still seemed possible that it might continue as a friendly and mutually advantageous association of most of the peoples of the old Empire.

13   LIBERAL REFORM, 1905–1914

THE YEARS of Liberal rule before the first World War were a time of great change. The Empire was developing into a voluntary association of self-governing nations (pp. 54–6). Britain was moving out of 'splendid isolation' towards alliance with France and Russia (p. 78). Her navy was rebuilt on a massive scale and her army was reformed. The power of trade unions developed strikingly (pp. 182–3), and women were demanding a new status in the community (p. 362). Conflict between the government and the House of Lords brought about the biggest constitutional development since 1832 (p. 73). And the government legislated not only for social reform on a new scale but also for social reform of a new type, for it insisted on the principle that the community as a whole has an obligation to look after the welfare of its members, and took the first steps towards constructing what was later called 'the Welfare State'.

Imperial affairs

South Africa: As soon as Campbell-Bannerman came to power he devoted himself to the affairs of South Africa. Instructions were immediately issued for ending 'Chinese slavery' (p. 51). Self-government was granted to the Transvaal by the end of 1906 and to the Orange River Colony six months later, and this policy was so successful that in 1909 they agreed to unite with Cape Colony and Natal to form the Union of South Africa.

India: The Morley–Minto reforms of 1909 (p. 332), which were the first real step towards self-government in India, were also the first step towards genuine self-government by any non-white people in the British Empire.

Ireland: In the whole of the Empire only Ireland was a source of imminent trouble. Asquith hoped that he could conciliate Ireland with his Home Rule Bill of 1912 (p. 66) as Campbell-Bannerman had conciliated South Africa. But the Protestant Irish of Ulster and the Roman Catholics of the South could not be reconciled as easily as the Boers and the English settlers of South Africa had been. In 1914 Ireland seemed ready for civil war, and her future was still unsettled when the first World War broke out.

Foreign policy

Sir Edward Grey was Foreign Secretary throughout the years leading up to the first World War. He took office during the Tangier crisis (p. 85) and only resigned in December 1916 when

Lloyd George replaced Asquith as leader of the coalition government. His principal aim was to maintain British security, and since the main threat to that security was the possibility of German domination of Europe he sought to strengthen good relations with France and Russia, for those two nations could be relied on to oppose an extension of German power in Europe.

At the same time he tried to avoid antagonising the Germans, and it was largely for this reason that he tried to reach agreement on limiting naval building, gave Russia no support during the Bosnian crisis of 1908–9 (p. 86), and supported Austria-Hungary's demand at the London Conference of 1912–13 (p. 101) for the establishment of an independent Albania. But Grey did not make the sort of mistakes the appeasers were to make in the thirties (pp. 252–5). He stood firm when it was necessary, as over Morocco (pp. 85 and 87), he helped to build and strengthen the Triple Entente so that when it was eventually necessary to fight, Britain, France, and Russia stood together, and although up to the last moment he struggled to keep the peace, he had for years made it clear that Germany could not rely on British neutrality if she attacked France.

Haldane's army reforms

While Grey tried to keep the peace Haldane, the Secretary for War, ensured that Britain would have an efficient army if she needed to fight. In 1906 he gave the army a general staff. In 1907 the Territorial and Reserve Forces Act provided for a regular Expeditionary Force of six infantry divisions and one cavalry division, with its own artillery, transport, and other supporting arms, all ready for rapid mobilisation. It also provided for home defence by a Territorial Army of civilian part-time volunteers. In 1909 Officers' Training Corps in schools were formed. As a result of these reforms it was possible to mobilise rapidly in 1914, provide trained men to replace the heavy casualties in the early weeks, and provide a steady stream of officers throughout the war.

Social reform

Much of the most lasting work of the Liberals was in the field of social reform, and some of the more important measures in this field were concerned with labour conditions, trade unions, children, and the penal system.

Labour conditions: In 1906 a Workmen's Compensation Act extended the Act of 1897 (p. 48) to cover all workers earning less than £250 a year, and included industrial diseases as well as accidents. A Merchant Shipping Act of the same year improved conditions for seamen, and in 1908 the Mines Act fixed the miners' working day at eight hours. Both the Labour Exchanges Act and the Trade Boards Act were passed in 1909. The first set up over a hundred labour exchanges to put unemployed men in contact with employers with vacancies. The second set up boards to put an end to 'sweated' labour by fixing minimum wages for those who worked in small workshops or even at home and lacked the opportunity for trade union organisation. In 1911 a Shops Act gave shop assistants a weekly half holiday.

Trade unions: The government's legislation affecting trade unions was designed to free them from the restrictions imposed on them by two legal judgments. In 1906 the Trade Disputes Act had the effect of reversing the decision of the House of Lords in the Taff Vale Case of 1901 (p. 182) and in 1913 the Trade Union Act similarly reversed the Osborne Judgment of 1909 (p. 182).

Children: A new interest was taken in the welfare of children. In 1906 local authorities were empowered to provide meals for needy schoolchildren, and in 1907 they were compelled to provide regular medical examinations. Then in 1908 most of the existing legislation affecting children was gathered together in the Children Act, or 'Children's Charter', which also introduced severe penalties for the neglect or maltreatment of children, set up separate courts to deal with young offenders, prohibited the imprisonment of anyone under fourteen, and revised the system of reformatories.

The penal system: Penal reform was not limited to measures affecting children. In 1907 the probation system was introduced, and this, together with another measure of 1914 which established that a reasonable time should be allowed for the payment of fines, helped to reduce the numbers in prison. In 1908, the same year as the 'Children's Charter', the attempt to reform young offenders rather than merely punish them was carried further by the introduction of the Borstal system.

The beginnings of the Welfare State

Most of this reforming legislation was in the nineteenth-century tradition of protecting the individual from exploitation or maltreatment by others. But some, such as the measure introducing school meals, which was, significantly, introduced by a Labour member, implied a new attitude that one function of government was to compel the individual to contribute to the social welfare of other members of the community.

The Old Age Pensions Act of 1908: This attitude was apparent in the Old Age Pensions Bill, introduced by Asquith in April 1908, the month in which he became Prime Minister and in which he also introduced his last budget. From the beginning of 1909 men and women over seventy with an income of 10s. or less were to get a pension of 5s. a week, while a married couple in this position would get 7s. 6d. between them. In a sense this was unremarkable. It was a reform which had long been advocated, and it was on a very small scale. The significant thing about it was that Asquith found the money for the scheme in the budget, and thus accepted the principle that the government could tax the rich in order to redistribute their money to the poor.

The People's Budget of 1909: This principle was carried even further a year later when Lloyd George introduced his first budget —the famous People's Budget. He had to find more than £15 million extra taxation. This was not because the government's reforms had been expensive. Some, such as the introduction of the probation system, saved money, and Haldane had even been able to cut the army estimates while reforming the army. The only expensive measure so far was the Old Age Pensions Act, which would cost nearly £5 million in a full year. Most of the money was needed to pay for the eight new Dreadnoughts which public opinion had demanded should be built (p. 86).

Lloyd George, instead of cutting expenditure drastically to help pay for the Dreadnoughts, decided that he would provide even more money in his budget to pay for new schemes such as road improvement and the establishment of labour exchanges, and that the main burden of the extra taxation needed would fall on the rich, and especially on unearned wealth. He therefore proposed an increase of the income tax (from 1s. to 1s. 2d.) a new super-tax on incomes over £3,000, increased death duties on estates over £5,000, increased taxes on drink and tobacco, new taxes on cars and petrol, and a new land tax.

It was these proposals which brought to a head the struggle between the government and the House of Lords which was only concluded by the Parliament Act of 1911 (p. 73).

The National Insurance Act of 1911: The Old Age Pensions Act and the People's Budget had established one essential principle of the Welfare State: that the rich should be taxed not merely to provide revenue but in order that their money may be redistributed to the poor. The National Insurance Act established the other essential principle: that the members of a community may be compelled to insure themselves against future mishaps.

Again it was only a small start. The Act made insurance compulsory only for workmen earning less than £160 a year. It provided only the workman, and not his family, with free medical treatment, and it provided a weekly benefit while out of work only to men in certain jobs in which unemployment was a recurrent hazard. But it laid the foundations on which later governments built.

Failures and achievements

The achievements of the Liberals in the pre-war period were great, but so were their failures. For all Sir Edward Grey's attempts to maintain peace, the years of Liberal rule culminated in a World War; and it was only the war which saved the government from domestic troubles with which it was unable to cope. A belief in the effectiveness of violence as a political weapon seemed to be replacing the traditional belief in parliamentary democracy. In the years immediately preceding the first World War trade unionists were seeking to bring about social revolution by organising strikes on a scale previously unknown (p. 183), suffragettes were trying to get votes for women by means of a campaign of crime and violence (p. 362), and while Ireland was preparing for civil war the leaders of the Unionist opposition in England seemed to be encouraging Ulster to rebellion and the army to mutiny (p. 66). To none of these problems had the government yet found a solution. Even in the sphere of domestic social reform the Liberals failed in some ways. There was a pressing need for legislation to regulate the development of the country's housing, but the Housing and Town Planning Act of 1909 obstructed rather than encouraged planning, and the failure to make a start in this field in the pre-war years was partly responsible for the chaos of unplanned building under the National government in the thirties.

But for all their failures the Liberals achieved far more in the decade they were in power than any of the governments in the preceding twenty years or in the twenty years between the wars. Their reforms helped to lay the foundations of a new society. The Conservatives, who had opposed most of the Liberal reforms when they were introduced, later accepted them and eventually included even the Welfare State, and the principles on which it is based, among those aspects of society which are worth conserving. The Labour Party, which took over much of the Liberal support after the first World War, also took over much of the work the Liberals had started, and many of its reforms after the second World War were along paths the Liberals had first tentatively trodden.

IN the twelfth century Ireland was conquered by Normans from England, and for the next seven centuries the Irish were ruled as a subject people. Except in the Northern province of Ulster, which was colonised by English and Scots settlers in the seventeenth century, most of the land was owned by English absentee landlords and was rented from them in smallholdings by the Irish peasantry. The Irish resented bitterly the frequent abuse by the landlords of their power to raise rents and evict tenants, and by the 1880s this resentment frequently resulted in acts of violence.

Possible solutions to the Irish problem

By this time two quite different solutions were being proposed to the problem of how Ireland should be ruled.

(1) Gladstone, who was Prime Minister for the second time in 1880–85, believed that the solution was to reform the law affecting land tenure and at the same time act firmly against anyone committing acts of violence. So in 1881 he introduced a Land Bill, which greatly improved the terms on which Irish tenants held their land, and a Coercion Bill, under which suspects could be imprisoned without trial.

(2) Charles Stuart Parnell, who led a group of Irish Nationalist M.P.s in the House of Commons after 1878, believed that the solution was to allow Ireland to rule herself. He tried to force the British government to grant Home Rule partly by means of obstructionist tactics in the House of Commons, where the Irish members made long irrelevant speeches, and partly by encouraging active opposition in Ireland, as a result of which he was imprisoned for six months under Gladstone's Coercion Act of 1881.

The Irish Nationalists faced the difficulty that they were inevitably a minority party. Ireland had only been represented at all in the British parliament since 1801, and even then most of the hundred Irish M.P.s were merely spokesmen for the Protestant English land-owning class. But as a result of the Ballot Act of 1872 (p. 360) it had become possible to form a small Irish Nationalist Party which genuinely represented the Irish people. Being a small minority group the Irish Nationalists could scarcely hope to get Home Rule by constitutional means unless they could convince either the Liberal or the Conservative Party of the need for it; and there seemed little likelihood of their being able to do so. Thus by the time Lord Salisbury took over from Gladstone as

Prime Minister in June 1885 there appeared to be a deadlock in Irish affairs, and partly because of this many Irishmen were prepared to use unconstitutional methods to get their liberty.

Political upheaval, 1885–6

But the events of the next year proved to be a turning-point in the history of the struggle for Home Rule. As a result of the Franchise Act of 1884 (p. 361) the Irish Nationalists were able to extend their influence in the general election of December 1885, and Parnell returned to parliament at the head of a tightly knit party numbering 86. By adding their votes to those of the 249 Conservatives they were able to balance the 335 Liberals exactly and thus keep in office the Conservative ministry of Lord Salisbury, which seemed better disposed towards them than had the previous Liberal government led by Gladstone.

But meanwhile Gladstone had privately changed his mind about the Irish problem and was prepared to accept the solution demanded by the Irish Nationalists. He saw that although land reform might solve an important social problem it would not obliterate the desire of the Irish to rule themselves; and he realised that coercion, which would remain necessary so long as the Irish were not allowed to rule themselves, would only increase the bitterness in Anglo-Irish relations.

As soon as this change of attitude became known the Irish changed sides in the House of Commons, with the result that Salisbury's government was defeated in February 1886. Gladstone, who now took office for the third time, introduced an Irish Home Rule Bill in June.

But another effect of Gladstone's change of attitude was that the Liberal Party split into a majority group, which followed Gladstone, and a minority group, which was not prepared to accept the change of policy and therefore joined forces with the Conservatives against it. The result was that the Home Rule Bill was defeated and that there developed a permanent Unionist alliance between this minority group, whose members were known as Liberal Unionists, and the Conservatives.

The Conservatives, despite their flirtation with Parnell during Salisbury's first ministry, were adamantly opposed to the idea of Home Rule, and ironically they were in the process of accepting Gladstone's old answer to the Irish problem at just the time that he was deciding to abandon it in favour of Parnell's answer.

Most Englishmen were opposed to giving Ireland Home Rule.

The result was that Gladstone was heavily defeated when he fought a general election on the Home Rule issue in July 1886, and this in turn meant that the Irish problem, instead of being settled, remained a major issue in British politics for nearly thirty-six years. One immediate effect was that the Conservative Party gained so much added support from the Unionist vote that it was able to dominate British politics for nearly twenty years, while the Liberal Party was tied to the unpopular Home Rule cause and to a permanent alliance with the Irish Nationalists.

Parnell

When Lord Salisbury took office for the second time in July 1886 he set out to solve the Irish problem by providing 'twenty years of resolute government', and his nephew, A. J. Balfour, who soon became Chief Secretary for Ireland, ruled the country firmly but with justice.

The most important developments during Salisbury's second ministry concern Parnell, for public sympathy for the Home Rule movement was closely related to the fluctuations in his personal prestige. His reputation suffered in 1887 when *The Times* published a facsimile of a letter said to have been written by him condoning the murder in 1882 of Lord Frederick Cavendish, Chief Secretary for Ireland in Gladstone's second government. But in 1889 it was shown that the letter was a forgery, and sympathy for Parnell produced so much increased support for Home Rule that a general election at this time would probably have produced a large Home Rule majority.

In 1890, however, the Home Rule movement suffered from the shattering of Parnell's public reputation when he was cited as co-respondent in a divorce case, and the damage was all the greater because he did not resign the leadership of the Irish Nationalist Party and consequently split it. Although Parnell died in 1891 the split in his party could still not be mended and it harmed the Home Rule cause in the 1892 election.

Twenty years of stalemate

Despite this setback to the Home Rule movement the Liberals and the Irish Nationalists had a majority of forty over the Unionists when parliament reassembled, and Gladstone, now Prime Minister for the fourth time, was able in 1893 to steer a second Home Rule Bill through the House of Commons. But the Home Rule movement now encountered a further obstacle, for the House of Lords rejected the Bill by 419 votes to 41. The Liberal government did not feel strong enough to challenge this decision, and a few months later, in March 1894, Gladstone retired.

This ended the Liberal attempt to give Ireland Home Rule for another sixteen years. From 1895 until 1905 the Conservatives were in power again and continued the policy of trying to solve the Irish problem by a combination of firm government and land reform. They were unsuccessful, for the Irish would be satisfied with nothing less than Home Rule. But meanwhile opinion in England was so much against Home Rule that the Liberals dropped it from their election programme in 1905. It was only after the election of January 1910, when the Liberals needed the support of the Irish Nationalist members to retain their control of the House of Commons, that Asquith, now the Liberal leader, promised to introduce a third Home Rule Bill. By the time this Bill passed the Commons in 1912 the Parliament Act of 1911 (p. 73) had ensured that it could not be vetoed by the Lords but could merely be delayed for two years.

Ulster and the Amending Bill of 1914

At this point a further complication became apparent. The Protestants of Northern Ireland feared that 'Home Rule means Rome Rule', and many also feared that the industrialised area of Ulster would suffer economically if it were divided from England and dominated by the backward and agricultural South. So in 1912 more than 200,000 Ulstermen signed a covenant pledging themselves to use 'all means which may be found necessary' to defeat Home Rule, and a volunteer army known as the Ulster Volunteers was formed. The Conservative leader, Bonar Law, appeared to be encouraging them to resort to armed rebellion, and in the spring of 1914 a number of army officers stationed in Ireland declared that they would rather be dismissed than be ordered North against the Ulsterman. Meanwhile another private army, the National Volunteers, was rapidly growing in the South, and civil war seemed imminent.

Even at this stage neither the North nor the South wanted to see Ireland partitioned. The South wanted Home Rule for the whole of Ireland, and the North wanted to maintain the union of the whole of Ireland with Great Britain. But in June 1914 Asquith attempted to solve the problem by introducing an Amending Bill to exclude most of Ulster from Home Rule. It was difficult to decide exactly what area should be excluded, so in July a conference of party leaders met to attempt a settlement. The conference lasted four days and broke up in disagreement on 24th July. There the matter rested, for on the previous day Austria-Hungary had sent her ultimatum to Serbia, and within a fortnight Britain was at war.

'The Troubles'

During the war Anglo-Irish relations deteriorated. The Irish lost faith in their Irish Nationalist leaders, who had decided to support the war against Germany, and turned to an extremist organisation, *Sinn Fein* ('We Ourselves'), which organised an unsuccessful rising in Dublin during Easter Week of 1916, and after the war won 73 seats in the general election of December 1918.

The *Sinn Feiners* refused to go to Westminster and instead set up their own government in Dublin. The Labour leaders in England and Asquith, who was now in opposition, suggested that Ireland should immediately become a self-governing Dominion within the Empire. But the coalition government, which consisted mainly of Unionists, even though it was led by Lloyd George, set out to subdue Ireland and reinforced the Royal Irish Constabulary with British volunteer units of ex-servicemen. For more than two years there was a form of civil war between these volun-

SCOTLAND

BELFAST

THE IRISH FREE STATE

The United Kingdom of Great Britain and Northern Ireland

DUBLIN

WALES

Independent: Dec.1921
Named 'Eire': 1937
Republic: 1948

Northern Ireland granted Home Rule in 1920

Three counties of Ulster not included in Northern Ireland in 1920

teer units, commonly known as the Black-and-Tans, and the Irish Republican Army.

In 1920, while this fighting was at its height, Lloyd George introduced a Government of Ireland Bill which proposed the setting up of two separate governments in Ireland: one in Belfast ruling most of Ulster, and one in Dublin ruling the South. The North accepted the offer, and thereafter Northern Ireland has settled her domestic affairs in her own parliament, while continuing to send representatives to Westminster where matters such as foreign policy and defence are decided. But the South rejected the offer and demanded complete independence, so the British government seemed to be faced with the choice of either evacuating Ireland or else undertaking its reconquest.

Independence

However, in December 1921 the British government and the Irish leaders agreed to a treaty establishing the Irish Free State as a self-governing Dominion within the Empire. This took the problem of Southern Ireland's future out of the hands of the British government, but it did not solve it, for one of the principal Irish leaders, Éamon de Valéra, would not accept the treaty, partly because it involved separating Northern Ireland from the rest of the country, and partly because the Free State was not to be a republic. This resulted in an Irish Civil War which ended in May 1923 with the defeat of de Valéra and the republicans.

Until 1932 the Free State government adhered scrupulously to the terms of the treaty, and meanwhile the British government had voluntarily accepted the principle that each of the self-governing Dominions was 'equal in status' with Great Britain (p. 56). But in 1932 de Valéra returned to political life and won a general election at the head of a new party, the *Fianna Fail* ('Soldiers of Destiny'), and pursued a 'policy of pinpricks' aimed at destroying the treaty and breaking every link between Ireland and Britain. In 1937 he promulgated a new constitution. No mention was made of the monarchy, so from this time Ireland was in effect a republic. At the same time the name of 'Eire' was adopted.

Eire sent no representative to the Imperial Conference of 1937, in April 1938 she persuaded Britain to give up her right under the 1921 treaty to use certain Irish harbours as naval bases in time of war, and she was the only Commonwealth country to remain neutral in the Second World War. In 1948 she finally cut herself off from the Commonwealth by the Republic of Ireland Act.

15 THE LORDS AND THE CONSTITUTION

GREAT BRITAIN has no written constitution. This does not mean that she has no constitution. But it does mean that her constitution consists of a curious mixture of law and precedent. It is, for example, by virtue of a law passed in 1872 that voting in British elections is by secret ballot. But, on the other hand, there is no law that a prime minister must resign or ask for a dissolution if he ceases to be able to command a majority in the House of Commons; it is the precedents for this which make it constitutionally binding upon him to do so.

Constitutional precedents do not have to be long established. As soon as Stanley Baldwin became prime minister in 1923 and Lord Curzon was passed over it became firmly established that in future prime ministers would have to be in the Commons.

Sometimes law and precedent appear to conflict. For example, no law has ever been passed to restrict the monarch's right of veto over legislation, but in practice the royal veto has not been exercised since 1708. Legally the right of veto still exists—constitutionally it does not.

Many of the most important aspects of the constitution are based on precedent rather than law. But if a dispute arises about a constitutional issue it eventually becomes necessary to define the position by law, and in the last resort the decision about what the law shall be rests with the will of the people as expressed in a general election. In 1910 the electorate had to express its will on an issue which produced one of the most important constitutional disputes in British history: the question of the relationship between the two Houses of Parliament.

Lords and Commons

Towards the end of the nineteenth century the relationship between the House of Lords and the House of Commons was still based on constitutional precedent rather than on legislation. The principal difference between the two houses lay in their composition. Members of the House of Commons were elected for the duration of a parliament, which was fixed by a law of 1716 at no longer than seven years, while membership of the House of Lords was hereditary.

Cabinet ministers could be in either house. In each of the four cabinets in office during 1885 and 1886 the number of ministers in the Lords balanced the number in the Commons fairly evenly, and although the Chancellor of the Exchequer was usually in the Commons, the Foreign Secretary was usually in the Lords. Moreover, since the Great Reform Act of 1832 the Prime Minister had just as often been in the Lords as in the Commons. New legislation could be introduced in either house, and each could amend and veto the legislation of the other.

The only accepted constitutional difference in their powers lay in the fact that for two hundred years the Lords had never amended any Bill initiated in the Commons which dealt with money matters. Therefore the House of Commons, as a result of its control over the nation's finances, had tended to become more important than the House of Lords. Consequently the majority of important legislation was initiated in the Commons, and the main function of the House of Lords came to be the criticism and revision of untidy legislation.

The inactivity of the Lords, 1886–92

However, during the period of Conservative rule from 1886 to 1892 the House of Lords neglected its function as a revising chamber and did not amend a single government Bill. This was partly because over the centuries many peers had forgotten that their position entailed a duty to participate responsibly in the government of the country, although they still assumed that they had a right to take part when their own interests were affected. But it was primarily the effect of the secession of the Whig element from the Liberal Party as Liberal Unionists in 1886 (p. 186), for that resulted in such overwhelming Unionist domination of the Lords that there was little effective opposition to the government.

The Lords and the Liberals, 1892–95

After the Liberals took office in 1892 the House of Lords was not merely useless but positively harmful, for the Unionists used their permanent majority there to destroy Liberal legislation. When they rejected the second Home Rule Bill in February 1894 (pp. 65–6) many Liberals felt that the House of Lords must be 'mended or ended', and Gladstone wished to resign and fight an election on this issue. But he allowed himself to be overruled by his colleagues who feared the consequences of an open constitutional conflict, and in March he retired and was succeeded by Lord Rosebery.

The Lords now used the veto indiscriminately, and in the election of July 1895, after Rosebery had given up the struggle and resigned, the government's feebleness in failing to challenge the Lords earlier was rewarded with a heavy defeat and then with ten years in opposition.

'The watch-dog of the constitution'?

It is possible to justify the Lords' veto of the second Home Rule Bill on the grounds that one function of the House of Lords was to act as 'the watch-dog of the constitution' and ensure that the will the people was not overridden by the Commons; and at least in England public opinion was opposed to the Home Rule Bill, which depended, as did all other government measures in the period of Liberal rule from 1892 to 1895, on Irish Nationalist votes.

But when the Liberals returned to power after ten years in which the Lords had again completely neglected their function as a revising chamber the same excuse could not be offered. After the 1906 election the Liberals had an overall majority and also the support of the Irish Nationalists and the Labour Party, while the Unionists had less than a quarter of the seats in the Commons. But Balfour and Lord Lansdowne, the Unionist leaders, decided to make use of the permanent Unionist majority in the House of Lords to obstruct the work of the government.

'Mr. Balfour's poodle'?

They knew that they were playing a dangerous game and that if they were to win the next election it was important not to lose such working-class support as they had, so in 1906 they accepted certain measures, such as the Workmen's Compensation Act (p. 59) and even the Trade Disputes Act (p. 182). But in the same year they destroyed an Education Bill, regarded by the government as the most important measure of the year, and a Plural Voting Bill, designed to prevent someone who owned property in more than one constituency from voting more than once.

So in 1907 Campbell-Bannerman carried a resolution in the Commons warning the Lords that their powers would have to be restricted by law if they continued to flout the will of the people. Despite this they went on to destroy the government's plans for land reform, and in 1908 they rejected an important Licensing Bill.

Lloyd George and the budget

By 1909 the government was clearly in danger of being hamstrung by the House of Lords as Lord Rosebery's government had been, and at the same time the government was experiencing the swing of public opinion against it which was the usual lot of the party in power. But at this stage Lloyd George, the Chancellor of

the Exchequer, chose to stand and fight, and like a good general
he chose the ground on which to fight.

The proposals in his 1909 budget laid a heavier burden than
usual on the rich, and in particular the new land taxes were aimed
at the landowning aristocracy. Unionist opposition in the Commons was bitter, and Lloyd George answered it not merely in the
Commons but also in the country at large by turning the issue of
the budget into the issue of the Lords' power of veto. It was he
who referred to the House of Lords as 'Mr. Balfour's poodle'; he
asked whether these 'ordinary men, chosen accidentally from
among the unemployed', should be allowed to flout the will of the
people; and in effect he challenged them to reject the budget.

The Lords made the mistake of accepting the challenge. They
rejected the budget at the end of November, and by doing so put
themselves at a disadvantage in two ways in fighting for the powers
of their house: they appeared as men acting both selfishly, in
attempting to avoid taxation, and unconstitutionally, in interfering
with a Bill dealing with money matters.

1910. 'The Lords *versus* the People'

In December 1909, after Asquith had carried through the Commons a resolution that the Lord's rejection of the budget was 'a
breach of the constitution and a usurpation of the rights of the
Commons', parliament was dissolved, and in January 1910 a
general election was fought. The Liberals only won two more
seats than the Unionists and therefore became dependent on the
support of the Irish Nationalist and Labour Parties. To get the
support of the Irish for the budget they had to promise them Home
Rule, but they were not unwilling to do this, and in April the
1909 budget was passed by both the Commons and the Lords,
who had accepted the verdict of the election.

By this time the government had taken the issue further by introducing a Parliament Bill to restrict the powers of the Lords.
But the death of King Edward VII resulted in a lull in party strife,
and the new king, George V, persuaded the Liberal and Unionist
leaders to try to settle their differences amicably in a Constitutional Conference.

Both the question of the powers of the House of Lords and the
question of its composition were discussed. The Unionists, who
wished to retain its powers, were prepared to accept changes in
its composition. The Liberals, who wanted to restrict its powers,
were less interested in reform of its composition. The conference
eventually broke down because the Unionists insisted that the

Lords must at least have the right of vetoing any constitutional change until a referendum showed it to be the will of the people. The Liberals could not accept this, because their promise of Home Rule for Ireland entailed constitutional change.

King George V now promised Asquith that if another general election showed the country to be still in favour of restricting the powers of the Lords, and if the Lords would nevertheless not accept the Parliament Bill, he would create enough new peers to enable it to be passed. So in December 1910 another general election took place.

The Parliament Act of 1911

This second general election of the year produced hardly any change in the composition of the house, so the Commons passed the Parliament Bill again and sent it to the Lords. Its principal terms were that the Lords should have no power to reject or amend money Bills, that they should be able to delay other Bills for no longer than two years, and that the maximum duration of a parliament should be reduced from seven to five years.

The Lords, faced with a choice between voting for the Bill or being swamped with new peers, eventually accepted it by 131 votes to 114. The vital constitutional issue of the relationships between the Lords and the Commons had been settled. From now on the House of Lords could not even delay legislation for its own abolition for more than two years.

Further restriction and reform

Before the first World War the Lords used the delaying power to hold up the third Irish Home Rule Bill and a Bill for disestablishing the Welsh Church. They had no need to use it in the years of Conservative dominance between the wars, and they accepted most of the Labour government's legislation after 1945. But in 1947, when the government decided to nationalise iron and steel, it became clear that the Lords would delay this on the grounds that it had not been mentioned in the Labour Party's election programme. So a Bill was introduced to reduce the delaying power of the Lords to one year, and under the operation of the Parliament Act of 1911 it became law in December 1949.

In 1958, when the Conservatives introduced life peerages, a first step was made towards reforming the composition of the House of Lords. But apart from the Peerage Act of 1963, which made it possible for a peer to give up his title, nothing more was done. Nor were any further limits placed on the powers of the House of Lords.

Section III International Affairs, 1890–1919

16   'SPLENDID ISOLATION'

IN the late nineteenth century Great Britain was the most powerful nation in the world. Her Empire spread into every continent and included a quarter of the world's population. In the mid-1880s she was still producing more coal and steel than any other country. London was the hub of the world's trade and banking. Half the merchant shipping of the world was British; and she had by far the strongest navy in the world.

The origins of 'splendid isolation'

In this position of strength Great Britain maintained an isolationist foreign policy. On 16th January 1896 a member of the Canadian government described this policy as splendid, and on the same day a member of the opposition asserted that Britain's isolation was in fact dangerous rather than splendid. The reason British foreign policy was being discussed in the Canadian House of Commons was that Britain's isolation had become very obvious a fortnight earlier when the Jameson Raid (p. 268) had ended in fiasco and had been followed the next day by Kaiser Wilhelm II's telegram of congratulation to President Kruger of the Transvaal.

The phrase 'splendid isolation' was soon widely used, and isolation came to be regarded as Britain's traditional policy in the nineteenth century.

Splendid or dangerous?

The reason for regarding isolation as 'splendid' was that Britain was thought to be so strong that she did not need allies. In 1889 she had adopted the Two Power Standard—a policy of keeping the Royal Navy superior to the combined strengths of any two other navies, and it was felt that the navy, with its widespread bases, could protect Britain and the Empire from any likely enemy.

The reason for regarding isolation as 'dangerous' was that if Britain persisted in keeping free from any alliance with another great power, and at the same time pursued an expansionist colonial policy, she might one day find a formidable alliance ranged against her. Isolation, in fact, did not merely mean having no allies. It could also mean having no friends.

The nature of isolation

Perhaps few men stopped to think what it was that Britain was isolated from. Those who did probably assumed that isolation meant keeping freedom of action by avoiding the commitments which alliances would impose. Certainly it did not entail a refusal to have any agreements with other countries. Indeed, Britain had an alliance with Portugal and she was also a guarantor of the neutrality of Belgium.

Isolation, in fact, was not a rigid doctrine but a practical policy. Alliances have the disadvantage that they commit one to giving help to one's ally. Isolation has the advantage that it entails no obligation to defend anyone else. Consequently, so long as one does not need any assistance oneself isolation is a sensible policy. But as soon as one's problems get too large to be dealt with on one's own isolation becomes dangerous.

A threat to Britain

It was at about the time that the phrase 'splendid isolation' came to be widely used that the British government began to realise that isolation might be dangerous. The Triple Alliance of Germany, Austria-Hungary, and Italy had existed since 1882, and with this alliance Britain had no quarrel. But in June 1895 a Dual Alliance of France and Russia was publicly announced, and Britain had many causes for dispute with both France and Russia, for they were the other two main colonial powers at the time.

One answer to this was to join forces with the Triple Alliance. But this would have the disadvantage of committing Britain to intervene in quarrels, such as Austro-Russian rivalry in the Balkans, which did not directly concern her.

The attempt to relieve pressure

Therefore, when the British government began to feel anxious for the security of the British Empire, it did not look for an alliance but instead tried to relieve the pressure on it by means of agreements.

As early as 1887 Lord Salisbury, who was Foreign Secretary as well as Prime Minister, had entered into the Mediterranean Agreement with Italy (p. 95) and had reached a tentative agreement with Germany on spheres of influence in East Africa; and in 1890 he signed agreements about the partition of Africa with France and Portugal as well as with Germany.

In 1897 this policy was carried a step further by the Niger Conference at Paris, which came to an end in June 1898 after drawing the boundaries between French and British possessions in West

Africa. But a month later occurred the clash at Fashoda between Kitchener and Marchand (pp. 91–2), and consequently the last years of the nineteenth century saw increased rather than decreased Anglo-French tension.

The year 1898 also saw an attempt to reach agreement with the Russians about North China in order to lessen the commitments of the British Far East fleet. But the Russians would not come to to an agreement, and a fortnight later they seized the Chinese port of Port Arthur in the Liao-tung peninsula.

Thus in 1898 Anglo-Russian relations as well as Anglo-French relations deteriorated instead of improving. The attempt to improve Britain's position by means of agreements with those powers with whom she had reasons for quarrelling had failed.

Approaches to Germany

This failure drove Britain into the only other possible course of action: that of seeking to come to terms with the Triple Alliance, and in particular with Germany. So in 1898 and again in 1899 and 1901, Joseph Chamberlain, the Colonial Secretary, with the consent of Lord Salisbury, proposed an alliance to Germany. The attempt was a failure:

(1) Britain would not commit herself to defending Austria from Russia, and Germany was equally unwilling to commit herself to defending the British Empire from Russia.

(2) Britain was asking Germany to limit her naval building at the very time (April 1898) when Germany was planning to treble the size of the Imperial Fleet within six years.

(3) Most important of all, the German government understandably expected Britain to quarrel so badly with France and Russia that she would eventually be driven to offer far more for German assistance than she was prepared to at the time.

Thus at the beginning of the twentieth century Britain's relations with France and Russia were very strained, and her approaches to Germany had been rejected. In this situation, with all the European powers against her, Britain fought the Boer War of 1899–1902 (pp. 268–9).

The Anglo–Japanese Alliance

The Boer War made it clear to Britain's leaders that isolation was dangerous rather than splendid, and the Marquess of Lansdowne, who succeeded Salisbury as Foreign Secretary in October 1900, therefore looked for an ally. He found one on the other side of the world, and in January 1902 signed a treaty with Japan by which Britain and Japan promised each other assistance if either of them should be attacked by more than one power. Thus if Russia went to war with Japan Britain would remain neutral, and if France assisted Russia Britain would help Japan.

The end of isolation?

It was generally assumed at the time that Britain had abandoned her policy of isolation. In one sense this was true, for Britain had at last committed herself to an alliance which could involve her in war with one of the powerful European alliances. But in another sense it was not true, for the treaty with Japan enabled Britain to continue her isolation from the European alliances, and it was not until August 1914 that she joined one of them. In this sense the Anglo-Japanese treaty was merely the first important step out of isolation, and the story of British foreign policy from the time of that treaty in 1902 until the outbreak of the first World War in 1914 is the story of how Britain gradually moved further out of isolation and closer towards an alliance with France and Russia.

Towards a European alliance

Lansdowne continued Salisbury's policy of seeking to relieve pressure on the British Empire, and in 1904 reached a friendly understanding, an *entente cordiale*, with France about colonial matters (p. 80), in which he promised diplomatic support for French ambitions in Morocco. This was not an alliance, but inevitably it brought Britain closer to the Dual Alliance, and Lord Rosebery, the Liberal ex-Prime Minister, accurately estimated that it would lead to 'war in ten years'.

In 1907 Sir Edward Grey, the Liberal Foreign Secretary who had taken over from Lansdowne in December 1905, took the policy of relieving pressure on the Empire even further by negotiating an *entente* with Russia (p. 83), though once again there was no alliance.

In 1906, as a result of a diplomatic clash with Germany over Morocco (p. 85), Grey had already allowed secret conversations to take place between British and French military leaders about combined action in the event of their countries being jointly at war with Germany. And as a result of another Moroccan crisis in 1911 Great Britain and France drew even closer together: it was agreed in the Anglo-French Naval Convention of 1912 that Britain should withdraw most of her Mediterranean fleet into the North Sea, while France withdrew her fleet into the Mediterranean. This put Britain at least under a moral obligation to defend France from any German naval attack on her Atlantic coast. The *entente* was coming to look suspiciously like an alliance.

Into war

But despite Britain's closer ties with both France and Russia she retained the freedom of action which her isolation from the European alliances gave her throughout the events leading up to the outbreak of war. Even on 1st August 1914, the day on which Germany declared war on Russia, the British cabinet was still not agreed on the necessity for Britain to enter the war. But Sir Edward Grey was convinced that British intervention was essential; and German violation of Belgian neutrality gave him the support of the cabinet, of parliament, and of the country. On 4th August Britain declared war on Germany and thus, by joining a military alliance, took the final step out of the now long out-dated policy of isolation.

17   THE TRIPLE ENTENTE

France and Russia in 1890

DURING the early years of the Third Republic France was without an ally. But by 1890 she felt the need of one, partly because of her weakness in relation to Germany, and partly because she was increasingly coming into conflict with Great Britain and Italy (Ch. 19) over colonial matters.

Russia had a tradition of alliance with Germany, but she had come to realise that whenever Austrian and Russian interests clashed in the Balkans Germany was likely to support Austria. Therefore in 1890 when her existing treaty with Germany (p. 10) lapsed she did not renew it.

The Dual Alliance, 1893

At the same time Russia was drawn towards an alliance with France by the knowledge that France could supply money for projects such as the Trans-Siberian railway. So in 1893 Russia and France signed a treaty of military assistance.

(1) If France were attacked by Germany alone, or by Germany and Italy, Russia would go to her aid.

(2) If Russia were attacked by Germany alone, or by Germany and Austria-Hungary, France would go to her aid.

This constituted the Dual Alliance, and in 1895 it was made public that such an alliance existed.

Germany and the Dual Alliance

Apparently this alliance was directed primarily against Germany. But in practice this was not so. France had no intention of attacking Germany to regain Alsace-Lorraine, and Russia had no direct cause for a quarrel with Germany.

But France had clashed with Italy in Africa and wanted an ally lest Germany should support Italy. And Russia's interests clashed with Austria's in the Balkans, and she therefore wanted an ally lest Germany should support Austria.

Moreover, Germany had at this time no wish to clash with either France or Russia, and for years she had pursued a policy of diverting France from the question of Alsace-Lorraine by encouraging her colonial adventures in Africa, and of diverting Russia from the Balkans by encouraging her expansion eastwards into Asia, while at the same time restraining Austria-Hungary from aggression in the Balkans.

Great Britain and the Dual Alliance

Thus France and Russia did not come into conflict with Germany and Austria-Hungary in the last years of the nineteenth century. Instead, being imperialist colonising nations, they clashed with Great Britain, the greatest imperial power in the world, standing in 'splendid isolation'. It was only in the twentieth century, as Germany became more powerful, that France and Russia were driven to come to terms with Great Britain.

Great Britain and France

Relations between Britain and France had been strained ever since 1882 when Britain had occupied Egypt, and they had deteriorated further after the Dual Alliance was made public in 1895, for Britain was very suspicious of Russia, and therefore France was now doubly suspect—in her own right and as the ally of Russia.

The traditional British scorn of the French was increased by the Panama Scandal (p. 26) and the Dreyfus Case (p. 27). French indignation resulting from British control of Egypt came to a head in 1898 when Kitchener clashed with Marchand at Fashoda (p. 91); and the French found a further cause for indignation against Britain in the Boer War of 1899–1902 (pp. 268–9).

The *entente cordiale*

Under these circumstances it seems surprising that Lansdowne and Delcassé, the British and French ministers responsible for foreign affairs, reached a friendly understanding, an *entente cordiale*, in 1904. But there were three good reasons why it should happen: (1) For years Britain had been anxious to relieve pressure on her Empire. She was especially anxious to reach agreement with France about Egypt, as this would relieve her of the increasingly distasteful necessity of relying on German diplomatic support. Thus as soon as the French wanted an *entente* the British government was likely to welcome it.
(2) The Fashoda crisis had shown the French that rivalry with Britain did not pay. They had asked both Germany and Russia for support, and neither had given it, so France, too weak to oppose Britain alone, had had to climb down. Delcassé therefore realised the desirability of settling all outstanding disputes with Britain.
(3) The Anglo-Japanese Alliance of 1902 (p. 77) was obviously directed against Russia, and France saw the danger of being involved as Russia's ally in a war against Britain, the ally of Japan.

Thus in January 1902, the same month that the Anglo-Japanese treaty was signed, negotiations for the *entente* began. The numerous outstanding disputes were settled by the practical method of both sides making concessions, and the final agreement was signed in April 1904. Britain made concessions over Senegal and Madagascar, France over Siam and Newfoundland. Most important, France accepted that Egypt was a British sphere of influence, while Britain promised diplomatic support for French ambitions in Morocco.

Great Britain and Russia

The hostility between Britain and Russia was more deep-rooted than that between Britain and France. The British regarded Russia's expansionist ambitions as a threat to their Empire, while

Russia blamed Britain for blocking her expansion to a 'warm-water' port which her ships could use in the winter. Their interests conflicted in the Eastern Mediterranean, in the area North of the Indian Ocean, and in the Far East.

(1) *The Eastern Mediterranean:* For centuries expansion towards

the Mediterranean had beeen a permanent feature of Russia's foreign policy. Britain had constantly opposed this, for she feared the consequences of Russia being able to block her trade route to India. Since she had gained control of Egypt in 1882 Britain had less cause to fear Russia, but her anxiety increased as a result of the Franco-Russian Dual Alliance, for the British Mediterranean fleet would not want to fight the French and Russian fleets combined.

(2) *Afghanistan and Persia:* The next nearest outlet to the sea for Russia was the Indian Ocean. In less than two centuries the Russians had expanded 2,000 miles into Southern Asia, and in 1885 a Russian force crossed the border of Afghanistan at Penjdeh. They were prevented from encroaching any farther by a threat of war from Gladstone in March, but the consequence of this was that they diverted their ambitions towards Persia and towards the Far East.

(3) *The Far East:* By the 1890s Russian ambitions had spread across Asia to include Manchuria and even North China. After the formation of the Dual Alliance and the construction of the Trans-Siberian railway to Vladivostock the British government became increasingly apprehensive.

The Russo-Japanese War

The rivalry in the Far East was settled first. In 1898 Britain tried to reach agreement with Russia. When she failed she turned for support to Germany (p. 76), but again was unsuccessful. In the end she found the solution to her problem in an alliance with Japan (p. 77).

One direct result of this alliance was that in 1904 Japan, knowing that France could not assist Russia without involving herself in war with Britain, attacked Russia. Her forces invaded Manchuria and at the end of the year took Port Arthur. Then in 1905 they defeated the Russians on land at Mukden and at sea in the Straits of Tsushima (map, p. 76).

The war was ended the same year by the Treaty of Portsmouth (U.S.A.), by which Russia handed over South Sakhalin and her lease of Port Arthur to Japan, evacuated Manchuria, and recognised Korea as a Japanese sphere of influence.

As far as Britain was concerned, Russia no longer constituted a threat in the Far East.

The *entente cordiale* and Russia

The danger of conflict in the Eastern Mediterranean declined at the same time. In the first place, Russia had been so weakened as a result of her defeat by Japan and the subsequent revolution at home (p. 21) that she was unlikely to take any action over the Straits without the assent of the other great powers. In the second place, Russia was unlikely to get support from France for any action which threatened British interests, partly because France had now settled her own disputes with Britain, and partly because now that Russia's military and naval weakness had been demonstrated it was all the more necessary for France to keep Britain as a friend—especially in view of the growing hostility and strength of Germany.

The Anglo-Russian *entente*

Thus by 1907 the way was fairly clear for an agreement between Britain and Russia. There were still difficulties in the way of such an agreement. For example, Britain was still allied to Russia's recent enemy, Japan, and the Liberal government which had taken office in December 1905 was strongly opposed to the autocratic nature of Tsarist rule. But these were not insuperable obstacles, for Britain and Russia did not intend to negotiate an alliance but merely to settle outstanding disputes.

In 1907 they reached agreement. Both would leave Tibet alone; Russia agreed not to intervene in Afghanistan; and spheres of influence in Persia were defined: Russia dominated the more valuable North, but was excluded from the coastal area, which came under British influence, and from the central area, which was left to the Persians.

The Triple Entente

As a result of this *entente* Britain was on friendly terms with Russia as well as France. She still did not have an alliance with them, but after 1907 it becomes increasingly useful to think in terms of what may be called the Triple Entente.

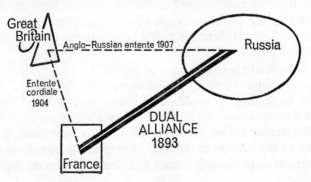

18 'WELTPOLITIK'

German foreign policy before 1890

SINCE 1882 Germany, Austria-Hungary, and Italy had been linked together in the Triple Alliance. The Italian aspect was always a minor feature of the alliance, whose importance lay in the military agreement dating from 1879 (p. 9) by which Germany was bound to assist Austria-Hungary if she were attacked by Russia. But Bismarck, the German Chancellor, believed that it was necessary for Germany to remain friendly with Russia as well as with Austria-Hungary, and in 1887 he had negotiated with Russia the Reinsurance Treaty (p. 10), in which Germany promised to uphold Russia's interests in the Balkans.

The change of policy

In 1890, when Kaiser Wilhelm II dismissed Bismarck, German foreign policy underwent a drastic change, for after that date, and even more so after the formation of the Dual Alliance, the fundamental assumption on which German foreign policy rested was that Britain would one day have to fight France and Russia. This assumption was a reasonable one; and towards the end of the nineteenth century Britain came so much into conflict with France and Russia that in 1898, the year of the Fashoda crisis (p. 91) and of the Russian acquisition of Port Arthur (p. 92), Joseph Chamberlain approached Germany with suggestions for an alliance.

But the assumption had three important consequences:
(1) Germany allowed the Reinsurance Treaty to lapse in 1890, and thereafter neglected her traditional policy of alliance with Russia.
(2) Germany scorned the British offers of alliance, believing that Britain was so much in need of support against France and Russia that she would eventually have to pay a far higher price for Germany's support than she was willing to at the time.
(3) In 1898 Germany began building an Imperial Fleet capable of challenging the Royal Navy, so that when Britain clashed with France and Russia Germany would be able to intervene decisively in any settlement.

The effects of these changes of policy

These changes of policy were disastrous for Germany:
(1) By neglecting her traditional alliance with Russia Germany drove Russia to conclude the Dual Alliance with France (p. 79).
(2) By scorning Britain's offers of alliance Germany drove Britain to protect her Empire in the only other possible way: by settling her various disputes with France and Russia by negotiation.

(3) By building a large battle fleet Germany forced a naval building race on Britain and at the same time drove Britain even closer towards friendship with France and Russia.

Thus Germany's leaders misjudged the diplomatic situation at the end of the nineteenth century badly. By their *Weltpolitik*, a policy of aiming at leadership or even domination of the world, they helped to create friendly relations between the very powers against whom Germany went to war in 1914.

The Tangier crisis, 1905

The first indication that Germany's policy was miscarrying was when the Anglo-French *entente* was concluded in 1904. The immediate German reaction was to attempt to break up the *entente*, and the Kaiser tried to do this by demonstrating to France that she could not rely on Britain to keep her promise of support for France over Morocco. He went to Tangier, the capital of Morocco, and made a dramatic speech in which he declared that the Sultan was absolutely free.

Germany then demanded an international conference to settle the future of Morocco, and Delcassé, the French Foreign Minister, who opposed this demand, had to resign.

The Algeciras Conference, 1906

The conference was arranged to take place in Spain at Algeciras in January 1906. In the previous month the Liberal Sir Edward Grey had succeeded Lord Lansdowne at the Foreign Office, but Britain's policy remained constant, and as a result of British support for France, Germany was outvoted at the conference and control of most of Morocco was handed over to France, though a small area in the North, including Tangier which was placed

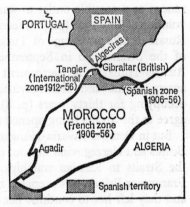

under international control six years later, was reserved for Spain.

The result of this crisis was that Britain and France, instead of being split apart as the Kaiser intended, came so much closer together that in January 1906, the same month as the Algeciras Conference, secret conversations began between British and French military leaders.

Naval rivalry

In the next month, February 1906, Britain launched the first *Dreadnought*-class battleship—the type which dominated the seas in the first World War. This put Germany at a disadvantage, both because the *Dreadnought* was incomparably more powerful than any other battleship in existence at the time, and also because even after the Germans had built comparable ships they would not be able to use them effectively until the Kiel Canal from the North Sea to the Baltic was enlarged.

This, combined with the new concentration of the Royal Navy nearer home (p. 47), stimulated German naval rivalry and resulted in the German Navy Law of April 1906 providing for six new battleships comparable with the *Dreadnought* and for the widening of the Kiel Canal; and this in turn eventually caused such widespread concern in Great Britain that in 1909 a reluctant Liberal government, which had begun by cutting naval building, was driven by public opinion to start building eight new Dreadnoughts.

The Bosnian crisis

Increasing suspicion of Germany had also helped to drive the British government to seek friendship with Russia, and in 1907 the Anglo-Russian *entente* was concluded. One effect of this was to leave Russia only the Straits from the Black Sea to the Mediterranean as a possible outlet to warm water. The Young Turk revolution of July 1908 (p. 307) seemed to provide an opportunity for Russia to take advantage of Turkey's difficulties and gain control of the Straits. So in September 1908 Russia negotiated with Austria–Hungary an agreement that Austria–Hungary should annex Bosnia and Herzegovina, which she had already been occupying for thirty years (p. 8), and that in return she should agree to the Straits being opened to Russian warships.

But in October Austria-Hungary forestalled Russia by annexing Bosnia and Herzegovina without making any provision for opening the Straits to Russian warships. Russia protested, but neither France nor Britain was prepared to support Russia over this issue, and they left her to continue her complaints alone.

Germany and the Bosnian crisis

Germany's original position was embarrassing, for by supporting Austria-Hungary she would be offending Turkey; but once Turkey had been compensated with a money payment and with the return of the *sanjak* of Novibazar, which Austria-Hungary had also been occupying since 1878, Germany felt free to support

Austria-Hungary against Russia. In March 1909 she sent an ultimatum to Russia, and Russia, lacking the support of either France or Britain, was obliged to climb down.

Apparently Germany had been successful, for Russia had suffered a diplomatic defeat as the result of the failure of the other *entente* powers to support her. But in the long run Germany's policy had the opposite effect from that which was intended. Although it temporarily humiliated Russia, it also caused the Russians to build up their army so much that when another crisis occurred in the Balkans in 1914 they felt strong enough to take a firm stand. Although it temporarily split the Triple Entente, in the long run it strengthened it, for the crisis showed the Tsar the danger of standing alone, and shortly after the crisis he said to the British ambassador, 'We must keep closer and closer together.'

The Agadir crisis

After 1909 there was some relaxation of international tension until, in the summer of 1911, Germany provoked another crisis over Morocco.

There had been some point to German action in the Tangier and Bosnian crises. There was far less point to her action in 1911. In June the German government sent a gunboat, the *Panther*, to Agadir on the Moroccan coast and demanded a large part of French Equatorial Africa, in return for acceptance of French control over Morocco.

The British government was alarmed both by this threat to French interests in Morocco and by the possibility that Germany intended to establish a naval base at Agadir. Three weeks later Lloyd George, the Chancellor of the Exchequer, made a speech declaring that Great Britain would not be treated 'as if she were of no account'. The German government, unwilling to go to war, accepted a far smaller area than it had demanded.

Once again German provocation of a crisis over Morocco had driven Britain and France closer together, and one result of the Agadir crisis was the Anglo-French Naval Convention of 1912 (p. 78).

Anglo-German rivalry

The international situation remained tense after the Agadir crisis, which was followed by the Italo-Turkish War of 1911–12 (p. 94) and by the Balkan Wars of 1912 and 1913 (pp. 101–2). But relations between Germany and Britain improved. They co-operated amicably at the London Conference of 1912–13 (p. 101) and moved towards agreement on those matters which had embittered their relations in recent years.

Trade rivalry had caused tension between them, but in the years before the war, when British trade was booming and Germany was developing new markets in Asia Minor, Africa, and South America, it was becoming obvious that there was plenty of room in the world for both of them. Consequently in July 1914 the two governments reached an agreement about the Berlin to Baghdad Railway, and businessmen of both nations, fearing that war would disrupt trade, pressed their governments to keep the peace.

Colonial rivalry also caused tension. Germany resented the extent of Britain's colonial empire and felt that she too should have 'a place in the sun'. But she had always settled her colonial disputes with Britain amicably, and in July 1914 they reached an agreement for the eventual partition of Portugal's colonies.

Naval rivalry was probably the factor which caused most ill-feeling. But even in this sphere tension was decreasing, for in 1914 Britain informally accepted a German proposal that Dreadnoughts should be built in the ratio of ten German to sixteen British.

The effects of German policy

Thus when Britain eventually declared war on Germany on 4th August 1914 it was not because of any direct quarrel between the two countries. Britain was hoping to settle her differences with Germany in the same way that she had settled her differences with France and Russia—by agreement. But she was not prepared to let any one country dominate Europe. In the past she had fought Philip II of Spain, Louis XIV of France, and Napoleon Bonaparte for this reason; and now she was prepared to fight Germany for the same reason. Fear of Germany had driven Britain into the arms of France and Russia, and German policies had produced a situation in which the great powers of Europe were divided into two opposing armed camps: the Triple Alliance and the Triple Entente.

One would expect the Triple Alliance to be a more closely knit group than the Triple Entente. In fact it was the other way round. For Italy, the third and weakest member of the Triple Alliance, was linked to Germany and Austria-Hungary only by the terms of a treaty which bound her little. But Britain, the third and strongest member of the Triple Entente, was bound to France and Russia by self-interest. She could not afford to let Germany defeat them and thereafter dominate not just Europe but the whole world.

THE LATER years of the nineteenth century saw the beginnings of a scramble to acquire colonies by many of the technically more advanced nations of the world. Of those countries which were later involved in the first World War Britain, France, Germany, Belgium, and Italy were involved in the scramble for Africa, and Britain, France, Germany, Russia, and Japan were involved in the scramble for the Far East.

But the first World War was not caused by colonial rivalry, for all the colonial rivals except Germany, which was a comparatively minor participant in the scramble for colonies, were on the same side in the war. The relevance of colonial affairs to the outbreak of war is that the war was only able to take place when the principal colonial rivals had settled their differences enough to be able to unite against the growing power of Germany.

Great Britain clashes with France and Russia

The three main imperialist powers in the late nineteenth century were Great Britain, France, and Russia. They valued colonies in this period partly as a source of prestige, partly as strategic bases, but primarily as sources for raw materials and as markets for their manufactures.

Britain and France had two advantages over most other nations. They already had overseas possessions, which were often useful bases, and they were already highly industrialised, and thus had a natural demand for raw materials and for markets for their goods.

Russia had the advantage over all other nations of being able to spread into the great land-mass of Asia, where she was unrivalled until she approached the coast in the South near Afghanistan or Persia, or reached the coast in the Far East near Manchuria.

There was no reason for France and Russia to clash over colonial matters, for in the Far East Russia's interest was in the North while France had her ambitions in the South, and in Africa, which was the main sphere of colonial activity for France, Russia had no interest at all.

Britain, on the other hand, had such extensive colonial interests that she clashed with France in Africa and with both France and Russia in the Far East.

Britain and France in Africa

The main outline of British and French possessions in Africa were established by 1890.

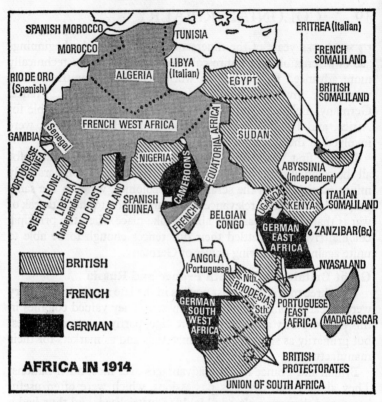

AFRICA IN 1914

France: France dominated inland West Africa from the Mediterranean to the Equator, though more than half of the Atlantic coast was in other hands. She also held a small area at the southern end of the Red Sea, cut off from the rest of her colonies by the Sudan and Abyssinia, and some Frenchmen dreamt of an Empire stretching across Africa from the Atlantic to the Red Sea.

Great Britain: In the same way some Englishmen, such as Cecil Rhodes, had dreamt of a British Empire stretching from Egypt, which Britain had occupied in 1882 together with the Sudan, to Cape Colony. By 1890 this dream was no longer feasible, for although Rhodes had pushed British influence nearly 2,000 miles northwards from the Cape, Britain had withdrawn from the Sudan in 1885 and in 1887 had agreed to divide East Africa with Germany, thus losing the chance of linking her Northern and Southern possesssions.

But though Britain avoided any possibility of a clash with Germany by accepting her authority in German East Africa, there was still a danger of a clash with France, for joining Egypt to East Africa remained possible, and this would cut across the French ambition.

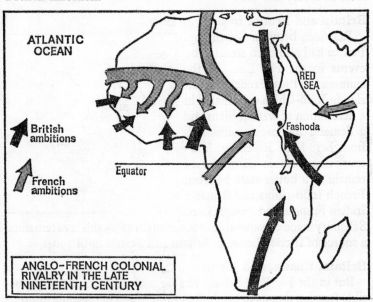

ATLANTIC OCEAN

RED SEA

Fashoda

➡ British ambitions

➡ French ambitions

Equator

ANGLO-FRENCH COLONIAL RIVALRY IN THE LATE NINETEENTH CENTURY

The Fashoda Incident

Britain and France were already on bad terms over African affairs. They had been estranged by the British occupation of Egypt in 1882, for France had always felt that she should have a share. Tension had developed in West Africa, where France resented the numerous British colonies, Gambia, Sierra Leone, the Gold Coast, and Nigeria, which kept France away from much of the coast. And their rivalry came to a head in 1898 when an Anglo-Egyptian army under Sir Herbert Kitchener was reconquering the Sudan. In 1895 the British government had made it clear that it would regard any French expedition across Africa towards the Nile as 'an unfriendly act'. But in 1896 a small French expedition under a Captain Marchand set out from Senegal on the Atlantic coast and in July 1898 reached Fashoda, a town in the Sudan on the Upper Nile. Marchand claimed it on behalf of France. A fortnight later Kitchener arrived with five gunboats and two thousand men. Marchand would not give way, but Kitchener refrained from using force and left the settlement of the crisis to the French and British governments. For a while war seemed likely, but the French government realised that there was little point in quarrelling with

Britain over 'the sands of the desert', and in March 1899 Marchand was withdrawn. But relations between the two countries had reached a very low ebb.

Britain and France in the Far East

Relations between Britain and France had also been strained by events in the Far East. In the summer of 1893 French expansion in Indo-China culminated in a declaration of war on Siam and a demand for large concessions from her. Lord Rosebery, however, insisted that Siam should remain as a buffer state between French Indo-China and Britain's Indian Empire, and though Lord Salisbury made considerable concessions in 1896, this area remained a source of friction between Britain and France until 1904.

Britain, Russia, and Japan

But in the Far East Britain was far more concerned about possible Russian threats to her Indian Empire and her trading interest. She had checked the Russian advance South-East towards the Indian Ocean at Penjdeh in 1885 (p. 33), and for the next twenty years the main thrust of Russian expansion was eastwards towards North China (map, p. 81).

But the situation in the Far East was complicated by the rising power of Japan. In a war between Japan and China in 1894–5 Japan had acquired Korea, the Liao-tung peninsula at the southern end of Manchuria, and Formosa (map, p. 76). At this stage Germany, France, and Russia had acted together to force Japan to return the Liao-tung peninsula to China. Russia gained from this, for China now allowed her to build the Chinese Eastern Railway through Manchuria to Vladivostock, and in 1898 she acquired a lease of Port Arthur on the Liao-tung peninsula and began to build the South Manchuria Railway.

Although Britain and France each gained a lease of a Chinese port as compensation, it was increasingly obvious to Britain that Russia and Japan, being adjacent to China, were better placed than any other powers to extend their influence over her, so Britain, fearing an extension of Russian power, concluded a treaty with Japan in 1902 (p. 77).

The Triple Entente and Germany

Thus at the beginning of the twentieth century Britain was on very bad terms with both France and Russia, and if any war between European powers seemed likely it was a war between Britain and the Dual Alliance. But in fact they had all realised that it was not worth fighting each other over colonies. Britain had declined to fight Russia over Port Arthur in 1898. In the same year France had declined to fight Britain over Fashoda. And in the next decade a diplomatic revolution took place. In 1904 Britain and France settled their colonial differences and concluded the *entente cordiale*, and in 1907 Britain and Russia reached a similar understanding thus bringing the Triple Entente into existence.

This diplomatic revolution made European war more, rather than less likely, for when Britain, France, and Russia had settled their colonial differences they naturally turned their attention nearer to Europe, and thus came into conflict with Germany.

(1) *Great Britain:* The *entente cordiale* and the defeat of Russia by Japan enabled Britain to reduce her naval strength in the Mediterranean and the Pacific and concentrate her fleet in home waters. This had the effect of stimulating German naval rivalry and helped to provoke the German Navy Law of April 1906 (p. 88).

(2) *France:* The *entente cordiale* gave France the support of Britain over Morocco, and the result of this was that Germany provoked the Moroccan crises of 1905 (p. 85) and 1911 (p. 87).

(3) *Russia:* The Japanese War (pp. 312–3) and the Anglo-Russian *entente* checked Russia's ambitions in the East and turned her towards the Balkans. As a result she came into conflict with Austria-Hungary, and consequently with Germany, in 1908 and again in 1914.

Thus one effect of forming the Triple Entente was to stimulate German antagonism, for Germany regarded it as an anti-German alliance. In this sense Germany can be said to have gone to war in 1914 against '*entente* imperialism'.

Italian colonialism

The rivalry in Africa between France and Italy had equally little direct effect on the outbreak of the first World War. Once again the colonial rivals eventually fought on the same side.

The French annexation in 1881 of Tunisia, on which Italian colonial ambitions had been centred, had so inflamed Italian politicians that in 1882 Italy had allied with her traditional enemy,

Austria-Hungary, and with Germany. For the next thirty years Italy's tortuous foreign policy was aimed primarily at the eventual acquisition of Tripoli, the only part of the North African coast which Turkey had not yet lost. But during this time Italy re-established friendly relations with France, and when in 1911 she invaded Tripoli, which she renamed Libya, it was not France but Italy's allies who disapproved of her action.

Germany objected partly because Italy was attacking Turkey, whose ties to Germany were very close by 1911, and partly because, since Tripoli was part of the Turkish Empire, Germany had begun to regard it as a sphere of influence for herself.

Austria-Hungary objected because she suspected Italy of coveting Turkish lands in Europe which Austria-Hungary regarded as a field of expansion for herself, and she therefore told Italy that the war must not come near the Balkans.

This mild colonial rivalry between Italy and her allies had no influence on the outbreak of the first World War, in which Italy was not involved for most of the first year. But the Italo-Turkish War, which was only made possible by the ending of colonial rivalry between France and Italy, did have an indirect effect on the outbreak of the first World War, for the Balkan nations saw it as an opportunity to attack Turkey, and the Balkan Wars which resulted (pp. 101–2) increased the tension in the Balkans which eventually snapped and produced the first World War.

Colonial rivalry and the first World War

Thus colonial rivalry did not cause the first World War, for the only colonial power to fight against the Triple Entente was Germany herself, who was scarcely involved in colonial disputes until the Moroccan crises; and even the Moroccan crises were not really colonial disputes but were both deliberately provoked for the very different reason of trying to split the *entente cordiale* and establish Germany's predominance among the great powers.

Germany's allies in the war were even less concerned in the scramble for colonies. Austria-Hungary had no interests outside Europe, and Turkey's loss of the last of her African possessions to Italy in 1912 had no connection with her entry in 1914 into a war in which at the time Italy was not involved.

The only direct connection between colonial rivalry and the first World War is that it was only when Russia, Britain, France and Italy had settled their differences that it became possible for them to co-operate against Germany.

20 'SACRED EGOISM'

IN the years following the unification of Italy, which culminated in the seizure of Rome from the Pope in 1870, Italian politicians began to think of their country as a great power; and one consequence of this was that they felt that Italy should dominate the Mediterranean and acquire colonies.

After France annexed Tunisia in 1881 they saw France as their principal rival for the control of the African coast of the Mediterranean, so in the following years their foreign policy was directed towards finding friends who would support them against France.

The Triple Alliance, 1882

The first step in this direction was the Triple Alliance of 1882 between Germany, Austria-Hungary, and Italy. Germany and Austria-Hungary both promised to support Italy if she should be attacked by France, and in return Italy promised to support Germany if she were attacked by France, and Austria-Hungary if she were attacked by both France and Russia.

Italy gained little advantage from the alliance, for there was little or no chance of France attacking her; and the friendship with Austria-Hungary to which the alliance committed Italy was a disadvantage, for Austria-Hungary still controlled the predominantly Italian-speaking areas of Istria and the Trentino, and the alliance prevented an Italian demand for these unredeemed lands, or *terre irridente*.

Italy and Great Britain

The other nation Italy turned to for support against France was Great Britain. In the terms of the Triple Alliance Italy had stipulated that her promises should not commit her to going to war with Great Britain. From the point of view of Germany and Austria-Hungary this was reasonable, for neither of them saw any likelihood of being involved in war with Great Britain; and Italy made this proviso partly because as a peninsula jutting out into the Mediterranean she was peculiarly vulnerable to British sea-power, but also because she regarded Britain as a natural friend.

The anti-French aspect of this friendship is clear from the Anglo-Italian agreement of 1887 in which each country promised 'mutual support in the Mediterranean' in any dispute with a third country. This amounted to a promise of mutual support against France. Italy would support Great Britain over Egypt if Britain would support Italy's ambitions in Tripoli.

An Italian *entente* with France

But towards the end of the nineteenth century Italy gradually resolved her quarrel with France. In 1896 she recognised French control of Tunisia, and in 1900 she recognised French interests in Morocco in return for a free hand in Tripoli. There were now no real grounds for a quarrel with France, and in 1902 Italy made France a secret promise, which conflicted with the terms of the Triple Alliance, that she would not go to war with her. In 1906 at the Algeciras Conference on the future of Morocco (p. 85) Italy kept to her agreement of 1900 by voting against her allies, Germany and Austria-Hungary.

An Italian *entente* with Russia

Meanwhile Italy was also seeking to come to terms with the other great power against whom the Triple Alliance was directed. In 1900 she secretly agreed to support Russia's aim to have the Straits opened to Russian warships in return for Russian support over Tripoli, and in 1909 Italy and Russia signed another secret agreement, recognising each other's interests in the Balkans and promising support for each other's policies.

The best of both worlds

Thus Italy, like Great Britain, was drawing closer to France and Russia. But there was an important difference between Italian and British foreign policies. While Britain was in some ways driven apart from Germany Italy managed to maintain her alliance with both Germany and Austria-Hungary. In December 1912 she renewed the Triple Alliance for the fourth time in thirty years, and as late as March 1914 she concluded new military and naval agreements with Germany and Austria-Hungary.

It was possible for Italy to maintain the Triple Alliance while at the same time establishing friendly relations with the Dual Alliance because in the years before the first World War most diplomacy was conducted in secret, the terms of treaties were seldom public, and sometimes their very existence was unknown. Italy took advantage of this situation unscrupulously. In 1900, for example, she promised Austria-Hungary that she would not make any agreements with another country without her knowledge, yet her promise of neutrality to France in 1902 and her agreement with Russia in 1909 were both made without informing Austria-Hungary. But Italy did this not because she was preparing to throw over her allies but because she wanted if possible to be friendly with their enemies as well as with them.

The weak link in the Triple Alliance

Nevertheless the Triple Alliance was doomed, because in the event of a major conflict of European powers Italy had more to gain from fighting against Germany and Austria-Hungary than from fighting with them.

Italy had only joined the Triple Alliance to get support for her immediate objective—the acquisition of an African Empire. By 1914 she had got as far in Africa as she could for the moment, and her principal and latest advance, into Tripoli in 1911–12 (p. 94), had been unsupported and even frowned on by her allies.

But forming the Triple Alliance had not solved the problem of the *terre irridente*, which in the long run were more important than African colonies to the Italians. France no longer blocked any Italian ambitions in Africa, but Austria-Hungary did still block Italian ambitions in Europe.

Neutrality, August 1914–May 1915

When the first World War eventually began Italy declared herself neutral, as she was entitled to do under the terms of the Triple Alliance for three reasons:

(1) As the war began by Austria-Hungary attacking Serbia it could be regarded as a war of aggression.

(2) Italy had not been informed of her allies' intentions in advance, nor had she been offered compensation.

(3) She was not bound to fight in any war involving Great Britain

Italy then felt free to take any action which seemed to be in her own interest. She abandoned the idea of joining Germany and Austria-Hungary after the defeat of the first German onslaught in the battle of the Marne (p. 110); but throughout 1914 she continued negotiating with them to see what land she could get in return for a promise of 'friendly non-belligerence' or even merely of continued neutrality.

However, the Triple Entente powers could offer Italy more than Germany and Austria-Hungary would, for above all Italy wanted the *terre irridente*, and it cost the Allies nothing to promise them to her in the event of victory, whereas Austria-Hungary, fighting to preserve her crumbling Empire, would not concede any ground.

The Treaty of London, April 1915

At last in March 1915 Germany got Austria-Hungary to agree to make some concessions. But already in February Salandra, the Italian Prime Minister, who in October described his policy as *sacro egoismo*, had opened negotiations with Great Britain, and in April of the same year the Treaty of London was concluded.

In return for entering the war the next month Italy was to get the Trentino, together with the part of the German-speaking Tyrol which lay South of the Alps, the Istrian peninsula, including Trieste but excluding Fiume, part of the Dalmatian coast, most of the islands of the Adriatic, part of the Turkish Empire if it were partitioned, and an undefined area of Africa if Germany's colonies were annexed.

In accordance with the treaty Italy declared war on Austria-Hungary in May 1915, though it was not until August 1916, more than a year later, that she declared war on Germany as well.

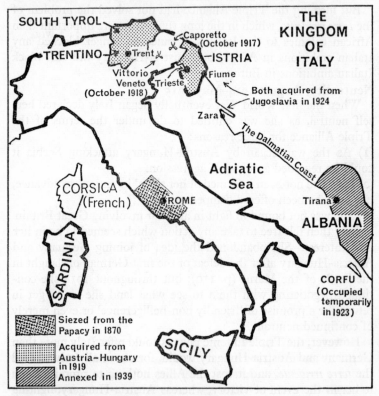

SOUTH TYROL

THE
KINGDOM
OF
ITALY

Caporetto
(October 1917)

TRENTINO — Trent

ISTRIA

Vittorio
Veneto
(October 1918)

Trieste

Fiume

Both acquired from
Jugoslavia in 1924

Zara

The Dalmatian Coast

CORSICA
(French)

ROME

Adriatic
Sea

Tirana

ALBANIA

SARDINIA

CORFU
(Occupied
temporarily
in 1923)

Siezed from the
Papacy in 1870

Acquired from
Austria–Hungary
in 1919

Annexed in 1939

SICILY

Italy at war

Italy played a comparatively small part in the fighting. When she went to war all her plans were still based on the assumption that she would be fighting on the same side as Austria-Hungary rather than against her, and even after declaring war the only new plans she made were for defence.

Nevertheless, for two and a half years her help was valuable to

the Allies, for it kept numerous Austro-Hungarian troops occupied
on the Alpine front. But in October 1917 the Italians suffered a
disastrous defeat at Caporetto, losing more than half a million men,
and were driven back into the plain of Lombardy. As a result the
Allies had to send reinforcements to prop up the Italian front.

It was not until the war was almost over that the Italians had any
success. At the end of October 1918 they attacked in the North-
East and won the Battle of Vittorio Veneto; and at the beginning
of November, as Austria-Hungary collapsed, their army took
Trent and their navy took Trieste.

The post-war territorial settlement

Italians later claimed that although their country had won the
war she had 'lost the peace', for Italy did not gain all that she had
been promised in the Treaty of London. This was inevitable, for
the circumstances after the war were very different from those of
1915. Austria-Hungary had disintegrated, her subject peoples
were asserting their independence, and the new state of Jugoslavia
inevitably claimed much of the land which Italy coveted. Moreover
the U.S.A. had entered the war in 1917 and afterwards was determined to view all territorial claims, including those of Jugoslavia
and Italy, in the light of the principle of self-determination.

All the same Italy gained most of her demands on her Northern
and North-Eastern frontier. She acquired the Trentino, the South
Tyrol, and the Istrian peninsula, including Trieste, though not
Fiume, which she had neglected to claim in 1915 but demanded
after the war. But farther afield Italy did less well. Most of
the Dalmatian coast and the Adriatic islands went to Jugoslavia;
Turkey was not partitioned; and Italy was not given a mandate
over any Turkish or German colonies, and received negligible
compensation in Africa (map, p. 249).

The reward of 'sacred egoism'

But more important to Italy than the territorial settlement was
the fact that Austria-Hungary, her natural and traditional enemy,
even though ostensibly her ally for over thirty years, had disintegrated. Great Britain, France, and even Russia had been fighting
principally against the growing power of Germany; and twenty
years later Germany was ready to fight them again. But Italy had
been concerned with the power of Austria-Hungary, and after the
first World War Austria-Hungary no longer existed. If anything
can justify Salandra's policy of 'sacred egoism' this does, for Italy
gained more from the war than any of her European allies.

21 THE BALKANS

Precarious stability

IN the last years of the nineteenth century the European lands of the crumbling Ottoman Empire were coveted by both Austria-Hungary and Russia, and also by a number of small independent Balkan states (Serbia, Montenegro, Greece, and Bulgaria) which claimed these lands on the strength of historical, linguistic, and racial ties with the peoples living there.

But for the thirty years after the Congress of Berlin in 1878 (p. 7) the only important change in the Balkan territorial settlement was the union of Eastern Roumelia with Bulgaria in 1885 (p. 9). *Russia* avoided making trouble for fear of provoking against her not only Austria-Hungary but also Germany, and possibly Great Britain as well.

Austria-Hungary was kept in check by the knowledge that Germany would only help her against Russian aggression and would not support her in a more ambitious Balkan policy.

The Balkan states were disunited, and none of them was strong enough to attack Turkey successfully on its own.

The main development during these years was that Germany replaced Great Britain as the power on which Turkey was most dependent. In 1889 and again in 1898 Wilhelm II visited Constantinople, and as a result of the second visit the project of a railway from Berlin to Baghdad was agreed, and arrangements were made for a German company to build the railway through Turkey to the Persian Gulf.

The effects of the Bosnian crisis of 1908-9

It might have been expected that German support for Austria-Hungary in the crisis over Bosnia from 1908 to 1909 (p. 86) would have alienated Turkey from Germany. But by then the ties between the two countries were too close to be easily snapped, and once Turkey had been compensated it did not make much difference to her whether Austria-Hungary merely administered Bosnia, as she already had for thirty years or actually annexed it.

The effect of the crisis on Russia was that her government determined not to suffer another diplomatic defeat of this sort and therefore began to increase the size of her army, while at the same time determining to regain her influence in the Balkans.

The effect on Austria-Hungary was that Germany's support encouraged her to feel able to pursue a far more reckless Balkan policy.

The most important effects of the crisis concern Serbia:

(1) Relations between Serbia and Austria-Hungary became more strained, because up to 1908 Serbia had been hoping eventually to acquire Bosnia. So now she encouraged anti-Hapsburg terrorism in Bosnia.

(2) Serbia and Russia drew closer, because Serbia now hoped for Russian aid in the event of a clash with Austria-Hungary.

(3) Since Serbia's aim to acquire Bosnia had been thwarted, her ambitions turned southwards towards Macedonia; and the effect of increased Serbian interest in Macedonia was to revive the traditional enmity between Serbia and Bulgaria, for ever since 1878 Bulgaria had been hoping to acquire Macedonia from Turkey.

Thus after 1908 the Balkans were even more a potential source of trouble than before.

The First Balkan War, 1912

In 1912 matters came to a head:

(1) The Young Turk revolution of 1908 (p. 307) had resulted in increased unrest in Macedonia, for the new Turkish government was more efficient and consequently more oppressive.

(2) The enmity between Serbia and Bulgaria was temporarily ended by the good offices of Russia, who believed she could increase her influence in the Balkans at the expense of Austria-Hungary in this way, and in 1912 the Balkan League of Greece, Bulgaria, Serbia, and Montenegro was formed.

(3) At that time Turkey was occupied in defending Tripoli, which had been invaded by Italy in 1911; so the Balkan League took the opportunity of attacking her in Europe.

The armies of the League attacked in October and swept through Macedonia. In December the Turks, who had been driven back as far as Adrianople, asked for an armistice.

The London Conference, 1912–13

At this stage the great powers intervened and insisted on a conference, which met in London. Austria-Hungary was determined that Serbia should not get an outlet to the sea, and therefore demanded the setting up of an independent state of Albania. Britain supported this demand, so a new country came into existence on the Eastern shore of the Adriatic. Russia was determined that Bulgaria should not get Constantinople, and the conference therefore insisted that Turkey should keep it. The area in between was left to the victorious Balkan League, and in May 1913 a peace treaty was drawn up in London.

AUSTRIA–HUNGARY

The independent Balkan states
before the Balkan wars

RUSSIA

ROUMANIA

SERBIA

Southern
Dobruja

BULGARIA

The Black Sea

MONTENEGRO

MACEDONIA   THRACE

THE OTTOMAN EMPIRE

Aegean
Sea

The arrows show
which countries
fought against
the Ottoman Empire
in the first Balkan
War of 1912

GREECE

On the whole the great powers had behaved with moderation.
The reason for this was probably that they saw the danger of war,
and some were genuinely anxious to avoid war, while others were
not yet ready to fight.

The second Balkan War, 1913

Only a month after the conclusion of the Treaty of London the
second Balkan War broke out. The members of the League had
not reached any clear agreement before the first war on how to
divide up the lands they were intending to take from Turkey. In
the event Bulgaria, which was nearer the base of Turkish power,
bore the brunt of the fighting, while the armies of Serbia and
Greece occupied more territory. Then the creation of an independent Albania had the effect that Serbia, prevented from expanding
South-West, became more anxious to expand South-East, and
therefore insisted on retaining the large area of Macedonia which
her troops had occupied, but which was inhabited mainly by

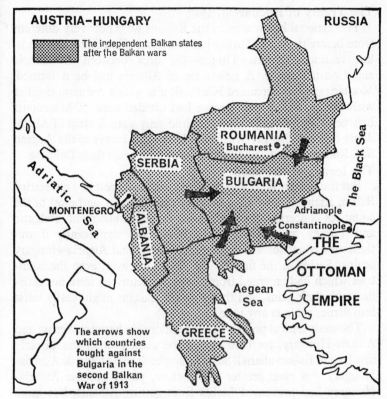

AUSTRIA-HUNGARY   RUSSIA

The independent Balkan states
after the Balkan wars

The Black Sea

ROUMANIA
Bucharest

SERBIA

BULGARIA

Adriatic Sea

MONTENEGRO

ALBANIA

Adrianople

Constantinople

THE

OTTOMAN

Aegean
Sea

EMPIRE

GREECE

The arrows show
which countries
fought against
Bulgaria in the
second Balkan
War of 1913

Bulgars and which was regarded by Bulgaria as her rightful share
of the spoils.

In June 1913 Bulgaria attacked Serbia, but she soon found herself surrounded by enemies:

Greece, seeing herself as Bulgaria's next victim, attacked from the
South.

Turkey attacked from the East in order to try to regain Adrianople,
which had gone to Bulgaria in the Treaty of London.

Roumania, the only other country bordering on Bulgaria, saw a
chance of acquiring the Southern Dobruja, and attacked from the
North.

Just as Turkey had been surrounded by Greece, Bulgaria, Serbia, and Montenegro in 1912, Bulgaria was surrounded by Greece,
Serbia, Turkey, and Roumania in 1913. Just as Turkey had been
defeated in a few weeks in 1912, Bulgaria was defeated in a few
weeks in 1913; and in August the war was ended by the Treaty of
Bucharest.

The Treaty of Bucharest, 1913

The national boundaries in the Balkans were now very different from before the wars. Turkey had lost most of her European lands, but retained Eastern Thrace—the area between Adrianople and Constantinople. A new state of Albania had been formed. Montenegro had expanded North-East to gain a common frontier with Serbia. Serbia and Greece had divided most of Macedonia between them. Bulgaria had acquired only a small strip of Macedonia but did also get Western Thrace and access to the Aegean Sea. Roumania had gained the Southern Dobruja from Bulgaria.

The legacy of the wars

But the Balkan Wars and the Treaty of Bucharest had not settled Balkan affairs. They had merely rearranged them, and most of the countries concerned were eager for further adjustment. Bulgaria and Turkey were bitterly dissatisfied, and significantly it was these two countries which joined Germany and Austria-Hungary against Serbia in the first World War. Moreover, even the countries which had emerged from the wars victorious were not satisfied with their gains, and therefore the Balkans might easily burst into flames again at any time.

The most critical point was the relationship between Serbia and Austria-Hungary, for here one of the great powers was directly involved in Balkan affairs. Serbia's aggressiveness towards Austria-Hungary was even greater than before, partly because Austria-Hungary had prevented Serbia from getting Albania, but more because now Serbia had expanded to include the Serbs who had been under Turkish rule, she was even more eager to expand to include all the South Slavs (Serbs, Croats, and Slovenes) under Austrian control. Austria-Hungary, realising that this would mean the end of her Empire, determined to destroy Serbia.

The international repercussions of this situation could be vast. If Austria-Hungary attacked Serbia, Russia would feel obliged to oppose her. But Austria-Hungary would only attack if she knew she had the support of Germany. German intervention would entail the participation of Turkey, over whom Germany's control was now very tight, for Turkey bestrode the Straits and could thus cut Russia off from France. France, of course, was committed to Russia, and Great Britain, linked to France and Russia by the *ententes*, would probably join in as well. Even Japan, bound to Great Britain by the Treaty of 1902 (p. 77), might join in. If a fire started in the Balkans it could easily spread all over the world. All that was needed was a spark to light the fire.

THE EVENT which precipitated the crisis leading up to the first World War was the assassination on 28th June 1914 of the Hapsburg Archduke Franz Ferdinand when he was visiting the town of Sarajevo in Bosnia. At the time few people expected this incident in the Serb campaign of violence against Austria-Hungary (p. 101) to lead to a general war. But although other international crises in recent years had been settled without war, the combination of circumstances in the summer of 1914 was such that this one set in motion a series of events which plunged Europe into chaos.

Nationalism and economic change

The idea of Nationalism had altered the balance of power in Europe drastically during the nineteenth century. On the one hand it had brought Germany and Italy into existence, and on the other it was threatening to destroy both the Turkish and Austrian Empires. It was a threat to the territorial integrity of all those great powers which ruled another European people. Polish Nationalism, for example, was a threat to Germany, Austria-Hungary, and Russia alike. Irish Nationalism was a threat to Great Britain. And Serb Nationalism was so great a threat to Austria-Hungary that the Austrian government believed that the survival of its Empire depended on the destruction of Serbia.

Economic developments helped to alter the balance of power. Industrial progress had helped to make Germany the strongest power in Europe, while Austria-Hungary was so undeveloped industrially that it seemed likely that she would soon not have the strength to maintain her position as a great power.

Thus Nationalism and economic change between them produced a situation in which Austria-Hungary was desperately anxious to maintain not merely her position as a great power but even her very existence, and in which Germany wanted to acquire a position of political dominance in the world which corresponded to her actual strength. Both of these circumstances created tension in relations with the other great powers, and the tension was increased by the fact that these two powers, one declining and the other rising, were linked together in a military alliance.

The military situation in 1914

This tension between the great powers was heightened in the years before the war by an arms race. France and Russia attempted to maintain their security by competing with Germany, and in

1914 the German General Staff believed that Germany was in danger of becoming relatively weaker than she had been hitherto, and that 1914 was the last year in which she could win a continental war rapidly. The reorganisation and build-up of the Russian army, which was begun after the Bosnian crisis (pp. 86–7), was not yet completed in 1914, nor were the Russian strategic railways on the Polish front. The three-year service introduced by France in 1913 was not yet in full operation in 1914. The German army, on the other hand, reached a peak of strength in the summer of 1914 which could not be permanently maintained in peace-time. Consequently Moltke, the Chief of the German General Staff, who believed that a war between the Triple Alliance and the Triple Entente was inevitable, also believed that it was in Germany's interest to start the war in the summer of 1914.

Thus just as there was an element in Austria-Hungary which believed that a war was necessary to forestall political collapse, there was an element in Germany which believed that war was necessary to forestall military weakness.

Motives for going to war

Nationalism and economic developments had upset the balance of power in Europe enough to create new political problems, and it was this together with the build-up of powerful armies which created an explosive situation in 1914.

The existence of two opposing alliances made it likely that if one great power become involved in a war in Europe the others would be involved as well. But the mere existence of the alliances did not precipitate the war, for after all the alliances had existed side by side for twenty years without war.

Colonial rivalry, trade rivalry, and naval rivalry all helped to create tension in international relations, but none of them contributed directly to causing the outbreak of war.

In the event each of the European countries which went to war in July or August 1914 fought either for survival or else to prevent something which it regarded as a greater evil than war:

Austria-Hungary wanted to maintain her territorial integrity and her position as a great power, and believed that this could only be done by destroying Serbia. She knew the danger that war would bring revolution and the disintegration of her Empire, but she was prepared to risk being destroyed in a long war in the hope of being strengthened by winning a short one.

Serbia fought to avoid extinction or domination by Austria-Hungary.

Russia fought to prevent any further extension of Austrian influence in the Balkans.

Germany fought to prevent the destruction of Austria-Hungary, for that would weaken Germany by giving Russia control of the Balkans and cutting Germany off from Turkey and the Middle East.

France fought to prevent the defeat of Russia, which would leave her at the mercy of Germany.

Belgium fought to defend herself against a German invasion.

Great Britain fought to prevent Germany defeating the Dual Alliance, for that would make Germany so powerful that Britain and the Empire would be defenceless against her.

War aims

None of these countries went to war for an expansionist or aggressive motive, but some of them had expansionist ambitions, and the war provided an opportunity for those ambitions to be satisfied. Since 1871 France had looked forward to the recovery of Alsace-Lorraine, and now she included it in her war aims. For even longer Russia had wanted control of the Straits and of Constantinople, and now she included that in her war aims. Germany had recently been aiming at economic, military, naval, and political predominance in the world. She had no fixed intention of fighting to establish that predominance, and had not taken previous favourable opportunities for fighting, such as the Tangier crisis of 1905 (p. 85), when the Dual Alliance was seriously weakened by Russia's defeat in the Russo-Japanese War (p. 312) and by the subsequent revolution in Russia (p. 21), and when the *entente cordiale* had only just been concluded and no arrangements had yet been made for joint Anglo-French military action. But once the war had started Germany found herself fighting for domination of the world.

The political crisis of July 1914

The war did not begin until a month after the assassination of the Archduke. On 5th July, one week after the assassination, Bethmann-Hollweg, the German Chancellor, encouraged Austria-Hungary to act firmly against Serbia, hoping to win another diplomatic triumph over Russia like that of 1909 (pp. 86–7), and trusting that any fighting which did result would not spread outside the Balkans. It was the failure to win this diplomatic victory which precipitated general war, for Bethmann-Hollweg found himself faced with the alternatives of retreat or war, and in this situation the army was able to insist on war.

On 23rd July Austria-Hungary sent Serbia an ultimatum which was intended to be unacceptable. On the 25th Serbia accepted most of the terms, but made minor reservations. Austria-Hungary treated this as a refusal, declared war on her on the 28th, and on the 29th attacked her and bombarded Belgrade, the Serbian capital.

Meanwhile Russia had ordered partial mobilisation, but the Russian army had no plans for partial mobilisation, so on the 30th the order for general mobilisation was issued.

By this time Bethmann-Hollweg was so worried about the impression created in other countries by Austria's action that on the 30th he pressed Austria to halt and negotiate after occupying Belgrade, and even telegraphed that Germany 'must decline to be dragged into a world conflagration by Vienna'. Unfortunately he was no longer in complete control in Berlin, and on the same day Moltke urged the Austrian army to mobilise instantly against Russia, and promised German support. The result of these conflicting injunctions from Germany was that on the 31st, in response to Bethmann-Hollweg's message, the Austrian government at last expressed its willingness to negotiate, but on the same day, in response to Moltke's message, general mobilisation of the Austrian army was ordered.

The Schlieffen Plan

Meanwhile, also on the 31st, news was received in Germany of the Russian mobilisation ordered the previous day. Military requirements now produced an ultimatum to Russia, for Moltke insisted on the need to move swiftly in order to be able to strike first. The ultimatum demanded that Russia should demobilise, and the next day, 1st August, Germany declared war on her.

Military requirements also produced an ultimatum to France on the 31st, for Germany's ready-made war plans, which had been drawn up in 1905 by Count von Schlieffen, who was then Chief of the General Staff, were based on the assumption that Germany would go to war with France as well as Russia. It was intended to defeat France in six weeks, before Russian mobilisation was completed, and then turn East and spend six months in crushing Russia. Since the object of the plan was to ensure a rapid victory in the West and avoid fighting on two fronts at once, it was essential to find some way of bringing France into the war quickly. So the ultimatum to France demanded a guarantee of neutrality in the event of a war between Germany and Russia. France declined to give the guarantee, and on 3rd August, after a delay in which the

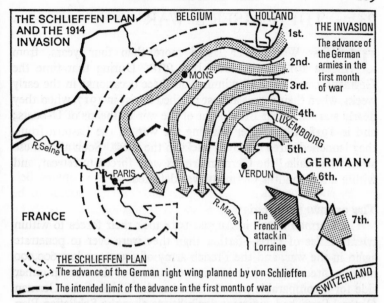

German government tried to induce Britain to remain neutral, Germany declared war on France.

Another aspect of the Schlieffen Plan was a flanking attack through Belgium and Luxembourg intended to encircle and crush the French left flank. Therefore on 3rd August, the day that Germany declared war on France, she also sent an ultimatum to Belgium demanding free passage for her troops. Thus purely military requirements also involved Germany in war with Belgium and ensured that Britain would move against her. For it was the violation of Belgian neutrality which Britain had promised to maintain in 1839 which enabled Sir Edward Grey to convince the cabinet, parliament, and public opinion that Britain should go to war. On 4th August the German invasion of Belgium was launched, and the same day Britain declared war on Germany.

Armageddon

Within a fortnight Japan, seeing an opportunity for expansion in the Far East at Germany's expense, declared war on her. Turkey closed the Straits to the *entente* powers, who declared war on her on 1st November. By the time Bulgaria had joined the Central Powers (October 1915) and Italy (May 1915) and Roumania (August 1916) had joined the *entente* powers most of Europe was at war. When the U.S.A. joined the *entente* powers in April 1917 all the great powers of the world were at war.

23   THE KAISER'S WAR

THE first World War lasted more than four years, from August 1914 until November 1918. During that time the Germans came close to winning on three occasions: in the early weeks, when their forces almost reached Paris; in 1917, when they nearly starved Great Britain out of the war by means of U-boats; and in 1918, when, after winning the war on the Eastern front, they launched three massive attacks in the West. Soon after these attacks had failed the German armies were forced to retreat, and within a few months Germany was defeated.

The opening campaign

The German attack in August 1914 took their forces to within twenty miles of Paris—farther than they were ever to penetrate again in the war, and the French army of 1,300,000 lost 600,000 men in three weeks—the heaviest casualties of the war on either side for a comparable period. Moltke, the Chief of the German General Staff, had sufficient flexibility to alter the Schlieffen Plan (p. 108) to meet unexpected circumstances: he diverted some troops to help deal with a rapid Russian attack in the East and others to help hold a French attack in Lorraine. But he lacked the self-assurance to keep a firm control of the operation, and by September the German armies, which had inevitably lost impetus after so long a march, were in a disorganised line stretching eastwards roughly along the valley of the Marne from Paris to Verdun, about 130 miles away.

The French now counter-attacked, and in the battle of the Marne in the first ten days of September forced the Germans to withdraw about 40 miles and dig in. Flanking attacks by both sides resulted in a line of trenches stretching from Switzerland to the North Sea. The Germans tried to reach the Channel ports and cut the supply line from England to the British and French forces on the continent. But while Germany's armies on the Eastern front, under Generals Hindenburg and Ludendorff, were defeating and driving back the Russians, her forces in the West were unable to break past the British Expeditionary Force entrenched at Ypres.

War on two fronts

The result of failure to win the war in 1914 by means of a swift well-planned *Blitzkrieg* was that the Germans now had to fight on two fronts at once—the very situation which the Schlieffen

Plan had been designed to avoid. But they had two great strategic advantages which they retained throughout the war. One was that their forces were established in enemy territory in both East and West, so that they could afford to make tactical withdrawals while the Allies were committed to standing firm to prevent any further loss of their own territory. The other was that Russia was cut off from supplies from her Western allies, except via the peril-ous Arctic route, because Turkey, which was allied with Germany, controlled the Straits leading to the Black Sea.

This second strategic consideration, together with the wish to establish a base from which to strike at 'the soft under-belly of Europe', caused the British to embark in 1915 on the unsuccessful Gallipoli campaign (p. 167). The failure of this attempt was dis-astrous for the Russians, for while the Turks held the British at Gallipoli, Falkenhayn, the German commander who replaced Moltke soon after the battle of the Marne, agreed to the demands being made by Hindenburg and Ludendorff that the German forces should stand on the defensive in the West and attack in the East; and during 1915 the German armies drove the Russians back across Poland, taking a million prisoners and thus dealing them a blow from which they never really recovered.

The war of attrition

The effect of the German failure to win in the West in 1914 and of the British failure to open a more mobile front in the Balkans in 1915 was that both sides settled down to a long drawn-out war of attrition on the Western front—an attempt to win by wearing down the enemy's resources of men and armaments. And the failure of the British to open the Mediterranean supply route to Russia meant that Russia would eventually be defeated and that attrition on the Western front would decide the war.

In 1916 Falkenhayn turned the bulk of the German war effort westwards again. In the first half of the year he set out to wear the French down by attacking them at Verdun—an ancient town and fortress, which, he rightly guessed, the French were prepared to defend even at the cost of very heavy losses. It was only after nearly five months, when the British launched an attack farther North in the area of the River Somme that he called the attack off. By then each side had lost more than 300,000 men—the French rather more than the Germans. The battle of the Somme, which lasted from July to November, was even more costly of life, and although the British gained some ground they did not break through the German lines, and strategically the situation remained unchanged. There was complete deadlock.

The war at sea

In 1916 and 1917 the Germans made an attempt to break the deadlock by means of their navy, for the Allied forces on the Continent were dependent on supplies from Britain and so could easily be defeated if their supplies were cut off. But this involved denying the use of the sea to British merchant ships.

The most obvious way of doing this was by defeating the Royal Navy and seizing control of the sea, and this was attempted in May 1916 when the German fleet came out into the North Sea and fought the battle of Jutland. But although the British losses in tonnage and men were twice as great as the German losses, the Germans were driven to realise that their fleet was simply not big enough to defeat the British at sea.

An alternative method entailed U-boat warfare against British merchant shipping. This had already been attempted early in 1915, but the U.S.A. objected to 'unrestricted' U-boat warfare (p. 169), and the Germans abandoned it because they lacked sufficient U-boats for it to be worth the risk of American intervention. However, by 1917 they calculated that they had sufficient U-boats to win the war before the U.S.A. could intervene. It was a disastrous miscalculation, for although Germany came nearer to victory than at any time since the early weeks of the war, Britain survived the U-boat campaign, and after April 1917 the U.S.A. was in the war as well and in time would come to the aid of her allies.

The last bid for victory

The Germans had one further opportunity for winning the war. The Bolshevik Revolution in Russia in November 1917 was followed by German victory in the East early in 1918, and as a result the Germans were able to concentrate their forces in the West and achieve superiority of numbers for the first time since 1914. Falkenhayn had been replaced at the end of August 1916, in the middle of the battle of the Somme, and Hindenburg was now Chief of the General Staff. But the real commander of the German forces was First Quartermaster-General Ludendorff; and it was he who organised and launched a series of three attacks in the spring and summer of 1918. The first, in March, was aimed at separating the British and French; the second, in April, was aimed at cutting the Allies off from the Channel ports; and the third, in May, was an attempt to split the French forces and reach Paris.

All three were initially successful, but they lost their impetus as the lines of communication lengthened, and each of them was held after a desperate week's fighting. Moreover, since the U.S.A. had declared war the allies had been able to buy war supplies from American firms with money borrowed from the American government, and although American troops were not in

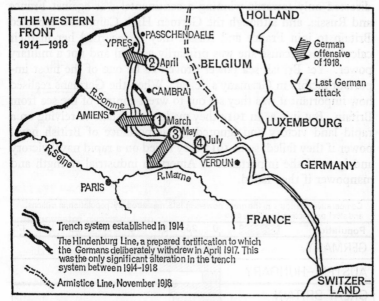

THE WESTERN FRONT 1914–1918

HOLLAND
YPRES
PASSCHENDAELE
② April
BELGIUM
CAMBRAI
AMIENS
① March
③ May
④ July
R. Somme
R. Seine
PARIS
R. Marne
VERDUN
LUXEMBOURG
GERMANY
FRANCE
SWITZER-LAND

German offensive of 1918.

Last German attack

Trench system established in 1914

The Hindenburg Line, a prepared fortification to which the Germans deliberately withdrew in April 1917. This was the only significant alteration in the trench system between 1914–1918

Armistice Line, November 1918

action in large numbers until June 1918 it was clear even before that month that the manpower resources of the Allies were virtually inexhaustible.

In July the Germans launched a last attack. It was a hopeless dying effort. The French counter-attacked and dealt the Germans a major blow at the second battle of the Marne, and from 8th August, when the British attacked near Amiens, until November 11th, when the armistice was signed, the Germans were perpetually retreating. While they were being driven back across Belgium, Bulgaria collapsed, the Austrians were defeated at Vittorio Veneto, the Turks were pushed back through Syria, the German fleet mutinied, revolution broke out, and the Kaiser abdicated and fled to Holland. Defeat had become collapse.

The reasons for Germany's defeat

The Schlieffen Plan failed in 1914 partly because it was mismanaged but more because the Germans underestimated the opposition they would meet. The U-boat campaign of 1917 failed because of British sea-power. By 1918 Germany was exhausted by four years of fighting, and the attacks launched in the spring and summer of that year drained her last reserves of energy.

Germany's only real war aim had been domination of the world. Yet her military plan, as distinct from her political plan, was directed only towards winning a continental war against France and Russia, and although the German High Command expected Britain to join France and Russia they disregarded her in their calculations because she was primarily a naval and not a military power. Yet British sea power proved to be one of the most important factors in Germany's defeat. When the Germans realised how important it was they set out to wrest control of the sea from Britain. But just as in 1914 they made the mistake of relying on a rapid land victory and ignored the importance of British naval power if they failed, so in 1917 they relied on a rapid naval victory and ignored the importance of American industrial strength and manpower if they failed.

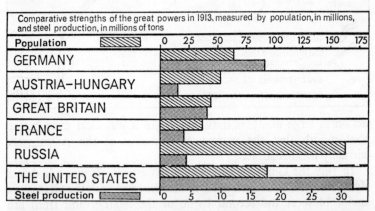

Comparative strengths of the great powers in 1913, measured by population, in millions, and steel production, in millions of tons

The result was disaster. The German High Command had never intended to fight for as long as a year. But in the end Germany had to fight for over four years, and by the end of that time her strength was exhausted. German industrial strength and manpower had made a victorious *Blitzkrieg* seem possible in 1914. Superior industrial strength and greater manpower eventually defeated her, for a war which was intended to be a continental *Blitzkrieg* turned into a war of blockade and attrition.

THE FOURTEEN POINTS AND PEACE

IN JANUARY 1918 President Wilson of the U.S.A. made a speech to Congress in which he announced Fourteen Points, in accordance with which peace should be made. The first four of these were concerned with the way in which he believed international relations should be regulated in respect of diplomatic, naval, economic, and military matters after the war. The next nine were concerned primarily with the territorial adjustments which he thought would be necessary at the end of the war. The last was a proposal for the establishment of 'a general association of nations'.

Brest-Litovsk to Versailles

Germany ignored these proposals, and in March 1918 imposed on the new Bolshevik government of Russia the crippling Treaty of Brest-Litovsk (p. 219). Germany now poured troops into the Western front in a last desperate bid to win the war, but by the autumn the German General Staff knew that they were beaten. So on 5th October the German government asked President Wilson to arrange an armistice and proposed that peace negotiations should be on the basis of his Fourteen Points.

When the British and French Prime Ministers were consulted Lloyd George insisted that Britain could not accept the second of the Fourteen Points, a demand for freedom of the seas both in peace and war, because British security depended on commanding the sea in time of war, and Clemenceau insisted that Germany should be made to pay for the damage done to civilian property during the war.

The Germans were informed that the Allies would conclude peace on the lines of the Fourteen Points, subject to these two reservations, and at 11 a.m. on 11th November, 1918, an armistice took effect. The German army withdrew across the Rhine, and Germany surrendered her fleet and so much military equipment that it was militarily impossible for her to resume fighting.

The Peace Conference

The Peace Conference did not begin until January 1919, and when it met not all the main belligerents were represented. In one sense this was inevitable, for the strains produced by war and defeat had created a completely new situation in Europe in which four of the great Empires which had gone to war in 1914 had disappeared. The Dual Monarchy of Austria-Hungary had completely disintegrated, the Turkish Empire was breaking up, Russia was plunged in civil war, and the German Empire had been replaced by a democracy. But it was not merely the representatives of these Empires who were excluded from the conference. Even the representatives of the new democratic republics of Germany, Austria, and Hungary were allowed no part in the drawing up of the treaties which they eventually had to sign, and the new Bolshevik government of Russia was ignored, although Russia was affected by the peace treaties.

The main task of drawing up the settlement was undertaken by the five victorious allied powers: the U.S.A., Great Britain, France, Italy, and Japan. But Italy and Japan were concerned only with those aspects of the settlement which affected themselves, and neither of their Prime Ministers remained throughout the negotiations. Thus the principal authors of the settlement were Clemenceau of France, Wilson of the U.S.A., and Lloyd George of Great Britain. Clemenceau wanted to provide permanent security for France from any future German attack. Wilson dreamt of 'a world made safe for democracy'. And Lloyd George wanted a practical settlement which would satisfy as many people as possible.

Time and the treaties

All of them were influenced by the pressure of time, for they had to attempt to solve Europe's problems peacefully at a time when many other men were trying to settle those problems by force. During 1919 there was still widespread fighting in Eastern Europe, there were short-lived Communist revolutions in Berlin (p. 140), Munich, and Budapest (p. 19), many prisoners-of-war were still in captivity, and many thousands of people were starving. All these factors helped to create a feeling that it was more important to reach decisions quickly than to reach the right decisions, and it was hoped that any mistakes could be put right later.

Three treaties were completed in 1919: the Treaty of Versailles with Germany, the Treaty of Saint-Germain with Austria, and the Treaty of Neuilly with Bulgaria. The other two, the Treaty of Trianon with Hungary, which was now completely separate from Austria, and the Treaty of Sèvres with Turkey, were not completed until 1920. These five treaties established new territorial boundaries, dealt with the questions of reparations and disarmament, and set up the League of Nations.

The German reaction

From the first the Germans objected to the Treaty of Versailles. They resented Article 231, the war-guilt clause, in which they had to admit that the war had been caused by 'the aggression of Germany and her allies'. They resented the demand that the Kaiser and war criminals should be brought to trial. They disliked the territorial losses they suffered (p. 216), and they complained that the disarmament clauses were unjust and that the reparations demands were excessive, vindictive, and impossible to satisfy. Above all they condemned the treaty as a *Diktat*. The Allies, they said, had deceived them by agreeing to make peace in accordance with the Fourteen Points, and then, after tricking Germany into disarming, had imposed on her a dictated settlement.

The Fourteen Points

Certainly the treaties were not strictly in accordance with the Fourteen Points, but this was not because the peacemakers made no attempt to adhere to them.

The first four points were impracticable. In effect they were demands for:

(1) *an end to secret diplomacy and secret treaties;*

(2) *freedom of the seas both in peace and war;*

(3) *international free trade;* and

(4) *general disarmament.*

The second point was, of course, ruled out by Great Britain, but in any case there was little that the peacemakers could do to ensure that the nations of the world acted in accordance with any of these points.

The next nine points nearly all needed modification to meet changing circumstances. Only two were not changed at all:

(8) *the return of Alsace and Lorraine to France;* and

(13) *the establishment of an independent Poland.*

Two more were modified very little:

(7) *the restoration of Belgium.* Belgium gained a little land from Germany (p. 216).

(9) *the rectification of Italy's frontier on the basis of nationality.* Italy gained the German-speaking South Tyrol.

The idea of making colonial areas captured from Germany and Turkey into 'mandated territories' resulted in drastic modification of two other points:

(5) *the 'impartial adjustment of all colonial claims'.* The Germans lost all their colonies.

(12) *'secure sovereignty' for the Turkish portions of the Ottoman Empire and independence for the subject peoples.* The subject peoples did not gain independence until much later, and even the Turks had to fight to get 'secure sovereignty' in Anatolia (pp. 308–9).

The break-up of Austria-Hungary and the seizure of power in Russia by the Bolsheviks (p. 124) resulted in the modification of the three other clauses concerned with territorial arrangements:

(6) *the evacuation of Russia.* The Germans did evacuate Russian territory, but little of it was regained by the Russians.

(10) *self-government for the peoples of Austria-Hungary.* In practice the peoples of Austria-Hungary gained complete independence.

(11) *the restoration of Roumania, Serbia, and Montenegro.* Roumania was both restored and enlarged. Serbia and Montenegro were restored, united, and enlarged to form Jugoslavia (p. 218).

The last of the Fourteen Points was carried into effect:

(14) *the establishment of 'a general association of nations'.* But Germany and Russia were not allowed to join the League of Nations, and the consequences of this were disastrous. In 1919 these two great powers were neither destroyed nor conciliated. Instead they were both treated as outcasts, and as a result they were both dissatisfied and anxious for revision of the peace settlement.

Ideal and reality

But Germany and Russia were not the only countries which were dissatisfied with the treaties. Under the circumstances it was impossible to satisfy anyone, let alone everyone. This was particularly so because the treaties so often fell short of the ideals proclaimed by Wilson. He had promised 'a peace without humiliation of the defeated'. But unfortunately defeat entails humiliation. He had promised 'self-determination of nations'. But in some cases this was an impossibility. Compromises were frequently necessary, and invariably they seemed to be an abandonment of principles for the sake of expediency. The lack of representation of the defeated nations increased this impression of unfairness.

But this does not mean that the treaties were bad. The peacemakers tried hard to draw up a peace which was just, and in large measure they succeeded. They made a genuine attempt to make a new start in international relations by trying to get the League of Nations to take the place of the principle of 'balance of power' as a means of keeping the peace. And the treaties failed to produce a more stable world not because they were unjust but because the most was not made of such justice as there was in them.

Section IV Europe between the Wars

25 THE SPREAD OF DICTATORSHIP

AFTER the first World War parliamentary democracy was fashionable in Europe. The war had been won by an alliance of democracies, and the autocratically ruled Empires of East and Central Europe had been defeated. Consequently parliamentary constitutions were widely adopted by both old and new nations, and most of Europe came to be ruled by parliamentary governments.

But by 1939 democracy survived only in the North-West. This was partly because many other areas of Europe still had a peasant economy, together with a low standard of living and widespread illiteracy, and thus lacked the conditions which had enabled democracy to develop naturally. Another reason was that many constitutions were quite unsuited to the conditions in which they had to operate. Proportional representation, for example, made it difficult to get stable government, and many democratic governments lacked adequate powers to deal effectively with the problems which faced them. Furthermore, the right to vote every few years gives a man little control over his government, and consequently people in countries which lacked a democratic tradition rapidly became impatient and disillusioned with parliamentary rule, especially when its achievements were small.

The authoritarianism of the Left

The process of overthrowing parliamentary government began even before the end of the war when the parliamentary system which had been established in Russia in March 1917 was overthrown by the Bolsheviks in the following November. But the only other significant headway made by the Communists in Europe between the wars was the establishment of a short-lived Communist government in Hungary from March to July 1919.

The authoritarianism of the Right

It was far more usual for parliamentary government to be overthrown by right-wing authoritarian movements, of which there were three main types.

(1) The most extreme manifestations of right-wing authoritarianism were seen in the Fascist movement, which brought Mussolini to power in Italy in 1922, and the Nazi movement,

which brought Hitler to power in Germany in 1933. Both glorified the use of force and each offered a super-human leader as the solution to all problems.

(2) A more moderate form of authoritarianism evolved in Portugal. In the sixteen years after the overthrow of the monarchy in 1910 Portugal had forty-four different governments, so in 1926 a group of army officers who wanted to see stable government had overthrown parliament. They turned for assistance in ruling the country to an economist, Dr. Salazar, who in 1932 became Prime Minister with complete control over policy. He established a one-party police state with rigid restrictions on individual liberty but without the private armies, aggressive Nationalism, and pompous ceremonial of Fascist Italy and Nazi Germany. The dictatorship established by Dr. Dollfüss in Austria in 1933 was on similar lines, as was that imposed on Spain by General Franco in the Civil War of 1936-9. All three based their government on close association with the Roman Catholic Church and justified it by reference to the papal bull *quadrigesimo anno* of 1931, in which Pope Pius XI attacked both Socialism and *laissez-faire* Capitalism, which was associated with Liberalism, and tried to suggest a middle way between them which would involve co-operation between the classes and increased state intervention.

(3) In South-East Europe there was a return to traditional monarchical government:

In *Hungary* a Regent, Admiral Horthy, ruled in accordance with the old constitution even though the neighbouring countries would not tolerate the return of a Hapsburg monarch to Hungary.

In *Albania* years of chaos culminated in the assumption of the Presidency in 1925 by a young army officer, Ahmed Zogu, who in 1928 proclaimed himself King Zog I.

In *Bulgaria* parliamentary government survived with difficulty until 1934, and then there was a year of military dictatorship until in 1935 King Boris III assumed supreme power.

In *Roumania* unstable parliamentary government gave place in 1930 to a harsh form of military dictatorship which was itself overthrown in 1937 when King Carol II seized control of the country into his own hands.

Greece was particularly unstable as the result of a split during the first World War between the pro-German King Constantine and the pro-British Prime Minister, Venizelos. After years of upheaval a republic was established in 1923, but in 1935, after a civil war, King George II returned to the throne and appointed as

Prime Minister General Metaxas, who ruled as dictator over what he called 'the Third Hellenic Civilisation'.

Albania was annexed by Italy in April 1939. Hungary, Bulgaria, and Roumania all became allies of Germany in the second World War, and Greece was conquered by Germany in April 1941.

Jugoslavia

The new Balkan kingdom of the South Slavs, or Jugoslavia, was a nation formed by the expansion of Serbia into the vast Southern tracts of Austria-Hungary, and with the later addition of Montenegro. It was divided against itself by race, religion, and history. The Serb majority were Orthodox by religion, their history included a long period of subjection to the Turks, and they were still a comparatively primitive people. The Croats and Slovenes were mostly Roman Catholic, for centuries they had been under Hapsburg rule, and in many ways they were more advanced than the Serbs. They were conscious of their position as minorities and wanted a federal constitution which would give them self-government in internal matters.

But the Serbs insisted on centralised government. So the Croats and Slovenes were discontented, and their discontent was intensified in 1929 when the Serb King Alexander suspended the constitution and began to rule as a dictator. In 1934 he was assassinated by a Croat terrorist, and his young son, Peter II, became King. But Alexander's brother, Prince Paul, ruled the country as Regent until March 1941 when he was overthrown by army leaders as soon as he gave in to pressure from Hitler to join an alliance with Germany. The new government was determined to resist Hitler, but the German invasion was too swift and powerful for them, and on 17th April, eleven days after it was launched, Jugoslavia surrendered.

Czechoslovakia

The new country of Czechoslovakia was even more divided racially than Jugoslavia. It was a miniature replica of Austria-Hungary, out of which it had been carved, including, besides Czechs and Slovaks, Germans, Magyars, Poles, and Ruthenians. Surprisingly this did not make parliamentary government unworkable, and parliamentary democracy was far more successful in Czechoslovakia than in most states of Central and Eastern Europe. This was partly due to the personality and prestige of Tomàš Masaryk who had first become famous as the leader of an army of Czech prisoners-of-war in Russia. They had fought for the Russians and then, during the revolution, had fought their way across Siberia to Vladivostock and returned to Europe by sea. Masaryk, who represented the new Czechoslovak republic at Paris in 1919, was devoted to democratic principles and was President of Czechoslovakia from 1918 until 1935. Another reason was that already under the Hapsburgs industrialisation and education had produced a large urban population, including an educated middle class, in the provinces of Bohemia and Moravia, thus making them fertile soil for democracy to grow in.

In the end democracy was overthrown in Czechoslovakia by German intervention, and although the minorities in Czechoslovakia were exceptionally well treated it was the minorities issue which made this possible. The demand of the German minority for Home Rule led to the Munich agreement of September 1938 (p. 245) and a subsequent break-down of firm government in Czechoslovakia. The desire of many Slovaks for independence provided Hitler with the excuse for destroying Czechoslovakia in March 1939.

Poland

While Masaryk, an Austrian Czech, had led Czech troops fighting for Russia against Austria-Hungary, Piłsudski, a Russian Pole, had led Polish troops fighting for Austria-Hungary against Russia. Each of them was fighting against the power which he saw as the main obstacle to the Nationalist aspirations of his own people, and Piłsudski was as much the founder of modern Poland as Masaryk was of modern Czechoslovakia. From 1918 to 1922 he was Chief of State of the new Polish nation which emerged from the Paris Peace Conference and which nearly doubled its size in the wars it fought against Lithuania and Russia. Then he handed over a large and potentially powerful country to parliamentary government.

But the new Poland had been formed from territories belonging to three different Empires and was not naturally cohesive. It also had a serious minorities problem, for although Poles made up the majority of the population there were large German, Russian, Lithuanian, Ruthenian, and Jewish elements, none of which would willingly be assimilated and most of which were badly treated. These divisions were accentuated by the adoption of the principle of proportional representation, which produced large numbers of conflicting parties in parliament, and by 1926 the parliamentary system was working so badly that Piłsudski unwillingly emerged from retirement and ruled virtually as a dictator until his death in 1935, when control of the country passed to a group of army leaders.

The minorities problem which complicated the internal politics of Poland was linked to the question of her relations with her neighbours. In the West Germany resented the existence of the Polish corridor (p. 216). In the East the U.S.S.R. resented the loss of the lands seized by Poland in the Russo-Polish War of 1920–1 (p. 228). In the North Lithuania resented the Polish annexation of Vilna (p. 229) And in the South Poland herself resented the fact that the Poles living in Teschen were controlled by Czechoslovakia. Germany and the U.S.S.R. were powerful enough for Poland to have cause to fear them, so she naturally looked for friendship and support to France. But the Four Power Pact of 1933 (p. 248) shook Poland's faith in France, and Piłsudski decided that he would have to choose between Germany and the U.S.S.R. It was not an easy choice, for it entailed choosing between Hitler and Stalin—and either choice would have been a mistake. In the event Piłsudski accepted Hitler's offer of a non-aggression pact, which was signed in January 1934. In September 1938, at the time of the Munich Conference, Poland acquired Teschen from Czechoslovakia as the result of Hitler's patronage. But Hitler was a dangerous friend. In August 1939 he reached an agreement on the partition of Poland with Stalin, and in September they divided Poland between them.

The Baltic States

The three small Baltic states, Estonia, Latvia, and Lithuania, were all established as parliamentary republics. As in Poland the system of proportional representation made the formation of stable governments difficult. The social and economic problems raised by the war and the Russian revolution created great difficulties for the governments which were established, and Lithuania, which was also under perpetual pressure from the expansionist ambitions of Poland, sought stability and security under a dictatorship as early as 1926. Estonia and Latvia maintained democracy longer, but their fate reflects what seemed to many people the inevitable course of history in the thirties: their internal difficulties were increased by the problems created by the great depression; the example of authoritatian movements and governments abroad encouraged the development of their own Communist and Fascist Parties; and faced with the threat of force the only answer seemed to be force. Estonia became a dictatorship in 1934 and Latvia in 1935 in order to avoid going to either authoritarian extreme. Paradoxically the only practical alternative to dictatorship seemed to be dictatorship.

Marxism

THE Bolshevik Revolution in Russia in November 1917 had its origins in the writings of Karl Marx, a German Jew who spent much of his life in exile in London and who believed he had found a scientific explanation of history and of the future. The economic structure of a society, he said, determined its political structure, and political institutions merely reflected the stage of economic development which a society had reached.

Feudalism: In the peasant economy of the Middle Ages political power was in the hands of the landlord class at whose head was the supreme landlord, the king.

Capitalism: This feudal system was gradually broken down by the rise of a money economy until eventually political power was in the hands of a capitalist class—the property owners who were represented in a parliament elected on a severely limited franchise.

Socialism: Marx argued that in a capitalist economy there was a natural tendency towards the development of vast combines and that the number of capitalists would consequently decrease. These few capitalists would get richer, and the numerous workers, the industrial proletariat, would get poorer until eventually their poverty and misery would cause them to rise against their oppressors, and their numbers would enable them to establish 'the dictatorship of the proletariat' and a Socialist economy, in which the means of production would be owned by society as a whole.

Communism: The final stage of this historical process would come with the establishment of a classless society governed by the Communist principle, 'from each according to his ability, to each according to his needs'.

The Social Democratic Party

However, Marx's law of increasing misery which was going to produce Socialist revolution in the capitalist countries did not work out in practice. Instead the industrial proletariat tended to share in the rising level of prosperity and most of the Social Democratic parties formed in the late nineteenth century under the influence of Marx's ideas turned to parliamentary methods and aimed at gradual evolution towards Socialism.

In Russia, which was primarily an agricultural country, Marxist ideas had little appeal to the peasantry, whose support generally went to a quite different party, the Socialist Revolutionaries, or

Essaires. On the other hand, some industry had recently developed and conditions were so bad that the small Russian working-class of recently urbanised peasants was exceptionally inclined towards revolutionary action—all the more so because Russia had a strong tradition of violence in political life.

In 1898 the Russian Social Democratic Party was formed, and one of its leaders, Vladimir Ilyich Ulyanov, better known by his revolutionary pseudonym of Lenin, won a majority at a party conference in London in 1903 for a constitution which would make the party a small disciplined organisation of active revolutionaries. This produced a split between Lenin's group, which called itself the *Bolshevik*, or majority, party, and the more moderate group, who came to be known as the *Mensheviki*, or minority men.

The November Revolution

The division between the two groups came to a head in 1914. While the Mensheviks supported the war, Lenin vigorously opposed it, arguing that the international working class should not fight each other on behalf of capitalists and imperialists. The German government saw the advantage of letting Lenin loose in Russia, so in April 1917, the month after revolution had broken out in Russia, they transported him from Switzerland, where he had spent most of the war, through Germany, so that he was able to reach Petrograd via Sweden and Finland.

Although the Bolsheviks were only a minority in the *soviets*—the committees of workers and soldiers which had sprung up in the March Revolution, and which were dominated by the Mensheviks and *Essaires*—Lenin believed that a sufficiently revolutionary programme would gain them support among the workers, and as soon as he got back to Petrograd he explained his programme: immediate peace; all land to the peasants; all power to the *soviets*.

In the long run he was proved right. Although a Bolshevik rising in July was crushed by the provisional government, they gained control of the Petrograd Soviet in October and Trotsky, an outstanding personality who had joined them in the summer, was elected its President. By that time many peasants were seizing land for themselves and many soldiers were deserting. The Bolsheviks were the only revolutionary group in no way associated with the failings of the provisional government, which had been led since July by Alexander Kerensky, a moderate Socialist who had joined the *Essaires* in March, and at the end of October their leaders formed a 'military–revolutionary committee'. On 7th November they seized control of Petrograd, and the members of the provi-

sional government either fled or were imprisoned. Theoretically
power was handed over to the *soviets*. In practice, it rested with a
Council of People's Commissars consisting of the Bolshevik leaders
and led by Lenin.

The Civil War

The Bolsheviks now had to establish control over the rest of the
country, and this involved them in three years of civil war.

Their opponents included Russian political enemies of every
complexion, certain minority groups, and armies of intervention
from Great Britain, France, Japan, and the U.S.A. But they could
generally rely on the industrial workers, from whom they had
always derived their main support, and increasingly the peasants
supported them as well because of their policy of letting the
peasants take over the land for themselves. They were acceptable to
the Baltic peoples because they disclaimed territorial ambitions on
coming to power and in 1920 signed treaties of friendship with
Finland, Estonia, Latvia, and Lithuania, which most of their
opponents openly wished to reincorporate in Russia. Among the
mass of the Russian people they derived popularity from ending
the war with Germany in March 1918, and later, somewhat ironically, they acquired popularity as a patriotic party defending
Russia from foreign armies of intervention.

The Bolsheviks also had the great advantage that their enemies
were disunited. Not only did the various different anti-Bolshevik
groups have quite different war aims, but also the forces of General
Denikin in the South, General Yudenitch in the Baltic area, and
Admiral Kolchak in Siberia, themselves made up of various different anti-Bolshevik elements, were never able to establish contact
with each other, for the Bolsheviks always controlled the vital central
area around Moscow. And this also meant that the Bolsheviks
were fighting on internal lines and were able to transport their
troops and supplies far more conveniently than their enemies could.

Another reason for the Bolshevik victory was the single-minded-
ness, vigour, and ruthlessness of their leaders. The Council of
People's Commissars maintained the internal security of the area
its forces dominated by means of an Extraordinary Commission
for Combating Counter-revolution and Sabotage, generally known
from its initials as *Cheka*, which was set up as early as December
1917. And Trotsky, as Commissar for War, used general conscription, rigid discipline, and even the expertise of former Tsarist
officers, to build the Red Army, which was formed in January 1918,
into the largest and most effective fighting force in Russia,

War Communism

At the end of 1920 the Bolshevik Party, which since March 1918 had called itself the Communist Party, emerged victorious. But by then Russia was devastated. Industrial production was down to a sixth of what it had been before the first World War, the land had been laid waste, the system of communications had broken down, the only means of trade was barter, and hunger had driven a third of the urban population into the countryside to seek food.

During the war the Bolsheviks had tried to solve the food problem by sending out special foraging detachments to requisition food and crops from the peasants to feed the Red Army and the hungry in the towns. The peasants were forbidden to sell their surplus produce, and had to hand over to the government everything other than what they needed for themselves. But they rebelled against this policy of 'war communism' by hiding their surplus or else failing to produce any more than they needed. This intensified the famine, and when a drought in the Volga basin in 1920 caused the wheat crop to fail the danger of widespread starvation came close.

The New Economic Policy

The complete breakdown of the economy brought about by the civil war caused Lenin to introduce the New Economic Policy, or N.E.P. From March 1921 each peasant had to produce a quota of goods for the state, but any surplus could be sold for profit. Then in 1922 peasants were given security of land tenure and were permitted to sell or lease their land and even hire labour to work it. Small individual enterprises were encouraged to develop on a traditional capitalist basis, and a new class of small-scale capitalists and middle-men known as *nep*men got trade going again. The state bank issued a new currency and re-established the orthodox financial practices of capitalist societies. Trade with other countries was encouraged, and foreign capitalists were encouraged to invest in Russian industry.

In some ways the Bolsheviks seemed to be returning to a capitalist economy. But N.E.P. was not so much a return to capitalism as an admission that Socialism could not be built overnight. It was no more than a tactical withdrawal, for heavy industry, transport, and foreign trade remained under state control, and thus the Bolsheviks retained a firm base from which to advance to Socialism.

Lenin

Lenin had always believed in the inevitability of the historical process foretold by Marx, but he also believed that planning, organisation, and vigorous action by a nucleus of dedicated Marxists was essential, and having led his party successfully through revolution he then set out, while still in the midst of civil war, to plan for world revolution and for the construction of Socialism in Russia.

The International Working Men's Association founded by Marx in 1864 had fallen apart after ten years largely because of internal dissension, and the Second, or Social Democratic, International, founded in 1889, disintegrated on the outbreak of war in 1914. So in 1919 Lenin established the Third International, or Comintern—a far more rigidly disciplined body than its predecessors, aimed specifically at world revolution.

At the same time he reorganised the Communist Party to adapt it to its new role of ruling Russia and building Socialism, providing it with the Political Bureau (*Politburo*), the Organisation Bureau (*Orgburo*), and a Secretariat.

He always intended that the Communists should retain control of the country and had no respect for the will of the majority as expressed in elections. Consequently he had an elected Constituent Assembly dissolved in January 1918, the day after it met, because it would not do as he wished, and the Communist constitution adopted in July was no more than a propaganda gesture. Although it provided for the election of a Congress of Soviets by most people over eighteen, the Congress of Soviets was only to meet once every two years, the indirect system of voting gave the electors no choice over who eventually represented them, 'obvious enemies of Socialism' were excluded from the franchise, and the representation of the peasants in proportion to their numbers was only a fifth that of the more reliable townsfolk.

Similarly the transformation of Russia in 1923 into the Union of Soviet Socialist Republics, a federation of seven republics, gave control only over local matters to the Communist leaders among the non-Russian peoples and left ultimate power with the Communist rulers of the whole U.S.S.R.

The formation of the U.S.S.R. was one of Lenin's last achievements. In May 1922 he had suffered a serious stroke, and in January 1924 he died. From the Communist standpoint he had speeded history along its inevitable course. To many non-Communists, who were less convinced that Marx had provided an infallible guide for the future, he seemed to have achieved even more: by his personality, ability, and ruthlessness he had altered the whole course of history.

The struggle for power

AFTER LENIN's death in January 1924 power in Russia lay with Lev Bronstein, better known as Trotsky, Zinoviev, Bukharin, Joseph Djugashvily, better known as Stalin, and Kamenev—the five members of the *Politburo*. Trotsky, the most obviously brilliant among them, had won so great a reputation as the man who had organised the Red Army and won the civil war that some saw him as a potential new Napoleon, whose control over the army might enable him to seize absolute power.

By comparison Stalin, who eventually won the struggle for power, seemed, as Trotsky later described him, 'the outstanding mediocrity of the revolution'. But he was a skilful and ruthless politician, and since Lenin's first stroke in May 1922 had built himself a particularly strong position from which to manoeuvre for power. One member of the *Politburo* had to be in the *Orgburo* to ensure co-operation between the two bodies. Stalin was that member. Then in 1922 he gained direct control of the party organisation throughout the country by undertaking the apparently tedious job of General Secretary, and as the leading member of the *Orgburo* he was the only person in a position to check his own activities as General Secretary.

Lenin had seen the danger of this, and in his will left a warning against the enormous power accumulated by Stalin since he had become General Secretary, saying, 'I am not sure that he always knows how to use that power with sufficient caution,' and suggesting that he should be removed from the position. But Lenin's warning was ignored, partly because the other Communist leaders underestimated Stalin, and partly because they were far more suspicious of Trotsky.

Zinoviev and Kamenev made the mistake of joining Stalin against Trotsky, and once Stalin had with their help got rid of Trotsky, who accepted that a majority of the party leaders opposed him and resigned his post as Commissar for War, he used his position as General Secretary to pack the party leadership with men dependent on himself, turned for support to Bukharin, and before the end of 1924 was able to overthrow Zinoviev and Kamenev.

In 1926, too late, Zinoviev and Kamenev joined Trotsky against their common enemy, Stalin. But in 1927 their attempt to rally an effective opposition foundered against the rock of party discipline, and Trotsky, who refused to acknowledge his errors, was exiled.

With Trotsky, Zinoviev, and Kamenev out of the way Stalin turned against Bukharin, who in 1929 followed the example of Zinoviev and Kamenev by publicly acknowledging his errors.

Policy differences

Questions of policy were intimately involved in this struggle for power. In the years 1924–7 Stalin was destroying the left-wing leadership of the party. While Trotsky wanted to stimulate world revolution Stalin preferred to concentrate exclusively on the internal affairs of Russia and in the autumn of 1924 adopted the slogan, 'Socialism in one country'. But this slogan was misleading in terms of domestic politics, for while Stalin agreed with Bukharin about the need to build Socialism gradually, Trotsky, Zinoviev, and Kamenev all wanted to replace N.E.P. (p. 182) rapidly with genuine Socialist policies.

	External policy	*Domestic policy*
TROTSKY:	World Revolution	Establish Socialism
STALIN:	'Socialism in one country'	Maintain N.E.P.

However, in 1928 Stalin determined on a policy of imposing Socialism with a crash programme involving collectivisation of agriculture and central planning for industry of the sort Trotsky had always advocated, and it was this that involved him in 1928–9 in an attack on Bukharin and the right wing of the party.

The economic crisis of 1927

Part of the reason for this drastic change of policy by Stalin was that by 1927 a serious fault in the Russian economy had become apparent. Although agriculture had recovered rapidly from the ravages of war and revolution, so that by 1927 food was abundant, industry was recovering so slowly that by 1927 industrial production had only just recovered to the pre-1914 level. This meant that food was so cheap and manufactured goods so expensive that it was not worth the while of the class of more prosperous peasant farmers, or *kulaks*, to sell their surplus crops to the towns, because the money they got for them was too little to buy manufactured goods. The *kulaks* therefore hoarded their surplus produce in order to force prices up, the towns went without food in a time of plenty, and the countryside went without manufactured goods because the few that were produced were too expensive.

Stalin saw that the only solution was a massive development of industry. But industrialisation on the scale that was needed would only be possible if the state could ensure that a regular supply of food for industrial workers would not dry up because of *kulaks* hoarding food to push prices up. So in 1928 Stalin decided to break the grip of the *kulaks* over the economy.

Collectivisation

Collectivisation was intended to provide an agricultural system which would not only be easier to control than the system of individual peasant holdings but also more efficient. Stalin's policy was that each group of sixty to two hundred households should merge its individual holdings into a collective farm, or *kolkhoz*. This was popular with the poorer peasants, who stood to gain, but it was bitterly opposed by the *kulaks*, many of whom destroyed their crops and livestock rather than give in. It took Stalin till 1932 to destroy the opposition, and then he only did it at the cost of about five million lives and more than half the livestock of Russia. After 1932 collectivisation proceeded smoothly and rapidly, and by the end of the decade most agricultural land had been collectivised. In the long run it was a more efficient system—especially when the establishment of Machine Tractor Stations gave each *kolkhoz* access to heavy machinery. And it also had the important side-effect of enabling millions to leave the land, thus providing more manpower for the newly developing industries of Russia.

The Five Year Plans

In October 1928 N.E.P. was officially abandoned and replaced by a Five Year Plan, the object of which was to develop the industry and transportation system of the U.S.S.R. so as to construct a self-sufficient economy. Emphasis was on such things as the construction of hydro-electric power stations, steel works, and machine-tool factories, and by the end of 1932 Russian industrial production had more than doubled.

A second Five Year Plan which ran from 1933 to 1937 was intended to place a greater emphasis on the production of consumer goods, but the growing threat of war in the thirties increasingly diverted emphasis to heavy industry, and in the end production of capital goods and war materials was considerably greater than originally intended and production of consumer goods considerably less. By the end of this second plan the total volume of Russian industrial production had overtaken that of Great Britain and was the third largest in the world—next after the U.S.A. and Germany.

A third Five Year Plan followed, but it was interrupted in 1941 by the outbreak of war.

The Stalin constitution

In 1936 Stalin gave the U.S.S.R. a new constitution which he described as 'the only truly democratic constitution in the world'. It established universal suffrage over the age of eighteen, did away with the previous bias against rural voters, replaced the old indirect system of electing a Congress of Soviets with direct voting for a Soviet of the Union, and introduced secret ballot. But only candidates nominated by the Communist Party were allowed to stand for election, and there was not even a choice between them.

The great purges

Meanwhile the security police, which had undergone various changes of name and organisation since the establishment of *Cheka* (p. 126) and was now known as the N.K.V.D., retained a rigid grip over the country. And the assassination in December 1934 of Sergei Kirov, the Leningrad Party Secretary (Petrograd had been renamed Leningrad in 1924), was followed by a wave of trials and executions of prominent people.

In January 1935 Zinoviev and Kamenev were tried for treason and conspiracy and given long prison sentences, and in the middle of 1936 they were tried again together with several other party leaders and executed. Early in 1937 more senior party leaders were tried and most of them sentenced to death. In the summer Marshal Tuchachevsky, a great Red Army hero of the civil war, and seven other generals were tried by a military tribunal and executed. In 1938 Bukharin and the old right wing of the party were destroyed, together with Yagoda, who had controlled the N.K.V.D. until 1936. In 1939 Yezhov, who had followed Yagoda as head of the N.K.V.D. and organised most of the purge, was executed. And in 1940 Trotsky, in exile in Mexico, was assassinated. Meanwhile hundreds of thousands of people suspected of disloyalty, including thousands of army officers and members of the Communist Party, were executed or sentenced to forced labour in Siberia.

The Great Patriotic War

One effect of Stalin's internal policies was to make Russia capable of surviving when the Germans invaded in 1941. Not only had Russian industry been vastly expanded but also a great industrial region had been built up beyond the Urals. Potential opposition had been eliminated by crushing the *kulaks* in 1928–32 and by the great purges of 1935–9. And although the Red Army had been seriously weakened by the purges, by 1941 it had been reorganised and built up to a strength of five million men.

Nevertheless, the Germans advanced deep into Russia and did immense destruction. In all probably thirty million Russian lives were lost and a quarter of all Russian property destroyed. But although the German armies reached Leningrad, Moscow, and Stalingrad, they never took any of them, the Red Army and the mass of the people remained loyal, and during 1944 the Germans were driven out of Russia.

The post-war era

In 1945, after the sufferings of the war, the main desire of the Russian people was for an improved standard of living. But Stalin was anxious to strengthen the U.S.S.R. in relation to the capitalist countries which had recently been his allies, and the fourth and fifth Five Year Plans, introduced in 1946 and 1951, were, like their predecessors, more concerned with the construction of heavy industry and the production of capital goods and military equipment than with the production of consumer goods.

Stalin was also anxious to reassert the influence of the Communist Party over all aspects of life, for the control of the party had to some extent been modified during the war, especially in the areas occupied by the Germans. So after the war the U.S.S.R. was rigidly cut off from contact with the capitalist world, and not only were the press and wireless controlled by the government but also literature, music, art, and even science were expected to conform to the attitudes laid down by the Communist Party.

This does not mean that the country was seething with discontent. On the contrary, most Russians were probably proud of their nation's achievements since the revolution, particularly now that the U.S.S.R. was so obviously one of the two great powers of the world. And much discontent was diverted by the practice of 'self-criticism', whereby people were permitted and even encouraged to criticise the manner in which policies were carried out, though they were not, of course, allowed to criticise the policies themselves. Moreover, Marxist–Leninist theory could always provide an intellectual justification or rationalisation of what the government did, and by the time Stalin died in March 1953 most Russians probably accepted the essentials of Marxism–Leninism as automatically as most Englishmen accepted the liberal democratic tradition. But at the same time many of them, including many of the Communist leaders, were anxious to have the higher standard of living which could only come from the production of more consumer goods, and at the same time wanted greater freedom of expression.

DESPITE its geographical unity it was not until 1861 that most of the Italian peninsula was unified as the new nation of Italy, and it was not until 1870 that Rome was seized from the Papacy to be its capital. The tardiness of this unification was at the root of many of the problems which beset Italy in the early years of the twentieth century.

(1) There was a permanent conflict between Church and State. In 1870 Pope Pius IX had refused to accept the seizure of what remained of his lands, and he forbade Italian Roman Catholics to vote in elections or take office.

(2) There was a permanent conflict between the backward agricultural South, with its population of poverty-stricken illiterate peasants, and the comparatively prosperous North, where industrial development was producing a new middle class and an urban working class.

(3) Both the peasants of the South and the industrial workers of the North were discontented, for the franchise was restricted to about $2\frac{1}{2}$ per cent of the population until after the election of 1913. Then universal manhood suffrage was introduced and prepared the way for revolutionary change.

(4) Social and economic distress was increased by a rapid growth of population which resulted in heavy immigration to the U.S.A. and also in a demand for colonies.

(5) The demand for colonies was mixed up with a desire for national prestige which led Italy into a tortuous foreign policy culminating in the Italo-Turkish War of 1911–12 (p. 94) and in Italy's participation in the first World War (pp. 97–98).

Post-war unrest

When the war ended the Italians were thoroughly dissatisfied with the territorial settlement, and their dissatisfaction centred on the East coast of the Adriatic. By the end of the war Italy was occupying Albania, and in September 1919 the nationalist poet D'Annunzio, with the connivance of the weak Italian government, seized Fiume with a private army. But in 1920 the Italian government withdrew its troops from Albania, and at the end of the year it agreed with Jugoslavia that Fiume should be a Free City and drove D'Annunzio out.

The discontent felt by the Italian people with what seemed a weak foreign policy was matched by their discontent with domestic politics. The new principle of universal manhood suffrage had the effect that after the general election of 1919 most seats in the Chamber of Deputies were held by two parties which appealed to the working class: the Socialists, whose support was from the industrial workers of the North, and the Popularists, a Catholic Party whose support was among the peasantry. But papal condemnation of Socialism in 1864 made co-operation between the two parties impossible, and since the anti-clerical Liberals who had dominated politics before the war would co-operate with neither of them, effective parliamentary government became impossible.

The Socialists, influenced by the fact that they were the largest single party, by the post-war unrest, and by the success of the Bolsheviks in Russia, were inclined to take direct action, and in the autumn of 1920 the workers in the North seized control of six hundred factories. But they had no clear revolutionary programme. After ten weeks the difficulties they encountered compelled them to reach agreement with their employers, and soon after this the Socialist Party split into three separate parts.

Government followed government in quick succession, for no combination was able to maintain a majority in the Chamber of Deputies. Inflation developed. Law and order was breaking down. And in this situation there was presented a new solution to Italy's problems: Fascism.

Fascism

In March 1919 Benito Mussolini, an ex-corporal who had been wounded and invalided out of the army, had formed a league of ex-servicemen, the *fascio di combattimento*, and three-and-a-half years later, as the leader, or *Duce*, of the Fascists and as the prophet of Fascism, he was to become ruler of Italy.

Fascism was a remarkable paradox: it was conservatism pretending to be revolutionary. The Fascists were concerned to assert nationalist ambitions and maintain traditional property rights and the capitalist economic system against the threat of international Socialism, but they seemed revolutionary because their leader, their methods, and the support on which they depended were all quite different from what one would expect from an essentially conservative, or even reactionary, movement:

(1) Mussolini, far from being an aristocrat, was the son of a blacksmith and had been one of the leaders of the Socialist Party and the editor of the official Socialist newspaper before 1914.

(2) The casual and uncontrolled brutality of the Fascist Black Shirt gangs was scarcely what one would expect from men con-

cerned to protect established property rights. But they felt that parliamentary methods were ineffective against the threat of Socialism and expected force to be more effective.

(3) The support on which the Fascists depended was not just those with a vested interest in the old traditional society, who feared that it was crumbling in the face of Socialism and saw Fascism as a better defence than parliamentary government. It was also anyone who could be inflamed by talk of national pride and national destiny: those who were discontented with the peace settlement and with weak parliamentary government, those who had been coarsened by war and saw force as the best solution to problems, and those with illusions of grandeur who saw themselves as a superior race. In the end Mussolini managed to get support from almost every direction: from rich and poor, Monarchists and Socialists, liberal idealists and thugs, anti-clericals and priests.

The Fascists had no clear policy, but this was no disadvantage in a country with a recently enfranchised and uneducated mass electorate. On the contrary it had the advantage that it made attacks on Fascist policies difficult, especially as Mussolini was prepared to change his tack whenever he sensed a change in the direction of the political wind. At first he was both anti-clerical and anti-Liberal, but by June 1921 he was declaring himself the friend of Catholics and Liberals. In the general election of May 1921 he had still been a republican, but in September 1922 he announced his support of the monarchy. In August 1922 he signed an agreement with the Socialists, but in November, after coming to power, he renounced it.

Mussolini was far more concerned with the acquisition of power than with policies, and he adjusted his propaganda to appeal to all discontented groups. He managed to look progressive, but at the same time was at pains to give his movement an appearance of respectability, and the emphasis he placed on discipline and Nationalism made him acceptable to conservative middle-class elements and even to some parliamentary leaders.

The establishment of Fascist rule

In the elections of May 1921 the Fascists only won 35 seats out of 535—and those only because the government had welcomed Fascist co-operation and violence in the election as a way of beating the Socialists. What eventually brought Mussolini to power was the fact that in a situation in which parliamentary democracy seemed to have broken down no one had sufficient faith in it to fight in its defence against what seemed to be a more virile system.

In October 1922 it was clear that the Fascists were preparing an attempt to seize power, and at the end of the month the Prime Minister, Facta, asked King Vittorio Emanuele to proclaim martial law. The king refused and instead called on Mussolini to form a government. The Black Shirts made the symbolic gesture of a March on Rome, and Mussolini arrived by train to form a coalition government in which he himself took the posts of Prime Minister, Foreign Minister, and Minister for Home Affairs.

At first Fascist rule was quite moderate—and this was not even particularly surprising, for no one had any previous experience of Fascist rule. The other parliamentary parties continued in existence, and the press and the trade unions still had some freedom.

However, at the end of 1923 a new electoral law provided that any coalition which got 25 per cent of the votes in a general election should have two-thirds of the seats in the Chamber of Deputies, and in April 1924 the Fascists, who had Black Shirts on duty at the polling booths, understandably won the election.

In June a Socialist deputy called Giacomo Matteotti, who had protested against the new electoral law and the use of force, was murdered by the Fascists. Most of the non-Fascist deputies walked out of the Chamber in protest, and the crisis nearly brought about Mussolini's fall. But the king hesitated to dismiss him because of his own responsibility for bringing him to power, and Mussolini survived the crisis by disowning the murderers and then imposing a rigid censorship of the press.

Having once survived this crisis it became easier to consolidate his power. At the beginning of 1925 he accepted responsibility for Matteotti's murder and defied what was left of the opposition in the Chamber to attempt to take action against him. He refused to allow those who had walked out to return, banned criticism of himself in the Chamber and the press, and appointed a committee to reform the constitution.

The Corporate State

During 1925 Mussolini strengthened his position by giving the Federation of Italian Industrialists virtual control over the economy in return for their support, and later he got the support of agricultural and commercial employers in the same way.

Eventually Italy was reorganised as a 'corporate state' in a way reminiscent of Syndicalism (p. 181). But the syndicates which the workers were compelled to join also represented the owners, theoretically as a way of reconciling class conflict, and the workers

neither owned nor controlled the industries. The local syndicates
of an industry were grouped into nation-wide corporations, which
were in turn grouped into a National Council of Corporations.
And after 1928 the corporations had the function of nominating
about a thousand parliamentary candidates. Mussolini and the
Grand Council of Fascists which he nominated then chose four
hundred and asked the electorate's approval of the list.

In 1929 Mussolini managed to get papal approval of his 'corporate state'. Already religious services, including the Mass, had been
introduced into public ceremonies. Now, by the Lateran Treaty,
Pope Pius XI recognised the united Italian kingdom while Mussolini recognised Roman Catholicism as the official religion of Italy
and agreed that the state would enforce Church laws on matters
such as marriage. The Papacy was also given a large number of
state bonds as compensation for the lands lost in 1870, thus acquiring a financial stake in the Fascist régime, and the final seal of
respectability was set on Mussolini when Pius XI declared publicly
that Fascism, unlike Liberalism and Socialism, was compatible
with Christianity.

Fascist economic policy

In his economic policy Mussolini drifted from the extremes of
laissez-faire to the idea of a planned economy in which Italy would
be self-sufficient. In 1926 he inaugurated a 'battle for grain' aimed
at self-sufficiency, which in 1932 he claimed to have achieved.
But wheat production on this scale was uneconomic for Italy, since
wheat could have been bought far cheaper from the U.S.A., and
as a result the Italian people had less to eat. A public works
scheme, which involved draining the Pontine Marshes near Rome
and building new motorways, gave a good impression to foreigners,
but it covered up a grossly inefficient system in which, by the end
of the twenties, wages were the lowest in Western Europe and
public money was regularly finding its way into private pockets.
Finally one of the most pressing economic problems in Italy was
its excessively high population, but strangely enough Mussolini's
only policy in this sphere was to inaugurate a 'battle for births',
with financial incentives to have children—a policy which was as
unsuccessful as it was ill conceived.

Totalitarianism, militarism, and collapse

Despite its failings Fascism came to be widely accepted in
Western Europe as more suitable for Italy than parliamentary
democracy. At last Italy had stable government. Mussolini

seemed on good terms with the monarchy, the industrial leaders, and the Papacy, and in foreign affairs there was no repetition of the aggressiveness of the Corfu incident (p. 229) for another ten years.

But all the while the grip of an authoritarian one-party system was tightening over Italy. The Black Shirts became an official voluntary militia. And in the thirties Fascism was increasingly becoming a religion in which the State and the *Duce* were worshipped. In schools children were taught to repeat the Ten Commandments of Fascism, including 'Mussolini is always right', and, as Mussolini wrote in the *Enciclopedia Italiana* in 1932, Fascism recognised the individual 'only in so far as his interests coincide with those of the state'.

But there seemed nothing capable of bringing the Fascist régime down, and in the end it was only overthrown as the result of defeat in a war into which Italy had been thrown to justify Mussolini's militarist propaganda. In a speech at Milan in 1932 he had declared, 'The twentieth century will be the century of Fascism, the century of Italian power, the century during which Italy will become for the third time the leader of mankind.' And in accordance with this attitude he had invaded Abyssinia in 1935, Albania in 1939, France and then Egypt in 1940, and Greece in 1941.

The later phase of this policy, which involved fighting as the ally of Germany in the second World War, was peculiarly misguided, for in the long run Italy had as much to lose as any other European country from German victory. Even in the short run it was grossly mistaken, for Fascism was an extraordinarily inefficient and corrupt system of government and depended for its reputation not on achievements but on bluff, and in particular on Mussolini's own undoubted gift for publicity. But Mussolini himself was deceived by the façade of lies which his officials constructed, and believed that he had three thousand aircraft when he had less than a thousand, and that he could mobilise eight million men when he could scarcely mobilise two million—and those armed with nineteenth-century rifles.

In 1940 he plunged into a war for which the Italian people had no enthusiasm. But they showed no inclination to rebel. They accepted first the war and then military defeats with neither obvious loyalty nor disaffection, and in the end it was Mussolini's own Grand Council of Fascists which overthrew him. It met late in July 1943, when the Allied forces were already in Sicily, and voted that it had no confidence in him. The same day Mussolini was arrested and twenty years of Fascist rule in Italy came to an end.

ON 3RD NOVEMBER 1918, with defeat imminent, revolution broke out in Germany. It spread rapidly through the country, and on 9th November, two days before the armistice was signed and took effect, the Kaiser abdicated and Ebert, the leader of the Social Democratic Party, formed a provisional government.

But the Social Democratic Party had been divided ever since the beginning of the first World War, for Karl Liebknecht, the leader of a minority group of the party, had called on workers in all countries to refuse to fight their fellow-workers in other countries. Although there was only a small response to this call, in April 1917 200,000 German workers reacted to the news of the outbreak of revolution in Russia by going on strike and demanding democratic government and a peace with 'no annexations'. Moreover, when Workers' and Soldiers' Councils were formed in November 1918 they looked for leadership not to the Majority Socialists, who now formed the government, but to the more extreme Minority Socialists and to the Spartacists, or Communists.

Another important factor in post-war Germany was the existence of free-lance military units whose formation was encouraged by the Social Democratic government. There were probably about 400,000 men in these Free Corps, most of them fighting on the unsettled Eastern frontiers, and in January 1919 the government called in one of them, under General von Lüttwitz, to put down the Spartacists, who had seized control of Berlin.

The Weimar constitution and the political parties

In the same month took place the elections for the assembly which met at Weimar in February to draft a new constitution, and which established the sovereignty of a parliament, or *Reichstag*, to be elected on the basis of proportional representation. One effect of this system was that no one party was ever able to dominate the assembly, and all governments were coalitions until Hitler abolished the party system in 1933. Another effect was that the number of German political parties grew ever larger until in July 1932 there were twenty-four parties taking part in the general election.

The Social Democrats, or *Majority Socialists,* were always the largest left-wing party, and they were also the leading party in the government until 1923.

The German Nationalist People's Party represented big business interests and was the main right-wing party during the twenties.

The Catholic Centre Party, which represented the interests of the

Roman Catholic Church, consistently got about four million votes
out of a total of approximately thirty millions, and formed an
important part of most coalitions.

The Nazis and *the Communists* were both anti-democratic
parties, and only became important during the last years of the
Weimar Republic.

The Kapp *Putsch*

The Social Democrats had survived an attack from the Left at
the beginning of 1919 when they were the provisional government,
and early in 1920, when they were in office under the Weimar constitution, they had to face an attack from the Right. In March a
political adventurer called Kapp and General von Lüttwitz, who
had put down the Spartacists the year before, tried to take advantage of the nationalist feelings of those Germans who blamed the
government for accepting the Treaty of Versailles, and made an
attempt to seize power. They held Berlin for a few days, but
then the attempt collapsed, largely because of a general strike.

However, the moderate Socialist government realised that its
position was precarious, and it was so anxious to do nothing which
might offend the right-wing nationalist elements in the country
that it failed to punish those who took part in the *Putsch*.

Economic collapse

Another effect of the government's unwillingness to offend the
right wing was that it failed to tax the rich at all heavily. Consequently it was unable to balance its budget, failed to maintain its
reparations payments, and in the end stood by while the German
economy collapsed (p. 233).

This collapse of the economy discredited the government, and
for many of the middle class it was a worse disaster than the war
had been, for all their savings became valueless. Many of them
turned against the whole idea of democratic government, and it
was at this stage, with the abortive Munich *Putsch* of 1923 (p. 145),
that Hitler and the Nazi Party first became prominent.

Gustav Stresemann

But in 1923 the Nazi Party was still a new and minor element in
German political life, and it was the German Nationalist People's
Party which benefited from the swing against the Socialists.

At the height of the crisis, in August 1923, Gustav Stresemann,
the leader of the Nationalist People's Party, had become Chancellor. His aims were economic recovery, reconciliation with
France, agreement over reparations, and admission to the League

of Nations. In September he brought to an end the strikes in the Ruhr which had broken out in protest against the Franco-Belgian occupation (p. 233), he then established a new currency, the *Rentenmark*, with an exchange value of twenty to the pound, and in August 1924 he accepted the Dawes Plan for reparations (p. 233). In October the German government received its first loans under the Dawes Plan, and in November the occupation of the Ruhr was ended.

During the next five years Germany's economy recovered rapidly. Foreign money poured in and was used partly to make some reparations payments, partly to expand Germany's industry, and partly to extend social amenities.

At the same time Germany's international position improved. Stresemann had only remained as Chancellor for a few months, but he kept the post of Foreign Minister until he died in October 1929, and in that capacity he achieved much. In 1925 he proposed and concluded the Locarno Treaties (p. 235). In 1926 Germany entered the League of Nations and became a permanent member of the Council. In 1929 reparations were reduced by the Young Plan (p. 233), and arrangements were made for the last Allied troops to leave the Rhineland by the end of June 1930.

Stresemann's success in overcoming the 1923 crisis and the subsequent success of his foreign policy combined to restore the credit of the democratic republic. But in the long run his policy was dangerous. He encouraged German Nationalism and sought to gain support both for the Weimar Republic and his own party by obtaining concessions in foreign policy. And he only agreed to the Locarno Treaty affecting Germany's Western frontier in order to establish the possibility of an eventual revision of the Eastern boundaries. But if the credit of the democratic republic was to be restored by gaining concessions through foreign policy, its credit would have to be maintained with further concessions; and a time might come when a more extreme nationalist group, such as the Nazis, would outbid the Nationalist People's Party.

The Brüning government

In October 1929 Stresemann died, and in the same month came the Wall Street crash (p. 283). Soon the slump hit Germany. The number of unemployed increased rapidly. Germans feared a repetition of 1923, and six years had not been long enough to build up faith in parliamentary democracy.

In March 1930 Field-Marshal Hindenburg, who had been elected President in 1925, called on Brüning, one of the leaders of the Catholic Centre Party, to form a government. This marks the end of democratic government in Germany, for Brüning, lacking a majority in the *Reichstag*, ruled by emergency decrees.

During the next six months the economic situation deteriorated further, and meanwhile Brüning's government ruled in the interest of the aristocracy, the army leaders, and the industrialists. Its rule was unconstitutional, oppressive, and increasingly unpopular and the consequence of its unpopularity was that in the election of September 1930 both the anti-democratic parties received increased support. The Nazis now held 107 seats out of a total of 576 and the Communists 77. The government still lacked a majority, but since the country was now ruled by emergency decree instead of by decision of the *Reichstag* the election result could not bring the government down, and Brüning remained in office.

During 1931 matters got worse. The collapse of *Kredit Anstalt* (p. 283) was followed by bank failures all over Germany. Then the devaluation of British currency in September (p. 211) damaged Germany's export position badly, and German employers demanded the same sort of economies that the new National government was making in Britain: cuts in public expenses, such as the salaries of state employees, and cuts in social insurance expenditure, including unemployment benefit. By the beginning of 1932 the total number of unemployed in Germany had risen to approximately eight million, both the Nazis and the Communists were organising riots against the government, and eventually in May Hindenburg dismissed Brüning.

The von Papen government

The main reason for dismissing Brüning was that General von Schleicher, an army leader with a gift for political intrigue, had persuaded Hindenburg to appoint as Chancellor Franz von Papen, a diplomat who had been expelled from the Centre Party. Most of the ministers in this new government were proposed by von Schleicher, who himself became War Minister. He then made an unsuccessful attempt to get the Nazis in the *Reichstag* to support the new government, but by the general election which took place at the end of July the brown-shirted Nazi *Sturmabteilung* was organising riots on an even larger scale than before.

The Election of 31st July 1932

Support for the Nazis had been growing rapidly since the previous general election in September 1930, and now the Nazi vote more than doubled, reaching 13,700,000, and the Nazis became the largest party in the *Reichstag*, with 230 seats out of 608. The Communist vote also increased (they won 89 seats), and just over half the total votes went to these two anti-democratic parties.

Meanwhile most of the other parties declined. The Social Democrats lost 10 seats, though the combined Social Democrat and Communist vote increased slightly. But the right-wing parties declined rapidly, for they were losing votes to the Nazis. The

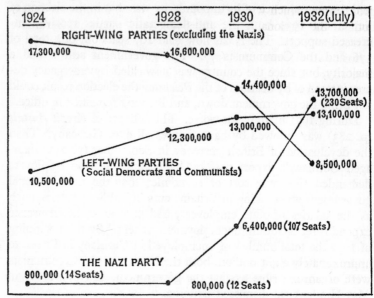

only party whose position remained constant was the Catholic Centre Party, which even increased slightly until it had more votes than all the other right-wing parties, except the Nazis, put together.

The end of the Weimar Republic

As soon as the new *Reichstag* met the Nazis and Communists acted together to defeat a vote of confidence in von Papen. This resulted in the dissolution of the *Reichstag*, new elections in November, and in a series of intrigues and political manoeuvrings (pp. 147–8) which culminated on 30th January 1933 in the appointment of Hitler as Chancellor at the head of a right-wing coalition government in which von Papen was his Vice-Chancellor.

This coalition won another general election five weeks later (p. 149) and then brought before the *Reichstag* a Bill for granting the government unlimited power. On 23rd March the Bill was passed. The Weimar republic had committed suicide.

The National-Socialist German Workers' Party

IN APRIL 1919 in a beer-cellar in Munich a thirty-year-old ex-corporal, Adolf Hitler, was enrolled as seventh committee member of the small German Workers' Party. He was soon its leader, or *Führer*, and he provided it with its National-Socialist programme, which was intended, as the word implies, to appeal both to the Nationalist and the Socialist elements in Germany. Hitler appealed to Nationalists by demanding, for example, the union of all German-speaking peoples in one state and the rejection of the Treaty of Versailles. He appealed to Socialists by demanding measures such as the abolition of all unearned income.

The Munich *Putsch*

It was during the economic collapse of 1923 (p. 233) that the Nazi Party first became prominent, and in November, the same month that the mark finally collapsed completely, Hitler made an unsuccessful attempt to seize control of Munich, and was arrested, tried, and imprisoned. He used his trial was an opportunity for propaganda against the government, and his imprisonment, which only lasted a few months, as an opportunity for starting to write *Mein Kampf*, in which he openly proclaimed his ambitions.

Election results

Hitler was out of prison in time for the general election of May 1924, in which the Nazi Party gained its first great success, winning 32 seats in the *Reichstag*. But in the new elections of December, when the success of Stresemann's policies (p. 141) was already apparent, the number of seats held by the Nazis fell to 14.

In the increasing prosperity of the twenties the Nazi Party could not hope to thrive, and in 1928 the number of Nazi seats in the *Reichstag* declined even further to 12.

But then in 1930 the slump hit Germany, and in the election of September the Nazi vote increased eightfold from a mere 800,000 to 6,400,000, and with 107 seats the Nazis suddenly became the next largest party in the country after the Social Democrats.

In April 1932, when Hindenburg stood for re-election as President, Hitler felt strong enough to oppose him, and though Hindenburg gained more than nineteen million votes and took office for a second term, over thirteen million votes were cast for Hitler.

Three months later, when there was another general election, the Nazis won an even greater success by gaining 230 seats out of

608, thus becoming the largest party in the *Reichstag*, with nearly a hundred seats more than the Social Democrats.

The reasons for the rise of the Nazis

The effects of the depression: One important reason for this Nazi success was that many Germans were disillusioned with what seemed to be the failure of democratic government and of the capitalist economic system. As the slump deepened and unemployment increased, support for the anti-democratic parties, the Nazis and Communists, also increased.

The weakness of German democracy: Moreover, democratic government had no very deep roots in Germany and had only been established there in 1918 as the result of defeat in war. Nor had it proved very successful. Already in March 1930 Brüning's government (p. 197) had in effect abandoned democracy by ruling through emergency decrees.

The division of the left-wing: But since it was not only the democratic political system which was breaking down but also the capitalist economic system it might be reasonable to expect a swing towards the Social Democrats and Communists rather than the Nazis. Part of the reason this did not happen was that the left-wing in Germany was bitterly divided. The Social Democrats remained the largest working-class party, but they were more committed than any other party to the idea of democratic government, which so many people felt was unsatisfactory, and consequently their support declined. The Communists were never able to supplant them as the main working-class party, but nevertheless they gained votes at the Socialists' expense.

Nationalism: This Communist rise helped the Nazis, for they were able to portray themselves to the middle-class as a bulwark against Communism. Most Germans preferred Nazism to Communism, for it was Nationalist instead of internationalist; and the Nazis were able to play on German national pride by, for example, explaining away the defeat in the first World War as the fault of Jews and Communists who, they said, had stabbed the army in the back by stirring up revolution in November 1918.

The Socialist aspect of Nazism: Moreover, the Nazi Party had an advantage over the other Nationalist parties in Germany in that it combined aggressive Nationalism with a vague form of Socialism which appealed not only to the unemployed factory-hand but also to many of the middle class who did not want to be associated with either Communism or Social Democracy.

Militarism: The Nazis as a matter of policy both spoke and acted violently, and their brown-shirted Storm Detachment, the *Sturmabteilung,* or S.A., provided an outlet for the militarism which had been latent in Germany and which could now be let loose on convenient scapegoats, such as Jews and Communists.

Propaganda: Hitler made utterly unscrupulous use of modern propaganda methods and deliberately distorted the truth on a vast scale because he believed that 'even the grossly impudent lie always leaves traces behind it'.

Hitler's personality: Finally, Hitler himself, with his conviction of his own genius and with his gift for swaying crowds by his oratory, had just the personality needed to portray himself as a super-human leader who would lead Germany out of its troubles to what he later described as a 'National Reawakening'.

Nazi difficulties and von Papen

The combination of all these reasons gave the Nazis more than a third of the total votes cast in the election of July 1932. But despite this striking success it was by no means inevitable that Hitler should come to power. Even in this election the Nazis had gained less than 38 per cent of the votes, and in the following months their support declined. As the economic crisis blew over Nazism could well have faded back into obscurity, and indeed in the new elections of November 1932 the Nazi Party lost two million votes and 34 seats. Moreover, it was by now heavily in debt, for within eight months it had had to bear the expenses of a Presidential election and two general elections.

In the end Hitler was only able to come to power because many right-wing leaders were prepared to collaborate with him against the Social Democrats and Communists, and tried to use him in their intrigues against each other.

Von Papen, who had been Chancellor since May, still only commanded 10 per cent of the *Reichstag's* votes, so he opened negotiations with Hitler and offered him the position of Vice-Chancellor. When Hitler refused von Papen decided that the Nazis must be crushed by unconstitutional means, and on 1st December he proposed this to President Hindenburg and General von Schleicher, the very influential War Minister.

Von Schleicher and the Left

But von Schleicher was not prepared to use the army to do this, because he thought he could split the Nazi Party by detaching from it the genuinely Socialist elements led by Gregor Strasser and Roehm. So he now became Chancellor himself and on 3rd December offered the post of Vice-Chancellor to Gregor Strasser. Strasser wanted to accept, but Hitler forbade him to do so, and the outcome of this crisis in the Nazi Party was that Strasser resigned from the party but made no attempt to split it.

Now that von Schleicher had failed in his aim of arranging a combination between the army and the Socialist wing of the Nazi Party, he attempted to forge an even more surprising alliance— one between the army and the Social Democrats. But he failed to get the support of the Social Democrats, and at the same time he alienated the other army leaders by making the attempt.

Hitler becomes Chancellor

Meanwhile many of the landowners and industrialists, whose principle aim was to preserve the old social and economic structure, had felt since the decline of the Nazi vote in November that they had less cause to fear Hitler and might well be able to use him and his still considerable electoral support. On 4th January 1933 there took place a meeting between Hitler and von Papen, who was determined to get back into office, and after this meeting many of the big industrialists began paying money to the Nazi Party, which was able to pay off its election debts and increase its propaganda.

Because of his flirtation with the Social Democrats von Schleicher was now unable to rely on the army against this combination, and at the end of January, when he had not yet been in office two months, he was dismissed.

Since Hitler now had the support of von Papen and also of the Nationalist People's Party, President Hindenburg felt that he had no option but to offer him the Chancellorship. On 30th January Hitler accepted and formed a right-wing coalition government in which only two of the other ten members of the cabinet were Nazis. But even this coalition was only able to muster 42 per cent of the *Reichstag* votes. So Hitler demanded a dissolution and new elections were fixed for 5th March.

The *Reichstag* Fire

The election campaign was fought in an atmosphere of civil war, with frequent street fights between the S.A. and the Communists. Then on 27th February, six days before the election, the *Reichstag* building was set on fire by a Dutchman, Marinus van der Lubbe, and the Nazi leaders seized the opportunity of blaming the Communists. As a result President Hindenburg was persuaded the next day to issue an edict revoking all constitutional guarantees of personal freedom. This edict of 28th February placed very extensive power in the hands of the police—and the police were under the control of the two Nazi members of the cabinet, Frick and Goering. So the Communist press was promptly banned and four thousand Communist officials were arrested.

The election of 5th March 1933

In the election five days later Hitler's coalition government won a majority. The Nazi Party with 288 seats and the Nationalist People's Party with 52 held 340 out of a total of 647. But this was not enough for Hitler, for he wanted to pass an Enabling Bill, which would give him unlimited power, and since this entailed changing the constitution it needed a two-thirds majority.

The other three largest parties were the Social Democrats with 120 seats, the Catholic Centre Party with 73, and the outlawed Communists who had managed to win 81 seats. Even though the Communists were not allowed to take their seats and vote, Hitler was still far short of a two-thirds majority.

The Enabling Bill

But then the Catholic Centre Party agreed to vote for an Enabling Bill in return for a promise that the edict of 28th February suspending individual liberty would be revoked. The promise was given, though never kept, and on 23rd March 1933 the Weimar Republic voted itself out of existence. The lead given by the Catholic Centre Party was followed by the smaller parties, and in the end only the Social Democrats voted against the Bill, which was carried by 441 votes to 94.

The end of Trade Unions and political parties

As soon as Hitler had supreme power he took steps to dispose of potential enemies. In May numerous union leaders were arrested, all union property was confiscated, and then all unions were suppressed. In June Hitler suppressed the Social Democratic Party, and during the next two weeks the other main parties dissolved themselves. On 14th July the Nazi Party was declared by law to be the only political party in Germany.

'The night of the long knives'

Now that all other political parties were suppressed the divisions among the Nazi leaders came to the fore, and Hitler's next blow struck down Roehm, the Chief of Staff of the S.A., who differed from Hitler on three important issues:

(1) he believed in the Socialist aspect of the party's programme;

(2) he wanted agreement with the Western powers, and especially with France;

(3) as leader of the S.A. he wanted the S.A. and the army merged into one National-Socialist People's Army.

It was this last point which was crucial, for Hitler felt that he had to choose between the S.A., which had helped to bring him to power, and the army, which he would need in the future. He chose the army, and in the early hours of 30th June 1934 numerous S.A. leaders were killed as well as many others whom Hitler wished out of the way, such as Gregor Strasser and General von Schleicher. Probably about two hundred died in all.

The development of the Nazi state

The S.A. now became a politically unimportant mass organisation, while Himmler's élite corps, the *Schutzstaffeln*, or S.S., which had carried out the massacre of 30th June, became more important; and in June 1936 all police, including the secret state police, or *Gestapo*, were placed under the control of Himmler.

Political enemies were imprisoned in concentration camps, anti-Semitism was encouraged, and in September 1935 the Nuremberg Laws were passed depriving the Jews of civil rights. In November 1938 hundreds of Jews were murdered in *pogroms* encouraged by the government, and during the second World War more than five million Jews were systematically exterminated.

Children were indoctrinated with Nazi ideas at school and in the Hitler Youth movement, and they went on from the Hitler Youth to do National Labour Service and from that to a period of service in the armed forces.

But there was little constructive development in Germany, and the old social and economic structure survived.

The popularity of the Nazi régime

Hitler's undoubted popularity rested on the ending of the unemployment problem, the overall recovery of Germany's economy during the thirties, and on the success of his foreign policy. When he declared himself President after the death of Hindenburg in August 1934, 84 per cent of the German voters approved his action in a plebiscite whose result the government had no need to falsify. Support on this scale probably did not continue throughout the next decade, but, as Hitler realised, his best justification was success, and until he ceased to be successful in the middle of the second World War the mass of the German people continued to support him.

Constitutional monarchy, 1874-1923

DURING the nineteenth century there was a long drawn out struggle in Spain between the monarchy, which wanted absolute power, and the Liberals, who wanted a parliamentary constitution. A republic which was established in 1873 was replaced by a constitutional monarchy in 1874, but neither the parliamentary system nor the monarchy was ever firmly established.

The parliamentary system came to an end as the result of a crisis caused by events in Morocco. The Algeciras Conference of 1906 (p. 85) had handed the northern strip of Morocco to Spain, but the Spanish had never occupied the whole of their area effectively, and in 1921 a Spanish army was routed by Moroccan tribesmen. Many Spaniards blamed King Alfonso XIII and the parliamentary government, and the result was widespread unrest.

The army leaders were ready to take matters into their own hands, so in 1923 the king destroyed the constitution by calling on General Primo de Rivera to rule as a dictator.

Dictatorship, 1923-30

Primo de Rivera pacified Morocco, and at home he pacified the trade unions so effectively that Largo Caballero, the Socialist leader, served on his Council of Ministers. But his government became increasingly unpopular, and like so many other governments it was unable to weather the world financial crisis which began in October 1929. In January 1930 the king dismissed him.

The republic, 1931-36

Alfonso XIII was now in a very difficult position, for in 1923 he had himself destroyed the constitutional system to which he hoped to lead the country back. A prolonged crisis ended with overwhelming defeat of the monarchists in all the main towns in the municipal elections of April 1931, and with the king leaving the country. Two months later in a general election the left-wing republican parties gained a majority, with 282 seats in the assembly, while the right-wing parties won only 60 seats and the moderate parties in the centre 112. A new constitution was drawn up, and in December the republic was proclaimed. But it only lasted four-and-a-half years before Spain plunged into civil war.

During the first two years, from December 1931 until December 1933, Spain was ruled by the left-wing parties which had won the election of June 1931. But a general election in December 1933

resulted in a violent swing of power. The left-wing parties gained
only 99 seats, the right wing rose from 60 to 207, and the parties
of the centre held the balance with 167 seats. So for the next two
years, from December 1933 until February 1936 Spain was ruled
by coalitions of the centre and the right.

In the general election of February 1936 there was another
violent swing. The Left won 258 seats, the Right 152, and the
Centre declined to 62. A left-wing coalition took office; but five
months later a rebel group of army officers attempted to seize
power by force, and Spain plunged into civil war.

The division of Spain

This came about primarily because the political divisions in
Spain were particularly intense. On the Left were many parties
which had in common the fact that they wanted change, but which
disagreed with each other about what change was desirable and
how it should be achieved. On the Right were a number of parties
committed in varying degrees to maintaining the traditional social
and economic structure of Spain. This is a situation common to
many countries, and one might expect it to result under a parliamentary system in gradual evolution as the result of compromise.
But when the Left was in power it aroused bitter opposition from
the Roman Catholic Church by attacking its privileges, from the
great landowners by attempting to nationalise large areas of land,
from the industrialists by attempting to introduce some measure
of state control into industry, and, most dangerous of all, from the
army leaders by attempting to destroy their political power. And
when the Right was in power it aroused bitter opposition from the
working class by trying to overthrow the work of previous left-wing
governments.

The effect of external influences

The enmity between the Left and Right in Spain was increased
by the idealogical conflict taking place in Europe.

The right wing had before it the example of Fascism in Italy,
which appeared to be efficient, and which seemed to have been
given the approval of the Pope both by the Lateran Treaty of
1929 (p. 138) and by the bull *quadrigesimo anno* of 1931 (p. 120).
So in 1932, the year after the proclamation of the republic,
Primo de Rivera's son, José Antonio, formed the Spanish Phalanx,
which acted as the Nazis were doing in Germany, exploiting the
difficulties and mistakes of weak governments.

On the other hand, the growing fear of dictatorship drove most of the left wing and moderate forces together in a Popular Front. The principle of forming Popular Fronts had been approved by the Seventh Congress of the Comintern in 1935 (p. 258), and it was a Popular Front coalition which won the election in Spain in February 1936 and then took office.

The Home Rule issue

The situation was further complicated by demands in some areas for Home Rule. Catalonia had been granted a measure of Home Rule as early as 1931, and the Basques were hoping for a similar measure. These areas associated themselves with the republic, and the supporters of the Popular Front government of 1936 included not only Socialists, Communists, Liberals, and Republicans, but also Basque Nationalists and the Catalan Left.

The appeal to force

During 1936 unrest increased, for the tradition of violence in Spanish political life was already well-established. In August 1932, during the first period of left-wing rule, a right-wing group led by General Sanjurjo had tried to seize power. In October 1934, during the period of right-wing rule, the extreme Left, and particularly the miners of Asturias, tried to overthrow the government by revolution. And in 1936 both extremes were prepared to resort to force. There were strikes, political murders, and widespread attacks on buildings and on people. So on the Right the army leaders felt it was their task to restore public order and social discipline, while on the Left Largo Caballero, the leader of the extremist wing of the Socialist Party, had refused to join the Popular Front government and preparing for revolution and demanding the dictatorship of the proletariat.

The war, July 1936–March 1939

The army leaders struck first. Their rising started in Spanish Morocco, and they soon gained control of two other areas— a number of towns in the South-West, and a far larger area in the North. The government held the rest of Spain, including the industrial areas of Asturias on the North coast, Catalonia in the North-East, and Madrid in the centre of the country.

At the beginning of the war the leadership of both sides changed hands. Sanjurjo was killed in an air crash, and his place as leader of the Nationalists, as the rebels called themselves, was taken by General Franco. On the government's side the influence of Largo Caballero was increased as the result of a decision to arm the trade

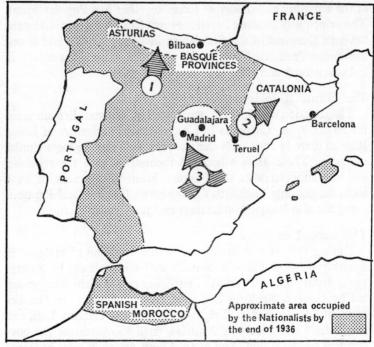

Approximate area occupied
by the Nationalists by
the end of 1936

unionists, and in September 1936 he became Prime Minister.

The military history of the war is the story of how the Nationalists rapidly united their own three areas and then split the government's territory in three, conquering each section in turn.

1936: In the early weeks of the war rebel troops had to be ferried across to Spain from Morocco by air, but by the middle of August Franco had gained control of the Straits and could use the sea. Also in August the rebels succeeded in linking their two mainland zones in the North and South-West by seizing a strip of land near the Portuguese border. Then in September they cut the Basques off from France. After this they advanced on Madrid, and although they failed to take it they did succeed in driving a wedge into the government's area by taking Teruel. By the end of 1936 Franco controlled rather more than half of Spain.

1937: Early in 1937 Italian troops landed in Spain to help him, but when in March they attacked Guadalajara, North-East of Madrid, they were checked by the first of the International Brigades of anti-Fascist volunteers, who had been recruited from all over Europe and North America. During the rest of 1937 most of the rebel effort was concentrated in the North. In June Bilbao in the Basque country fell, and by the end of October the whole of Asturias was occupied. Now only the large Eastern area was left to the government, which gained a great success at the end of the year by recapturing Teruel.

1938–9: This success was only temporary, for in March 1938 Teruel again fell to the Nationalists, who went on to reach the sea in the following month and thus divided the remaining government territory in two. By now it was clear that the Nationalists would eventually win. In January 1939 Catalonia fell, and the area controlled by the government dwindled rapidly until in March Madrid surrendered and the war was over.

The reasons for Franco's victory

Franco won the war for four reasons: he had much support within Spain, he had an initial military advantage, the government side was disunited, and he was assisted by foreign powers.

Spanish support: The monarchists, the Phalanx, the great land-owners and industrialists, the leaders of the Roman Catholic Church and of the army, and most of the professional middle class supported him. So did many of the Catholic peasantry and almost all the soldiers of the regular army.

The military advantage: At the beginning of the war Franco was able to use not only the army but also the middle-class Civil Guard and the well-organised forces of the monarchists and the Phalanx against the unprepared, unorganised, and largely untrained forces of the government. He lacked control of the sea at first, but was able to transport his troops by air, and by the end of 1936, while the government was still trying to organise an effective resistance, he controlled more than half of Spain.

Government disunity: The government's forces were never as united as those of the Nationalists, for the government was a coalition in whose army Liberals, Socialists, Communists, and Anarchists fought together for different ideals. Moreover, leadership of the government's forces fell increasingly into the hands of the left wing. Thus Largo Caballero became Prime Minister in September 1936, and although he was replaced in May 1937 by a more moderate Socialist, Dr. Juan Negrín, this was primarily because Negrín was personally more acceptable to the Communists.

Foreign intervention: Possibly the decisive factor was the extent of aid given by foreign powers to each side:

ITALY: Mussolini poured supplies into Spain to help Franco, and by mid-1937 had fifty thousand troops fighting there.

GERMANY: Hitler sent less troops than Mussolini but much valuable modern equipment, and it was thirty Junker transport planes which transported Franco's troops from Morocco in the crucial early days of the war.

PORTUGAL: Dr. Salazar was sympathetic towards Franco, and aid was able to reach the Nationalists through Portugal.

THE U.S.S.R.: Stalin, on the other hand, officially sympathised with the Spanish government, but privately he had reservations. Moreover, Russian military resources were limited, and Stalin was husbanding them for the future struggle with Germany which he thought inevitable, so the aid he gave was comparatively little.

GREAT BRITAIN: The National Government in Britain remained strictly neutral, partly because opinion in Britain was divided, but far more because as a matter of policy it tried to avoid giving offence to any other power.

FRANCE: Léon Blum, as leader of a Popular Front government, genuinely sympathised with the Spanish government, but he wished to avoid imperilling his domestic reform programme by antagonising the right wing in France. He therefore proposed to the League of Nations only two weeks after the beginning of the war that all states should refrain from intervention in Spain.

The result of this was that in September 1936 a non-intervention committee of twenty-seven states was set up. This effectively prevented the Spanish government from buying supplies from friendly nations but could not prevent the rebels from receiving aid from Hitler and Mussolini, neither of whom had any qualms about flouting the decisions of the non-intervention committee.

Franco's Spain

In the unsettled Europe of 1939 Franco's victory in March, the same month that Hitler took over Czechoslovakia (p. 246), appeared as a victory for Fascism and aggressive Nationalism over the rather shaky alliance of Liberalism and Communism.

Inevitably Franco was drawn into the orbit of Hitler and Mussolini. They had recognised his government as early as November 1936, and in the same month that he won the war he joined them in the anti-Comintern pact (p. 243). To many it seemed likely that he would join them in the second World War, but sensibly he remained 'non-belligerent'. Thus when the second World War brought Hitler and Mussolini crashing down Franco survived them and continued as Spain's ruler. He was still ruling Spain a quarter of a century later.

FRENCH POLITICS were as tangled between the wars as before 1914. But one important change was that the centre of gravity had shifted as the Monarchists disappeared on the Right and the Socialists gained strength on the Left. The Radicals, who had been the principal left-wing party in the early years of the republic, were now the principal element of the Centre. It remained impossible for any one party to rule on its own, and in practice power swung backwards and forwards from Right to Left, depending on which way the Radicals leaned.

But it is possible to discern some sort of pattern in this. After the resignation early in 1920 of Clemenceau, who had been Prime Minister since November 1917, the Right ruled for four years with Radical support. Then the elections of 1924 produced a victory for a Radical–Socialist combination, which lasted two years until the Radicals switched their support to the Right again. Right-wing governments continued in power with Radical support until the elections of 1928, and without Radical support for most of the next four years. In 1932 a new Radical–Socialist combination won another election and the pattern of 1924 to 1928 was repeated: Radical–Socialist rule for two years followed by two years of right-wing rule with Radical support. In 1936 the elec-

General Elections:	1920		1924		1928		1932		1936		
				1926				1934		1938	1940
RIGHT WING											
RADICALS											
SOCIALISTS											

tions were won for the third time since the war by a left-wing alliance, and for the third time it lasted only two years. When this Popular Front broke down in 1938 the whole system of parliamentary government seemed in danger of breaking down as well, and the French went into the second World War demoralised and in a state of political disintegration.

Right–wing rule, 1920–4

The two main issues around which French politics revolved between the wars were foreign policy, which involved the question of French security in relation to Germany, and financial policy, which involved the question of German reparations payments.

During the four-year period of right-wing rule from 1920 to 1924 France built up the system of alliances (p. 237) which was intended to give her security from Germany, but at the same time she was suffering financially from the effects of the war, which she had paid for with loans rather than by extra taxation. The franc declined in value, prices rose, and the government had to increase taxation.

The French felt that Germany had escaped with excessively lenient treatment from the war and wanted their own financial burdens lightened by the German payment of reparations. So in 1922 the government of Briand, who was felt to be soft about reparations, fell, and Poincaré, who had been President from 1913 to 1920, became Prime Minister, promising to extract full reparations payments from Germany. He was responsible for the occupation of the Ruhr in January 1923 (p. 233); but it failed to force the Germans to pay, and it cost so much that he had to increase taxation even further. As a result the Radicals switched their support to the Socialists in time for the general election of 1924.

Left (1924–6) and Right (1926–32)

The new Radical–Socialist government adopted a far more moderate foreign policy. It evacuated the Ruhr and adopted the Dawes Plan (p. 233), and in 1925 Briand returned to office as Foreign Minister, negotiated the Locarno Treaties (p. 235), and agreed to Germany joining the League of Nations.

Meanwhile, however, the franc continued to decline in value until many Frenchmen feared a complete collapse of the economy such as Germany had experienced in 1923 (p. 233). This had the effect that most of the Radicals transferred their support to Poincaré, who came back to power, ruled by emergency powers, and saved the franc from complete collapse by devaluing to a fifth of its pre-war value. His government gained the confidence of the people to such an extent that it survived the general election of 1928; and although Poincaré himself was forced by ill-health to resign in July 1929, right-wing governments were able to continue in office until the next election in 1932.

Left (1932–4) and Right (1934–6)

France suffered less from the world economic crisis than more highly industrialised countries such as the U.S.A., Great Britain, and Germany, but the dislocation of her economy was sufficient to turn public opinion against the right-wing groups in power. So a Radical–Socialist combination again won a majority at a time of increasing financial difficulties, and again it only lasted two years.

From May 1932 to February 1934 five different left-wing governments tried to cope with financial difficulties, while abroad a new threat to France emerged in the shape of Nazi Germany. Then the Radical–Socialist combination collapsed under a scandal involving a Russian Jewish swindler called Stavisky, who had apparently been able to continue his dishonest career under the protection of left-wing politicians who were involved with him. When he committed suicide it was widely believed that this had been arranged to avoid further disclosures. The Radicals switched their support to a respectable government of the Right, and the right wing continued in power—though with no great success—until the elections of 1936.

Left (1936–8) and Right (1938–40)

During 1936 the French were increasingly worried by the ambitions of the German and Italian dictators. Mussolini had tended to draw away from France and closer to Hitler after the breakdown of the Hoare–Laval Pact (p. 239), and Hitler's occupation of the Rhineland in March 1936 (p. 243) had brought the German military threat up to the borders of France. So in the face of the growing threat of international Fascism all the parties of the Left and Centre combined in a Popular Front (p. 258).

In the summer the Popular Front won the general election, and Léon Blum, the Jewish barrister who was the Socialists' leader, became Prime Minister. His government introduced paid holidays and a forty-hour week, and improved the social services—all reforms which were long overdue—but in doing so it hindered efforts to increase production, although increased productivity was essential if France was to survive economically and militarily.

In the end the Popular Front only lasted for about the same time as previous left-wing combinations. The Communists had refused to join the government and increasingly impeded its work, and after two years the Radicals again switched their support to the Right. But the right-wing government of the Radical Daladier, who became Prime Minister in 1938, was less effective than those which had taken over in 1926 and 1934, and France drifted helplessly towards war.

Disintegration

Militarily France was incapable of taking the offensive when the war began, for her military leaders were committed to a belief in a defensive strategy. So she merely awaited the German attack, and during the eight months of waiting French morale collapsed. On the Left the Communists wanted to come to terms with Hitler and put their trust in his new ally, Stalin. On the Right men like Pierre Laval and the veteran Marshal Pétain saw defeat as inevitable and they also wanted France to get what terms she could from Hitler. The mass of the French people remembered how high a price they had paid for victory in the first World War and wondered if victory was worth the price.

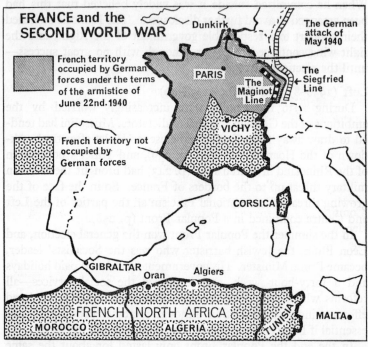

On 10th May 1940 Germany attacked in the West, and within less than a month the French army was beaten. Reynaud, who had taken over from Daladier as Prime Minister in March, wanted to continue the war either from Britain or from the French colonies in North Africa, but the army leaders would not agree. So he resigned on 16th June, and Marshal Pétain formed a government which accepted an armistice on Hitler's terms on the 22nd: North France and the Atlantic coast were to be occupied by Germany, and the French government, which moved South to Vichy, was to administer the whole of France and the French colonial empire. On 10th July the National Assembly handed over complete power to Marshal Pétain, and the Third Republic came to an end.

THE NINETEENTH-CENTURY Liberal tended to believe in a natural process of constitutional development which would eventually culminate in the establishment of parliamentary democracy throughout Europe. Demands for constitutional change usually involved demands for the extension of the franchise, and those who demanded such change were described as 'left wing', while those who obstructed it were described as 'right wing'. Thus it was right-wing parties which were open to the charge of being unconstitutional before the first World War. But the Bolshevik Revolution of 1917 (p. 125) changed this, for the Bolsheviks, who were an extreme left-wing party, overthrew parliamentary democracy in Russia, and their success encouraged the Left in other countries to adopt a more extreme position.

By now it was the Left which was obviously unconstitutional, and in Western Europe this tended to produce a revival of the Right and the election of essentially conservative parliaments after the war. In Italy traditionally conservative elements, who regarded saving the country from the threat of Bolshevism, or Communism, as more important than maintaining parliamentary democracy, co-operated with the Fascists in 1922 in bringing about the overthrow of democratic institutions (p. 136).

The success of the Fascists in Italy encouraged the extreme right wing in other countries to turn to direct action just as the success of the Bolsheviks in Russia had encouraged the Left. But it also made clear that the Right could still be unconstitutional as well as the Left. This helped to produce a revival of the Left and the election of left-wing governments, and in the mid-thirties, when the threat of international Fascism loomed large, those Socialists who regarded saving Europe from the threat of Fascism as more important than maintaining parliamentary democracy co-operated with the Communists. Thus a situation developed in Europe in which right-wing democrats tended to co-operate with Fascism and left-wing democrats with Communism. Fascists and right-wing democrats had in common that they both wanted to maintain the traditional structure of society and the economy, and the effect of their alliance was eventually to produce right-wing authoritarian governments throughout Central and Southern Europe. Communists and left-wing democrats had in common that they both wanted drastic changes in the traditional structure of society and the economy, and the outcome of their alliance was the Communist-inspired 'Popular Front' movement, which reached its peak in 1936 with Popular Front electoral victories in both France and Spain.

In this situation, attacked from both Left and Right, and betrayed by its own adherents, it was natural for parliamentary democracy to collapse. The only area of Europe where democracy survived until the outbreak of the second World War was the North-West, for that was an area of almost universal literacy, a high standard of living, and a tradition of parliamentary government.

Great Britain: In Great Britain it was always assumed that the maintenance of parliamentary institutions against the threat of authoritarianism was more important than the furtherance of particular left-wing or right-wing aims. Thus the support given by the right-wing press lords, Beaverbrook and Rothermere, to Sir Oswald Moseley's New Party (p. 205) in 1931 was short-lived once they appreciated the authoritarian nature of his movement, and the British Labour Party always resolutely refused to form a Popular Front with the Communists. Both Socialists and Conservatives faced the fact that the twentieth century had introduced a new conflict into politics. The old struggle between change and conservatism continued, and over this they opposed each other. But a new conflict had arisen between parliamentarianism and totalitarianism, and in this conflict they were on the same side. Both believed in parliamentary government, constitutional methods, individual liberty, and toleration of opposition. And as threats developed to these values, whether from Fascism or Communism, many of them came to believe that what they had in common was more important than their differences.

France: The only other European great power to retain parliamentary democracy between the wars was France. But French politics had long been unstable, and although parliamentary institutions survived during peace-time, the lack of stability in French political life helped to produce the disintegration of national morale which set in in the early stages of the second World War.

Belgium: The Belgians had had a parliament ever since the establishment of the country in 1830 after a successful rebellion in which they broke away from the United Kingdom of the Netherlands. Despite dissension between Catholics and Liberals and between the Flemish minority and the French-speaking majority Belgium managed to evolve a two-party system because she had large urban constituencies which tended to return several men of the same political persuasion.

In the 1890s the franchise was widened and a form of proportional representation was introduced whereby the seats in any constituency were allocated in proportion to the votes cast in that constituency. This made it possible for a large Socialist Party to join the other two main parties, the Catholics and the Liberals, and the Belgians managed to work a three-party system well.

The discontent of the Flemish minority remained a disruptive force in Belgian life even after 1932, by which time they had won the struggle for the official use of their language; and this, together with the development of a Belgian Fascist Party, the Rexists, tended to weaken Belgium's capacity to resist the Germans in 1940. Belgium's capacity to resist was further weakened by the change in her foreign policy after the German occupation of the Rhineland in 1936, for the Belgians abandoned their French alliance and reverted to their traditional policy of neutrality, and as a result they failed to co-ordinate their defence arrangements with France and Britain.

The German attack in 1940 caused chaos, and after eighteen days King Leopold III ordered his troops to surrender. This was done without the approval of the government, which fled to Britain, so after the war, when the parliamentary constitution was restored, resentment of the king's attitude continued until in 1951 he was forced to abdicate in favour of his son, Baudouin.

The Netherlands: Holland had always been naturally more stable internally than Belgium, but in 1918 the Dutch, who were neutral in the first World War, introduced an extreme form of proportional representation: the number of seats a party had in parliament was to be in proportion to the total votes cast in the whole country. In practice this resulted in a multiplication of parties in parliament, and soon the hundred members of the Dutch parliament were grouped in ten different parties. However, parliamentary government was so firmly established in the Netherlands that even this did not disrupt unduly the stable course of Dutch political life.

Switzerland: Switzerland also had a stable political life. The Swiss, who had no common language, but were made up of German, French, and Italian-speaking people, and were also fairly evenly divided into Roman Catholics and Protestants, had developed a tradition of tolerance and compromise. They also had a prosperous economy built on efficient agriculture and industry, and an established policy of neutrality which, unlike Belgium's, was made practicable by the mountainous nature of their country.

Eire: A new independent parliamentary democracy was formed in the British Isles between the wars when the Irish Free State, later Eire, was created in 1921 (p. 68).

Scandinavia: In Scandinavia the number of independent states also increased in the first half of the twentieth century as the result of developing Nationalist feeling. In 1905 the Norwegian parliament declared the union with Sweden at an end, and after a plebiscite Norway became an independent state with a member of the Danish royal family as king. Finland, which had had a form of parliamentary representation even when it was a Grand Duchy of the Russian Empire, was recognised as completely independent by the new Bolshevik government of Russia in January 1918. After a period of civil war it settled down as a parliamentary republic in the spring of 1919, and despite the divisive effect of adopting the Dutch system of proportional representation Finnish parliamentary institutions came to be firmly established. Iceland, which had been united with Denmark since 1380, gained Home Rule in 1918 and eventually, in 1944, became an independent republic.

The most striking development in the history of the main Scandinavian countries during the thirties was the domination of political life by Socialist parties, which introduced welfare services and extensive social reform. Most impressive of all was the Socialist government of Sweden which came to power in 1932 and devised a remarkably effective programme of economic recovery. It encouraged co-operative measures, while avoiding wholesale nationalisation, and it conquered unemployment, largely by means of a public works programme for which it paid by borrowing the money needed.

The survival of parliamentary democracy in North-West Europe until the second World War demonstrated the practicability of a constitutional system which offered a middle way between the two authoritarian extremes of Fascism and Communism. But constitutional stability depends on economic stability, and parliamentary democracy would only be able to survive after the war if it could rest on a sound economic basis. The fact that it could was demonstrated by Sweden, whose history showed that it was also practicable to adopt a middle way in economic policy between doctrinaire Socialism and *laissez-faire* Capitalism.

Section V   Great Britain, 1914–1945

34   BRITAIN AT WAR, 1914–1918

IN 1914 Great Britain's professional volunteer army was so much smaller than the armies of the other European powers that she was in no position to attack any of them, and her industry was not geared to war on land any more than her menfolk were trained as soldiers. On the other hand, the Royal Navy was more powerful than the fleet of any of the continental powers, and this meant that Britain was in a position to defend herself effectively against any likely attack. It also meant that if the navy could save Britain from rapid defeat it might be able to gain her the time to train a large army and turn her industry to producing the materials of war needed by her own and her allies' armies.

The Western Front

The British army played a significant though secondary part in the fighting in Western Europe.

The B.E.F.: The British Expeditionary Force which had been created by Haldane's army reforms (p. 59) and which was immediately shipped to the Continent in August 1914 numbered less than a hundred thousand at a time when Germany and Austria-Hungary could mobilise two million men each. But it was an efficient professional army. At Mons in Belgium it played an important part in holding up the German advance and disrupting the time-table of the Schlieffen Plan (p. 108). In the battle of the Marne (p. 110) it attacked through a gap between the first and second German armies and helped to compel the subsequent German retreat. Then it was transferred to the North to hold the coastal area, and in the battle of Ypres in the autumn it saved the Channel ports from falling to the Germans. The cost of this achievement was the lives of almost all the men of the original expeditionary force. But by this time reinforcements were arriving from Britain, and it was soon possible for British troops to hold the front as far South as the River Somme.

The Somme and Passchendaele: During 1915 the British forces were engaged in a series of inconclusive battles, but the French bore the brunt of the fighting until July 1916 when Sir Douglas Haig, now the British Commander-in-Chief, launched an attack near the Somme on the 1st of the month. The British army was still essentially a volunteer force, for conscription had only been introduced in January, and few of the conscripts had yet reached France. Nearly 60,000 men fell on the first day, and four months later, when the battle ended, there had been more than 400,000 British casualties—more than the total British losses, civilian as well as military, in the second World War.

In 1917, once more from July to November, the British army again attacked—this time at Passchendaele, near Ypres, and suffered 300,000 casualties. Neither the Somme nor Passchendaele produced any significant territorial gains, but it is possible to offer a justification for fighting them on two counts: one is that the Germans also suffered heavy losses; another is that each of them relieved pressure on the French at a time when there was a danger of a German break-through—in 1916 when the French armies were being battered at Verdun, and in 1917 when widespread mutinies had broken out in the French armies after a disastrous summer campaign.

The fighting of 1918: The heavy British losses at Passchendaele, together with the need to transfer troops to other fronts, had the effect that the British army on the Western front was smaller in the spring of 1918 than it had been a year earlier, and when the Germans attacked in March and April they achieved considerable initial successes. But in March the British prevented the Germans from splitting them from the French, and in April, fighting, as Haig told them, with their 'backs to the wall', they frustrated a renewed German effort to reach the Channel ports.

During the summer, while the Germans concentrated their attack on the French sector of the line, the British prepared for a counter-offensive, and this attack near Amiens on 8th August, which General Ludendorff called 'the black day of the German Army', started the German retreat which continued for the rest of the war.

The attempt to turn Germany's flank

The use of British troops on other fronts was potentially more important than their use in the West, where the trench system from the North Sea to Switzerland provided no opportunity for outflanking the enemy.

As early as 1914 Lloyd George and Winston Churchill were both advocating plans for turning Germany's flank by an attack in the East. Lloyd George wanted to land troops in the Balkans. Churchill wanted a direct attack on the Ottoman Empire, starting with the seizure of the Straits in a combined naval and military operation. Both plans would enable the Allies to strike at the Cen-

tral Powers through 'the soft under-belly of Europe', give assistance to the Serbs, and possibly at the same time encourage the
other Balkan countries and even Italy to join the Allies. Churchill's
had the supreme advantage that it was a way of reopening the
supply route to Russia.

But the insistence of the military leaders that troops could not be
spared from the Western front resulted in February 1915 in a
purely naval attempt to force the Straits. This was unsuccessful,

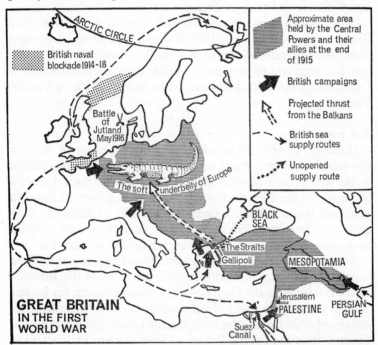

and by April, when troops were eventually landed on the Gallipoli
peninsula, the Turks were ready for them. The attempt to seize
the peninsula continued throughout the year without any success
and cost 250,000 casualties before it was abandoned in December.

Had this campaign succeeded the war might well have been
ended in 1915. Its failure was a major disaster for the Allies.
Bulgaria, instead of joining them, allied with the Central Powers in
October 1915. Serbia was conquered by the end of the year.
Greece and Roumania delayed joining the Allies until it was too
late for their assistance to be of any value. Most important of all,
Russia remained cut off from supplies from the West and was
eventually defeated.

The subsidiary theatres of war

Another effect of the failure to drive the Ottoman Empire out of the war was that Britain had to maintain armies in the Middle East to defend the Suez Canal and her oil supplies in the Persian Gulf. Already in 1915 a British army had advanced through Mesopotamia only to be surrounded and forced to surrender in 1916. But in 1917 the conquest of Mesopotamia was resumed, and in the same year a British cavalry force based on the Suez Canal advanced into Palestine and took Jerusalem.

These advances continued in 1918, and in September 1918 British troops took part in a swift Balkan campaign which brought about the surrender of Bulgaria, while in October British troops who had been sent to prop up the Italian front after the disaster of Caporetto (p. 99) helped the Italians to win the battle of Vittorio Veneto.

Sea power

However, all of these remained subsidiary theatres of war, for Germany's flank was never turned. She was eventually defeated by the slow process of wearing down her resources until she could be beaten on the Western front, and the most important factor in achieving this was British control of the sea, for although Germany was less immediately dependent than Britain on supplies from overseas, she could not survive a blockade indefinitely.

As early as 1898 the German government had recognised the importance of sea power with its decision to build the Imperial Fleet. But traditionally Germany was a military power, her leaders thought primarily in terms of land warfare, and the Schlieffen Plan was aimed at destroying the French army rather than at seizing the Channel ports and cutting France off from Britain. Only after the Schlieffen Plan had failed did the German High Command try to seize the Channel ports, and even then they made no use of their fleet. Moreover, their only important pre-war naval calculation was mistaken. They assumed that the British fleet would try to blockade Germany close inshore, where it would be vulnerable to minefields and torpedo attacks by small boats. But in fact the Royal Navy established a remote blockade by closing the English Channel and the North Sea between Scotland and Norway, thus effectively cutting Germany's sea communications without exposing itself to the danger of defeat by entering German waters. The result was that most of Germany's battle fleet remained inactive and impotent in harbour until May 1916, when Admiral

Scheer took it out and fought the battle of Jutland. And after that, having learnt that it could not wrest control of the seas from the Royal Navy in an open battle, the Imperial Fleet never ventured out again until it came out to surrender.

Scheer drew the conclusion from Jutland that Germany must return to a policy of trying to starve Britain out by destroying her merchant fleet with submarines, or U-boats. They had already attempted this as early as January 1915, but then the U.S.A. had demanded that they should keep to international agreements on the conduct of war, such as that merchant ships should only be sunk after a warning, and in May 1915, after the U.S.A. had protested at the sinking without warning of a British liner, the *Lusitania*, which had a hundred American citizens on board, Germany abandoned 'unrestricted' U-boat warfare.

But while Britain's supply lines remained open Germany's were closed, and the blockade of Germany was so effective that the German High Command concluded by the beginning of 1917 that Germany would not be able to stand the strain of war on two fronts more than another year. So they at last accepted Admiral Scheer's demand for a renewal of unrestricted U-boat warfare, trusting that the three hundred U-boats they had built would be sufficient to win the war before the strength of the U.S.A. could be felt in Europe.

Unrestricted submarine warfare began in February 1917 and was so successful that in April, the month in which the U.S.A. declared war, one ship in every four which left Britain never returned. At that rate British merchant shipping would have been completely destroyed and the war won by Germany within six months. But with new methods of anti-submarine warfare, the use of the convoy system, and American and Japanese naval help, together with an expansion of ship-building, an increase in domestic food production, and the imposition of food rationing, Britain managed to survive the crisis.

Meanwhile Germany was suffering more and more from the British blockade, which was even tighter now that the U.S.A. was in the war and no longer upholding the right of neutrals to trade with Germany. The British siege of Germany was less dramatic than the German U-boat campaign, but in the end it was more effective.

Industrial power

Britain's ability to make use of the seas throughout the war while denying its use to the enemy, and her ability to continue the war on land, depended on her industrial strength. Her munitions industry needed to be developed, but she had the industrial capacity to do this, and Lloyd George as Minister of Munitions from May 1915 to July 1916 geared British industry so effectively to the production of war materials that after the ceaseless bombardment in the battle of the Somme, the British army had more guns and ammunition than it had started with.

Important new weapons were developed. U-boats, which at the beginning of the war could only be sunk by ramming, were being attacked in 1917 with depth charges. An armoured fighting vehicle was developed, and in October 1917 381 of these vehicles, which were soon known as 'tanks', attacked at Cambrai and breached the German line over a 6-mile front for the loss of only 1,500 men. The success was not followed up, but more ground was gained, even though only temporarily, than in the whole battle of Passchendaele, which was still being waged farther North at a cost of two hundred times as many losses. The effectiveness of the tank was apparent, and 450 were used in the British attack near Amiens on 8th August 1918 which started the German retreat.

The ability of Britain's allies to continue the war also depended on Britain's capacity for supplying them with war materials. Those of her allies who were cut off from her, Russia, Serbia, and Roumania, were all defeated by the Central Powers. Both manpower and industrial strength were needed, but Russia's vast manpower was unavailing when her industrial strength was exhausted.

The importance of attrition

In restrospect it can easily seem that Germany was defeated by the overwhelming industrial strength and manpower of the U.S.A. But in fact the U.S.A. only needed to commit her resources to war on a very limited scale to tip the balance in the war either way, for all the European belligerents were exhausted by their long struggle. Britain had tried to gear all her national resources to war, and had raised massive conscript armies as well as fighting the war at sea and subsidising and supplying her continental allies; and as a result she was so exhausted that she was nearly defeated in 1917 by the German U-boat campaign and in 1918 by the German armies. But Germany was worn down at the same time, and an important part in this process of attrition was played by the naval blockade and by the men who fell in battles such as the Somme and Passchendaele.

35 GREAT BRITAIN IN OUTLINE, 1915–1945

DURING the forty years from 1915 to 1955 Great Britain was ruled for slightly more than half the while by coalition governments, formed in times of military or economic crisis. But political parties continued, and after the second World War the traditional system of party government was as firmly established as it had been before the first World War.

The first period of coalition rule lasted seven and a half years, from 1915 to 1922, and during the last six years the Conservatives were the dominant party in the government. Then for nearly nine years after 1922 there was a three-cornered struggle between the Conservative, Liberal, and Labour parties, and two periods of Conservative rule alternated with two periods of rule by the Labour Party with Liberal support. In 1931 another coalition was formed, and for the next fourteen years Britain was again ruled by coalitions in which the Conservatives predominated.

The end of the second World War saw a return to party politics. It also saw a return to the traditional two-party system which had been disrupted ever since the general election of December 1885, when the Irish Nationalists had become a significant element in the House of Commons. After 1945 the only large groups in the Commons were the Labour and Conservative parties. For the first six years after the war the Labour Party was in power, and then in 1951 there began a thirteen-year period of Conservative rule.

Asquith's war-time coalition

Great Britain had entered the first World War with a Liberal government led by Asquith. The general election which was due before the government's five-year term ran out at the end of 1915 was postponed until the war should be over. But there was nevertheless a change of government in 1915, for in May, when the government was heavily criticised for its conduct of the war, Asquith gave in to Conservative pressure and formed a coalition government. Despite the changes made at this time discontent with the government's conduct of the war continued, and by the end of 1916 Asquith's leadership was particularly criticised.

The establishment of Lloyd George

In December he was replaced by Lloyd George, another Liberal, who reconstituted the government drastically and prosecuted the war with far greater vigour. For a long while the extent

of Lloyd George's support in the House of Commons was uncertain. And his position was eventually challenged by Asquith in
the Maurice debate of May 1918 (p. 192), in which Lloyd George,
was accused of deliberately starving the Western front of troops.
But the challenge was unsuccessful, and the debate had two
important effects:

(1) It produced an open breach in the Liberal Party, for half the
Liberals voted with Lloyd George while the other half voted with
their party leader, Asquith.

(2) Since most of the Conservative Party supported Lloyd George,
it greatly strengthened his position and cemented his alliance with
the Conservative leaders.

The 'Coupon Election' of 1918

In December 1918, a month after the armistice, Lloyd George
fought a general election. The combined effect of his personal
ascendancy as the man who had led the nation to victory, of the
split in the Liberal Party, and of the changed political attitudes of
the Irish (p. 67), was to return a parliament quite unlike that
which had preceded it.

Bonar Law, the leader of the Conservative Party, had agreed to
continue the coalition, and in effect the election was fought on the
issue of whether one was for or against Lloyd George. A letter of
approval, signed by him and Bonar Law, was given to a number of
candidates who were pledged to support the coalition, and this
'coupon', as Asquith called it, was issued to only 159 Liberals.

The coalition won an overwhelming victory. The largest opposition group was the Labour Party with 63 seats; the official
Liberal Party, led by Asquith, won only 28 seats; and only 7 Irish
Nationalists were elected, for 73 of the seats which they traditionally held had been won by *Sinn Fein*, whose members refused to
come to Westminster.

The end of the coalition

But the post-war coalition government was unable to cope
effectively with the enormous problems which the war had created,
and dissatisfaction with it increased both in the country at large
and among the mass of Conservative M.P.s, who met together in
October 1922 and voted in favour of ending the coalition. Lloyd
George immediately resigned the premiership, and Bonar Law
formed a Conservative government—though some of the leading
Conservatives who had wanted to continue the coalition, such as
Austen Chamberlain and Balfour, did not take office.

Bonar Law and 'tranquillity'

The Conservatives already had a comfortable majority in the House of Commons, but the changed political situation which resulted from the ending of the coalition made it desirable to hold a general election as soon as possible. Bonar Law went to the country promising 'tranquillity', and the election, held in November 1922, resulted in a clear victory for his party, which gained an overall majority of 79 seats. But Bonar Law only held office for six months. In May 1923, a dying man, he retired, and was succeeded by his Chancellor of the Exchequer, Stanley Baldwin.

Baldwin and Protection

On this occasion Baldwin was not Prime Minister for much longer than Bonar Law had been, for in December he fought another election on the issue of Protection and lost it. The Protection issue had the effect of re-uniting both the Liberal and Conservative Parties. The Lloyd George and Asquith Liberals united under Asquith to defend Free Trade, while the coalition Conservatives joined the rest of their party in campaigning for Protection. But it was the Labour Party which came to power. Like the Liberals it had been defending Free Trade, and it had won more seats than the Liberals. Although the Conservatives had won more seats than either of them, the combined vote of the two Free Trade parties was enough to defeat the Conservative government, and this happened as soon as Parliament met in January 1924.

The first Labour government, 1924

Asquith had already declared that the Labour leaders should take office, and he had added that although the Liberals would not join a coalition they would co-operate with a Labour government. So when Baldwin resigned Ramsay MacDonald, the leader of the Labour Party, formed a government which depended for its existence on Liberal votes.

Bonar Law had held office for six months and Baldwin for eight. MacDonald was to remain Prime Minister for ten months. In October the government was defeated in a vote concerning its withdrawal of the prosecution of a Communist journalist (p. 202), and MacDonald asked for a dissolution. At the end of the month there took place the third general election within two years.

The Conservatives had dropped Protection from their programme because of its unpopularity, and Baldwin offered 'sane, commonsense government' as an alternative to Labour. Liberal disunity was meanwhile increasing, and in the event the Conservatives won a massive victory. MacDonald resigned and Baldwin became Prime Minister again.

Baldwin's second ministry, 1924-9

With an overall majority of 215 Baldwin was able to remain in office for a full term. But the late twenties were a time of industrial unrest and increasing unemployment in Britain, and the popularity of the government was whittled away by its failure to provide any long-term solution to these problems. Baldwin had to have a general election before the end of 1929, so in May he went to the country with the slogan 'Safety First'. But for the only time in all seven elections between the wars the Conservatives failed to win more seats than any other party; and the Labour Party, at last the largest party in the Commons, took office for the second time.

The second Labour government, 1929-31

Although the Labour Party had won more seats than any other party it again lacked an overall majority, so it again depended on Liberal support. But this time it was not an adverse vote in the Commons which brought the government to an untimely end but a division of opinion in the cabinet. During the financial crisis of the summer of 1931 (p. 205) MacDonald was unable to convince many of his colleagues in the cabinet of the need for certain economies, and he therefore resigned.

The formation of the 'National' government

A strong government needed to be formed rapidly in order to deal with the immediate crisis, and there was no time to wait for a general election. The Liberals were prepared to join a coalition under MacDonald, though not under Baldwin, who accepted the situation and announced the willingness of the Conservatives to serve under MacDonald as well.

King George V therefore asked MacDonald to form a 'National' coalition government, and he agreed to do so. All the Conservatives supported the new government, and so, for the moment, did all the Liberals. But most of the Labour members went into opposition, and the result of this was that the Conservatives now dominated a coalition led by a Labour Prime Minister just as, during the premiership of Lloyd George, they had dominated a coalition led by a Liberal Prime Minister.

The National government, 1931-40

In October MacDonald gave in to Conservative pressure to hold a general election, and the National government won an overwhelming majority. When Parliament reassembled there were

555 members supporting the government faced by a meagre opposition of 60. 471 of the government's supporters were Conservatives, and there were only 13 National Labour members.

Dominated in this way by his Conservative allies MacDonald nevertheless continued as Prime Minister, with Baldwin as his deputy, for nearly four years. Not till in June 1935 did he resign. Baldwin then succeeded him as leader of a government which was really Conservative. The government won its second general election five months later in November 1935, and its majority, though cut by a half from 495 to 247, was still very large indeed.

The next year there was something of a constitutional crisis. When George V died in January 1936 he was succeeded by his eldest son, a bachelor of 41, who became king as Edward VIII. Later in the year King Edward told Baldwin that he intended to marry a divorced American woman, Mrs. Wallis Simpson, who was now divorcing her second husband. This would have given offence to many of his subjects. So Baldwin insisted that he could not both marry Mrs. Simpson and remain king. Edward decided to abdicate. On 11th December, only a week after the news of the crisis became public, he was succeeded by his brother, the Duke of York, who became King George VI.

By this time Baldwin was nearly seventy. So in May 1937 he resigned, and for the next three years the National government, by now almost entirely Conservative, was led by Neville Chamberlain, the son of Joseph and half-brother of Austen Chamberlain. In September 1939, when Britain plunged into the second World War, Chamberlain made several changes in his government. but neither the Labour nor Liberal Party was prepared to join a coalition under him, and in May 1940, after many of his own party had voted against him, he resigned.

Churchill and Attlee

Winston Churchill now formed a coalition government in which the Labour Party leader, Clement Attlee, became Deputy Prime Minister. This government continued until in May 1945 the war against Germany came to an end. In the same month Churchill ended the coalition and parliament was dissolved. The Conservative government which he then formed lasted only two months, for in the general election of July 1945, the first for nearly ten years, the Labour Party gained a clear majority in the House of Commons for the first time. Churchill resigned and Attlee took office less than two weeks before the war with Japan came to an end.

36   THE BRITISH ECONOMY

Booms and slumps

IN the late nineteenth century Britain was increasingly an industrial rather than an agricultural country. Capital goods, such as factories, were owned by private individuals, and this capitalist economy was vulnerable to the economic fluctuations known as booms and slumps, which are the result of production and consumption failing to keep pace with each other. Manufacturers, who naturally want to expand as much as possible in order to make more profit, borrow money to do so, sometimes at a high rate of interest. Sometimes the expansion is excessive, and this results in over-production, decline in demand, the building up of stocks, and then decreased production and unemployment. In this situation, which is known as a slump, there is less demand to borrow money, and interest rates become lower. Eventually stocks run down, demand increases, and in order to increase production to meet the increased demand men are re-employed, money is borrowed, and industry expands. Rapid expansion is known as a boom.

The boom produces another slump and the slump in turn produces another boom. The whole process is known as 'the trade cycle' and was generally thought in the late nineteenth and early twentieth centuries to be inevitable. The only consolation was that each slump did always seem to be followed by a boom.

The balance of payments

The situation was complicated by the fact that Britain needed to import food and raw materials from abroad and had to pay for them with exports. To have a healthy economy it is necessary to have an income from exports at least as great as the cost of one's imports—i.e. one must maintain a balance of payments. And although Britain had what is known as an adverse balance of trade, because she imported more goods than she exported, she kept a favourable balance of payments because she was more than able to pay for the surplus imports with her income from invisible exports—i.e. her receipts for services such as merchant shipping, banking, and insurance, and the interest on capital invested abroad.

Britain's economy before the first World War

However, the health of Britain's economy depended more on her actual than her invisible exports, and thus it depended on her industrial efficiency. In 1871 Britain was the leading industrial nation of the world, responsible for a third of the world's industrial production. In the mid-1880s she was still producing three times as much coal and more than twice as much steel as Germany, and she was even producing more coal and steel than the U.S.A. But both Germany and the U.S.A. were rapidly catching up.

Moreover, coal and steel, which formed a high proportion of Britain's export trade, were commodities which enabled the countries which bought them to build up their own industries. Eventually they no longer wanted from Britain goods which they could make themselves, and they even became competitors. This meant that Britain was perpetually driven to look for new markets. As it happens world consumption was increasing rapidly, and there were still wide markets to which she could sell her goods, even after German and American industry had overtaken hers. But if world consumption should ever decline the health of Britain's economy would be seriously affected.

The effects of the first World War

During the first World War, when much of British industry was producing armaments instead of goods for export, Britain paid for imports of food and raw materials by selling many of the overseas assets from which she had previously drawn the large income which helped to maintain a favourable balance of payments. Eventually she resorted to large-scale borrowing as well, and she emerged from the war a debtor nation instead of a creditor nation.

This made it even more important than before to export on a large scale in order to be able to pay for imports. But world consumption had declined drastically, and in 1919 Britain exported less than half as much as in 1913:

(1) The financial and social chaos in Central and Eastern Europe deprived her of a large pre-war market.

(2) Countries such as Japan and India had developed their own industries in the war and now had less demand for British goods.

(3) The U.S.A. and some of these newly industrialised countries retained a large share of the markets which they had taken over from Britain during the war.

(4) Some countries which wanted to buy British goods were unable to because they had to use their money to repay American war loans.

(5) Britain found it all the more difficult to sell her goods because other countries were raising tariff barriers to protect their home industries.

The effect of all this was not felt immediately by the British economy, which experienced a short boom in 1919 as the result of the heavy demand at home for consumer goods after the austerity of the war years. But by 1920 the home demand had declined and world trade was so badly dislocated that Britain's exports were only 60 per cent of what they had been even in 1919.

The balance of payments problem in the twenties

Since Britain still needed imports on a large scale, she found it difficult to maintain a balance of payments. There were three obvious ways of solving this problem: by exporting more, by importing less, and by increasing invisible exports.

The only way to export more was to produce more goods more cheaply, and this could be achieved either by greater efficiency or by reduction of costs. Both methods were tried. Some industries achieved greater efficiency by mass production, while others reduced costs by making employees work longer hours for less pay. These developments alleviated the problem but did not solve it.

The obvious way to reduce imports was by raising tariffs against foreign goods, but when Baldwin fought an election on this issue in 1923 (p. 207) he lost because the electorate still regarded tariffs as a way of taxing food.

Invisible exports could only be increased by restoring world confidence in Britain's currency and financial security. Two Conservative Chancellors of the Exchequer tried to achieve this:

(1) In 1923 Baldwin undertook that Britain would honour her war debts to the U.S.A. But this necessitated a high rate of taxation which in the long run increased the cost of British goods and thus harmed the ordinary export trade.

(2) Then in 1925 Winston Churchill returned Britain to the gold standard (p. 211), fixing the value of the pound at the same rate in relation to the dollar as before the war. This had the disastrous effect of making British exports a further 10% more expensive.

The balance of payments problem continued throughout the twenties and was only partially solved in 1931 when the National government took Britain off the gold standard and devalued the pound.

Unemployment in an unbalanced economy

The closely related problem of unemployment also had to be faced in the twenties. By the summer of 1921 more than two million men were out of work, mainly in the cotton area of South Lancashire, the coal-mining areas such as South Wales, and the ship-building areas of Clydeside and Tyneside. Thus unemployment was concentrated in Britain's main export industries, each of which was suffering as the result of the war. Many textile markets had been lost to Japan and India. The decline in world trade caused a decline in demand for shipping and coal, and the coal industry also suffered from competition from other fuels such as oil and electricity.

Meanwhile new industries, such as rayon, cars, and electrical engineering, were developing. Most of them did not need coal, so they tended to develop near their principal market, which was usually London. Thus while there was a slump in South Lancashire, South Wales, Clydeside, and Tyneside there was a boom in places like Slough and Dagenham. This further increased the population in the London area and thus in turn produced an even greater consumer market and stimulated a building boom.

The new industries did comparatively little to help solve the balance of trade problem, for only cars became a major export. They also did comparatively little to alleviate the problem of unemployment in the old industrial areas, for a skilled craftsman from Tyneside might find it difficult to get a different job in London, and in any case probably could not afford the expense of moving.

Thus during the twenties Britain's economy was badly out of balance. While some of her light industries in the South boomed, the old heavy industries on which her export trade depended suffered a long drawn-out slump. They could not work to capacity because they could not sell their products, so both capital and labour were unemployed. The capital, such as machinery and factories, was useless for any other purpose, and the labour could not easily be diverted into other channels. This explains why in 1929, at the height of the so-called boom, Britain was still exporting less than she had in 1913 and still had over a million unemployed, with one miner in every four and one man in every five in ship-building out of work. Britain's economy was still very largely geared to the circumstances of the late nineteenth century.

The Keynesian solution

John Maynard Keynes, the Cambridge economist, offered a revolutionary solution to the problem of how to prevent unemployment and slump. He accepted the orthodox view that it was necessary to stimulate investment in capital goods and spending on consumer goods, but argued that in the past too much emphasis had been put on purely monetary policies. More money had been injected into the economy in the expectation that it would be spent, but in practice many people preferred to save. Interest rates had been lowered as an incentive to investment, but in practice a man's decisions about long-term investment depended far more on his degree of optimism about the future volume of spending. Monetary policies, in fact, could not ensure increased investment and increased spending. But the government could ensure increased investment by itself investing in a public works programme, and this in turn would stimulate spending—especially if taxes were kept low. The government would have to borrow heavily and spend lavishly. It would not be able to balance its budget.

Keynes' ideas were accepted by Lloyd George even before the Great Slump, but the Liberals were heavily defeated in the general election of 1929 and the Labour and Conservative Parties adhered to more orthodox economic theories. Neither was prepared to finance a public works programme by accumulating a large government debt, and the National government's solution to Britain's economic problems was drastic economies, protection from foreign competition, and orthodox financial measures, such as enforcing low interest rates and imposing heavier taxes.

Precarious recovery during the thirties

There was some recovery during the thirties, partly because of the increasing efficiency in British industry, but mainly as the result of the natural operation of the trade cycle which was affecting the whole world. But neither the balance of payments problem nor the problem of permanent unemployment was solved. In 1937, at the height of the recovery from the slump, Britain's total exports were 28 per cent less than in 1913 while her total imports had increased 32 per cent, and there were still nearly one and a half million unemployed. Then in 1938 a recession began, and it was possibly only the approach of war which prevented another serious slump. As it was the recession was soon checked by a rearmament programme which gave the ship-building, coal, iron and steel, car, and aircraft industries the sort of boost which Keynes had argued a public works programme would give, and this, combined with conscription, assimilated most of the surplus manpower in 1939. But rearmament could not provide a permanent solution to economic difficulties, for it does not provide goods for home consumption or exports, and indeed it diverts industry away from the production of consumer goods. Thus the second World War merely postponed Britain's economic problems, and from 1945 onwards the Labour government had to face the task of controlling the economy so as to balance exports against imports and maintain full employment.

The London dock strike of 1889

ALTHOUGH the Trade Union Congress, or T.U.C., was formed as early as 1868, only the skilled workers in Britain were then organised in unions. Trade unionism did not spread to unskilled workers until the dockers in London, where large numbers made organisation more easily possible, formed a union in 1887 and in 1889 went on strike to get a minimum wage of 6*d*. an hour. The success of this struggle for 'the dockers' tanner' produced a great extension of trade unionism among unskilled workers, and by the turn of the century there were two million members of unions affiliated to the T.U.C.

Capitalism, Syndicalism, and Socialism

Thus by the beginning of the twentieth century it was already clear that trade unions were becoming a powerful force in society. It was far less clear how that force was likely to be used, for three different courses of action seemed open to the unions.

Acceptance of Capitalism: They could maintain the traditional trade union policy of accepting the capitalist social and economic system, with private ownership of capital goods, and seek to obtain for their members a greater share of the benefits of Capitalism.

Syndicalism: They could seek to bring about a social and economic revolution by direct action—strikes and even armed force. This was the policy of those who believed in Syndicalism—a belief that the workers in any industry should own it and run it for their own profit, and that government should be through trade union representatives rather than through the representatives of territorial constituencies.

Socialism: They could seek to bring about a social and economic revolution by using established political methods. This was the policy of those who believed in Socialism (p. 196), which, like Syndicalism, had the appeal that it rejected the idea of the inferiority of labourers to employers and aimed at overthrowing the capitalist system, of which recurring slumps seemed an integral part.

These three social and economic systems are theoretically incompatible, but in practice the trade union movement never committed itself exclusively to any one of them. There seemed little immediate prospect of overthrowing Capitalism, so trade unions usually tried to improve the standards of living of their members by negotiation with employers, while making little contribution to helping the capitalist system to work efficiently. In times of adversity they tended to resort to Syndicalism, but in general this essentially selfish doctrine, which was later adopted in a modified form by the Italian Fascists (p. 137), had less appeal than Socialism; and during the twentieth century trade unionism has been increasingly associated with Socialism and the Labour Party.

The Unions and the Labour Party

In 1899 the T.U.C. passed a resolution calling for 'an increased number of Labour members in the next parliament'. This resulted in the meeting at which the L.R.C. was established (p. 197), and right from the beginning the unions had considerable control over the embryo Labour Party, partly because the L.R.C. depended for its income on a levy from union members, and partly because the unions' large membership gave them the dominant voice at the annual conferences of the party. Soon, when the unions' interests were affected by two legal judgments, they found the value of having a specifically working-class party in parliament.

The Taff Vale Case: In 1901 the unions' assumption that they were not legally and financially responsible for the acts of their members was upset when the House of Lords, acting as the High Court of Appeal, awarded £23,000 damages to the Taff Vale Railway Company, which had sued the Amalgamated Society of Railway Servants after a strike by some of the society's members. This was a serious blow to the right to strike, which would be made too expensive, and the strong feeling on this issue was largely responsible for the election of so many Labour M.P.s in January 1906. These Labour members promptly fulfilled the hopes of trade unionists by persuading the Liberal government to pass the Trade Disputes Act of 1906, which reversed the Taff Vale decision.

The Osborne Judgment: In 1907 a member of the Amalgamated Society of Railway Servants called Osborne, who was a Liberal, objected to contributing to the levy which financed the L.R.C. A legal decision in Osborne's favour was confirmed by the House of Lords in 1909, and it had the effect of making the whole political levy illegal. Once again the Labour M.P.s exerted pressure on the Liberal government, which in 1913 passed the Trade Union Act, legalising the political levy subject to the right of individuals to 'contract out' if they did not want to pay.

Direct action—pre-war and post-war

Meanwhile the decline in Britain's industrial supremacy in the early twentieth century had caused wages to stand still while prices rose, and this turned many trade unionists towards Syndicalism. From 1910 to 1912 there was a series of strikes on a larger scale than Britain had ever known before. Some were nation-wide and brought the strikers into direct conflict with the government, which intervened in 1911 to end a railway strike at the time of the Agadir crisis (p. 87) and in 1912 to force the Miners' Federation to go to arbitration. In 1913 the railwaymen's, dockers', and miners' unions formed a 'Triple Alliance' with a view to combined action in the future, but nothing ever came of this, for in 1914 war broke out, and during the war the unions generally co-operated with the war effort.

When the war was over, however, many unionists, encouraged by the success of the Russian Revolution, still favoured militant action. In 1919 there was an average of 100,000 workers on strike each day, in 1920 the London dockers refused to load a ship called the *Jolly George* which was to sail for Poland with munitions to be used in the war with Russia (p. 228), and later in the year a Council of Action was set up.

But the unions refrained from unconstitutional action, and a more important development at this time was the tendency of small unions to amalgamate in large bodies, such as the Transport and General Workers' Union, or T.G.W.U., which was formed in 1921 with Ernest Bevin as its general secretary. The trade union movement was further strengthened in 1921 by the establishment of the General Council. But the economic situation after the war (p. 177) put massive difficulties in the way of unions trying to improve the lot of their members.

The problems of the coal industry

The coal industry suffered particularly in the post-war years. In 1919 a commission investigated it and recommended nationalisation, but although the government had already taken control of the mines during the war (p. 192) nationalisation was impossible in a parliament dominated by Conservative businessmen, and in 1921, when coal prices collapsed from 115s. a ton to 24s., the government avoided the losses it would soon face by handing the mines back to private ownership. The mine-owners were faced with the losses which the government had avoided, and since their main expense was wages they announced that wages were to be reduced. The miners went on strike in April, but in June they accepted defeat and went back to work with less pay.

For four years there was frustration in the mines. Then in

April 1925 Winston Churchill's financial policy (p. 178) had the
effect of increasing the cost of British exports by 10 per cent, thus
making it even more difficult to sell coal abroad. The price of coal
had to be cut, so once again the coal-owners announced their
intention to cut wages.

The General Strike

Many of the miners were already living in poverty, so they refused to accept a further cut. The General Council of the T.U.C.
threatened a strike and promised the support of the transport
workers and railwaymen with effect from 31st July 1925. At the
last moment the government provided a temporary solution by
granting a subsidy to pay the difference between the old and new
wages for the next nine months until 1st May 1926 while a commission considered the problem.

When the commission eventually produced its report it was unacceptable to both sides in the dispute. But meanwhile the government had established an Emergency Committee on Supply and
Transport to co-ordinate plans in the event of a general strike.
The T.U.C. made no plans, but when the nine months were up
and there was still a deadlock in the negotiations it could see no
alternative to a strike. On 30th April the government adopted
emergency powers, and on 4th May all the workers in the major
industries were called out and came out on strike.

Right from the start the strike was doomed. The government's
emergency plans worked smoothly and could have gone on indefinitely. The strikers could not hope to win without resorting to
violence, so after nine days the T.U.C. leaders, who were just as
anxious as the government to avoid violence, gave in and advised
the men to go back to work.

The effects of the general strike

By surrendering the union leaders saved the country from serious
violence, but the failure of the strike was a serious blow to trade
unionism, and merely in terms of money cost the T.U.C. £4
million. The miners stayed on strike until the end of the year and
in the end went back to longer hours and less pay. Many other
strikers never got their jobs back. There were more than 3,000
prosecutions for making seditious speeches or for violence. And
in 1927 the government followed up its victory by passing the
Trade Union and Trade Disputes Act, which made all sympathetic
strikes illegal, established that the political levy should not be
paid except by those who chose to 'contract in', and forbade

civil servants from joining any union affiliated to the T.U.C.

Trade union leaders learnt the bitter lesson that direct action which involved challenging the government could not be effective unless one was prepared to go on to revolution; and since they were not revolutionaries the failure of the general strike had the effect of turning them away from direct action towards political action.

Ernie Bevin of the T.G.W.U.

Political action meant influencing the Labour Party, and in the thirties Ernest Bevin, with the massive block vote of the T.G.W.U. behind him, became a dominant figure at the annual conferences of the Labour Party.

In 1932 he attacked Herbert Morrison's contention that nationalised industries should be run by able men regardless of their politics. In 1933 he attacked Sir Stafford Cripps' proposal that a future Labour government should rule through emergency decrees. In 1934 he attacked Aneurin Bevan, who was trying to justify the rebelliousness of minority groups in the party. And in 1935 he attacked George Lansbury's pacifism with the effect that Lansbury resigned the leadership of the party.

In each of these matters Bevin was expressing an essentially trade unionist attitude—insisting on workers' control of industry, constitutional methods, solidarity in the party as in the unions, and a practical approach to foreign policy; and except on the first issue he was successful. His influence in the Labour Party increased even more after 1940 when he joined the war-time coalition as Minister of Labour, for a particularly close relationship developed between him and Attlee, who had succeeded Lansbury in 1935.

The Unions after the second World War

Bevin's position in the post-war Labour government, the repeal in 1946 of the Trade Union and Trade Disputes Act of 1927, and the fact that a third of the Labour M.P.s were union men, influenced the unions to support the government and even accept a policy of wage restraint. Syndicalism was a thing of the past. Socialism was a dream of the future. Meanwhile the unions, like the Labour government, accepted the capitalist society they lived in and tried to improve it. They sought better conditions for their members by negotiation with employers and, if necessary, by strike. But they realised that their members suffered from the industrial disruption caused by strikes, so they tended towards moderation not only under the Labour government but also under the Conservative governments which followed.

38 THE DECLINE OF THE LIBERAL PARTY

The secession of the Liberal Unionists

THE FIRST big split in the Liberal Party was caused by the issue of Irish Home Rule. Gladstone was able to form his third ministry in February 1886 partly because the 'unauthorised programme' of social reform (p. 37) advocated by Joseph Chamberlain in the election of December 1885 had resulted in the return of 86 more Liberals than Conservatives to parliament, and partly because his own conversion to Home Rule (p. 64) ensured him the support of the 86 Irish Nationalist members.

But in June, when he introduced the first Home Rule Bill, 93 Liberals voted against it, with the result that it was defeated by 343 votes to 313, and Gladstone again had to resign. Most of these 93 were the Whig element, led by Lord Hartington (a member of the House of Commons until he succeeded his father as Duke of Devonshire in 1891); but there was also among them a smaller number of Radical social reformers led by Joseph Chamberlain, who commanded considerable electoral support.

This division became a permanent one. The Whig and Radical rebels, who were jointly known as Liberal Unionists, supported Salisbury's second ministry from 1886 to 1892, and when Salisbury formed his third ministry in 1895 Hartington, now Duke of Devonshire, took office as Lord President of the Council, and Joseph Chamberlain became Colonial Secretary.

The 'Celtic fringe'

The split over Irish Home Rule made the remaining Liberals, who only numbered 191 after the election of 1886, increasingly dependent on the 'Celtic fringe' of Irish, Welsh, and Scots. Only once in the future, from 1906 to 1910, were they ever able to command a majority without Irish Nationalist support, and of the Liberals themselves some, like the young Lloyd George who entered parliament after a by-election in 1890, were really Welsh Nationalists under another name, and could not be relied on to give regular support to the Liberal leaders.

In power, 1892–5

Consequently in 1891, five years after the defection of the Liberal Unionists and less than one before the next election, the Liberals adopted the 'Newcastle programme' (p. 43). Thus when they came to power in 1892 and found themselves dependent on the

Irish vote they were also committed to a policy of Home Rule for Ireland to which the majority of Englishmen objected. Although the Commons passed the second Home Rule Bill in September 1893, the Lords threw it out by 419 votes to 41, and Gladstone could not persuade his cabinet to fight a general election on the issue of reform of the House of Lords. In March 1894 Lord Rosebery succeeded Gladstone as Prime Minister, and in June 1895 he took the opportunity of a snap vote of censure on Campbell-Bannerman, the Secretary for War, to resign.

The I.L.P. and the 1895 election

In the subsequent election which the Conservatives and Liberal Unionists won with a majority of 152, the new Independent Labour Party (p. 196) made its first challenge. None of its twenty-eight candidates won a seat, but some of them split the anti-Conservative vote and thus helped to increase the scale of the Liberal defeat.

In opposition, 1895–1905

During the years of opposition at the end of the nineteenth century the Liberal party tended to split wider apart. For example, by the turn of the century the Liberal Imperialist ex-Prime Minister Lord Rosebery was even prepared to contemplate the extremely illiberal measure of conscription, while John Morley, who was Secretary of State for India after 1905, was virtually a pacifist.

But in the twentieth century the Liberals gradually drew closer together. Most of the party was behind Campbell-Bannerman when he inveighed during the Boer War against 'methods of barbarism' (p. 269). Then in 1902, when Lloyd George led the opposition to Balfour's Education Act (p. 51), most Liberals united in an attempt to save non-conformists from having to pay towards the upkeep of Anglican schools. And between 1903 and 1905 Joseph Chamberlain's campaign for Protection (p. 52) drove the Liberals close together to defend the principle of Free Trade.

Labour and the Irish before the war

The election of January 1906 saw a great victory for the Liberals, but it also saw the arrival of 53 Labour members. The elections of January and December 1910 resulted in a Liberal victory over the House of Lords (p. 73); but one effect of abolishing the Lords' power of veto was to clear the way for a possible Labour administration in the future. Another result of the 1910 elections was the reduction of the number of Liberals in the Commons from 377, which gave them a majority of 64 over all other parties, to 272—parity with the Conservatives. This made them again dependent on the Irish vote, so to secure Irish support Asquith had to give Redmond, the Irish Nationalist leader, a promise of Home Rule, which had been dropped from the Liberal programme in 1905.

The War

But it was neither the rise of the Labour Party nor the issue of Home Rule which dealt the most crippling blow to Liberal fortunes. In 1914 Asquith was Prime Minister and leader of a parliamentary party with more than 260 members. In 1919 he was leader of a small group of 28, part of the opposition to a coalition government in which 136 other Liberals were swamped by 338 Conservatives. This collapse was the result of disagreements among Liberal leaders about the conduct of the war.

Asquith had been a great peace-time Prime Minister. He was not an effective war leader. In the summer of 1915 he gave in to Conservative pressure to remove two of his ablest ministers, Churchill and Haldane, from the offices they held and to form a coalition. Then, as the military disasters of 1916 continued, pressure for Asquith's resignation grew, and in December Lloyd George, now Secretary for War and increasingly eager to get control of the direction of the war for himself, resigned. This was followed the next day by Asquith's resignation, and two days after that Lloyd George became Prime Minister with the support of most Conservatives and some of the Liberals.

Asquith refused to join a government headed by Lloyd George, and in March 1918, a critical time in the war when the German forces were starting their last bid for victory (pp. 112-13), he and 97 other Liberals opposed a vote of confidence in the government.

Post-war disunity

Lloyd George was determined to remain as Prime Minister after the war, so he fought and won the election of 1918 (p. 172) as leader of a coalition in which the Conservatives predominated. Eventually in 1922 the Conservatives threw off Lloyd George (pp. 206-7), but the Liberals were still bitterly divided, and they fought the election in the autumn as two separate groups, each of which won 59 seats. By now the Labour Party was larger than both Liberal groups combined, and with 142 seats became the official opposition party.

Reunion

Baldwin's threat to Free Trade in 1923 (p. 207) drove Lloyd

George and Asquith to patch up an uneasy alliance, and in the election of December 1923, under the leadership of Asquith, the Liberals won 159 seats and found themselves in a position of balance between 191 Labour members and 258 Conservatives. They agreed to support a Labour government, but during the ten-month rule of the first Labour government they failed to act as a united party. 'Forty vote with the government,' wrote Austen Chamberlain, 'twenty with us, and the rest (including the leaders) walk out or absent themselves.' In the election of October 1924 their number slumped to 42.

Lloyd George's Party Fund

By now another factor was increasing Liberal disunity. Lloyd George had amassed large sums of money in a Party Fund, but he kept complete control of the money himself and maintained his own separate organisation. The Asquith Liberals always resented this, and in particular they attributed their lack of success in the 1924 election to Lloyd George's unwillingness to spend freely enough for the campaign. In 1926 Asquith, realising that it was impossible to maintain party unity 'under a system of rival authorities, with separate organisations and separate funds', gave up the struggle and resigned the leadership to Lloyd George.

The 1929 election

In 1929, united now under Lloyd George, the Liberals went into the election with a vigorous policy for conquering unemployment by a public works programme, inspired by the ideas of the Cambridge economist John Maynard Keynes (p. 179). The Conservatives fought the election with the unambitious slogan 'Safety First', and the Labour Party also lacked a clear-cut policy. But although Lloyd George spent his Party Fund so lavishly that there were 512 Liberal candidates, and although they gained nearly a quarter of the total votes cast, they won only 59 seats out of 615.

The divisions of the thirties

It was the last gasp of the old Liberal Party. In the election of 1931 after the formation of the National government (p. 174) seventy-two Liberals were returned to the House of Commons. Four of them (a family group of Lloyd George, his son, his daughter, and a relation by marriage) were in opposition. The rest supported the predominantly Conservative government with its Labour prime minister, and even they were not united. Thirty-five, led by Sir John Simon, were prepared to accept tariff reform, and these gradually became nothing more than Conservatives under another name. Thirty-three, led by Sir Herbert Samuel, maintained the Liberal principle of Free Trade and therefore ceased to support the government in 1932 as a result of the Ottawa agreements (p. 212).

This group declined to seventeen in the 1935 election, and as Sir Herbert Samuel lost his seat it was afterwards led by Sir Archibald Sinclair. The Lloyd George family party of four survived, but it was still separate from the rest of the party. The Simon Liberals, sitting on the government benches, won thirty-three seats.

The second World War

The war tended to bring all parties together. At the outbreak of war Sir John Simon was already Chancellor of the Exchequer. In the coalition formed by Churchill in May 1940 he became Lord Chancellor and Sir Archibald Sinclair became Air Minister. Even Lloyd George was offered a place in the cabinet, though, aged seventy-seven by now, he refused.

Labour takes over

But the end of the war marks the final stage of the Labour victory over the Liberals. Throughout the twenties and thirties the Liberals were losing votes to the Labour Party. In December 1910, in the last general election before the first World War, they had won 272 seats while Labour had won only 42. But the election of November 1922, which resulted from the ending of the coalition, produced a very different situation. The disunited Liberals only mustered 118 seats while the Labour Party had 142. And in May 1929 the pre-war situation was reversed, for the Labour Party then gained 228 seats but had to rely on the support of 59 Liberals to keep it in office.

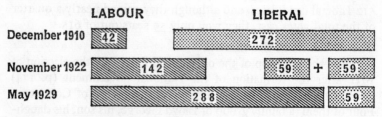

In 1945, when the Labour Party won 394 seats and found itself in as strong a position in the House of Commons as the Liberals in 1906, only twelve genuine Liberals were returned. In 1950 there were only nine, and in subsequent elections they seldom won more than six seats.

Asquith's coalition government

THE LIBERAL GOVERNMENT led by Asquith which took Britain into war in 1914 lasted until May 1915, when it was strongly criticised for a shell shortage on the Western front, and Lord Fisher, the First Sea Lord, resigned because he disagreed with the Dardanelles policy (pp. 166–7) of Winston Churchill, the First Lord of the Admiralty.

Asquith gave way to Conservative pressure to form a coalition. He met the complaints of shell shortage by creating a Ministry of Munitions and moving Lloyd George to it from the Exchequer, he met the Conservatives' objections to Winston Churchill by replacing him at the Admiralty with Balfour, the former Conservative Prime Minister, and he also encouraged the full co-operation of the working class in the war effort by bringing Arthur Henderson, the Labour Party chairman, into the cabinet.

During 1916 the government introduced conscription, and on the death of Lord Kitchener in the summer the far more vigorous Lloyd George took over as Secretary for War.

Lloyd George's war-time coalition

Before the end of the year Lloyd George was Prime Minister. Discontent with Asquith's leadership had grown so great, particularly among the Conservatives, that in December he resigned and Lloyd George, whom the Conservatives were prepared to support, formed a new government.

He believed that three main tasks needed to be accomplished:
(1) The enemy submarine menace had to be defeated.
(2) Unity of command had to be secured on the Western front.
(3) Vigour had to be given to the direction of the war effort.

The submarine menace: The threat to Britain's food supplies from enemy submarine warfare increased rapidly shortly after Lloyd George became Prime Minister, for in February 1917 the Germans adopted a policy of 'unrestricted' submarine warfare. Lloyd George believed merchant ships could be more easily defended if they travelled in convoy, but the Admiralty argued that a convoy was too large a target and would waste time. By April the situation was desperate (p. 169). Sir John Jellicoe, the First Sea Lord, was still opposed to convoys but he had nothing new to suggest. So at the end of the month Lloyd George himself took the responsibility of insisting on the adoption of the convoy system, and this tided Britain over the worst weeks of the crisis.

The Western front: On land as well as at sea Lloyd George came into conflict with the service chiefs, for he distrusted the whole military strategy of his own side. Like Churchill he was at heart an 'Easterner'. He wanted to turn Germany's flank by an attack in the East, and consequently he was at loggerheads with Sir Douglas Haig, the British commander on the Western front.

Ideally he should either have insisted on Haig's dismissal or else have supported him. He did neither and instead made Haig's job more difficult. In February 1917 he tried unsuccessfully to have Haig made subordinate to the French General Nivelle. Then in November he managed to have an Inter-Allied Supreme War Council established, and through this tried to limit Haig. And it is probable that in the winter of 1917–18 he tried to prevent Haig from launching an offensive by starving him of sufficient troops.

In March 1918, when a massive German offensive was launched, this issue came to a head, and Haig was induced to accept a subordinate position to Foch. But this was not the end of the matter, for General Sir Frederick Maurice in a letter to the *Morning Post* accused Lloyd George of starving the front of troops, and in May Lloyd George had to face an attack in the Commons from Asquith on this issue.

The direction of the war effort: The third task of giving greater unity and vigour to the nation's war effort was a very important aspect of Lloyd George's work as leader of the war-time coalition. As soon as he became Prime Minister he appointed a small War Cabinet of five members: himself, Bonar Law, Lord Curzon, Lord Milner, and Arthur Henderson. He also instituted a Cabinet Secretariat to record their discussions and decisions.

He brought men with administrative and business experience into the government, and when new ministries were created in 1917 with responsibility for such matters as the control of shipping, food supply, and labour relations, it was men with expert knowledge rather than politicians who were placed at their heads.

In order to bring greater efficiency to the mines, the railways, and other forms of transport they were brought under state control, and early in 1918 rationing was introduced.

The government was so successful in encouraging people to lend it their money that the National Debt, i.e. the total sum the government had borrowed from the people, increased during the war more than ten-fold to over £7,000,000,000. But private subscriptions alone could not possibly solve the financial difficulties of

the government in a modern war any more than voluntary recruitment could solve the army's need for manpower. So income tax
rose from 9d. in the pound before the war to 6s. in the pound at the
end, and the maximum rate for death duties rose from 8 to 40 per
cent. Increased revenue was also derived from very heavy taxes
on drink, and these, together with a reduction of licensing hours,
also helped to produce a more efficient use of manpower.

War-time reconstruction: By 1918 the goverment was also looking to the future. In that year a Ministry of Reconstruction was
formed and two major Bills were passed. The Representation of
the People Act gave the vote to women over thirty. The Fisher
Education Act raised the school leaving age to fourteen, forbade
the employment of children under twelve, extended the number
of free places in grammar schools, provided continuation classes
up to the age of eighteen for those who left school at fourteen, and
raised teachers' salaries.

The continuation of the coalition

When the war was eventually won in November 1918 Lloyd
George wished to remain in office to make Britain 'a fit country
for heroes to live in'. His personal prestige was so great that the
Conservative Party was willing to continue the coalition under his
leadership; and in the 'Coupon election' (p. 172) of December
1918 the coalition won a comfortable majority which enabled him to
remain as Prime Minister for nearly four more years.

The domestic policy of the post-war coalition

Lloyd George kept to his war-time practice of ruling through
a group of leading ministers, and he also kept the Cabinet Secretariat and several of the new ministries started during the war.

Two of the most important measures of post-war reconstruction
were the Housing and Town Planning Act of 1919 and the Unemployment Insurance Act of 1920. The first provided local authorities with financial assistance to enable them to build and rent out
what came to be called 'council houses'. The second extended
the national unemployment insurance scheme of 1911 (pp. 61–2)
to cover nearly all wage-earners.

But the post-war conditions and the political pressures which
accompanied them destroyed the government's chances of coping
successfully with domestic problems. The temporary prosperity
of the post-war boom was accompanied by a vigorous demand
from businessmen that the government should abandon the special
powers over industry which it had acquired during the war. Then

the slump which inevitably followed the boom was accompanied in 1921 by a demand for economies in government expenditure. The abandonment of controls wrecked the government's plans for the reconstruction of society after the war. The economies destroyed much of what it salvaged from the wreck.

Destruction of state controls: Rationing had come to an end in 1920, and by the end of the year the government had discarded most of its special war-time powers, though it retained control of the mines and railways. In 1919 the miners had demanded and a Royal Commission had recommended the nationalisation of the mines, but the government rejected the recommendation and in March 1921 handed the mines back to private ownership. In August the railways were also returned to private ownership, but here some progress was made, for whereas there had been a hundred and twenty different companies before the war all railways were now grouped into four large companies.

The 'Geddes axe': It was also in 1921 that the demand for economy developed. Inevitably the reforming measures introduced by the government were expensive. The education estimates, for example, which had been £19 million in 1918, were £43 million in 1920; and in 1921, when the slump put two million men out of work, the government was spending far more on unemployment benefit than it had ever received in insurance contributions.

So in August a committee under Sir Eric Geddes was appointed to make recommendations for cutting government expenditure 'with an axe'. It reported in February 1922, recommending drastic cuts in expenditure on the armed forces and on social services, such as education, public health, and the police. So several of the government's projected reforms were abandoned. The Fisher Education Act, for example, was in effect discarded, and the subsidies for building 'council houses', which had already been restricted in 1921, were stopped. As a result of the economies it was made possible to reduce income tax from 6s. to 5s. in the pound.

The unpopularity of the coalition

By the summer of 1922 opposition to the coalition government was building up.

Domestic policy: The government had become unpopular partly because of its extensive controls, and it became more unpopular when, by abandoning controls, it let loose chaos in the field of industrial relations. It had also become unpopular because heavy expenditure had resulted in high taxation, and it acquired further unpopularity as a result of the 'Geddes axe'.

Imperial policy: Meanwhile the goverment's Imperial policy gave offence both to those who regarded any grant of self-government to a subject people as a betrayal of the Empire and also to those who disliked repression. The Government of India Act of 1919 (p. 332) seemed to some a surrender, while the Amritsar massacre of the same year (p. 332) aroused dislike of Imperialism in others. Liberal opinion was also horrified by the atrocities committed by the Black-and-Tans in Ireland (pp. 67–8), while traditional Unionist feeling was opposed both to the Government of Ireland Act of 1920 and to the Irish Treaty of December 1921 (p. 68). The suppression of a revolt in Egypt in 1919, followed by the granting of independence in 1922, similarly had the effect of giving offence at home in two directions; and no one could be satisfied with the tangle in the Arab lands resulting from the conflicting promises made during the war (p. 345).

Foreign policy: Contradictions in the government's foreign policy also caused discontent. In 1918 Lloyd George had advocated imposing harsh terms on Germany, and had given the counter-revolutionary forces in Russia help against the Bolsheviks. But in 1919 he exercised a moderating influence on the demands made on Germany in the Treaty of Versailles, and began withdrawing the British forces from Russia. In the following years he increasingly tried to bring Germany and Russia back into friendly co-operation with the other European powers. But this policy was thoroughly unsuccessful, for it not only failed in its main object but also had the effect of estranging France from Britain.

The end of the coalition

Despite its failings the coalition government had good prospects for winning a general election in the autumn of 1922, partly because of the weakness of the opposition parties, which alone would probably have been enough to ensure an electoral victory for the coalition, and partly because of the developing Chanak crisis (p. 309), which might have enabled Lloyd George to rally the country behind him again. But in the event he never had the opportunity to fight another election at the head of the coalition, for the discontent in the country was reflected in many Conservative M.P.s, and the Chanak crisis brought it to a head.

In October a hitherto insignificant minister, Stanley Baldwin, persuaded the Conservative Party to leave the coalition, and in doing so he smashed not only the coalition but also the ministerial career of Lloyd George.

Socialism and social reform

THE British Labour Party was born from the marriage of Socialism with social reform.

Socialism is a belief that the means by which goods are produced, such as machines, distributed, such as railways, and exchanged, such as shops, should be owned by the whole nation (hence 'nationalisation') and should be used for the benefit of society as a whole (hence 'Socialism'). The first Socialist society in Britain was the Social Democratic Federation, or S.D.F., which was founded in 1881 by an Old Etonian stockbroker, H. M. Hyndman, with the object of establishing Socialism by revolutionary means; and in 1884 Sidney and Beatrice Webb formed the Fabian Society, which aimed not at revolution but at gradual evolution towards Socialism. Both of these societies were primarily middle-class organisations, and it was not until 1893 that Keir Hardie, a Scottish ex-miner who in the previous year had been the first working-class man to enter parliament without Liberal support, formed the Independent Labour Party, or I.L.P.—the first Socialist organisation in England whose membership was primarily working class.

Social reform was a far longer established movement in England. It was advocated in parliament by both Tory Democrats and Liberal Radicals, and at the same time the trade unions were much concerned with its promotion. Very few trade union leaders were Socialists. They were interested in practical piecemeal reform rather than in political or economic theories, and they believed that they could do more to improve conditions of life for the working class by influencing the two traditional parties than by attempting to form a new party. Thus in 1892, the year Keir Hardie entered parliament, fourteen trade union leaders were elected as Liberals.

The swing in trade union opinion

There could be no future for a separate Labour Party unless the trade unions, with their vast membership and financial resources, could be seduced away from the Liberal Party. As it happens the alliance between the Liberals and the trade unions was weakening during the last fifteen years of the nineteenth century. In 1886 Joseph Chamberlain, the leading advocate of social reform in the Liberal Party, had left the party over the Irish issue (p. 186); and in the following years Gladstone, who remained the Liberal leader until 1894, was more concerned with Irish Home Rule than with social reform, and Lord Rosebery, who followed him, was more concerned with Imperialism. Moreover, local Liberal associations would only adopt working-class men as parliamentary candidates in areas where a trade union was strong enough to dictate terms.

Meanwhile the I.L.P. was working hard to persuade the unions that it was desirable to have a Labour Party in parliament, and by the end of the century the time was ripe for the Socialist movement and the trade unionists who wanted social reform to join hands.

The L.R.C.

In 1900 delegates from the S.D.F., the Fabian Society, the I.L.P., and most of the trade unions, though not the important miners' union, attended a meeting in London. Keir Hardie's proposal that there should be 'a distinct Labour group in Parliament, who should have their own Whips and agree upon their own policy', was carried; so the Labour Representation Committee was formed, with an I.L.P. delegate, James Ramsay MacDonald, as its secretary.

The L.R.C. had no political programme of its own, its financial resources were small, and in the Khaki election (p. 40) eight months after its formation it was only able to spend £33 on the election campaign and only two L.R.C. candidates were elected. But during 1902 and 1903, largely as the result of the indignation aroused among the working class by the Taff Vale Case (p. 182), three by-elections were won by L.R.C. men, and in the general election of 1906 twenty-nine L.R.C. candidates were elected.

Moreover, sixteen miners' union officials were elected in 1906 with Liberal support, and another eight of the members elected had stood as Liberal–Labour candidates. At first it was far from clear whether the miners and Lib–Labs regarded themselves more as Liberal or Labour members; but in 1909 the Osborne Judgment (p. 182), which cut off the salaries paid by the miners' union to their M.P.s, had the effect of bringing them, the Lib–Labs, and the L.R.C. men together in what now became known as the Parliamentary Labour Party.

The Labour Party before the first World War

The Osborne Judgment also had the effect of making it financially difficult for the Labour Party to fight the elections of 1910, and the issues over which the elections were fought (p. 72) left the Labour Party outside the main body of the conflict, but it nevertheless emerged from them with 42 seats in the House of Commons.

Up till this time the parliamentary party had been very loosely held together. The chairmanship changed hands regularly—from Keir Hardie (1906–8) to Arthur Henderson (1908–10) to George Barnes (1910–11), and it was only when Ramsay MacDonald took over in 1911 that the chairmanship became in any sense permanent. When he became chairman MacDonald gave up the post of secretary to Arthur Henderson, and for the next twenty years he and Henderson dominated the party. Although they represented the two different elements in the party they worked very well together. MacDonald, a member of the Socialist I.L.P. and an exceptionally able parliamentarian, led the parliamentary party effectively, while Henderson, a trade unionist, had greater influence in the constituencies.

Labour and the first World War

The first World War made the first breach in the co-operation between them. MacDonald, in common with most of the I.L.P. and some European Socialists, was opposed to going to war. But the majority of the parliamentary party supported the government's decision to fight, so MacDonald resigned the chairmanship and Henderson took over.

In May 1915, when Asquith formed a coalition, Henderson entered the cabinet, and in December 1916, when Lloyd George became Prime Minister, he became one of the five members of the War Cabinet. But in the summer of 1917, after a disagreement with his cabinet colleagues which arose out of his belief in the possibility of a negotiated peace, he resigned. The Labour Party continued to support the coalition, but Henderson was replaced in the War Cabinet by George Barnes.

1918—a turning-point

The last year of the war was important in the development of the party in three ways:

(1) Henderson now had time to revise the structure of the party, and by building up a far more powerful organisation in the constituencies he enabled the party to put up 361 candidates in the Coupon Election of 1918 (p. 172)—more than six times as many as in 1910.

(2) A new Socialist constitution, with a fourth clause demanding 'common ownership of the means of production, distribution, and exchange', was drawn up by Sidney Webb and adopted; and Sidney Webb also drafted a new policy statement which called not only for nationalisation of industry but also for maintenance

of full employment, heavy taxation of high incomes to help pay both for the war and for social services, and an expansion of educational and cultural facilities for the mass of the people.

(3) The split in the party which had been caused by the outbreak of war was healed.

The post-war party

Unfortunately another split resulted from the Labour Party's decision to withdraw from the coalition at the end of the war, for George Barnes and some of the other Labour members in office decided to continue to serve under Lloyd George, and they were therefore expelled from the party.

Then the widespread success of the coalition candidates in the Coupon Election had the effect that the Labour Party only won 63 seats and that neither Henderson nor MacDonald was returned to parliament. But even so the Labour Party was now the largest opposition group in the Commons, and four years later, in the election of 1922, it won 142 seats.

Responsibility without power

Shortly after the 1922 election Ramsay MacDonald was re-elected chairman of the parliamentary party with the support of many of the extremists of the I.L.P. His position was strengthened by the fact that he was officially recognised as Leader of the Opposition and by the loyal support which Henderson and the trade union wing of the party gave him once he was elected; and it is from this time that the chairman of the parliamentary party was also known as the leader of the party.

Little more than a year later, and less than a quarter of a century after the formation of the L.R.C., MacDonald was Prime Minister. He took office in January 1924 (p. 201), but the Labour government lacked real power, for it had to rely on the Liberals for support, and when that support was withdrawn ten months later it fell.

After another five years in opposition the Labour Party at last became the largest party in the Commons and MacDonald formed his second government (p. 203). But the party had again failed to win an overall majority, and thus the government again depended on the Liberals for survival and had responsibility without real power. This time the Labour government lasted over two years in increasingly difficult circumstances, and came to an end when the cabinet was unable to agree on how to deal with the financial crisis of 1931 (p. 205).

Collapse and revival

The outcome of the 1931 crisis was a disastrous split in the party. The I.L.P. men who had engineered MacDonald's election to the leadership were already disillusioned with him, for his domestic policies had been conservative and unimaginative. Now they indeed tasted gall, for on 24th August MacDonald formed a new 'National' government with the support of the Conservatives and Liberals but very few of his own party. On the 28th Arthur Henderson was elected leader of the parliamentary party, and exactly a month later MacDonald and those who followed him into the National government were expelled from the Labour Party.

The general election of October inevitably brought a heavy defeat. Only forty-seven Labour members were returned to parliament, and only one ex-cabinet minister, George Lansbury, retained his seat. The I.L.P., which had become an increasingly extremist group, fought the election separately. Only five of its members won seats, and since these five were unwilling to commit themselves to voting with the rest of the Labour Party the I.L.P. was disaffiliated in 1932 and rapidly declined into insignificance.

Meanwhile Lansbury led the parliamentary party, but he was a pacifist and increasingly out of sympathy with the mass of the party over foreign policy. The Abyssinian crisis of 1935 (p. 230) brought this to a head and he resigned, with the result that the Labour Party was led in the election of 1935 by Clement Attlee.

By this time there had been some recovery in the party's fortunes from the disaster of 1931. Earlier in the year the Labour Party had gained control of the London County Council, and in the general election the number of Labour M.P.s was more than trebled.

1935–1945

But the 154 Labour members were still a small minority, and the postponement of the next general election as the result of the outbreak of war in 1939 meant that they remained a small minority until 1945. But their support in the country was increasing, and Churchill recognised this in May 1940 when he formed his wartime coalition by giving them a large share of the government posts.

By 1945 many of the Labour Party's leaders had valuable experience in office, and when Labour won a large overall majority in the general election of 1945 Clement Attlee, who had already proved a very able Deputy Prime Minister during the war, was able to form the first Labour government which had not merely responsibility for governing the country but also the reality of power.

41   LABOUR IN OFFICE

BETWEEN the two World Wars two Labour governments accepted the responsibility of governing Great Britain, although neither of them had a majority in the House of Commons. They were in office but not in power, and they could only remain in office if they kept Liberal support. Both of them fell long before completing a full term—the first when Liberal support was withdrawn, and the second as the result of a division of opinion in the cabinet.

The establishment of the first Labour government

In December 1923 191 Labour members and 159 Liberals were elected to parliament in a general election in which both their parties had defended Britain's traditional policy of Free Trade against the proposal of Baldwin's Conservative government to introduce Protection. As soon as Parliament assembled in January 1924 they combined to defeat the government, which now only had 258 supporters in the Commons. Baldwin resigned, and Ramsay

Election of December 1923	LABOUR 191	LIBERALS 159
	CONSERVATIVES 258	

MacDonald took office at the head of the first Labour government, with a promise from Asquith of Liberal support.

Domestic policy of the first Labour government

The domestic achievements of this government during its short ten months tenure of office were few. The most constructive achievement was a Housing Act which produced a great increase in the building of 'council houses' by increasing the government subsidies which had first been provided under the Act of 1919 (p. 193). But the government proved incapable of dealing with the problem of unemployment which overshadowed all other domestic issues. The only solution it could think of involved nationalisation of basic industries, and this was impossible for a government which depended on Liberal support. So the government merely raised unemployment benefit, thus making life more tolerable for those out of work, but it did nothing to reduce the extent of unemployment.

Foreign policy of the first Labour government

The government's foreign policy was more successful. Mac-Donald, who acted as Foreign Secretary as well as Prime Minister, tried to co-operate with the League of Nations, and although he rejected the Draft Treaty of Mutual Assistance (p. 234) on the grounds that it committed Britain to too much he encouraged the drawing up of the Geneva Protocol (p. 235).

He also tried to establish more friendly relations with the other European powers and was particularly successful in his dealings with France, with whom Britain's relations had been strained ever since the occupation of the Ruhr in January 1923 (p. 233). The improvement in Anglo-French relations which MacDonald managed to bring about enabled the Dawes Plan (p. 233) to be negotiated and accepted at a conference in London and also helped to produce the French agreement to evacuate the Ruhr within a year. These developments, which also brought about an improvement in relations with Germany, helped to create the period of calm in international affairs which lasted until the thirties.

Of less significance in relation to international affairs but of more significance in British domestic history was the improvement which took place at the same time in Britain's relations with the U.S.S.R. In February Britain officially recognised the Soviet government and invited it to send representatives to a conference in London. Early in August agreement was reached on both a trade treaty and a more general treaty, and a future loan to the Soviet government was proposed. But since both the Liberals and the Conservatives were opposed to this, it seemed likely that the Labour government would be defeated when the treaties came before parliament for ratification.

The fall of the first Labour government

In practice the government was defeated both in the Commons and in a general election before the Russian treaties came up for ratification. This arose out of a comparatively trivial incident. At the end of July a Communist journalist, J. R. Campbell, had written and published an article urging soldiers to refuse to fire on their fellow-workers. He had been arrested and charged with incitement to mutiny, but in the middle of August the proposed prosecution was withdrawn. Conservative and Liberal M.P.s criticised the government, implying that it was interfering with the course of Justice for political motives, and as soon as parliament reassembled at the end of September after the summer recess this question was raised in the House of Commons. A Liberal demand for a committee of inquiry was refused by the government but supported by the Conservatives, and as a result the government was defeated.

MacDonald decided to ask for a dissolution of parliament rather than resign, so three weeks later, on 29th October, there was a general election. Five days before the election another incident occurred which brought to the forefront of people's minds the question of the Labour government's relations with the U.S.S.R. The Foreign Office released to the press a copy of a letter said to be from Zinoviev, the President of the Comintern (p. 128), to the leaders of the British Communist Party giving them instructions for preparing for revolution. Zinoviev denied having sent the letter, and its authenticity was never established, but it was generally accepted at the time and helped to turn the electorate against the Labour government, which had placed so much importance on establishing friendly relations with Soviet Russia.

Thus the Russian trade treaties, the Campbell case, and the Zinoviev letter all to some extent associated the Labour Party in the public mind with revolutionary Communism. But this was not the main reason why the Labour Party lost the election. More important were the facts that the Conservatives had abandoned the unpopular policy of Protection, that Conservatives and Liberals avoided standing against each other in many constituencies, and that many people who had voted Liberal in 1923, but objected to Liberal support for the Labour government, now voted Conservative. Consequently the strength of the Labour Party in the Commons was decreased by 40, despite a gain of an extra half million votes, while the Conservatives won an extra two million votes and swept into power with an overall majority of 215.

The establishment of the second Labour government

Five years later there was a heavy swing of the political pendulum away from the Conservatives. In the general election of May 1929 the Labour Party won 288 seats, thus nearly doubling its number of seats and becoming for the first time the largest party in the

Election of May 1929	LABOUR 288		
	CONSERVATIVES 260		LIBS.59

Commons. But it still lacked an overall majority, and although MacDonald immediately took office when Baldwin resigned, his government once again had to rely on Liberal support.

Foreign and Imperial Policy, 1929-31

Again the Labour government appeared to be at its best when dealing with external affairs. This time Arthur Henderson, who had been Home Secretary in 1924, became Foreign Secretary. Diplomatic relations with the U.S.S.R., which had been broken off by the Conservatives in 1927, were promptly resumed, and a trade treaty was negotiated. Henderson then concentrated on trying to improve relations among the European powers by working through the League of Nations. As a result the occupying troops were withdrawn from the Rhineland in 1930, five years earlier than had been stipulated in the Treaty of Versailles, Britain accepted the principle of compulsory arbitration in international disputes, and in 1930 the Preparatory Commission began preparing the ground for the Disarmament Conference, which eventually met in 1932 under Henderson's chairmanship when he was no longer a member of the British government.

Meanwhile MacDonald, who had kept in his own hands matters concerning Anglo-American relations, managed to reach agreement with the U.S.A. and Japan on a further limitation of naval building. He also arranged for and presided over a Round Table Conference on the future of India in the winter of 1930-1, and although it came to an end in January 1931 arrangements were made for a second conference which eventually met in September 1931 when the Labour government was no longer in office.

Domestic policy of the second Labour government

The government was less successful in its domestic policy. It was hampered by having to rely on Liberal support in the House of Commons, and for lack of that support was unable to repeal even the most objectionable aspects of the Trade Union and Trade Disputes Act of 1927 (p. 184). It was also hampered by the continued Conservative domination of the House of Lords, by means of which an Education Bill which was intended to raise the school-leaving age to fifteen was frustrated.

The most useful measures passed were the 1930 Housing Act, which provided grants for slum clearance, and the Agricultural Marketing Act of 1931, which protected the interests of farmers by enabling marketing boards to fix prices. But the only Bill which was in any sense Socialist was Herbert Morrison's measure for establishing a public corporation with a monopoly of public transport in London. Ironically this measure was eventually passed in 1933 by the Conservative-dominated National government because it was a good practical solution to London's transport problem.

Another sphere in which nationalisation was even more necessary was the coal industry. But the government attempted to deal with the industry's problems with half-measures, and the Coal Mines Act of 1930 had little effect other than to fix the maximum length of a miner's working day at $7\frac{1}{2}$ hours.

The unemployment problem

The greatest problem the government had to face was that of persistent and rising unemployment. When it took office there were already well over a million unemployed. It promptly increased unemployment allowances again and made the payments from the Exchequer instead of from the Unemployment Insurance Fund, which was already heavily in debt. But this was no solution to the problem, and by the time the government fell just over two years later the number of unemployed had risen to over three millions. Meanwhile the only minister to produce a comprehensive scheme for attacking unemployment was Sir Oswald Moseley—an ex-Conservative who was now Chancellor of the Duchy of Lancaster and was already regarded by some as a possible future Labour Prime Minister. But his scheme seemed too revolutionary to most of his colleagues. It was rejected both by the cabinet and by the annual conference of the party, and as a result he resigned and formed the New Party.

The collapse of the second Labour government

Meanwhile the government plunged deeper and deeper into economic difficulties and by 1931 was spending £120 million a year more than its income. It became urgently necessary to raise a loan from the New York bankers, who would only make a loan if the British government would balance its budget—i.e. ensure that its expenditure was no more than its income. Since one of the main items of expenditure at the time was unemployment benefit some members of the government, including MacDonald and Philip Snowden, the Chancellor of the Exchequer, insisted that it was necessary to cut unemployment benefit. Others, such as Henderson, wished to raise the necessary money by a tax on imports, but, as MacDonald and Snowden pointed out, the Liberals would not agree to this solution of the problem. The cabinet reached deadlock.

For two years it had been trying to make the capitalist system work, while at the same time proclaiming that Capitalism could not work and must be replaced by Socialism. Now that the whole capitalist system of the world was breaking down its members found themselves arguing not about how to replace Capitalism with Socialism but about how best to prevent the capitalist system from breaking down completely. They could not agree on how to do this and therefore resigned—according to Moseley, their ex-colleague, like 'a Salvation Army which took to its heels on the Day of Judgment'.

THE CONSERVATIVE PARTY, which had been in power for most of the twenty years up to 1905, dominated the House of Commons again for most of the thirty years from 1915 to 1945. But for two-thirds of that period it dominated it as part of a coalition, and there were less than six years of exclusively Conservative rule.

In opposition, 1905–15

The leader of the Conservatives, when in opposition during the period of Liberal rule before the first World War, was at first A. J. Balfour, who had been Prime Minister from 1902 to 1905. His position as leader of the party had already been weakened when he was Prime Minister by his vacillation over the Protection issue (pp. 52–3), and his prestige suffered further from the disastrous result for the Conservatives of the election of January 1906. In opposition he led the party headlong into a constitutional conflict by using the House of Lords to wreck Liberal bills, and consequently he lost two more elections in January and December 1910. When the constitutional conflict ended in defeat for the Conservatives with the passage of the Parliament Bill in 1911 (p. 73) discontent with his leadership, expressed in the slogan 'B.M.G.' (Balfour Must Go), grew so great that he was driven to resign, and he was succeeded as leader by Andrew Bonar Law.

In coalition, 1915–22

In May 1915, when Asquith formed a coalition government (p. 191), Bonar Law became Colonial Secretary and Balfour First Lord of the Admiralty; and in December 1916, when Lloyd George became Prime Minister, Bonar Law entered the small War Cabinet and became Lloyd George's right-hand man.

At the end of the war the Conservatives agreed to continue the coalition, and for a while it looked as if all the supporters of the coalition would merge into one party. But after 1921, when ill-health caused Bonar Law to resign, discontent with the coalition among Conservative M.P.s increased, even though their new leader, Austen Chamberlain, was just as loyal to Lloyd George as Bonar Law had always been. This discontent was brought to a head in October 1922, when the President of the Board of Trade, Stanley Baldwin, made a speech at a meeting of Conservative M.P.s at the Carlton Club, in which he argued that the Liberal Party had already been 'smashed to pieces' by Lloyd George, who was now likely to do the same to the Conservative Party.

Austen Chamberlain spoke in favour of continuing the coalition, but the issue was settled when Bonar Law, who had for so long held the coalition together, gave his opinion against it. By a majority of a hundred it was decided that the Conservative Party would fight the next election under their own leaders and with their own policies. Lloyd George resigned the premiership the same day, and Austen Chamberlain, who had lost his chance of the premiership because of his loyalty to Lloyd George, resigned the leadership of the Conservative Party. Bonar Law resumed the leadership, formed a Conservative government, and fought and won a general election (p. 173).

Lord Curzon and Baldwin

The most eminent man in Bonar Law's cabinet was the Foreign Secretary, Lord Curzon, and since the other leading coalition Conservatives, such as Austen Chamberlain, did not take office, the Chancellorship of the Exchequer went to the almost unknown Stanley Baldwin. When ill-health caused Bonar Law to resign in May 1923 the choice of his successor was between these two. The dislike for Curzon felt by some of the Conservative leaders, together with the argument that the Premier needed to be in the Commons now that the Labour Party was the official opposition, resulted in Baldwin becoming Prime Minister.

He only retained the premiership for eight months, for in December 1923 he decided to fight another election on the issue of Protection. He had come to the conclusion that the solution to unemployment was the imposition of tariff barriers to protect home producers from foreign competitors, for if British goods could be sold cheaper than foreign goods there would be more work for British workmen. But the electorate was not yet ready for Protection. Even though the Free Trade vote was divided between the Labour and Liberal Parties (p. 201), with the result that the Conservatives remained the largest party in the Commons, there had been an overwhelming vote against Protection, and as soon as Parliament reassembled the Liberal and Labour Parties combined to defeat the government and Baldwin resigned.

Conservative achievements, 1922–3

Little had been achieved during the year of Conservative rule under Bonar Law and Baldwin. Baldwin, while Chancellor of the Exchequer, had negotiated somewhat unfavourable terms with the U.S.A. for repaying Britain's war debt (p. 282). And Neville Chamberlain, as Minister of Health, had arranged for subsidies to encourage an increase in the building of smaller types of houses.

Only in foreign affairs did the government's policy achieve distinction. The Chanak crisis (p. 309) had made clear the need for a new treaty with Turkey to replace the shattered Treaty of Sèvres (p. 219); and in the winter of 1922–3 Lord Curzon presided over the Lausanne Conference (p. 309) in a way that helped to restore Anglo-Turkish friendship as well as British prestige in Europe. He was unable to prevent the French occupation of the Ruhr in January 1923 (p. 233), but he did manage to frustrate a French attempt to build an independent buffer-state on the Rhine, and his demand for a realistic approach to reparations resulted in the setting up of the Dawes Committee in November 1923 (p. 233).

The new Conservatism

Although Protection lost the Conservatives the election in December 1923, it reunited the party, for the coalition Conservatives, such as Austen Chamberlain, whose father had begun the attack on Free Trade at the beginning of the century (p. 52), joined in the campaign for Protection.

When the Conservatives returned to power in November 1924, after the fall of the first Labour government, Baldwin brought Austen Chamberlain into the government as Foreign Secretary instead of Curzon, and Winston Churchill, who had been a Liberal less than a year before, became Chancellor of the Exchequer.

This government was the only Conservative ministry in a half century dominated by the Conservatives to live out its full span, and it marks a stage in the development of Conservatism from what it stood for in 1900 to what it stood for in 1950. No longer was the leadership of the party primarily aristocratic. Balfour had been replaced in 1911 by Bonar Law, an iron merchant, and Bonar Law was succeeded in 1923 not by the aristocratic Lord Curzon but by Stanley Baldwin, who was also in the iron industry. This change in leadership was accompanied by new attitudes.

The work of Baldwin's second ministry, 1924–9

Social Reform: The Conservatives now claimed to be a progressive party. They therefore introduced measures of social reform which one might have expected from a Liberal government: (1) The Pensions Act of 1925 reduced the age for receiving an old age pension, which was now ten shillings a week, from seventy to sixty-five.

(2) The Unemployment Insurance Act of 1927 provided that the weekly benefits paid to men out of work should continue until a

man was able to find another job, although it also reduced the amount of the benefits.

(3) The Equal Franchise Act of 1928 extended the right to vote to all women over twenty-one.

(4) The Local Government Act of 1929 extended the powers of county and county borough councils. At the same time an attempt was being made to stimulate agriculture and industry by exempting agricultural land from the payment of rates and by exempting industry from three-quarters of its rates. The local authorities were compensated for this loss of revenue by 'block grants' from the Treasury.

Private enterprise or state control? The Conservative Party was certainly becoming less conservative in its attitude. Increasingly its leaders thought of themselves as men uncommitted to any political doctrine, and they offered practical policies based on experience as an alternative to the doctrine of Socialism. They did have in common a belief in private enterprise as opposed to state intervention, but even this was thrown overboard when they decided that a measure of state control was the best practical solution to a problem. Thus they introduced some measures which might well have come from a Labour government:

(1) In 1926 an Electricity Act nationalised electricity supply and avoided the chaos to which private enterprise was leading by establishing a Central Electricity Board responsible for the generating and wholesale distribution of electricity.

(2) In the same year a royal charter transformed the British Broadcasting Company, which had been formed in 1922, into a public corporation financed by the revenue from wireless licences, and with a monopoly of broadcasting.

Foreign Policy: The sphere in which the government's policy at first seemed most different from that of the preceding Labour government was foreign affairs. A fortnight after taking office Austen Chamberlain informed the Russians that Britain would not ratify the Anglo-Russian treaties negotiated by the Labour government; and in March 1925 he rejected the Geneva Protocol (p. 221). But in its fundamentals Austen Chamberlain's policy was in the same tradition as Macdonald's—seeking reconciliation with Germany, security through the League, and friendship among the European nations. In October 1925 he joined with Stresemann of Germany, Briand of France, and Mussolini of Italy in negotiating the Locarno Treaty (p. 235) and agreed to support Germany's entry into the League of Nations in 1926; and in 1928 he signed the Kellogg–Briand Pact for the renunciation of war (pp. 235–6).

Imperial Policy: The Imperial Conference of 1926 marked an important stage in the development of the Commonwealth, for in response to pressure from Canada, South Africa, and the Irish Free State, Balfour, now in the House of Lords and still in the cabinet as Lord President of the Council forty years after first entering it, drew up the declaration that all self-governing dominions were 'equal in status' (p. 56). And in the following year a British Parliamentary Commission was sent to India to report on how far India was fit to govern herself.

Financial Policy: Perhaps the most unsatisfactory aspect of the work of the government was the decision by Winston Churchill in 1925 that Britain should go back on the gold standard. This had the effect of making British exports more expensive (p. 178), and thus increased economic difficulties and industrial unrest.

The General Strike, 1926: The industrial unrest of the twenties, which the government's financial policy had helped to provoke, culminated in the General Strike of May 1926. As the dispute between the mine-owners and the miners flared up the government did what it could to prevent a strike and meanwhile made preparations for dealing with it if it could not be averted. When it eventually happened the government was ready and the strike was broken in nine days. The next year the government followed up its victory by passing the Trade Union and Trade Disputes Act (p. 184), heavily curtailing the powers of trade unions.

1929–45

Discontent with the government's record from 1924 to 1929, and in particular with its failure to solve the problem of unemployment, resulted in its defeat in the 1929 election. Baldwin continued to lead the party for another eight years: two in opposition, four as Deputy Prime Minister in the National Government, and two as its Prime Minister. He was succeeded in 1937 by Neville Chamberlain, who was followed by Winston Churchill in 1940.

Thus at the end of the second World War the Conservatives were led by the some-time Liberal social reformer, Winston Churchill, who had been out of office during the thirties at first because he disapproved of the policy of eventually giving self-government to India and then because he attacked the government's defence and foreign policies. In 1945 he was a national hero, and was the Conservatives' greatest, though insufficient, electoral asset.

43 THE NATIONAL GOVERNMENT, 1931–1940

THE NATIONAL GOVERNMENT, which was formed as a temporary expedient in August 1931 to deal with the financial crisis (p. 205), lasted nearly nine years until May 1940. During those years the country slowly recovered from the depression and at the same time drifted towards war.

The financial crisis

The first and most pressing problem facing it was the financial crisis which had brought it to power. On 10th September 1931 Snowden, who had retained the office of Chancellor of the Exchequer which he had held in the preceding Labour administration, introduced new budget proposals. These consisted primarily of the economies and taxes needed for balancing the budget. He proposed to increase income tax from 4s. 6d. to 5s. in the pound, and to increase heavily the taxes on beer, tobacco, and petrol, to cut unemployment benefit by 10 per cent, and to cut the pay of state employees—school-teachers, for example, by 15 per cent, and some members of the armed forces by even more.

During the following week school-teachers campaigned against the 15 per cent cuts, and some sailors at Invergordon mutinied. On 21st September the government agreed that no cuts would be greater than 10 per cent.

The end of the gold standard: Meanwhile the Bank of England had still been obliged to sell gold for a fixed amount of British currency, for this is entailed in being on the gold standard. But the result of the continued crisis was heavy withdrawals of gold from London by people who were losing faith in British currency. The consequence of this was that on 21st September, the same day that the government agreed that no cuts should be greater than 10 per cent, it also checked the withdrawal of gold, and thus took Britain off the gold standard, and at the same time devalued the pound—the very steps it had been formed to avoid.

Coming off the gold standard would have seemed revolutionary if a Labour government had done it, but now the Bank of England actually advised it, and the change was accepted from a Conservative-dominated coalition without loss of confidence in the pound.

Neville Chamberlain as Chancellor

After the general election of October 1931 Neville Chamberlain succeeded Snowden as Chancellor of the Exchequer and held that post under Macdonald and Baldwin until he eventually became Prime Minister in May 1937. He aimed to secure the recovery of the British economy both by protecting it from foreign competition and by stimulating its expansion.

Protection and the Ottawa Conference: He protected it from foreign competition by abandoning Free Trade. A start was made in November 1931 by imposing heavy tariffs on foreign goods which the government claimed were being 'dumped' on Britain in 'abnormal' quantities; and in March 1932 a general tariff of 10% was imposed on most goods except those from the Empire.

The next step was the Imperial Economic Conference at Ottawa in August 1932. The British government hoped to build a tariff wall round the Commonwealth and turn it into a common market area. But the idea of Empire Free Trade was less attractive to the newly developing Dominions than to Great Britain, anxious to find markets for her products. Agreements were signed between Britain and the Dominions arranging preferential terms for each others' exports, but most of the concessions made by the Dominions consisted of making tariffs against foreign goods even higher than those against Great Britain. This benefited Britain comparatively little, for the tariffs against British goods were still often high enough to protect the infant industries of the Dominions from British competition.

However, a decisive move had been made away from Britain's traditional policy of Free Trade and the government now moved even further in that direction. Between 1932 and 1935 trade agreements were made with seventeen other countries, Great Britain agreeing to import fixed quotas of goods from those countries in return for tariff concessions for her own goods.

Cheap money: Chamberlain aimed to stimulate the expansion of the British economy by making money more easily available to industry. He disliked the idea of a public works programme, which savoured both of Socialism and of Lloyd George, and adopted the alternative approach of trying to encourage private enterprise by monetary policies. He forced interest rates down, so that industrialists and individuals could more easily borrow the money they needed, and he restricted investment abroad, so that British investors were driven to put their money into British industry.

Wages, prices, and consumption

But there were other factors, nothing to do with the government, which were helping the British economy to recover:

(1) Wages were generally lower as the result of the depression, and

the lower cost of wages to industry made it possible to produce goods more cheaply.

(2) Prices were even lower than wages, not only because of the low wages bill, but also because of improved technical efficiency and because the countries which produced food and raw materials had been so hard hit by the depression that Britain was able to buy her imports cheaply. This also helped to make British goods cheaper. So more were sold and British industry expanded.

(3) Consumption tended to increase because, despite lower wages, low prices enabled people to buy more goods. Therefore Britain's home market expanded as well as her export market.

Economic recovery

Slowly the British economy revived. This was partly due to the government's measures to protect industry by building tariff barriers and to stimulate it by providing 'cheap money'. But it was due far more to the other factors over which the government had no control. During the thirties Britain's traditional industries were gradually recovering, and new industries, such as electrical engineering and the manufacture of cars, developed rapidly. Above all large numbers of houses were built (more than two and a half million during the whole of the thirties). It was a disorganised development, as can be seen from looking at the sprawling suburbs of London and other great cities. There was no central planning. But there was recovery. The volume of production increased and unemployment decreased—particularly as a result of the housing boom. And Britain's recovery was not strikingly slower than that of other countries where a greater measure of state control had been imposed in dealing with these problems.

State intervention

Although the government was inclined to avoid state intervention and preferred to base recovery on private enterprise, it could not avoid it altogether. The imposition of tariffs is itself an example of interference by the state with the working of the economy. Further intervention followed. The government protected British agriculture by guaranteeing stable prices through the marketing boards originally set up by the Labour government in 1931, and it encouraged the production of milk, barley, oats, wheat and sugar beet by means of subsidies. Other subsidies were given to industry, one of the largest being the loan made in 1934 which made it possible for the Cunard liner *Queen Mary* to be completed. And in 1934 the government intervened in the economy with an Act aimed at improving conditions in the depressed areas. This was on too small a scale to achieve much, but some people were removed to areas where there was more work, and eventually, as the result of another Act in 1937, some new trading estates were built to help provide work in the depressed areas.

Even more remarkable were the three measures of nationalisation brought about by the National government.

(1) In 1933 it took over the Bill for nationalising transport in London which Herbert Morrison had introduced in 1931 (p. 204), and set up the London Passenger Transport Board.

(2) In 1938 coal royalties were nationalised. That is, the money paid by owners of coal mines, usually to landowners, for the right to work their mines, was now paid to the government. Those who lost this form of income were given a lump sum as compensation.

(3) Then in 1939 the government formed the state-owned British Overseas Airways Corporation by amalgamating two companies which had both been losing money by competing with each other.

Commonwealth affairs

The period of the National government saw a considerable development of the Commonwealth. In 1931 the equality of status of Great Britain and the Dominions was established by law when the Statute of Westminster (p. 56) was passed. In 1932 representatives of the Dominions negotiated with Britain at the Ottawa Conference on equal terms. And in 1935 the Government of India Act (p. 333) provided a great step towards India's eventual independence. The only obvious weakening of Commonwealth ties in this period lay in relations with the Irish Free State whose government was anxious to emphasise the complete independence of the Irish from Britain and in 1939 declined to join the rest of the Commonwealth in the second World War.

Rearmament

The most important and least successful aspect of the work of the National government was its foreign policy (pp. 252–5) Closely connected with this was its attitude towards armaments and defence, and in this sphere also its record is poor.

Until 1934, the year in which the government at last decided to increase Britain's rate of aircraft production, it had spent even less money on armaments than had the preceding Labour administration. Eventually, in March 1935, more than two years after Hitler had come to power in Germany, the government declared its intention to rearm, and in May Baldwin, who succeeded Macdonald as Prime Minister in the following month, announced a further expansion of Britain's rate of aircraft production. But in the general election campaign in October of the same year, in the middle of the Abyssinian crisis (p. 230), he promised 'there will be no great armaments'; and throughout the rest of his period in office, which lasted until May 1937, he kept his promise far too well. Although an expansion and modernisation of the army, navy, and air force was announced in March 1936, in the following budget year, from April 1936 to April 1937, Great Britain still spent less than a fifth as much as Germany on armaments.

However, the government gradually awoke to its responsibilities and took steps to prepare for war—especially after the Munich agreement of September 1938 (p. 245), which has sometimes been justified on the grounds that it bought Britain an extra year in which to prepare for war. During that year the rate of aircraft production increased from two hundred to six hundred a month, the coastal radar screen, for giving warning of approaching enemy aircraft, was completed, and eventually, on 26th April 1939, general conscription was introduced.

Even so by the outbreak of war in September 1939 the British army still only had sufficient equipment for five divisions against Germany's one hundred and six.

The end of the National government

The National government had been formed in 1931 to protect the pound. Yet within a month Great Britain was off the gold standard. It remained in power for nearly nine years, and although Britain gradually recovered from the Great Depression during these years, the government ignored the need for social reform. It pursued a foreign policy which was intended to be realistic, but which was in fact weak. It pursued a quite unrealistic defence and rearmament policy, and Britain went to war in 1939 unprepared. Inevitably the government lacked the confidence of the people, and increasingly it lacked the confidence even of its own supporters in Parliament. In May 1940, after the failure of the Norwegian campaign (p. 261), Leopold Amery, a Conservative ex-minister, ended a speech attacking the government with the words Cromwell had used when he dissolved the Long Parliament in 1653: 'You have sat here too long for any good you have been doing. Depart, I say, and let us have done with you. In the name of God, go.' Chamberlain went, and Churchill replaced him as Prime Minister at the head of a genuine coalition.

Section VI International Affairs, 1918–1945

44 THE TERRITORIAL SETTLEMENT

ONE of the most striking consequences of the first World War is the dramatic alteration of the map of Europe. In nineteenth-century Europe there had been a 'balance of power'. No one country was strong enough to attempt to dominate the Continent, and for a century there was no major war. But by 1914 the balance had been upset by the growing strength of Germany, and during the war which followed President Wilson promised a post-war territorial settlement in accordance with the principle of 'self-determination' instead of the principle of 'balance of power'. After the war, with a few exceptions, this promise was kept.

Germany

Germany lost little European land, and very little indeed in which the population was mainly German:

(1) Alsace and Lorraine, which had been seized from France in 1871, were returned to France.

(2) Two small areas around Eupen and Malmedy went to Belgium.

(3) North Schleswig, which was part of an area seized by Prussia from Denmark in 1864, went back to Denmark after a plebiscite.

(4) Most of Posen and West Prussia and, after a plebiscite, part of Upper Silesia went to Poland. The loss of West Prussia was the aspect of the territorial settlement most disliked by the Germans, for it had the effect of dividing East Prussia from the rest of Germany. But Poland was particularly anxious to acquire this area, which came to be known as 'the Polish corridor', for not only was most of the population Polish but also the chief port of the area, Danzig, could provide Poland with an outlet to the Baltic Sea. The situation was complicated by the fact that the population of Danzig itself was mainly German. So the peacemakers compromised: Danzig was made a Free City under the control of the League of Nations; the municipal government remained in German hands; the port was controlled by the Poles.

(5) The port of Memel and the surrounding land was also placed under international control in order to provide an outlet to the sea for Lithuania, which seized complete control of it in 1923.

(6) The Saar went to the League of Nations for fifteen years, so that France could have its valuable coal mines for that period as

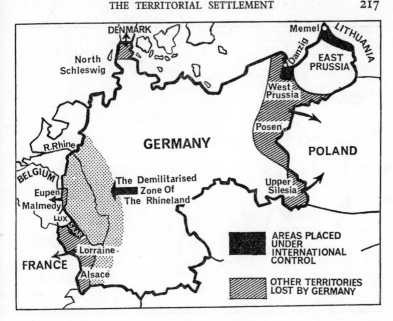

compensation for the destruction of her own coal mines by the retreating Germans in 1918. But after fifteen years the future of the Saar was to be decided by plebiscite (p. 242).

(7) The Rhineland remained part of Germany, but it was to be permanently demilitarised and there was to be an allied occupation until 1935.

Outside Europe Germany lost all her possessions, for her colonies all became mandated territories administered by other powers under the League of Nations. Her African colonies were divided between Britain, France, Belgium, and the Union of South Africa. Her possessions in the Far East were divided between Japan, Australia, and New Zealand.

Austria-Hungary

The Dual Monarchy of Austria-Hungary had disintegrated before the peace conference met, for the war had provided the opportunity for nationalist rebellions by the subject peoples. It was impossible for the Hapsburg monarchy to suppress the rebellions successfully while simultaneously fighting a European war; and in the last stages of defeat even the Germans of Austria and the Magyars of Hungary threw off Hapsburg control. Thus to some extent the Treaty of Saint-Germain with Austria and the Treaty of Trianon with Hungary merely confirmed what had already happened.

Austria was now a small weak republic with a total population of six millions. She lost two important German-speaking areas: the Sudetenland to Czechoslovakia and the South Tyrol to Italy.

Hungary was equally small and weak, and numerous Magyars found themselves living within the boundaries of foreign countries. More than a million went to Roumania, another million to Czechoslovakia, and many others to Poland and Jugoslavia. In all more than two and a half million Magyars, approximately a quarter of the total living in Europe, were placed under foreign rule.

Czechoslovakia was a completely new country created out of the Austrian provinces of Bohemia and Moravia and the Hungarian provinces of Slovakia and Ruthenia. Racially it was a miniature replica of Austria-Hungary, with a mixed population of six million Czechs, three and a half million Germans, two million Slovaks, a million Magyars, numerous Ruthenians, and some Poles.

Jugoslavia, another new state, was created out of a union of Serbia, and later Montenegro, with the extensive southern provinces of Austria-Hungary, such as Bosnia, Croatia, and Dalmatia.

Poland, an independent country for the first time since the eighteenth century, acquired from Austria the large province of Galicia, which was inhabited in the West by Poles and in the East by Ruthenians. The Curzon Line, Poland's provisional Eastern frontier, originally excluded Eastern Galicia from Poland; but the

Poles disputed this decision and seized Eastern Galicia during the Russo-Polish War of 1920–21 (p. 228).

Roumania acquired Bukovina from Austria and the large area of Transylvania from Hungary.

Italy acquired from Austria the Trentino and the Istrian peninsula, as well as the German-speaking area of the South Tyrol.

The Ottoman Empire

The Ottoman Empire had already lost most of her European lands in the Balkan Wars (pp. 101–3). In the Treaty of Sèvres she abandoned her Arab possessions, Syria coming under the control of France, and Iraq and Palestine under that of Britain. Even the Turkish portions of the Ottoman Empire, which had been promised 'secure sovereignty' (p. 118), were not left intact. Constantinople and the Straits were placed under international control, and Greece was allowed to occupy Smyrna and the surrounding area on the grounds that in Smyrna itself most of the population were Greeks (map, p. 308).

Bulgaria

Bulgaria lost very little either in land or population. By the Treaty of Neuilly a few small areas on her Western frontier went to Jugoslavia, and she lost to Greece the small strip of the Aegean coastline which she had gained from the Balkan Wars.

Russia

Germany and her allies were not the only countries which suffered territorial losses as a result of the first World War. By the Treaty of Brest-Litovsk with Germany in March 1918 Russia had lost an area of land containing a third of her population and more than half of her industry. Although the Germans withdrew at the end of the war Russia was not represented at the peace conference and most of the lost territory was not recovered. Her Baltic provinces became the independent republics of Finland, Estonia, Latvia, and Lithuania. Most of the new state of Poland was formed out of lands which had been part of the Tsarist Empire. And in the South the province of Bessarabia was transferred to Roumania. The only areas regained by the Russians were the Ukraine, the Crimea, Kars, which had been handed to Turkey, and Georgia, which had been recognised as an independent state.

The
Aaland
Islands
(see page
276)

FINLAND

ESTONIA

LATVIA

LITHUANIA

RUSSIA

To
POLAND

The Ukraine

Georgia
(Independent)

Bessarabia
(To ROUMANIA)

The Crimea

Kars
(To TURKEY)

AREAS LOST TO
RUSSIA BY THE
TREATY OF
BREST–LITOVSK,
BUT RECOVERED
AT THE END OF
THE WAR

AREAS LOST TO
RUSSIA BY THE
BREST–LITOVSK
AND NOT RECOVERED
AT THE END OF
THE WAR

Self-determination

Most of these changes were in accordance with the principle of self-determination, and as a result Germany and Bulgaria emerged from defeat almost intact, Austria-Hungary and the Ottoman Empire, both of which were multi-national Empires, were dismembered, and Russia lost her Western provinces, where the Tsars had ruled over non-Russian peoples.

However, the principle of self-determination will not bear exact application, and the peoples of Eastern Europe are so intermingled that it is impossible to draw national boundaries without leaving any minority groups. The million Magyars of Transylvania, for example, were surrounded on all sides by Roumanians. But the defeated countries could all justifiably claim that where the principle of self-determination was infringed it was infringed at their expense, for they all lost land, while none gained any. The fact that not only Italy and Roumania but also the new countries of Czechoslovakia, Poland, and Jugoslavia were treated as victorious allies at the peace conference, while Austria and Hungary were not allowed to send representatives, had the effect that all these countries gained at the expense of Austria and Hungary.

Self-determination also conflicted with particular strategic and economic needs. Consequently Italy was given the German-speaking South Tyrol because she demanded a strategic frontier on the Alps, and the German-speaking Sudetenland was included in Czechoslovakia partly for a similar strategic reason—to give her a mountain frontier with Germany—and partly because it formed an integral part of the economic unity of Bohemia.

The fact that exceptions of this sort were made helped to create the impression that principles were only adhered to when it was convenient. But in fact sound strategic and economic arguments were often subordinated to the principle of self-determination. The French demand for a strategic frontier on the Rhine was overruled. And Upper Silesia, an economic unity which was originally all going to Poland, was eventually divided between Germany and Poland as the result of a plebiscite.

The balance of power

The details of the territorial settlement are, of course, open to criticism. But in the main it was just. Its great failing was not that it failed to provide 'self-determination' but that it failed to provide a 'balance of power'. War had broken out in 1914 partly because a sufficient balance of power for ensuring peace had not been maintained. Yet Germany was now re-established as a united, potentially powerful state, with a population of seventy millions, flanked in the East merely by a string of small states instead of by two massive Empires. Although 'self-determination' had solved some of Europe's problems it was also creating new ones. Wilson realised this. He also realised that if the attempt to maintain a 'balance of power' were to be discarded it would have to be replaced by some other machinery for keeping the peace. This was why he cared so much about the League of Nations. He hoped that 'collective security' through the League would take the place of the 'balance of power' as a means of preserving peace. It did not, and Europe had to concede Hitler's demands in the thirties and eventually go to war again partly because the post-war territorial settlement had not provided a sufficient counter-weight to the potential power of Germany.

45   THE LEAGUE OF NATIONS

Origins

IN the chaos of the first World War men dreamt of a new and better world in which nations would live together in friendship and would settle their disagreements not by war but by negotiation; so they tried to establish machinery for international co-operation.

A committee set up by the British Foreign Office had been considering the idea of some sort of international organisation ever since 1916. The French were also interested in the formation of a league, though they wanted a permanent alliance which would provide 'collective security' for all its members. And in January 1918, in the last of his Fourteen Points, President Wilson called for 'a general association of nations'. So in 1919 the League of Nations was set up by the peace treaties.

Aims

The primary aim of the League was to maintain peace and security. It had, therefore, three main concerns:
(1) the reduction of national armaments;
(2) the preservation of its members from aggression;
(3) the settlement of any international disputes by peaceful means.

Since it was concerned with the general welfare of the world it also had numerous subsidiary aims, such as promoting good government of the mandated territories, ensuring reasonable treatment for minority groups, improving working conditions throughout the world, supervising the international armaments trade, stamping out unlicensed traffic in drugs, preventing the practice of trading in girls for use as prostitutes, providing help for refugees, fighting disease, and encouraging intellectual co-operation between people of different nations.

Besides this the League undertook to supervise all international organisations already in existence.

Organisation

The most important constituent parts of the League of Nations were the Assembly, the Council, the Secretariat, and the International Court of Justice; and there were also numerous subsidiary organisations.

The Assembly consisted of the representatives of all the member states (forty-two at the first meeting in 1920, fifty-five by 1924). Each state had one vote, and the Assembly could deal with any matter affecting the peace or general welfare of the world.

The Council was intended to consist of five permanent and four non-permanent members, with the victorious allies (the U.S.A., Great Britain, France, Italy, and Japan) occupying the permanent seats. In the event, any great power which was a member of the League was also a permanent member of the Council, and in practice this meant that by the end of 1936 the only permanent members were France, Great Britain, and the U.S.S.R. The non-permanent members were selected by the Assembly, and their number gradually increased until by 1936 there were eleven, thus greatly outnumbering the three permanent members. The Council heard any disputes brought before it and gave advice to the Assembly, but it had no power to take action.

The Secretariat, with a Secretary-General at its head, formed the permanent Civil Service of the League. As far as possible it included representatives of all member-nations, and it did most of the work of the League.

The International Court of Justice was established at the Hague in 1922 to deal with the interpretation of treaties and with the settlement of international disputes. It was not a court which tried criminal cases by Jury. It was rather a Court of Appeal, in which judges of various nationalities gave decisions on international disagreements brought before them.

The subsidiary organisations included bodies such as the International Labour Organization, or I.L.O., the Disarmament Commission, the Mandates Commission, and the Minorities Commission. These usually worked independently, although some, like the Mandates Commission, would make reports to the Council, and most were closely associated with the Secretariat.

The Weakness of the League

The League was born out of war and the chaos which followed war, and in the hurried atmosphere of the peace conference it acquired characteristics which weakened it as it grew. Since its Covenant formed the first twenty-six clauses of each of the treaties, the League was closely associated with the whole peace settlement and therefore with the faults of the treaties. Moreover, the peacemakers, believing that they were building a new and better Europe, created the League with apparatus only for maintaining the situation they established rather than for making any changes which might become necessary. In attempting to make history stand still they were attempting the impossible.

The League was also weakened by constitutional defects, by the absence of many great powers, and by lack of military strength.

Constitutional defects: There were several serious weaknesses in the machinery of the League. The Assembly met only once a year, and the Council only three or four times a year. Moreover, even when they did meet their decisions except on a few matters, such as admission to the League and questions of procedure, had to be unanimous. This made it very difficult to make any alteration to the constitution, and it also meant that it was usually impossible to decide anything of a genuinely controversial nature, for although no country was allowed to vote on a dispute in which it was itself involved, every other nation had the power of 'veto'.

The great powers: More important was the fact that many of the greatest nations of the world were not members of the League.

THE U.S.A. had retired into isolation again after the war, and it was because the Senate wanted the U.S.A. to keep out of the League that it refused to ratify the peace treaties, of which the Covenant of the League formed a part.

JAPAN, originally a member, announced her intention to leave in March 1933, after seizing Manchuria (p. 314).

GERMANY was excluded at first, and although she was granted membership in 1926 she left in October 1933 over disarmament.

ITALY, one of the original members, walked out of the League in May 1936 after conquering Abyssinia (p. 249).

THE U.S.S.R., unwelcome in the early years and also unwilling to join, became a member in September 1934 in order to gain allies against the new threat from Nazi Germany, and was expelled in December 1939 when she attacked Finland (p. 259).

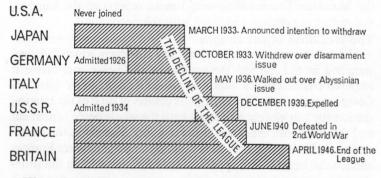

Thus the only two great powers who were members of the League throughout were Great Britain and France, and they disagreed about how the League should attempt to carry out its primary task of maintaining peace and security.

BRITAIN was unwilling to commit herself to future action in defence of other members of the League, partly because she wished to decide any future issue on its merits when it arose, and partly because she already had heavy responsibilities for defending her Empire, and had no wish to increase her commitments.

FRANCE, conscious of her own need for security, had hoped that an international force would be set up to provide 'collective security' for all members of the League. This was not done, and instead members merely promised to resist aggression. One understandable result of this was that France hamstrung the League's efforts to secure disarmament.

When it came to the point neither France nor Great Britain was prepared to act against an aggressor until a situation was reached in which they realised that their very existence was threatened.

Lack of power: In the last resort the weakness of the League lay in its lack of power. Law can exist only when it is backed by power, and international law can exist only when there is an international organisation strong enough to enforce it. Until such a power exists international laws are merely agreements which can be broken by anyone with sufficient strength.

Article 12 of the Covenant of the League provided for the settlement of international disputes by any of three methods:
(1) arbitration by a neutral power;
(2) judicial settlement by the International Court of Justice;
(3) an inquiry by the Council of the League.
But there was no way of compelling a nation to submit its case to arbitration or to a decision of the International Court of Justice or of the Council. More important, there was no way of compelling it to act in accordance with such a decision.

Even Article 16, which provided for diplomatic pressure, suspension of trade, and even armed force to prevent aggression, was merely a pious hope that these measures would be used. Usually they were not. On the only occasion when 'sanctions' were imposed, against Italy from October 1935 until July 1936, care was taken that Italy should not be seriously inconvenienced (p. 230).

Thus the League of Nations was never organised as a world police force. But it did provide a convenient apparatus which states could use for settling their disputes by mutual consent or for co-ordinating action against other states which threatened peace. When some of the great powers decided that they preferred to settle their affairs by force, and when the others declined to co-ordinate action against them, it became obvious that the League, at any rate as a peacemaker, was valueless.

The successes of the League

But although the League failed in its primary aim of maintaining peace and security, in other less ambitious spheres it achieved much. Its strength lay not in the Assembly or the Council, nor even in the International Court of Justice, but rather in the permanent Secretariat and in the various subsidiary organisations.

The I.L.O. drew up agreements on such matters as the freedom of workers to form trade unions, the limitation of night-work by women and children, and conditions of employment for seamen, and it induced many nations to accept these agreements. It also encouraged governments to provide such things as old age pensions and sickness and injury benefit for their peoples.

The reports submitted to the League by the Mandates Commission had the effect of reminding the mandatory powers that the rule of primitive peoples was, as the Covenant described it, 'a sacred trust of civilisation' and not an opportunity for exploitation.

Arrangements were made for the return home of 400,000 prisoners of war. Care was taken of refugees, and in 1923, after the war between Greece and Turkey (p. 227), the League arranged the settlement of over a million Greek refugees from Asia Minor and Eastern Thrace. Steps were taken to check disease—to prevent, for example, the spread of a Russian typhus epidemic in the early twenties, and to further research in leprosy. The indiscriminate sale of arms by private manufacturers was checked. Trade in dangerous drugs was controlled by international agreement. International co-operation was established in such things as transport and telegraphy. And meetings for exchanging ideas were arranged between scientists of different nations.

In 1923 Austria was rescued from economic collapse by loans of money to develop her agriculture and industry and re-establish her trade, and similar help was given to Hungary. The plebiscites after the war, and the one in the Saar in 1935 (p. 242), were conducted impartially, and for the fifteen years until it returned to Germany officials of the League managed the very difficult task of governing the Saar. They managed also, though with decreasing success after 1933, the even more difficult task of supervising the government of the Free City of Danzig until the German forces marched in in 1939.

Although any assessment of the work of the League of Nations must take into account its failure to maintain peace (pp. 227–31) it is only fair to place in the balance against that failure these many constructive achievements.

Pʀᴇsɪᴅᴇɴᴛ Wɪʟsᴏɴ of the U.S.A. had feared that the League of Nations would become merely 'an influential debating society' if its members did not give a guarantee to resist aggression. So in Article 16 of the Covenant members of the League undertook to combine against any aggressor. But even so the League turned out to be little more than 'an influential debating society' when dealing with its principal concerns. Disarmament was never achieved, aggression continued, and international disputes were not always peacefully settled. By the middle thirties the League was not even influential, and it was only in its subsidiary roles that it accomplished much (p. 226).

It was some time before the ineffectiveness of the League became widely apparent. In dealing with the comparatively small disputes of the twenties it seemed to have some success, for although the League generally accepted the easiest solution to any problem, regardless of right or wrong, at least peace was usually maintained. Not until the thirties was its authority openly flouted on a large scale, and therefore it was not until the thirties that it became obvious how completely powerless the League was.

The twenties

Disputes about the post-war territorial settlement were inevitable in the early twenties, and they were numerous.

The Aaland Islands: One of the first arose from the Finnish claim to the Aaland Islands in the Baltic (map, p. 220). For the century since the Napoleonic Wars both Finland and the Aaland Islands had belonged to Russia, but before that they were Swedish possessions, and in 1920 the inhabitants of the islands wished to return to Swedish control. The League, disregarding the principle of self-determination, handed them over to Finland.

The Graeco-Turkish War: Also in 1920 the Greeks, ambitious to increase their territory in Asia Minor, advanced beyond the area ceded to them in the Treaty of Sèvres (p. 219). They were encouraged in their aggression by Lloyd George, the British Prime Minister, while the French sold arms to the Turks. The war continued until August 1922, when the Turks routed the Greek army so completely that they were able to demand and get by the Treaty of Lausanne (p. 309) a complete revision of the peace settlement as it affected them. Throughout this affair the League neither did nor could do anything.

The Russo-Polish War: There was another act of aggression in 1920 when the Poles crossed their provisional Eastern frontier, which had been fixed by the British Foreign Secretary, Lord Curzon, in order to seize from Russia land which had once belonged to the old Polish monarchy, but in which the population was mainly Russian. After early successes the Poles were driven back almost to Warsaw by the Red Army, but then, with French assistance, they defeated the Russians in the battle of the Vistula in August 1920, and by the Treaty of Riga in 1921 Russia was compelled to surrender all the land which the Poles had coveted.

THE EXPANSION OF POLAND, 1919–1921.

Again the League did nothing. As in the war between Greece and Turkey, the country which was attacked was one which had been defeated in the first World War and was not a member of the League. Moreover, each of the aggressors in these wars was encouraged by one of the great powers in the Council of the League—Greece by Great Britain and Poland by France. Arguably the League had no obligation to resist aggression against a country which was not a member, but it boded ill for the future if aggression was not merely permitted but even encouraged by members of the Council.

Vilna and Memel: It was not only against Russia that Polish ambitions were directed in 1920. In October a Polish army seized Vilna, the capital of Lithuania, and the surrounding land. The League took no action, and in 1923, when a Conference of Ambassadors decided that Poland should keep it, the League accepted this decision. It also accepted the annexation by Lithuania in 1923 of Memel, which had originally been placed by the Treaty of Versailles under international control.

Peaceful boundary settlements: However, in 1921 the League had demonstrated that it could be useful, if its machinery were properly used, by settling a dispute between Germany and Poland over their boundary in Upper Silesia (p. 216), and two other boundary disputes between Albania and Jugoslavia, and Hungary and Czechoslovakia.

The Corfu incident: The first time one of the great powers openly flouted the League was in 1923. In August an Italian general and four men with him were murdered on Greek soil while drawing the frontier line between Greece and Albania. Mussolini demanded 50 million *lire* from the Greek government as compensation, and when this was refused he seized the Greek island of Corfu (p. 249). Greece appealed to the Council of the League, but Mussolini denied its right to deal with the matter. So once again it was the Conference of Ambassadors which settled the dispute, and the outcome was that Mussolini got the ransom he demanded.

Greece and Bulgaria: The League was more successful in 1925 when Greece invaded Bulgaria over a frontier dispute. Bulgaria appealed to the Council of the League, which for once took action. It made the Greeks withdraw and pay compensation to Bulgaria. Understandably the Greeks resented the fact that Italy had been able to attack them and get away with it, while they, merely because they were weaker, were not allowed to behave in the same way towards Bulgaria.

The thirties

Despite the inadequacies of the League in the twenties, its reputation in 1930 was high. At least none of the great powers had embarked on a career of conquest in defiance of the League. But in 1931 this reputation was shaken, and by 1936 it was lost.

Manchukuo: In September 1931 Japan invaded the Chinese province of Manchuria. The Chinese government appealed to the League, which sent out a commission of inquiry. Meanwhile, in March 1932, Japan had set up a puppet government in Manchuria headed by Pu-yi, the last Manchu Emperor (p. 319), who was now known as Henry Pu-yi. Manchuria was renamed Manchukuo, and a year later, when the League had condemned her action as aggression, Japan announced her intention of withdrawing from the League. No action was taken against her, and the Japanese continued to extend their influence into the North of China.

German Rearmament: In March 1935 Hitler made public the fact that Germany was rearming by announcing general conscription. This was an open breach of the Treaty of Versailles, and the heads of government of Britain, France, and Italy met in April at the Italian town of Stresa to condemn his action; but neither they nor the League did anything other than talk.

The Anglo-German Naval Treaty: In June 1935 a further breach of the Treaty of Versailles was condoned by the British government, which signed a naval agreement with Germany specifying that Germany's fleet should be no more than 35 per cent the size of the Royal Navy.

Twice in three months Hitler had been allowed to break the disarmament clauses of the Treaty of Versailles. The first time a protest was made. The second time he was encouraged. Under these circumstances it would be more difficult to take action in the future against any other breach of the treaty.

The Italo-Abyssinian War: In the same year the League of Nations faced a crucial test. At the beginning of 1935 Italy had demanded compensation from Abyssinia after a frontier incident on the border between Abyssinia and Italian Somaliland (map, p. 249). In March Abyssinia had appealed to the League of Nations. During April, the same month that Italy joined Britain and France in the Stresa Declaration against German rearmament, Mussolini was pouring troops into Italian Somaliland and Eritrea, which was also on the border of Abyssinia. In May Abyssinia appealed to the League again. In October Italy invaded. The League then acted swiftly, and many members agreed to prohibit the export of necessities of war to Italy. But coal, oil, iron, and steel, for lack of which the Italian operation might have failed, were not included in the 'sanctions'. In May 1936 Italy completed her conquest of Abyssinia and walked out of the League of Nations. In July 'sanctions' were withdrawn.

The end of the League

The failure of this attempt at collective security marks the end of any pretence that the League of Nations could keep the peace and protect smaller nations from aggression. Two months later the Council of the League did issue a declaration that no state should give assistance to either side in the civil war which had broken out in Spain in July—the same month that the sanctions against Italy were withdrawn. But Hitler and Mussolini ignored the declaration, and it was their help which enabled Franco to overthrow the government (pp. 155–6).

In March 1936 German troops had already marched into the demilitarised zone of the Rhineland, in March 1938 Hitler took over Austria, and in March 1939 he seized Czechoslovakia and forced Lithuania to hand over Memel. In July 1937 the Japanese had renewed their invasion of China, and in April 1939 Mussolini invaded and seized Albania. On none of these occasions did the League move, and as an organisation for opposing aggression it seemed to have ceased to exist.

Moreover, when the British and French at last acted they did so not as members of the League, and not in accordance with the provisions of the Covenant. Instead they gave guarantees of assistance against aggression to Poland, Greece, and Roumania; and when Hitler invaded Poland at the beginning of September the British Commonwealth and France declared war on Germany. But at the end of the year the League of Nations, so long apparently dead, made one last dying gesture. In November the U.S.S.R. had invaded Finland. In December she was expelled from the League.

After the expulsion of the U.S.S.R., Great Britain and France were the only great powers left in the League of Nations. In June 1940 France collapsed under the German onslaught; and with the British Commonwealth standing alone against a victorious Germany which had conquered most of Europe, the League was demonstrably a failure. The only future occasion on which the Assembly met was in April 1946 in order to disband it.

In the previous year the second World War had come to an end, and in the post-war world the two greatest powers were the U.S.A. and the U.S.S.R. The U.S.A. had never been a member of the League. The U.S.S.R. had been expelled. Consequently neither of them had wanted to revive the League; so when a new international organisation was formed in June 1945 it was given not only a new constitution but also a new name: the United Nations Organization.

THE PEACEMAKERS at Paris in 1919 had two main concerns other than rearranging the territorial boundaries of Europe and establishing the League of Nations. They wanted to arrange for reparations payments by Germany to the victorious allies and to reach agreement on the issue of disarmament. Neither issue was satisfactorily settled at Paris, and both dragged on into the early thirties when the attempts to reach satisfactory settlements were abandoned.

Reparations

The Allies had two reasons for imposing the payment of reparations on Germany: to punish her, and to extract from her a contribution towards the cost of the war. The French and Belgians, who had suffered most, were the most anxious to impose heavy reparations on Germany. The British government, which had just won an election with the slogan 'Make Germany pay', was inclined to support them. The U.S.A., which had suffered no damage at home from the war, was not interested in reparations but was interested in the repayment of the loans she had made to her allies.

The whole question of reparations was unsatisfactory from the start:

(1) The Germans resented having to pay, and as they had only accepted the Treaty of Versailles under compulsion they had no scruples about avoiding payment.

(2) There was no agreement in the treaty about how much Germany was to pay, so there were perpetual difficulties about how much the final sum should be and how quickly it should be paid.

(3) Even more important is the fact that a healthy economy depends on maintaining a balance between exports and imports, and thus the one-way payments of reparations tended to undermine the economic health of the world. Germany had to export to earn francs and sterling, for the allies demanded payment in their own currencies, but since she had to hand the money over as reparations payments she was unable to spend it on imports from France and Britain, whose economies therefore suffered.

(4) The question of American war debts, which were also one-way payments with a similar economic effect, is a further complication. So long as the European allies were going to take money from Germany the U.S.A. was not going to abandon her demand for the repayment of war loans, and so long as the European allies had to

pay large sums to the U.S.A. they were not going to abandon hope
of getting reparations from Germany.

In January 1921 they presented a demand for £11,000 million
to be paid over forty-two years. The Germans declared that this
was impossible and offered one-tenth as much. In April the demand was reduced to £6,600 million and the Allies occupied three
towns on the East side of the Rhine and threatened to occupy the
Ruhr unless payments began in August.

The Germans gave way and, with the help of loans from London
bankers, began paying in August. But the German government
found it necessary to sell marks in exchange for the currencies of
their creditors, and the result was a sharp decline in the value of
the mark. So Germany had to give up paying cash and instead
make payments in kind, such as coal. But this only made the plight
of the British coal industry, which was already bad, even worse.

During 1922 the British government came to regret the whole
reparations settlement, but the French and Belgians were still
anxious to collect, and in January 1923, by which time the Germans were badly behind with payments, they occupied the Ruhr.
The German reaction was a general strike to ensure that the
French should not profit. But German finances could not stand
the strain of this, and the mark declined in value so swiftly that by
November its value in relation to the pound and the dollar was
thirty million times less than in January. It was, in fact, valueless.

Already in September the Germans had given up passive resistance in the Ruhr, and in November the Dawes Committee, named
after its American chairman, was set up on the suggestion of
Lord Curzon, the British Foreign Secretary, to try to discover
what Germany could afford to pay. In August 1924 agreement was
reached on the basis of the recommendations of this committee:
the Ruhr was to be returned to Germany, the U.S.A. was to lend
her the equivalent of £40 million to help her economic recovery, and
after two years she was to start paying again. In 1929 this Dawes
Plan was replaced by the Young Plan, also drawn up by a committee under an American chairman. Germany was lent another
£60 million and was expected to go on paying until 1988.

Thus there evolved a ridiculous system whereby money chased
itself round the world in circles. The U.S.A. lent money to Germany, Germany paid reparations to the European allies, they paid
their war debts to the U.S.A., and the U.S.A. lent more money to
Germany. Instead of solving problems these arrangements helped
to bring the slump closer. Soon after the slump began in the

autumn of 1929 Germany was unable to pay her reparations and the Allies were unable to pay their war debts, and by July 1932, when a conference at Lausanne at last ended reparations, Germany had received approximately three times as much in unrepaid loans as she had paid out in reparations.

Disarmament and security

The reason that attempts were made at the Paris Peace Conference to make arrangements for disarmament was that many men believed that in the last resort the only effective way of preventing war was to remove the means of making war. Because of this the first aim specified in the Covenant of the League of Nations was 'the reduction of national armaments to the lowest point consistent with national safety.'

The first, and comparatively simple, step was the disarmament of Germany. Her army was limited to 100,000 men, she was allowed six battleships and some smaller craft, but no submarines and no aeroplanes. It proved more difficult to limit the armaments of other countries, for it was impossible to find an arrangement which was fair to both large and small countries and to both agricultural and highly industrialised countries. If France, a largely agricultural country with a population of forty millions, disarmed, she could no longer feel secure, for Germany, a highly industrialised country with a population of seventy millions, would be far better able to rearm. Consequently France blocked all schemes for disarmament, arguing that she could not be expected to disarm until she had some other assurance of security from Germany.

The Treaty of Washington, 1922: It did prove possible to achieve a measure of disarmament at sea. In 1922, at a conference in Washington, the naval powers fixed the relative sizes of their fleets in the ratio U.S.A. 100, Great Britain 100, Japan 60, France 35, Italy 35. And this was followed in 1930 by an agreement in London between the U.S.A., Britain, and Japan to limit the sizes of some of their larger ships.

The Draft Treaty of Mutual Assistance, 1923: Meanwhile various efforts had been made in the twenties to deal with the problem of providing security. The first significant one was a League of Nations proposal for a treaty under which nations would limit their armaments in return for a guarantee of rapid assistance if attacked. France welcomed the scheme, but Great Britain disliked it because under the proposed arrangements her possession of widespread territories would have resulted in her having proportionately wide commitments for giving assistance. So in

1924 Ramsay MacDonald, the British Prime Minister, rejected it.

The Geneva Protocol, 1924: Strenuous efforts were made to provide an alternative scheme, and during 1924 ministers in MacDonald's Labour government helped to draw up the Geneva Protocol—a proposal for the establishment of permanent machinery for the compulsory arbitration of international disputes. The French again welcomed the scheme, and it seemed certain that Britain would accept it as well, but in November the Labour government fell and in March 1925 the Conservative Foreign Secretary, Austen Chamberlain, rejected it partly because the Protocol would have infringed the right of a British government to decide any particular issue on its merits when it arose and partly because it might lay the British Empire open to interference in matters which the British government regarded as domestic issues.

The Locarno Treaties, 1925: After these failures hope now came from another direction. In 1925 Gustav Stresemann, the German Foreign Minister, made proposals which were welcomed by Austen Chamberlain and by Briand, the French Foreign Minister, about a settlement concerning Germany's frontiers, and before the end of the year a number of treaties were drawn up at a conference at Locarno. It was agreed that Germany's frontiers with France and Belgium should be maintained for ever, and that the Rhineland should remain permanently demilitarised; and Britain and Italy agreed to guarantee these arrangements. It was also agreed that no attempt should be made to alter Germany's frontiers with Poland and Czechoslovakia by force; and France agreed to guarantee these arrangements. At the time the Locarno Treaties were generally acclaimed as an important advance towards better international relations. In retrospect they look less impressive. The differences between the agreements about Germany's Eastern and Western frontiers implied that the Eastern frontiers could, and perhaps should, be altered—though not by war. Moreover, since the frontiers guaranteed by the Locarno Treaties were precisely those which had been established at Versailles, the Locarno agreements seemed to imply that the Treaty of Versailles was not fully binding by itself. However, the atmosphere of reconciliation in which the Locarno Treaties were negotiated helped to produce an atmosphere of international goodwill in which men could look with hope to the future.

The Kellogg–Briand Pact, 1928: In 1928, prompted by a French suggestion that their countries should promise never to fight each other, the Americans made their contribution to solving the problem of making the world secure by drawing up a pact which all nations could sign declaring that they intended to 'abolish war as an instrument of policy'. This also was generally welcomed, but it meant very little, especially as its originator, Kellogg, the American Secretary of State, expressed his opinion that any state might reasonably fight in self-defence. Sixty-two nations signed it, but the only effects that it seems to have had were that Japan preferred to call her seizure of Manchuria in 1931 an 'incident' and that Italy, when she invaded Abyssinia in 1935, claimed to be fighting in self-defence.

The Geneva Disarmament Conference, 1932: Despite all these efforts to negotiate agreements which would prevent war, and despite the calmer international atmosphere after Locarno, the fundamental problem remained the same: Europe must either disarm or rearm. In 1925, the same year as Locarno, the League had set up a commission to study the problems of disarmament and prepare the way for a disarmament conference. The problems were too complicated for this Preparatory Commission to achieve much, and in 1927, when no one was willing to accept a Russian proposal that all nations should start disbanding their armies, navies, and air forces without working out detailed arrangements, the U.S.S.R. had begun to enlarge her forces.

When the Disarmament Conference met at Geneva in 1932 numerous proposals were made. President Hoover of the U.S.A. wanted all armies cut by a third, and Ramsay MacDonald of Great Britain suggested that each great power should have an army of 200,000 men. But nothing came of these or any other proposals, so the Germans, who were complaining that they were the only European state which had disarmed, now demanded 'equality of status' in armaments with the other great powers. Eventually this was agreed in principle, but no details were worked out, and then the whole situation was altered when on 30th January 1933 Hitler became Chancellor of Germany. France in particular was both suspicious and frightened, and from then on blocked all schemes which would have involved her own disarmament, while doing everything possible to prevent German rearmament. In October 1933 Hitler withdrew both from the Disarmament Conference and from the League of Nations. It was clear that Germany was intending to rearm.

It was equally clear that the attempt to achieve disarmament had failed, and the inevitable sequel to its failure was rearmament. Europe began to prepare for the next war.

A T the end of the first World War the French had no illusions
that the might of Germany had been finally crushed, and they
believed that their best assurance of security lay in making an
attack on France militarily impossible for the Germans.

Therefore in the negotiations for the Versailles Treaty France
tried to get control of all land West of the Rhine, of the Rhine
itself, and of its bridges. Her allies would not tolerate this, and she
had to make do with an agreement for military occupation of the
Rhineland for fifteen years, followed by its permanent demilitarisation, together with a joint Anglo-American guarantee of assistance against German aggression. To many Frenchmen these
arrangements seemed insufficient to ensure security. 'This is not
peace,' commented Marshal Foch in 1919, 'It is an armistice for
twenty years.' Worse was to follow. In 1920 the American Congress declined to ratify the Treaty of Versailles, so the French lost
the American assurance of help; and then Britain, unwilling to
accept the commitment on her own, also withdrew. France, left
with neither the Rhine frontier nor the guarantee, felt cheated.

The French system of alliances

The result was that she tried to gain security from Germany by
encircling her with a system of alliances embracing all the European states which had benefited from the peace settlement and
were therefore interested in its maintenance. In September 1920
she concluded a military alliance with Belgium. In February 1921
she signed a treaty with Poland and at the same time gave Poland
assistance in her war against Soviet Russia (p. 228). By 1924 she
also had agreements with Czechoslovakia, Jugoslavia, and Roumania—the so-called 'Little Entente'.

Relations with previous allies

But this system of alliances was built up at the expense of a
deterioration in relations with Britain, Italy, and Russia. Britain
had no more wish to see the Continent dominated by France than
by Germany. Italy was discontented because France had failed
to transfer any colonial territory in Africa to her as compensation
for the French acquisition of mandates over some of Germany's
colonies, and also because France had supported Jugoslavia in
the dispute over Fiume in 1920 (p. 134). Russia was alienated
by the assistance France gave to Poland in 1921, and as a result

was driven into the arms of Germany, with whom in April 1922 she signed the Treaty of Rapallo (p. 257). Thus very soon after the first World War France was on bad terms with the three European powers in whose company she had fought the war.

The period of apparent French dominance

Despite this isolation from the other great powers France appeared in the twenties to be the dominant power in Europe, and her system of alliances helped to maintain this illusion. But no one knew better than the French leaders how illusory their dominance was. They were therefore very anxious to get 'collective security' through the League of Nations both for France and for her allies.

Consequently France zealously advocated the adoption both of the Draft Treaty of Mutual Assistance of 1923 (p. 234) and of the Geneva Protocol of 1924 (p. 235). The rejection of both of these agreements by Britain helped to increase in France the feeling that Britain could not be relied on for support against aggression. To some extent the French were reassured by the conclusion of the Locarno Treaties in 1925 (p. 235), for Germany voluntarily agreed to maintain her boundaries with France and the demilitarisation of the Rhineland, and Britain and Italy both guaranteed to assist France against any breach of this treaty. But even this had a drawback, for Britain and Italy would not join France in guaranteeing the arbitration treaties which Germany signed with France's allies, Poland and Czechoslovakia.

France did not get a sufficient sense of security from Locarno to risk either disarming or abandoning her system of alliances encircling Germany. So in 1929 she decided to build along her frontier with Germany the Maginot Line—a massive system of fortifications named after her Defence Minister, M. Maginot. And in 1931, when a customs union between Germany and Austria was proposed, France was so determined to prevent any increase in the strength of Germany that she exerted pressure on the Austrian government to ensure that the scheme was abandoned.

The effects of the rise of the Nazis

The accession to power in Germany of the aggressive anti-French Nazi Party inevitably had the effect of increasing French fears of Germany. It also had the effect of improving French relations with both Italy and Russia.

Italy: Hitler's ambition to incorporate Austria in Germany was contrary to Italian as well as French interest. As a result Italy and France drew closer during 1933 and 1934 until in January 1935 Mussolini and Pierre Laval, who had just become Foreign Minister in France, reached an agreement on numerous matters, including French acceptance of the idea of some form of expansion by Italy in Abyssinia.

Russia: Hitler's known ambition to colonise Eastwards, and his success in undermining the Franco-Polish alliance by concluding a non-aggression pact with Poland in January 1934 (p. 242), had the effect of bringing France and Russia together. France hoped that Russia would take Poland's place as her principal ally in the East. So during 1934 she advocated the admission of Russia to the League of Nations, and in September Russia was admitted. In May 1935 the new Franco-Russian friendship was cemented by a treaty of mutual assistance in the event of an attack by any European power, thus in a sense renewing the old Dual Alliance (p. 79).

Although the advent of Hitler to power in Germany resulted in an improvement in relations between the democratic French republic and the totalitarian régimes of Italy and Russia it did not at first bring France any closer to Britain—the other democratic European power. Britain did join France and Italy in April 1935 in the Stresa Declaration against German rearmament, but the Anglo-German Naval Treaty (p. 230) two months later inevitably increased the French doubts about the reliability of Britain as an obstacle to German aggression.

The effects of the Abyssinian War

When the Italians invaded Abyssinia a few months later and the League of Nations voted for the imposition of economic sanctions France found herself in a very difficult position. In the past she had always zealousy advocated making the League effective; yet now, when the League took action for the first time under Article 16 (p. 225), it was against a country which France did not wish to offend for fear of driving her into the arms of Germany.

In the event France agreed to impose certain economic sanctions, but at the same time tried to persuade the British government to agree to a solution which would be acceptable to Italy. The outcome of this was the Hoare–Laval Pact—a proposal for handing two-thirds of Abyssinia to Italy. When the indignation of British public opinion resulted in the British government withdrawing from this agreement, Anglo-French relations were strained even further; and Laval did not even have the consolation of maintaining good relations with Italy, for Mussolini was offended by the equivocal French attitude during the crisis and drew nearer to Hitler who had throughout approved his action.

The Rhineland and the Siegfried Line

In March 1936 Hitler took advantage of the disunity of Britain, France, and Italy to occupy the Rhineland (p. 243), and the French government took no action other than protesting to the League of Nations. Germany's occupation of the Rhineland and subsequent construction of the Siegfried Line opposite the Maginot Line was militarily and politically disastrous for France. Militarily it destroyed the basis of French strategic thinking by making it far more difficult for France to take effective action against Germany in the event of a German attack on her allies. Politically it weakened the relationship between France and her allies. In the first place, they had learnt that France could not be relied on to stand firm against a German breach of a treaty, even when her own interests were involved. In the second place, France was less valuable as an ally now that her military position was weaker.

Britain's shadow

Another effect of the increasingly apparent weakness of France was that she could no longer take the initiative in international affairs but was driven into merely following the lead of Great Britain. At first she was torn between Britain and the U.S.S.R., and when their policies differed, as for example over the Spanish Civil War, she tended to vacillate. But even there, although sympathetic to the Spanish government and inclined to join the U.S.S.R. in sending it assistance, she did in fact follow Britain in forbidding the sale of arms to both sides in Spain.

When Hitler annexed Austria in March 1938 France was in the middle of a political crisis and by then was in no position to do anything unless Britain gave a strong lead. The French government did take the opportunity of reaffirming its intention to defend Czechoslovakia from aggression. But later in the year, when the British government adopted a policy of appeasement over Czechoslovakia, the determination of the French crumbled, and they accepted first the Munich terms of September 1938 (p. 245) and then the final destruction of Czechoslovakia in March 1939.

In April 1939 France followed Britain's lead by giving guarantees of support against aggression to Poland, Greece, and Roumania, and then in September, when Germany invaded Poland, France again followed Britain's lead and declared war on Germany.

Hitler's aims

LONG before Hitler became Chancellor of Germany in January 1933 he had declared in *Mein Kampf* his determination that all German-speaking people should be incorporated in Germany, and his belief that Eastern Europe was a suitable sphere of colonisation for Germany. When he came to power he set out to achieve these aims as far as possible by diplomacy, and if necessary by war.

Germany's diplomatic position in 1933

The international situation which he found was a favourable one: Germany had been on friendly terms with Soviet Russia since the Treaty of Rapallo of 1922 (p. 257), with the U.S.A. since the Dawes Plan of 1924 (p. 233), and with Britain and Italy, and even to some extent France, since the Locarno Treaties of 1925 (p. 235). Some of Germany's grievances under the Versailles Treaty had already been settled:

(1) She had not regained any of the land lost at the end of the war, but the Locarno Treaties had made it clear that there was room for negotiation over revision of Germany's Eastern boundary.

(2) In 1926 Germany had been admitted to the League of Nations.

(3) The ending of reparations had been accepted in July 1932 at an international conference held at Lausanne in Switzerland.

(4) In December 1932 Britain, France, and Italy had agreed at the Geneva Disarmament Conference (p. 236) that Germany should be granted 'equality of status' with them over armaments.

The immediate effect of Hitler coming to power

To some extent the situation deteriorated as the direct result of Hitler coming to power. Although he declared to the world that he had no intention of trying to alter the peace settlement by force, he gave orders at home for accelerating rearmament and made little effort to conceal what was happening, so in the summer of 1933 France insisted that Germany should only be given 'equality of status' over armaments after a transitional period of four years.

The direct result of this was that in October 1933 Germany withdrew both from the Disarmament Conference and from the League of Nations, and again accelerated rearmament. For the moment Germany seemed to be once again in the dangerously isolated position in which she had found herself after the first World War and from which Stresemann had devoted all his energies to rescuing her (pp. 141–2).

The German-Polish non-aggression pact of 1934

But Hitler proclaimed his love of peace and his preference for bi-lateral over multi-lateral agreements; and then, just a year after becoming Chancellor, he achieved what amounted to a diplomatic revolution in Europe. In January 1934 he concluded with Poland a non-aggression pact to last for ten years. In one blow he had knocked away one of the main props in the system of alliances (p. 237) which France had so carefully built round Germany since the war, and at the same time had safeguarded his Eastern frontier so that he was able to concentrate on the acquisition of Austria in the South.

Failure to acquire Austria, July 1934

However, everything did not run smoothly for Hitler, for in March 1934, two months after the German-Polish non-aggression pact, the Austrian government attempted to safeguard itself from the threat of Hitler by putting itself under the patronage of Mussolini's Italy. For the moment this paid off, for in July, when the Austrian Nazis attempted a *Putsch*, Mussolini moved troops to the Austrian frontier and by this show of firmness dissuaded Hitler from taking action.

Hitler now changed his political strategy. He declared that he had no intention of ending the independence of Austria, nor even of interfering in her domestic affairs. He gave up threatening the Austrian government and encouraging the Austrian Nazis. And for nearly four years the question of Austria was shelved, together with the other vital issue of revision of Germany's frontiers in the East, while Hitler devoted himself to strengthening Germany in the West so that he would eventually be able to direct his attention South and East without fear of interference from the West.

The Saar and rearmament

Hitler had avoided attacking the Treaty of Versailles after coming to power, for the eventual return of the Saar to Germany depended on its terms (p. 217). In the plebiscite of January 1935 90 per cent of the votes cast were for union with Germany. So at the beginning of March the Saar was returned to Germany and Hitler declared that he had no further territorial ambitions in the West.

But now that he had the Saar he felt free to attack the Treaty of Versailles, and a fortnight later, on 16th March, he declared that Germany was no longer bound by the military clauses of the Treaty of Versailles and would raise a peace-time army of thirty-six divisions, more than half a million men, by conscription.

Although at this time there was still some measure of unity between Great Britain, France, and Italy, they did no more than issue the Stresa Declaration of April 1935 condemning Germany's action, and in June Hitler was able to follow up his success by winning Britain's agreement to a breach of the naval clauses of the Treaty of Versailles (p. 253). This also had the effect of helping to estrange France from Britain, and Hitler's friendly attitude towards Mussolini at the time of the Italo-Abyssinian War (pp. 249–50) had a similar effect in ensuring that Italy's breach with Great Britain and France would be permanent.

The occupation of the Rhineland

Thus by the beginning of 1936 the principal signatory powers of the Locarno Treaties were divided among themselves, and Hitler, who had helped create these divisions, was ready to take advantage of them. In March 1935, when he had repudiated the Treaty of Versailles on the grounds that it was a *Diktat*, he had declared his loyalty to the freely negotiated Locarno Treaties. But in March 1936 he proclaimed that the French had broken the spirit of Locarno by signing a treaty with the U.S.S.R. (p. 239), and he announced that German troops were already marching into the demilitarised zone of the Rhineland.

This was a calculated bluff. The German military leaders had advised against it, and the German forces had sealed orders to withdraw if they met resistance. But Hitler had calculated correctly. France could not rely on Britain to stand by her, and she was unwilling to fight without assistance from Britain. So no resistance was offered.

The occupation of the Rhineland placed Germany in a far stronger military position than before, for the construction of a massive system of fortifications, the Siegfried Line, facing the Maginot Line (p. 238), would enable Germany to hold any attack from the West while she fought in the East. It also had the political effect of weakening the French system of alliances (p. 240).

Hitler's diplomatic achievement by the end of 1936

Later in the year, when Franco led his rebellion in Spain (p. 153), Hitler gave him assistance and thus ensured a friendly attitude from Spain in the future. In October Hitler concluded with Italy an agreement for mutual co-operation which brought into existence what came to be known as the Rome-Berlin Axis. And at the end of November Germany and Japan signed the Anti-Comintern Pact, promising to support each other against Communism.

Thus by the end of 1936 Hitler had flouted the Treaties of Versailles and Locarno, divided France from her carefully acquired allies, gained the friendship of the governments of Italy and Japan and of the future government of Spain, had gained British connivance at his rearmament, and had ensured that Poland would take no military action against him. It was a remarkable achievement. Small wonder that his prestige was high at home.

1937

The achievements of the four years 1933–6 were the direct result of a vigorous foreign policy in which Hitler had seized and maintained the initiative. By contrast 1937 was a year of quiet and consolidation before the big moves of the next two years which culminated in war.

The *Anschluss*

By the beginning of 1938 Hitler was ready to take action over Austria. In February he demanded of Schuschnigg, the Austrian Chancellor, that the Austrian Nazis should be given a share in the government. Schuschnigg made considerable concessions, but on 9th March he announced his intention to hold a plebiscite in which the Austrian people would vote on whether or not they wished to remain independent. On the 11th Hitler threatened invasion unless Schuschnigg resigned. The same evening Schuschnigg did resign, but the next day German troops nevertheless marched in, and the day after that Hitler announced the *Anschluss*, or union, of Germany and Austria. He met no opposition either from Austria or any other nation.

This success encouraged Hitler to take action against his next victim: Czechoslovakia. And the *Anschluss* had increased his strategical advantage over Czechoslovakia, for it not only gave Germany added material resources and manpower, but also it had the effect of hemming Czechoslovakia in on three sides and making it possible for her to be attacked from the South as well.

The Sudetenland

As soon as Hitler had seized control of Austria he began stimulating unrest among the German-speaking peoples of Czechoslovakia, living in the area known as the Sudetenland. They demanded self-government, he supported them vociferously, and during the summer tension increased. The Czechs were frightened of a German invasion, and Britain and France were frightened of having to fight Germany in defence of Czechoslovakia.

In September the Czechs were persuaded by the British government to accept the German demand for self-government for the Sudetenland. But Hitler then demanded the transfer of the Sudetenland to Germany. The British and French governments persuaded the Czechs to accept the gradual transfer of all the areas where more than half the population were German-speaking; and on the 22nd Neville Chamberlain, the British Prime Minister, brought this agreement to Hitler. Hitler's reaction was to make further demands. He now insisted on immediate military occupation of the Sudetenland and on the further cession of other areas of Czechoslovakia to Hungary and Poland. This time the British and French did not insist that the Czechs should accept Hitler's demands, so the Czechs refused. On the 26th Hitler made it clear that he intended invasion. On the 29th Chamberlain, Mussolini, and Daladier, the French Prime Minister, met Hitler at Munich for a conference. The next day all Hitler's demands were accepted, and Chamberlain and Daladier informed the Czechs of the arrangements for the partial dismemberment of their country.

By gaining the Sudetenland Hitler also gained a further military advantage which would help him in the final destruction of Czechoslovakia, for the defence system which the Czechs had built in the mountain barrier of the North was now handed over to Germany, and Czechoslovakia was even more vulnerable to attack than before.

The destruction of Czechoslovakia

Hitler had declared at Munich that he had no further territorial ambitions in Europe. But a month later the *Wehrmacht* was given

secret instructions for 'finishing off the remainder of Czechoslovakia'; and all through the winter Hitler continued to provoke
unrest in Czechoslovakia among the minority groups.

On 14th March 1939 Slovakia proclaimed its independence.
The Czech President, Hácha, travelled to Berlin, where he was
intimidated into handing over his country to Hitler, and meanwhile German troops were crossing the border. The Czech areas
became the Protectorate of Bohemia and Moravia; Slovakia became a separate satellite state, and Ruthenia was handed to
Hungary.

Once again Hitler had gained a military advantage from his
move. Six months earlier Czechoslovakia had been militarily the
strongest state other than Germany in central Europe. Now Germany controlled all her military equipment and all her industrial
strength, including the great *Skoda* armaments works.

The last six months of peace

A week after the destruction of Czechoslovakia Hitler forced
Lithuania to hand over Memel, and at about the same time a
demand was presented to Poland for the return of Danzig to Germany and the creation of an extra-territorial belt of land linking
East Prussia to the rest of Germany. This met with a direct refusal
from Poland and provoked Britain on 31st March into giving a
guarantee of support for Poland against attack.

Then in April, when Britain introduced conscription, Hitler took
the opportunity of accusing her of aggressive intentions and renounced the Anglo-German Naval Treaty of 1935 and also the
German-Polish pact of 1934. In May he concluded non-aggression
pacts with Estonia, Latvia, and Denmark, bound Italy closer to
Germany by the 'Pact of Steel' (p. 251), and entered into trade
negotiations with the U.S.S.R. This last development was supremely important. If Hitler attacked Poland he was likely to be
involved in a war with France and Britain. He had no wish to
engage in a war on two fronts and therefore wanted to win rapidly
in the East before turning his attention West. This would not be
possible if the U.S.S.R. feared that he would advance through
Poland into Russia. He therefore set himself to allay Russian
suspicions, and in August succeeded. On the 23rd he concluded a
non-aggression pact with Stalin. This was an even more dramatic
diplomatic revolution than the German-Polish non-aggression pact
of 1934, and it also made war a practical possibility. Just a week
later, on 1st September 1939, Germany attacked Poland.

Mussolini's early years

MUSSOLINI was able to come to power in Italy in October 1922 partly because of Italian dissatisfaction with the peace settlement and with the weak foreign policy of the democratic government. He rapidly brought a new assertiveness to Italian foreign policy, and the first indication of this assertiveness came in August 1923 with the Corfu incident (p. 229). In the following year Mussolini was able to reach a favourable settlement with Jugoslavia, whereby Italy got Fiume and the port of Zara in return for giving up her claim to the rest of the Dalmatian coast. Then in 1927 he strengthened Italy's influence over Albania by concluding a defensive alliance, the Treaty of Tirana, with her.

Friction between Italy and France

Italy's resentment of the peace settlement gave her common ground with those countries which wanted the settlement revised, and turned her away from the countries which were interested in its maintenance. Thus the natural direction of Italian policy in the twenties was towards friendship with Germany, Hungary, and Bulgaria, and friction in relations with France and the 'Little Entente' of Czechoslovakia, Jugoslavia, and Roumania.

Another cause of friction between Italy and France was Italian jealousy of the French colonial empire. This dated back to 1881, when the French had annexed Tunisia, where Italians were still discontented with their status; and the friction was increased by the failure of France to honour her obligations under the Treaty of London of 1915 to give Italy land in Africa as compensation for the French acquisition of mandates over some of Germany's colonies.

Italian resentment of France was also stimulated by the fact that the French had supported the territorial claims of Jugoslavia against those of Italy at the peace conference, and had backed Jugoslavia over the question of Fiume in 1920 (p. 134). But the principal issue was the question of the peace settlement and Italy's dislike of the system of alliances by which France was determined to maintain it.

The success of Mussolini's policy

The consequence of this was that a cardinal point of Mussolini's foreign policy in the decade after he came to power was the restoration of Germany to a position of equality with the other European powers. It was for this reason that he joined in the Western Locarno Treaty of 1925 (p. 235), which Germany negotiated on terms of equality, and that he welcomed Germany into the League of Nations in 1926. This policy reached its culmination in March 1933, the same month that Hitler gained absolute power in Germany, when Mussolini proposed a Four-Power Pact between Italy, Germany, Great Britain, and France, providing for the co-ordination of foreign and colonial policies, consideration of the revision of the peace treaties, and the recognition of Germany's right to rearm if the other powers failed to disarm.

This was, of course, acceptable to Germany, and the British government saw no reason to object to it, but it dealt a shrewd blow against France and her allies. Although France managed to make it harmless by negotiation, she did not reject it outright for fear of offending both Italy and Great Britain, and this gave offence to her allies: Poland resented being excluded from the Pact when she felt that she had just as much right as Italy to be regarded as a great power; and the confidence of the 'Little Entente' in French determination to protect their interests was weakened.

The effect of Hitler's advent to power

But just as Mussolini succeeded in this way in undermining the French system of alliances his foreign policy underwent a drastic change. Strangely enough the advent to power of Hitler in Germany, far from drawing Italy and Germany closer together, had the effect of driving them apart and of pushing Italy temporarily into the arms of France.

The security of Italy's Northern frontier, and especially the newly acquired area of the South Tyrol, depended on Austria either remaining independent or coming under Italian domination; and Hitler's ambition to include Austria in the German *Reich* constituted a potential threat to Italy. Consequently Mussolini was determined to establish Italian rather than German influence in Austria. In March 1934 he succeeded in gaining considerable control over both the foreign and domestic policies of Austria; and then in July 1934, when the Austrian Nazis killed Dollfüss, the Austrian Chancellor, he rushed troops to the frontier and succeeded in dissuading Hitler from attempting to seize Austria.

Rapprochement with France

Meanwhile relations between France and Italy improved until in January 1935 Mussolini and Laval, the French Foreign Minister, reached agreement on most of the issues which had prevented friendly relations between their countries, and agreed to co-ordinate their policies on German rearmament and the independence of Austria.

They soon had cause to co-ordinate their policies in regard to German rearmament, for in March 1935 Hitler announced the introduction of conscription in Germany. But although they joined in the Stresa Declaration condemning Germany's measures, they took no action against her.

The annexation of Abyssinia

The reason for Mussolini's disinclination to do anything to offend Hitler at this stage was that he was plotting the annexation of Abyssinia, an independent East African state which lay between the Italian colonies of Eritrea and Italian Somaliland, and this made him anxious to keep free from European entanglements.

Italy had gained control of Eritrea by 1885 and of Italian Somaliland in 1889, and had made an attempt to link them in 1896 by an expedition into Abyssinia, only to be defeated by Abyssinian

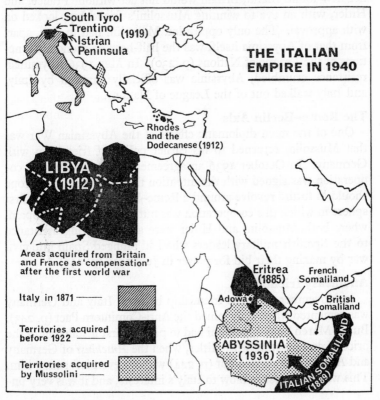

THE ITALIAN EMPIRE IN 1940

South Tyrol
Trentino (1919)
Istrian Peninsula

Rhodes and the Dodecanese (1912)

LIBYA (1912)

Areas acquired from Britain and France as 'compensation' after the first world war

Italy in 1871 ——

Territories acquired before 1922 ——

Territories acquired by Mussolini ——

Eritrea (1885)
Adowa
Abyssinia (1936)
French Somaliland
British Somaliland
ITALIAN SOMALILAND (1889)

tribesmen in the battle of Adowa. After the first World War Italy's ambition to expand in Africa was thwarted by the opposition of France. So in the twenties Mussolini attempted to extend Italian influence there by friendly co-operation: in 1923 he supported the admission of Abyssinia to the League of Nations, and in 1928 he concluded a treaty with her in which he promised that any dispute they might have would be submitted to arbitration. But by the end of 1933 he had plans ready for an invasion; in December 1934 he took advantage of a frontier incident on the border between Abyssinia and Italian Somaliland to demand an indemnity from her; and he then began building up forces in Eritrea and Italian Somaliland. In the next month, January 1935, he reached his agreement with France, and this included a vague French acceptance of some extension of Italian influence in Abyssinia.

It was not until October that he actually invaded, and then he found that he had calculated correctly that none of the great powers would use force against him. France was unwilling to act against her new-found friend, Britain would not act without France, and Hitler, with an eye to winning Mussolini's friendship, looked on with approval. The only opposition Mussolini had to face, apart from that of Abyssinia itself, was the half-hearted economic sanctions of the League of Nations (p. 230). In May 1936 Abyssinian resistance crumbled, Abyssinia was officially annexed by Italy, and Italy walked out of the League of Nations.

The Rome–Berlin Axis

One of the main diplomatic effects of the Abyssinian War was that Mussolini returned to his earlier policy of friendship with Germany. In October 1936 an agreement for Italo-German co-operation was signed with the intention that the affairs of Europe should in future revolve around a Rome–Berlin Axis, and the first sphere in which this co-operation was put into practice was Spain, where both Mussolini and Hitler were already giving assistance to the Spanish military leaders who had plunged Spain into civil war by making their bid for power in July 1936 (p. 153).

An uneasy friendship

In November 1937 the friendship between Italy and Germany was cemented when Italy joined the Anti-Comintern Pact (p. 243). But in March 1938 Mussolini had to pay the first instalment of the price of co-operating with Hitler, when the *Anschluss* of Germany and Austria was carried out (p. 244) without even informing him. This was, of course, a blow to Italy's interests, and it was very unpopular in Italy, but by now Mussolini felt too closely committed to Hitler to oppose him.

When in March 1939 Hitler added another humiliation by destroying Czechoslovakia without informing him, Mussolini reacted in the following month by invading and annexing Albania. But in May he bound himself closer to Hitler by concluding the 'Pact of Steel', in which Italy and Germany promised mutual assistance in any war.

Italy, however, was in no position to fight a major war (p. 139), so on 25th August 1939, when war was obviously imminent, Mussolini told Hitler that Italy was not yet ready to fight and decided for the moment to be 'non-belligerent'.

Italy's war, June 1940–September 1943

Consequently it was not until 10th June 1940, more than nine months after the beginning of the war, when France was almost beaten, that Mussolini, anxious to get his share of the spoils, declared war on her. He was too late. In the few days before France collapsed thirty-two Italian divisions were only able to push the six French divisions facing them back a few hundred yards, and in the armistice Hitler would not allow Mussolini any more territory than he had already gained.

Mussolini soon had to face the humiliating fact that militarily he was just as much tied to Hitler's coat-tails as he was diplomatically. In the early stages of the war he did make two unsuccessful attempts to act on his own initiative. In October 1940 Italian forces invaded Greece, this time without informing Hitler, but they were rapidly driven back into Albania. Already in September 1940 an Italian army had invaded Egypt, but by mid-February 1941 it had been driven almost out of Africa. Meanwhile in January 1941 the British had attacked Italy's East African Empire, and in May they finally conquered it.

Italy now had to depend for the recapture and defence of Libya on the German *Afrikakorps*, but after this was defeated in the second battle of El Alamein in October 1942, both the Italian and the German forces were rapidly swept out of Africa.

In July 1943 Anglo-American forces landed in Sicily, and later in the month Mussolini was overthrown by his own Fascist Grand Council. At the beginning of September, when the British Eighth Army crossed to the mainland, Italy surrendered unconditionally, and a week later, after three years and three months at war as the ally of Germany, Italy changed sides and fought against the German army as it was driven North.

51   APPEASEMENT

THE eight years before the second World War, when Britain was ruled by the National government, were a time of weakness and vacillation in foreign policy. Unlike the eight years before the first World War, when one man, Sir Edward Grey, had directed a consistent foreign policy, these years saw three Prime Ministers (MacDonald, Baldwin, and Chamberlain) and five Foreign Secretaries (Lord Reading, Sir John Simon, Sir Samuel Hoare, Anthony Eden, and Lord Halifax), each groping with the problems produced by the rise of dictatorship in Europe. They appreciated that Nazi Germany and Fascist Italy were a threat to the peace of Europe, but they were also conscious of a different threat from Soviet Russia; and they failed to act firmly against Germany and Italy, partly because they hesitated to destroy a bulwark against Communism, and partly because they lacked the military strength and the support of public opinion necessary for taking action.

Public opinion and the fighting services

Public opinion as a whole felt that Germany had been too harshly treated in the peace settlement, and right up to the destruction of Czechoslovakia in March 1939 (p. 245) it was possible for Englishmen to regard Hitler's aggression as a justifiable attempt to redress genuine grievances. Public opinion was also strongly inclined towards pacifism, and since it was widely believed that the first World War had resulted from the build-up of armaments it was also opposed to rearmament. The effect of this was that Britain was in no position to fight another great power even if she wanted to. Her army was dismantled, her air force was not yet developed, and even at sea she was no longer supreme. The limitations imposed by the Washington Naval Treaty of 1922 (p. 234) meant that Britain was no longer in a position to challenge either the U.S.A. or Japan in the Pacific, and Britain had not even built up to the limits agreed in the treaty.

The effects of naval weakness were felt within a few weeks of the National government taking office. When the Japanese invasion of Manchuria in September 1931 was condemned by the League of Nations Britain did not feel strong enough to undertake the responsibility of naval operations on the other side of the world.

Collective security or conciliation

Despite this failure of both Britain and the League, the British government continued to proclaim its belief in 'collective security'.

But it was hoping that Europe's problems could be solved by the conciliation of Germany, and after the Nazis came to power Britain, unlike France, still advocated 'equality of status' for Germany on matters of disarmament. Even after Hitler had announced the introduction of conscription in March 1935, Sir John Simon, the British Foreign Secretary, still visited him later in the month, thus appearing to condone his action.

Vacillation

At this point British foreign policy in relation to both Germany and Italy began to vacillate in a remarkable way.

Germany: In April Britain joined France and Italy in the Stresa Declaration, condemning Germany's action as a breach of the Treaty of Versailles. But immediately afterwards the British government took up a suggestion made by Hitler at his meeting with Simon and negotiated an agreement whereby Britain accepted that Germany could ignore the naval clauses of the Treaty of Versailles to the extent of building warships up to an overall strength of 35 per cent that of the Royal Navy, and with the same strength in submarines as Britain. This was signed in June—the month in which Baldwin succeeded MacDonald as Prime Minister and Sir Samuel Hoare succeeded Sir John Simon as Foreign Secretary.

Italy: Meanwhile the main issue in international affairs was the build-up of Italian forces on the borders of Abyssinia. At the time of the Stresa Declaration Britain had avoided bringing up the question of Abyssinia for fear of offending Italy. But in September Sir Samuel Hoare made a speech to the Assembly of the League of Nations declaring Britain's readiness to defend Abyssinia from 'all acts of unprovoked aggression'; and in November, the month after Mussolini's invasion, economic sanctions were imposed on Italy and Baldwin fought and won a general election on the principle of 'collective security'. Despite this, Hoare went to Paris in December and worked out with Laval, the French Foreign Secretary, proposals for ending the Abyssinian War whereby Italy was to be ceded nearly two-thirds of Abyssinia.

The reason for these vacillations is that the British government was genuinely uncertain what to do. The explanation of the Anglo-German Naval Treaty and the Hoare–Laval Pact is that the British government was inclined to deal with foreign policy as if it were making a business deal. On purely practical grounds there was a lot to be said for this approach. The Anglo-German Naval Treaty secured a German promise to limit naval building, and the Hoare–

Laval Pact would at least not have given Mussolini the whole of Abyssinia. But the drawbacks to this approach are that it assumed that the dictators would keep their promises and that it ignored principles such as the sanctity of treaties and the inviolability of independent states. Even on practical grounds the agreement to have parity in submarines was scarcely sensible.

Thus in 1935 British foreign policy did not merely lack any clear direction; it also lacked any clear principles. Sir Samuel Hoare had to pay the price for this in December when the terms of the Hoare–Laval Pact became known, for public opinion was so incensed that Baldwin was only able to keep his government in office by disowning the pact and replacing Hoare with Anthony Eden.

Eden and Chamberlain

Eden was inclined to take a firm line with the dictators. But Britain was scarcely in a position to oppose Hitler's breach of the military clauses of the Treaty of Versailles when he occupied the Rhineland in March 1936, partly because she had herself accepted the breach of the naval clauses in the previous year, and partly because public opinion would not have tolerated firm action on this particular issue. And in May 1937 British foreign policy was complicated by the fact that Neville Chamberlain, who then succeeded Baldwin as Prime Minister, had a different foreign policy from that of his Foreign Secretary. It was a policy of appeasement of the dictators. Believing that the dictators had limited aims and that Europe would have peace if those aims were satisfied, he wanted to try to win their friendship by making concessions. His differences with Eden came to a head early in 1938 when he wanted to negotiate an agreement with Italy, which was eventually signed in April, and in which Britain promised, among other things, to try to get other states to recognise Italian sovereignty in Abyssinia. Eden resigned in protest against this in February.

Appeasement

Two days after Eden's resignation Chamberlain indicated his attitude publicly by declaring that it would be wrong to encourage small nations in the belief that they would be protected from aggression by the League of Nations. Less than three weeks later Hitler annexed Austria.

In the summer Chamberlain decided to take a positive line in his policy of appeasement by trying to mediate in the quarrel between the Germans and the Czechs over the Sudetenland; and in September he persuaded the Czech government to accept most of the German demands. When Hitler reacted by increasing his demands Chamberlain persuaded Daladier, the French Prime Minister, to join him in insisting to the Czechs that they should accept Hitler's new demands, and on the 22nd he flew to Germany to take the agreement to Hitler. Only when Hitler made yet further demands did Chamberlain agree with the French to support Czechoslovakia in the event of a German invasion. But even then he felt that it was not really worth fighting over the extra concessions Hitler wanted, so he asked Mussolini to arrange a conference. On the 29th he flew to Munich for the conference, and on the 30th he and Daladier accepted all Hitler's demands and then informed the Czechs (p. 245).

From appeasement to war

The Munich agreement included a British guarantee of the integrity of the rest of Czechoslovakia, but when it was seized by Hitler in March 1939 Chamberlain pointed out that Britain could not assist a state which no longer existed. Nevertheless, this was as far as he was prepared to let Hitler go. When in the same month Hitler made demands on Poland, Chamberlain announced that Britain would defend Poland against any threat to her independence; and in April, when Italy annexed Albania, Britain gave similar guarantees to Greece and Roumania. Later in the same month the government introduced conscription and began to call up men aged nineteen and twenty, and in the summer Britain joined France in trying to arrange with the U.S.S.R. for mutual assistance against any German attack.

Appeasement had at last been abandoned, but unfortunately in his zeal to make Britain's new position clear Chamberlain swung so far to the opposite extreme that he threw away the last diplomatic advantage which Britain possessed. The U.S.S.R. feared an attack by Germany, but Germany could only attack her by going through Poland or Roumania. Thus when Britain gave her guarantees to Poland and Roumania Russia was assured of Britain's assistance in the event of a German attack Eastwards, and had little more to gain from negotiations with Britain. In this situation Russia came to terms with Germany (p. 258), and towards the end of August signed a non-aggression pact. A week later, on 1st September Germany invaded Poland and Britain had to fulfil her pledge. Militarily she was incapable of doing so. Politically there was no alternative, and on 3rd September, when no reply was received to an ultimatum, Britain declared war on Germany.

The idea of World Revolution, 1917–21

THE BOLSHEVIKS who seized power in Russia in November 1917 were concerned above all with the promotion of world-wide revolution. They did not expect permanent success even in Russia unless the revolution spread, and they were prepared to subordinate the interests of Russia to the cause of international revolution. When their appeal for peace to all governments and peoples at war met with no response, they decided to make a separate peace with Germany, and in March 1918 they accepted the Treaty of Brest-Litovsk (pp. 219–20) on Germany's terms.

For the moment they faced such difficulties at home that it was impossible for them to do much to further world revolution. They were faced with military intervention in the North by Russia's former allies, who were prepared to assist any group willing to continue the war against Germany. They had to fight a civil war against the counter-revolutionary armies of Denikin, Kolchak, and Yudenitch. And they had to fight a war against Poland. But during 1919 and 1920 the Allied troops were gradually withdrawn, by 1921 the Bolsheviks had won the civil war, and later in the year they signed the Treaty of Riga with the Poles (p. 228).

Meanwhile there had been Communist revolutions in Berlin, Munich, and Budapest, but they had all been rapidly suppressed, and liberal democracy, the form of government of the victorious European allies, Britain, France, and Italy, seemed more firmly established than ever in the West. The Russian Bolsheviks realised that world revolution was not imminent and that they would have to settle down to consolidating their position at home.

Rapprochement with the West, 1921–30

They also realised that as the result of the troubles of the previous seven years Russia faced economic disaster. Part of the solution to this seemed to be to get economic assistance from the Western capitalist countries, and they calculated correctly that for the sake of a quick profit capitalists would be willing to subsidise and strengthen even a régime which intended eventually to destroy capitalism.

As early as March 1921 they were able to conclude a trade agreement with Britain. But it was with Germany that they established the closest ties in the twenties. This was natural, for Germany, like Russia, was without friends after the first World War, and the two outcasts naturally drew together. In 1921 arrangements were made for trade, and a secret agreement was reached whereby Germany was enabled to evade some of the disarmament clauses of the Treaty of Versailles in return for help in building up the Red Army. In 1922 this agreement was confirmed in the Treaty of Rapallo, which on the surface was merely an undertaking to help each other out of economic difficulties.

The trend in the foreign policy of Russia, which was known as the U.S.S.R. after 1923, away from the promotion of world revolution towards the establishment of friendly relations with other countries was carried further after the death of Lenin in January 1924. For Stalin, who was steadily increasing his power in the U.S.S.R., was concerned primarily with strengthening the Russian state and his own position at its head, and realised that this would be easier if relations with other countries were not strained. He therefore made little effort to assist Communists to seize power in other countries and instead tried to improve relations between the U.S.S.R. and the West. In 1927 Russia even began to take part in the non-political activities of the League of Nations. By the end of 1929 all the European great powers recognised the Soviet government, and in 1930 Stalin appointed a new Foreign Commissar, Maxim Litvinov, who particularly tried to establish friendlier relations with the West.

The strengthening of Western ties, 1930–6

During the early thirties the U.S.S.R. was given another reason for becoming friendly with the Western liberal democracies. In 1931 Japan began to reassert herself by annexing Manchuria, and in 1933 the violently anti-Communist Nazi Party came to power in Germany and signed a non-aggression pact with Poland in January 1934. The Soviet leaders feared that Japan intended to encroach on Russian territory in the Far East, and that Hitler was planning to regain for Germany the lands lost to Poland in the Treaty of Versailles by compensating Poland with land taken from Russia.

The effect of this was to put the U.S.S.R. in the rather surprising position of an upholder of the Treaty of Versailles, and to recreate the Franco-Russian alliance which had existed for twenty years before the first World War. In September 1934 the U.S.S.R. at last joined the League of Nations, which Germany and Japan had both left in 1933. In May 1935 Russia and France signed a treaty promising each other assistance in the event of an attack by a European power; and at the same time Russia promised to assist Czechoslovakia against aggression so long as France gave her help first. Another indication of this trend in Russian foreign policy was that in the summer of 1935 the Seventh Comintern Congress approved the formation of 'Popular Fronts'—that is, the collaboration of Communists with other parties against the possibility of right-wing dictatorship.

Disillusionment with the West, 1936–9

However, the Russians became increasingly disillusioned with their new friends in the West. In 1936 when civil war broke out in Spain the U.S.S.R. found that no other country was prepared to give active assistance to the Spanish government. In 1937 when Japan renewed her attack on China the U.S.S.R. found that no other country was prepared to join her in assisting the victim of aggression. And in 1938 when the Sudetenland crisis came to a head (p. 244) Chamberlain and Daladier never consulted with the U.S.S.R., even though Litvinov reaffirmed in September that Russia was willing to join France in defending Czechoslovakia. After the Munich agreement Stalin came to the conclusion that the British and French leaders were trying to turn Hitler towards the East and use Nazism to destroy Bolshevism, and he ceased to put any more trust in them than in Hitler.

The non-aggression Pact, 23rd August 1939

In April 1939 Stalin saw an opportunity for turning the tables on them. The British guarantees to Poland at the end of March and to Greece and Roumania in April (p. 255), all of which were followed by similar French guarantees, created a completely new diplomatic situation. Since it was a geographical necessity for German troops to go through Poland or Roumania to reach Russia, it followed that Hitler could not launch an attack on Russia without provoking an attack on Germany by France and Britain. This was a situation as displeasing to Hitler, who had no wish to fight a war on two fronts, as it was comforting to Stalin, who was placed in a very strong diplomatic position. He had little more to gain from France and Britain, and though negotiations with them for mutual assistance began in April he took little interest in them. But he had much to gain from Germany; so in May he replaced the pro-Western Litvinov as Foreign Commissar with Molotov, who immediately opened secret negotiations with Hitler.

On 23rd August 1939 Molotov signed a non-aggression pact with Ribbentrop, the German Foreign Minister, and in a secret protocol arranged a partition of Eastern Europe which would give

Russia approximately those areas lost to her as the result of the treaties of Brest-Litovsk and Versailles. Stalin knew that the non-aggression pact would result in a German attack on Poland within a few days. And he had no illusions that Hitler would maintain the non-aggression pact any longer than it suited him. But he was buying both land and time. After defeating Poland Hitler would turn West against France and Britain, and while all the capitalist powers of Europe, whether totalitarian or democratic, tore each other to pieces Stalin could extend his power over Eastern Europe and eventually choose his own time to intervene in the war.

The German War, June 1941–May 1945

At first everything went approximately as intended. Seventeen days after the German attack on Poland on 1st September the Red Army invaded from the East. At about the same time Stalin demanded concessions, which amounted to acceptance of Russian domination, from Finland, Estonia, Latvia, and Lithuania. Only Finland refused. This was Stalin's first set-back, for when the Russians invaded Finland in November 1939 they met determined and effective resistance. However, by March 1940 the U.S.S.R. was able to induce Finland to cede some small but strategically important areas of land and the use of bases in the Baltic. And in June 1940 the U.S.S.R. seized Bessarabia and northern Bukovina from Roumania.

Thus as a result of the non-aggression pact Stalin had gained a large cushion of land along Russia's western frontier. More important, he had gained nearly two years, for it was not until 22nd June 1941 that Hitler turned to the East again and invaded Russia.

But even two years was not enough to strengthen the Red Army enough to enable it to hold the German onslaught. During 1941 it was driven back almost to Moscow, and Leningrad was surrounded. And although the Germans were halted that winter and even driven back a bit, they continued their advance in 1942. At last in the winter of 1942 the tide turned. The Germans were defeated at the battle of Stalingrad, and during 1943, 1944, and 1945 the Russian armies advanced until they met the British and Americans half-way across Germany.

The Japanese War, 8th–15th August 1945

In February 1945 Stalin had met Churchill and Roosevelt at Yalta in the Crimea and had secretly agreed to declare war on Japan soon after Germany was defeated in return for the Kurile Islands and the territory and spheres of influence lost by Russia in the Russo-Japanese War of 1904–5 (p. 312). However, when Germany was defeated Stalin still delayed joining the war against Japan, preferring to let his allies expend their energies in the Far East while he consolidated his position in Europe.

Then on 6th August, just after the Potsdam Conference (p. 412) which confirmed the arrangements made at Yalta, the whole situation was changed by the dropping of the first atomic bomb on Hiroshima by his allies. Stalin saw the danger of losing the lands he wanted in the East unless he kept his part of the bargain, so he declared war on Japan two days later. The next day the second atomic bomb was dropped on Nagasaki. Within a week Japan had surrendered.

The Eastern lands and spheres of influence of the old Tsarist Empire had been recovered with scarcely any effort, and Stalin also managed to extend Russian influence into Outer Mongolia and the Northern half of Korea. The Western lands had only finally

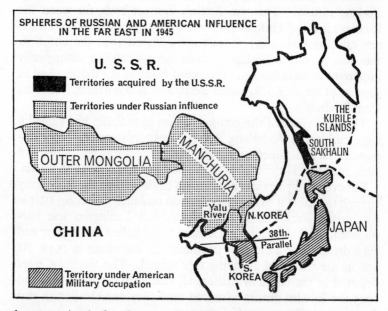

been regained after four years of bitter fighting. But in the West Russian influence had spread much farther into Europe than it ever had under the Tsars (see maps, pp. 220 and 393). Stalin's policy of building 'Socialism in one country' (p. 130) had paid dividends. There was no need to encourage Communist revolution in Eastern Europe from outside. He was able to impose it by force.

The destruction of Poland

ON 1st September 1939 Hitler launched his armies against Poland. This rapidly involved him in war with France and most of the British Commonwealth, but they were not militarily strong enough to take immediate action against him, and the attack in the East continued without any disturbance on Germany's Western frontier. It was the Poles who had to fight on two fronts, for on 17th September the Russians invaded, and by the end of the month Poland had been crushed between her two powerful neighbours and dismembered.

Already Germany and the U.S.S.R. were falling out over how to divide Eastern Europe between them, so Hitler now suggested to France and Britain that they should make peace and leave him a free hand in the East. When they refused he wanted to launch against them the same sort of lightning war, or *Blitzkrieg*, which had been so successful against Poland. But the approach of winter made this impossible. Instead there followed the months of inactivity known to the British as the 'phoney war' and to the Germans as the *Sitzkrieg*. And the German army prepared to attack France in the following spring.

Scandinavian diversion

In the spring of 1940, however, Hitler's attention was diverted North. Britain was making preparations for a landing in Norway, partly in order to open a supply route to the Finns, who had been attacked by the Russians in November 1939, and partly in order to cut Germany off from the Swedish iron ore on which German heavy industry depended, and which was transported to Germany via ports in Norway, such as Narvik, and then round the Norwegian coast. On 8th April the British began mining Norway's coastal waters. But on the 9th Hitler launched his attack on Scandinavia. Denmark fell without fighting. Sweden allowed the Germans to march through. Norway managed to hold out for six weeks.

Victory in the West

On 10th May, after a delay of only a month, the Germans attacked in the West. Holland collapsed on the 14th, and a direct thrust by the German armies through Luxembourg and South Belgium into France took them to the Channel coast in ten days. The British Expeditionary Force, the Belgian army, and many French troops were trapped between the advancing Germans and

the sea, and after a week, on 28th May, Belgium capitulated. By
the end of another week most of the British and some of the
French had managed to escape across the Channel to England.
The rest went into captivity. On 5th June the German armies
turned South, and within a fortnight the French had asked for an
armistice.

The Battle of Britain

By this time Hitler was already worried by the way the U.S.S.R.
was strengthening her position in Eastern Europe, and at the end of
July he gave orders for secret preparations to be made for an attack
on Russia. But he still wished to avoid fighting a war on two
fronts, and it was therefore necessary to defeat Britain first. But to
conquer Britain his armies would have to cross the English Channel in a fleet of towed barges which could not even move as fast as
Julius Caesar's invasion fleet two thousand years earlier. This
operation, and the subsequent maintenance of supply lines, would
only be possible if the German air force, the *Luftwaffe*, could
establish permanent air superiority over the Channel; and the
result was the Battle of Britain from August to October 1940 in
which the Royal Air Force and the *Luftwaffe* fought for control of
the skies. The Royal Air Force won. Hitler had met his first set-
back in the war, and by November he had decided that the invasion
of Britain would have to be postponed indefinitely. Britain would
have to be blockaded by U-boats, while priority was given to the
invasion of Russia.

Mediterranean diversion

Hitler wanted to attack Russia in the spring of 1941, but just as
he had been temporarily diverted to Scandinavia in 1940 so he was
now temporarily diverted to the Mediterranean area—this time by
the precipitous action of his Italian ally. Mussolini, who had taken
Italy into the war just in time for the collapse of France,
had invaded Egypt in September 1940 and Greece in October.
In each case the Italian forces were disastrously unsuccessful.
The British nearly drove them right out of Africa and the Greeks
pushed them back into Albania. So Hitler sent the *Afrikakorps*
under General Rommel to help the Italians hold Tunisia, and
when the British transferred some of their troops to Greece he
decided to invade the Balkans to ensure that the Roumanian oilfields would be out of reach of British bombers when he invaded
Russia.

On 6th April he attacked Jugoslavia and Greece, and although

Jugoslavia capitulated after eleven days and Greece after fifteen this still meant putting off the invasion of Russia until 22nd June, the anniversary of the fall of France. In the event the delay caused by this Balkan campaign was to be of great importance.

War with Russia and the U.S.A.

Hitler expected to defeat Russia before winter set in, and the German armies which swept East in the summer of 1941 as far as the outskirts of Leningrad and Moscow had no winter clothing.

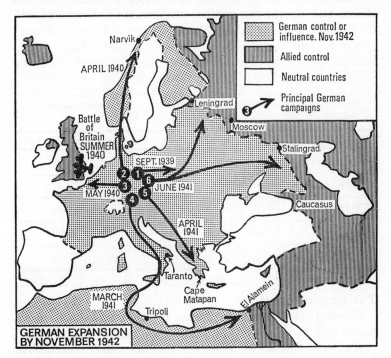

But in 1941 winter came early, and the Russians had destroyed their country behind them as they retreated, so that the German armies now had to endure a Russian winter with their lines of communication stretching hundreds of miles across hostile desolated countryside. Hitler had put himself in 1941 in a similar position to that which he had taken such care to avoid in 1939. He was fighting a war on two fronts—against Russia in the East and against Britain at sea and in Africa.

By the end of the year, when the German armies in Russia were suffering their first reverses, the overall situation was even worse than this. In September 1940, during the Battle of Britain, the

Anti-Comintern Pact had been transformed into a military treaty, the Tripartite Pact, whereby Germany, Italy, and Japan promised to give assistance to each other in the event of an attack by any power not then at war other than Russia. This was clearly directed against the U.S.A., and on 11th December 1941, four days after Pearl Harbor (p. 292), Hitler, who had already been contemplating attacking America because of the help she was giving Britain in the Atlantic, declared war on her.

Germany still had the advantage of the military strength she had already built up, the vast material resources she had captured, and the fact that Japan would divert some British and American energies away from Europe. But time was against her. The potential strength of an alliance including the British Commonwealth, the U.S.S.R., and the U.S.A. was overwhelming.

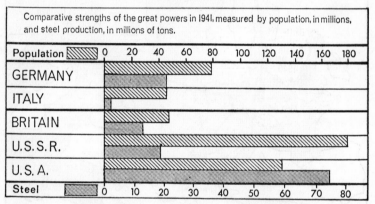

Comparative strengths of the great powers in 1941, measured by population, in millions, and steel production, in millions of tons.

The turn of the tide

However, in the summer of 1942 the German armies had renewed success. They drove the Russians back to Stalingrad and pushed down into the Caucasus, and they drove the British back in Africa as far as El Alamein. It seemed as if they might seize the whole Middle East in a vast pincer movement. But the farther they advanced the more difficult their supply problem became, and meanwhile both British and Russians were preparing for battle.

In October at El Alamein the British inflicted on the Germans their first serious military defeat, and in November Anglo-American forces landed in Morocco and Algeria and began to advance against the *Afrikakorps* from the West. In the same month the Russians struck at the German forces attacking Stalingrad and cut off 300,000 men, a half of whom were killed before the rest surrendered at the end of January 1943.

During the early months of 1943 the German and Italian troops in Africa were driven rapidly back from both East and West until in May 250,000 were trapped in Tunisia and had to surrender. By the end of the year Anglo-American troops had taken Sicily and were advancing North through Italy. Meanwhile the far larger German forces on the Russian front were also being driven back hundreds of miles.

The invasion of Normandy

On 6th June 1944 British and American troops landed on the Normandy coast, and by July, when they were firmly established, it was obvious that the Germans were beaten. The Russians had virtually cleared them out of the U.S.S.R., and were now advancing through Poland, Czechoslovakia, and Roumania. In the middle of July Rommel, who was now a Field Marshal, demanded that Hitler should recognise that Germany was defeated, and on the 20th an attempt on Hitler's life was made by Colonel Stauffenberg, Chief of Staff of the Reserve Army. But Hitler would certainly not consider surrender, and he survived the assassination attempt. In the next nine months until the war ended more Germans were killed than in the whole of the previous five years.

Defeat and surrender

At the end of July the American 1st Army broke out and after a rapid advance during August encircled and destroyed a large proportion of the German armour at Falaise. Then in the autumn, when the Allies were concentrating on strengthening their supply lines and were therefore advancing only slowly, Hitler made the mistake of thinking he could counterattack. Thirty divisions of what was left of his reserves struck through the centre of the advancing Allies. But this offensive in the Ardennes, like Ludendorff's July offensive in 1918, was a hopeless dying effort, and after an advance of 40 miles it collapsed.

For a long while the German towns had been subjected to heavy bombing and the whole country to an economic blockade. The last hope placed in new secret weapons, flying bombs and rockets, disappeared in the early months of 1945 as the Allies advanced across Germany from both East and West. On 25th April American and Russian troops made contact for the first time, five days later Hitler committed suicide, and on 7th May Germany surrendered unconditionally. As in the first World War Germany had been worn down by superior industrial strength and greater manpower, and in 1945 as in 1918 she collapsed completely.

Section VII Africa and America

54   THE BOER WAR AND THE UNION

The establishment of the Boer republics

DURING the Napoleonic Wars Great Britain seized Cape
Colony in South Africa, where there were about twenty-five
thousand *Boers*, or farmers, of Dutch descent. The British
government regarded the colony merely as a convenient station on
the route to India. They tended to neglect it, and in the 1830s two
thousand Boers who were discontented with British rule trekked
to the grassland areas of the interior, which were sparsely populated
by Bantu tribes, and founded two independent republics: the
Orange Free State, between the Orange and Vaal rivers, and the
Transvaal, between the Vaal and Limpopo rivers.

Annexation and the first Boer War

In 1877 the British government feared that one of the Bantu
tribes, the Zulus, was likely to overwhelm the Boer republics and
that this would later produce a threat to British territory. So
Britain annexed the Transvaal and then crushed the Zulus in the
Zulu War of 1879.

Gladstone, who was in opposition at the time, publicly condemned both the annexation and the Zulu War, but when he came
to power in 1880 he failed to give the Transvaal independence
immediately. The result was that the Boers of the Transvaal rose
under Paul Kruger and quickly defeated a British force at Majuba
Hill. Gladstone was in the difficult position of having previously
declared that the Transvaal should not have been annexed, so
instead of crushing the rising he granted the Transvaal its independence by the Convention of Pretoria in 1881.

Thus the Boers regained their independence in circumstances
which led them to believe that they had forced the British government to give in, made them contemptuous of the British army, and
embittered instead of improving Anglo-Boer relations.

British territorial expansion in South Africa

Further friction was caused by the way in which the Boers were
prevented from expanding either inland or to the sea by the extension of British influence in South Africa. In 1884 Bechuanaland
was annexed, thus blocking Boer expansion westwards. In 1889
Cecil Rhodes formed the British South Africa Company to develop

the area later known as Rhodesia, and in 1891 Dr. Jameson, one of the Company's agents, prevented the Boers from expanding North of the Limpopo river. Moreover, Cape Colony and Natal, which had been colonised by the British in the middle of the century, had by 1895 been extended to cover all the coast as far North as Portuguese East Africa, thus cutting the Boer republics off from the sea.

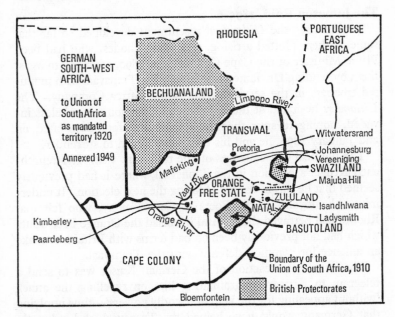

The gold of the Rand

The ill-feeling between the British and the Boers was brought to a head as a result of the discovery in 1886 at Witwatersrand in the Transvaal of large gold deposits which were so deep in the ground that the gold could only be extracted by someone with sufficient capital to pay for heavy machinery and a large, skilled labour force.

This meant that it tended to be Englishmen like Cecil Rhodes, who had already made a fortune out of the diamond mines at Kimberley, who were able to mine the gold of the Rand, and it also resulted in many Englishmen moving into the Transvaal.

The Transvaal government, which had previously been almost bankrupt, soon grew rich on the proceeds of a mines tax which produced nine-tenths of the country's revenue. But the Boers resented the new foreign immigrants, or *Uitlanders,* and would not grant them the same political rights as themselves. So in 1894 the *Uitlanders,* who by then numbered nearly a half of the male population of the country, presented a petition to the government demanding a constitution which would give them the right to vote, freedom of religion, free trade, and a system of justice free from political interference. Paul Kruger, now President of the Transvaal, refused to grant their demands.

The Jameson Raid, 1895–6

During 1895 the *Uitlanders'* resentment developed so far that some of them plotted a rising, and Cecil Rhodes, who had been Prime Minister of the Cape Colony since 1890, arranged to assist them by sending Dr. Jameson to invade the Transvaal with mounted troopers in the service of the South Africa Company. The *Uitlanders* hesitated at the last minute. Jameson nevertheless invaded, hoping to spur them to action. But four days later, on 2nd January 1896, he and his men were forced to surrender.

The political consequences of the raid were vast. It strengthened Kruger's position in the Transvaal, where it had previously seemed that he was in danger of losing the next election. It undermined the loyalty of the Boers of Cape Colony, who felt that Rhodes had betrayed them. And it caused the Orange Free State, which had not previously been on bad terms with Britain, to make an alliance for common defence with the Transvaal.

The immediate reaction of the German Kaiser was to send a telegram to Kruger congratulating him on repelling the attack 'without appealing for the help of friendly powers'—thus implying that Germany would have helped the Transvaal, and indirectly threatening the British. This encouraged Kruger to step up his armaments programme. In two years he more than quadrupled expenditure on arms, most of which were bought from Germany, and the Transvaal prepared and trained for war with the aim of driving the British out of South Africa.

The outbreak of the war, 1899

The *Uitlanders* were now persecuted by the Transvaal government, and when they sent a petition to the Queen the British government sent Sir Alfred Milner to try to negotiate better terms for them. When the negotiations broke down, Milner and Kruger both decided that war was inevitable, and while Milner advised the British government to send more troops to Cape Colony Kruger demanded the withdrawal of all British troops in the South of Africa. This was refused, so in October 1899 he declared war.

The period of Boer successes

The Boers began the war with a numerical advantage, but if they were to win they would have to do so before the British could transport their potentially far larger forces 6,000 miles across the sea; and then they would have to rely on diplomatic support from the European powers to prevent a British reconquest of South Africa.

They therefore attacked at once, and at first it looked as if they might succeed. But they were held up by the sieges of Ladysmith, Kimberley, and Mafeking, and because they were unwilling to continue their advance leaving these fortified strongholds to threaten their rear, they failed to reach the coast before the main British force arrived.

Despite this failure they continued to be successful, for the British army split up in an attempt to raise all three sieges, and in one week in December the Boers defeated each of the three groups.

The defeat of the Boers

But time was against them, and although they had won these tactical successes they had failed strategically, for the British lines of communication were still open, and in February 1900 the tide turned when a massive British army landed, led by Lord Roberts, with Sir Herbert Kitchener as his Chief of Staff.

In the same month Kimberley and Ladysmith were relieved and four thousand Boers surrendered at Paardeberg. In March the British took Bloemfontein, the capital of the Orange Free State, and then annexed the Orange Free State. In May they at last relieved Mafeking, which had been besieged since the beginning of the war, and in the same month they captured Johannesburg. At the beginning of June they took Pretoria, the capital of the Transvaal, and annexed the Transvaal. It seemed very much as if the Boers had been defeated after just eight months.

But although their armies had been defeated the Boers' spirit was unbroken, and they continued the war with guerrilla tactics for nearly two more years.

Kitchener was given the job of establishing effective control over the Boer territories. He did it by moving forward in stages, destroying crops, livestock, and farms, building blockhouses across the country and joining them up with barbed wire, and herding the women and children into concentration camps. He succeeded, but at the cost of twenty-six thousand women and children dying in the camps from disease—more than the total British losses in the war.

Peace and reconstruction

Eventually, in May 1902, the Boer leaders acknowledged British sovereignty in the Treaty of Vereeniging, and then Sir Alfred Milner, now Lord Milner, supervised the work of post-war reconstruction. £10 million and also a loan of £35 million were granted to repair the damage of war, and since there was a lack of native labour in the gold-mines of the Rand, which were the cornerstone of South Africa's economy, it was arranged to get them working again by importing Chinese coolies as labourers.

The Union of South Africa

In 1906, soon after a Liberal government took office in Britain, self-government was granted to the Transvaal, and in 1907 it was granted to the Orange Free State. Then in 1909 the governments of Cape Colony and Natal agreed to join the Transvaal and the Orange Free State in a Union of South Africa. The Union was established in 1910 by an Act of the British parliament, and Louis Botha, the Commander-in-Chief of the Boer forces during the war, became its first Prime Minister.

The Boer leaders, Botha and Jan Christian Smuts, wanted reconciliation with Britain and co-operation between the Boers and the English-speaking people of South Africa. Botha led South Africa into the first World War as the ally of Britain. Smuts similarly led South Africa into the second World War. But in 1948 a Nationalist Party won a general election, discouraged immigration from Britain, and eventually in 1960 made South Africa a republic. In 1961, fifty years after the formation of the Union, South Africa left the Commonwealth.

Apartheid

The issue on which the Nationalists won the election of 1948 was *apartheid*, or race segregation. Three and a half million white South Africans were outnumbered by fifteen million Bantu, or black South Africans. There were also two million people of mixed race, usually known as Coloureds, and half a million Asians. The aim of the Nationalist Party was to keep these races separate and maintain white supremacy.

It drew up a register to classify everyone by race, and it passed laws to forbid marriage between white and non-white, and to keep the races separate on public transport, on beaches, and in theatres, and in hospitals, schools, universities, and even churches. Among the white minority it was a popular policy, and in 1971 the Nationalist Party seemed likely to remain in power indefinitely.

55   BLACK AFRICA

African Nationalism

AT the beginning of the second World War in 1939 the European colonial powers controlled all of Africa except Egypt, the small state of Liberia which the Americans had founded in 1822 for freed slaves, and the Union of South Africa. Thirty years later, although much of Southern Africa was still controlled by white men, the land North of the Sahara was divided between five independent Arab states and the mass of the continent, inhabited by five hundred African tribes, was divided between more than thirty independent African states. What Harold Macmillan described in 1960 as a 'wind of change' had swept across the continent. It was the wind of African Nationalism.

The principal aim of African Nationalism was the liberation of the whole continent from foreign control. In practice the various African Nationalist leaders had to work within the old colonial boundaries, and the ideal of African unity, expressed in the Organization of African Unity created in 1963, was never strong enough to overcome these boundaries and create a greater African state. Instead powerful tribal feelings tended to pull the new states apart. Tribalism and African Nationalism were pulling in opposite directions.

Another aim of African Nationalism was to create a new African attitude, throwing off the old colonial mentality of subordination to white men, and taking a pride in what French-speaking Africans called *Négritude*. This did not mean reverting to tribalism. On the contrary, African Nationalists bitterly resented the attempt of the white rulers of South Africa to keep the Bantu separate in their traditional tribal culture. Instead they wanted to adapt European ideas and skills to African circumstances. Again, African Nationalism was in conflict with tribalism.

A third aim of African Nationalists was modernisation. They wanted to leap into the twentieth century and live on equal terms with Europe. This helps to explain why they developed sophisticated industries before they had a sound agriculture, and founded universities before they had widespread primary education. It also helps to explain their impatience with tribalism. Tribalism was the enemy of the ideal of African unity. Its primitive nature was an affront to the ideal of *Négritude*. And its association with traditional methods made it the enemy of modernisation.

All the same, tribalism was still a powerful force in Africa. Political parties often became tribal parties. And political opposition often appeared to be an expression of the enmity of one tribe towards another. European liberal democracy did not grow naturally in African soil. It needed careful tending.

The histories after independence of Zaïre, which was then known as the Congo, and of Nigeria, provide some illustration of the political problems which faced the new African states.

The Congo

The Belgian Congo seemed isolated from African Nationalism

in the decade after the second World War. The native *Force Publique* under its Belgian officers maintained order without difficulty, and no preparations were made for independence. But in 1957 the Belgians permitted a first step towards self-government by having elections for town councils. Political movements sprang rapidly into existence. In 1959 there was some serious rioting. And early in 1960 the Belgians decided to grant independence in June.

The Congolese politicians were divided over the issue of what sort of constitution the Congo should have. One of them, Patrice Lumumba, demanded a unitary state with power in the hands of the central government. Another, Joseph Kasavubu, wanted a federation. The result was a compromise. Ultimate power was to be in the hands of the central government, with Lumumba as prime minister. But provincial governments were to continue, and Kasavubu was to be President. Belgians were to remain in the administration and the *Force Publique* to help run the country.

On 30 June the Congo became independent. Five days later the *Force Publique* rebelled against its Belgian officers and rioting broke out. So the Belgian army re-entered the Congo. On 11 July Lumumba appealed to the United Nations against Belgian aggression, and only a week later the first United Nations troops arrived with the task of providing 'military assistance' to the government.

On the same day that Lumumba appealed to the United Nations Moise Tshombe, the provincial governor of the rich Southern copper-mining province of Katanga, encouraged by European business interests, declared Katanga independent. So in August Lumumba asked the U.N. forces to help him subdue Katanga. They refused. He then turned for help to the U.S.S.R. But in September the United Nations forces closed Leopoldville airport to stop the Russians transporting Lumumba's troops to fight the Katangese.

By this time President Kasavubu was trying to get rid of Lumumba. So the army Chief of Staff, Colonel Mobutu, arrested Lumumba, and early in 1961 Kasavubu had the captive Lumumba sent to Katanga, where Tshombe promptly had him killed.

Lumumba came to be identified after his death with the revolutionary Left, and the Russians renamed the Friendship University in Moscow for foreign students the Patrice Lumumba University. Tshombe, on the other hand, appealed to the Right. He was prepared to accept European influence in Katanga, and he used the money from the European business interests there to build up a largely French and Belgian mercenary army with which to assert Katanga's independence.

During 1961 the United Nations changed its policy over Katanga, and in September, the month in which the Secretary-General, Dag Hammarskjöld, was killed in a plane crash on his way to visit Tshombe, the U.N. forces entered Katanga. After more than a year's fighting against Tshombe's mercenary army the U.N. eventually brought the secession of Katanga to an end early in 1963, Tshombe went into exile, and in 1964 the U.N. force was withdrawn.

By then the Congo was disintegrating into chaos. In October 1964 Tshombe returned, and with a white mercenary army and the help of Belgian paratroops he succeeded in restoring order. But the next month he had to go into exile again. For at that point the army leader, Colonel Mobutu, seized power, and the Congo settled down to long years of military rule.

Nigeria

While the Congo seemed to exemplify the dangers and consequences of a sudden, unprepared grant of independence, Nigeria, which gained its independence just three months later, on 1 October 1960, seemed all through the years of trouble in the Congo a model of a successful independent African state. It was a large state. Its population of over fifty million was the largest in Africa. Its area was four times as great as Britain. Within its boundaries lived 150 different tribes. And for five years they lived at peace under a system of parliamentary democracy.

Then in 1966 began a series of events which demonstrated the powerful and disruptive force of tribalism in Nigeria. There were three particularly powerful tribes: the Hausa in the North, the Yoruba in the South-West, and the Ibo in the South-East. The 1960 constitution provided a federal system of government with three regions, North, West, and East, and in practice each of the three main tribes dominated a political party in its own region.

At first government was by a coalition of North and East, that is of Hausa and Ibo. But that broke down in 1964. Then early in 1966 a group of Ibo army officers killed the federal prime minister, Sir Abubakar Tafawa Balewa, and a number of other northern politicians. They were in their turn overthrown by the Commander-in-Chief of the army, General Ironsi, who restored order and abolished the federal system of government. But Ironsi was himself an Ibo. So many of the Northerners distrusted him. In the middle of 1966 the Hausas of the North began to massacre the many Ibos who lived there. And in July there was another military coup. This time Ironsi was killed and a Northerner, General Gowon, from the small tribe of the Angas, took over, restored the federal system, and appointed military governors for each region. Meanwhile two million Ibos were fleeing from the North to their homeland in the East.

The Ibos formed about two-thirds of the population of the Eastern Region, and another important element in the situation was that the rich Nigerian oilfields with an annual revenue of about £24,000,000 were there. The Ibos no longer trusted the central government. Nor did the central government trust them. A dispute over oil revenues led General Gowon to alter the constitution, divide the Eastern region into three, and take control of the coastal oil-producing areas away from the Ibos. So at the end of May 1967 the Ibo leader, Colonel Ojukwu, reacted to this by declaring that the Eastern region was now the independent state of Biafra.

This was followed by civil war. At first the Ibos advanced westwards. But Britain and the U.S.S.R. sent military equipment and technical aid to the federal government, and the federal army, which numbered only 8,000 at the start of the war, rapidly expanded in numbers and advanced into Biafra. After a year the Biafrans were surrounded in the Ibo heartland and in danger of being starved out.

At this point a number of countries, including France and South

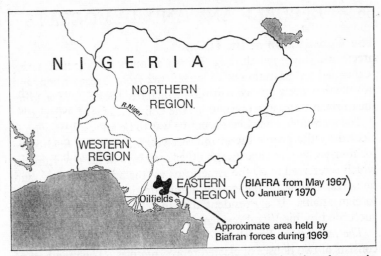

Africa, began flying arms into Biafra by night, and various humanitarian organisations flew food in. The effect was to keep the war going and prolong the process of slow starvation of the Ibo people all through 1969. The federal army continued to close in on the ever smaller area held by the Ibos. Then suddenly and unexpectedly in January 1970 Ojukwu fled and Biafra collapsed. General Gowon, at the head of an army nearly 200,000 strong, settled to the task of reconstruction in a Nigeria which was now divided into twelve regions, each under military control.

Military Government

Both the Congo and Nigeria had ended up with military government. And the same thing happened in a number of other African states. Just in the four months from November 1965 to February 1966 there were military coups not only in Nigeria, but also in Dahomey, Togo, the Central African Republic, Upper Volta, and Ghana. All governments of newly independent African states were faced with the problems of maintaining national unity in states which were not natural units, and of developing the economy to raise the standard of living. Their task was made more difficult by political opposition and public criticism. So they usually suppressed opposition and created one-party states. Thus the only way of changing the government was by force, and the only institution with sufficient force to change the government was the army. African governments which kept control of the army stayed in power. Those which lost the confidence of the army leaders fell,

The Constitution of the U.S.A.

ON 4th July 1776 thirteen British colonies in North America issued a Declaration of Independence from Great Britain, and in 1787 they drew up a constitution which had the effect of welding the thirteen states into one nation: the United States of America.

The executive: The chief executive was to be a President, who is elected by the people on an indirect voting system to hold office for four years. He chooses the other members of his government, which is referred to by the Americans as 'the administration', and he is responsible for day-to-day administration and the conduct of foreign affairs. If a President dies in office he is automatically succeeded by his Vice-President.

The legislature: Legislative power rests with Congress, which consists of two houses of elected representatives. The members of the lower house, the House of Representatives, are congressmen elected on a population basis, thus satisfying the desire of larger states for representation in proportion to their size. The upper house, known as the Senate, contains two Senators from each state, regardless of size, thus allaying the fear of the smaller states that their interests might be swamped by those of the large states. All laws require a majority in both houses.

The judiciary: The highest judicial body in the U.S.A. is the Supreme Court, which consists of judges appointed for life by the President. It is the final authority on all legal and constitutional issues, such as how far the President's powers extend, and it may even declare laws passed by Congress unconstitutional.

Although the personnel of the three functions of government are kept rigidly separate, so that, for example, a member of Congress may not be a member of the administration, the various functions of government overlap. Thus a two-thirds majority is needed in the Senate for the ratification of any treaty negotiated by the President, while the President has an extensive right of veto over legislation.

The separate states control their own domestic affairs, and each has its own executive, headed by a Governor, and its own legislature and judiciary. The question of how far state powers extend and of how far federal powers extend is one of the main sources of constitutional disputes in the U.S.A.; but the indissolubility of the Union was established by the defeat in the Civil War of 1861–5 of eleven Southern states which attempted to secede.

The parties in the late nineteenth century

In the period after the Civil War the Republican Party, under whose leadership the North had won, had a virtual monopoly of power. Republicans tended to emphasise the essential unity of the U.S.A. and to admire the virtues of individual enterprise and self-reliance by which they felt it was being built up. Businessmen contributed to the party funds, and the Republican administration looked after business interests by imposing high tariffs and even by making grants of money to enterprises such as railways. During the nineteenth century the industrial North-East remained 'rock-ribbed Republican'.

The Democratic Party, which emphasised the rights of the separate states, derived much of its support from groups which felt themselves oppressed or underprivileged. It had been led before the Civil War by the aristocratic slave-owners of the South, who saw their interests threatened by the business interests of the North, and defeat in the Civil War tended to make it all the more the party of the dissatisfied elements in American life. Thus the Deep South and the sparsely populated interior, where poor farmers had to pay high freight rates to monopolistic railway companies, voted Democrat.

The 'Progressive' movement

But the twentieth century brought changes in party allegiance. The urban working class in the North-East tended to shift its support to the Democrats, and as the Republican Party lost this support it developed a 'Progressive' movement which appealed to the increasingly more prosperous farmers of the mid-West and to the rapidly growing middle class.

The first President in this 'Progressive' tradition was Theodore Roosevelt, who held office from 1901 till 1909. Although a Republican he took vigorous steps to break the monopolistic position of some great industrial trusts and to enforce lower fares and freight rates on the railways. In a time of growing prosperity there seemed every reason why a progressive Republican Party should remain in power indefinitely, and in 1908 Roosevelt, who had declined to stand for a third term, virtually nominated his own successor: William Howard Taft. But by the time of the next Presidential election in 1912 Roosevelt and Taft had quarrelled. Taft, the more conservative of the two, was nominated as the Republican candidate, and Roosevelt also stood as a 'Progressive'. The result was the election of the Democratic candidate, Woodrow Wilson.

From Wilson to Roosevelt

In his domestic policy Wilson was in the Progressive tradition. In 1913 he managed to get some reduction of tariffs, the introduction of income tax, and a reform of the banking laws; and in 1916 he was elected for a second term, partly because of his successful domestic policy, and partly because he had kept the U.S.A. out of the war raging in Europe. Ironically, within a few weeks of beginning his second term Wilson took the U.S.A. into the war, and in doing so he abandoned the traditional American policy of isolation from Europe. His attempt at the end of the war to keep the U.S.A. intimately involved in European and world affairs by advocating joining the League of Nations helped to lose the Democrats the Presidential elections of 1920.

The successful Republican candidate, Senator Harding, called for a return to 'normalcy', and under his leadership the U.S.A. returned to an isolationist foreign policy and an economic policy of *laissez-faire*. 'The business of America is business,' declared his successor, President Coolidge, and so long as business boomed the Republican Party stayed in power.

But in 1929 the Great Slump hit America, and by 1932 the national income had been halved and fifteen million people were out of work. There was a swing away from the Republican belief in a free economy in which prosperity would eventually seep down from the rich to the masses, and the Presidential election of 1932 was won by a Democrat, Franklin D. Roosevelt, a distant cousin of Theodore Roosevelt, who promised 'a new deal for the American people'.

The New Deal

In a special session of Congress from 9th March to 15th June 1933, known as the 'Hundred Days', a series of laws were pushed through extending the powers of the federal government and providing for extensive measures of reform and relief of suffering.

The activities of banks and the Stock Exchange were regulated. The gold standard was abandoned and the dollar devalued. Pensions and the salaries of government officials and employees were cut. An organisation was established to provide relief for the aged, the infirm, and the unemployed. Loans were given to farmers and householders to prevent foreclosures on mortgages, and financial measures were taken to restore health to the country's agriculture. The railways were reorganised. A body was set up to plan and organise the development of the Tennessee Valley. The

Civilian Conservation Corps was established to provide work for a quarter of a million young men in projects such as flood control. And above all there was passed the National Industrial Recovery Act, which sought to regulate pay and conditions and hours of work, and which arranged for federal expenditure on projects such as building roads, bridges, dams, and airports.

The New Deal continued with further measures in the same tradition as those passed during the Hundred Days, and public works schemes were organised on such a scale that at one time the state was employing approximately seven million people.

Twenty years of Democratic rule

Inevitably these measures created bitter opposition. Roosevelt was accused of being a dictator and a Socialist, and the Supreme Court even declared certain New Deal measures unconstitutional. But Roosevelt had given the Americans new hope as well as a New Deal, and he won an overwhelming victory in the Presidential election of 1936. During his second term domestic issues were still important, but foreign affairs pressed themselves on the attention of Americans as the second World War approached, and they dominated the Presidential election of 1940. Roosevelt was then elected for a third term—an unprecedented event in American history; and in 1944, when the U.S.A. was still at war both in Europe and the Pacific, he was re-elected yet again.

After Roosevelt's death in April 1945, the new President, Harry S. Truman, had the difficult task of trying to hold the Democratic Party together. By this time the Deep South was unenthusiastic about any legislation in the tradition of the New Deal, and while the Negro vote in the North had tended to go to the Democrats since 1932, the Southerners still very largely kept the Negro disenfranchised. So in the Presidential election of 1948 the Southern Democrats put up a separate States' Rights candidate. And the Democratic Party was further split by a former Vice-President standing as a Progressive. All this, together with the fact that the Republicans had won control of Congress in 1946, produced a general expectation that the Republican candidate would win. Nevertheless, Truman won the election comfortably and returned to office for what some people spoke of as 'Roosevelt's fifth term'.

Party alignments in the mid-twentieth century

Despite the fact that the Democrats had also won a majority in both houses of Congress in 1948 Truman was unable to rely on the support of Congress. The Southern Democrats and the mass of the Republicans united to oppose 'creeping Socialism' and any measure on civil rights for Negroes; and some Presidential measures were only carried by the moderate Republicans voting with the mass of the Democrats.

The traditional party alignments were plainly out of date and indeed it was the Democrats, traditionally the defenders of states' rights, who had extended federal powers during the New Deal; but this did not necessarily herald a dramatic reshaping of American politics, for American political parties had never been rigidly disciplined cohesive bodies. They had developed out of the practical necessity of gathering maximum support for the election of a President, and were not held together by any clear political principles. On the whole, a prosperous middle-class Protestant whose family had been in the U.S.A. for generations would tend to vote Republican, while a poor Jewish trade unionist whose family had recently immigrated would be likely to vote Democrat. A practical man who believed in the virtues of rugged individualism would usually be a Republican, while an intellectual who believed in the need for social welfare legislation would probably be a Democrat. But these generalisations are merely indications of tendencies which did not even apply throughout the country.

Any Presidential candidate in the U.S.A. needs to be able to gather support throughout the country. And since there are wide variations in ways of life and traditions in different parts of the U.S.A., and since there is a large measure of local autonomy, it is essential for him to avoid rigid political principles, which are more likely to alienate support than accumulate it, and instead build a broad-based coalition which will incorporate as many different attitudes and interests as possible.

Ike

This flexibility in American politics helps to explain the election of the Republican candidate, General Eisenhower, as President in 1952, for he was essentially a non-party man—likeable, moderate, and acceptable to numerous Democrats. The Americans had had Roosevelt's New Deal, a World War, and Truman's Square Deal. Now they were happy to settle down to respectable, benevolent, middle-class government by Eisenhower. It might be dull, but that was a pleasant change. Four years later many Americans who disliked the Republican Party were still able to declare enthusiastically, 'I like Ike.' They showed their feelings in the elections. In 1956 the Republicans lost control of both houses of Congress. But Eisenhower retained the Presidency.

By the end of the nineteenth century the industry of the U.S.A. was developing rapidly. As early as 1890 she was producing more coal than Britain, and by the first World War more iron and steel as well. Most of her industrial products were absorbed by her large home market, so she played a relatively small part in world trade and in 1914 was still a debtor nation, spending more on imports than she was able to earn from exports.

The first World War

But the U.S.A. was sufficiently involved in world trade to find economic isolation less attractive than political isolation, and her wish to continue 'business as usual' during the first World War involved her first in a quarrel with the British, who insisted on limiting her trade with Germany, and then in so serious a quarrel with the Germans over unrestricted U-boat warfare that in April 1917 she went to war with Germany.

Even before the U.S.A. entered the war she had a considerable impact on it, for Britain and France bought large quantities of food and war materials from America and also borrowed $2 million in order to do so, and after the U.S.A. entered the war this flow of supplies increased, for the American government was prepared to lend virtually limitless money.

The vast demand for American goods by her European allies produced a rapid expansion of American industry, and the U.S.A. was also able to capture markets which the European countries were unable to satisfy because their industries were geared almost exclusively to war-time needs. Thus the war stimulated the economy of the U.S.A. while at the same time disrupting the economy of Europe; and the U.S.A. emerged from the war outstandingly prosperous.

The American Relief Administration

After the war the U.S.A. used her prosperity to alleviate the distress in Central and Eastern Europe, where the war had so disrupted agriculture and industry that millions were threatened with starvation. Herbert Hoover, who later became President, organised the American Relief Administration, which took control of communications in the parts of Europe most disrupted by war and distributed food from America to the peoples of twenty-one different countries—especially Russia, where revolution and civil war had resulted in famine affecting twenty-five million people.

War debts

But at the same time the U.S.A. adopted financial and economic policies which had a disastrous effect on the economy of Europe. She was owed a total of over $10,000 million by her former allies, and in particular Britain, and she expected payment in full and with interest. The situation was complicated by the fact that Britain, which had been the principal supplier of war materials to her allies in the early years of the war, was owed even more by her allies than she herself owed to the U.S.A., and in 1922, when the Americans began to seek repayment of their war loans, the British government, hoping for the cancellation of all war debts, issued a declaration in what was known as the Balfour Note, telling her debtors that she would demand from them no more than she was herself required to pay to the U.S.A.

The U.S.A. declined to take the hint and continued to press for payment. So in 1923 the British Chancellor of the Exchequer, Stanley Baldwin, arranged with the U.S.A. for Britain to pay off her debt, with interest at the rate of 3 per cent, by 1985. The other countries in debt to the U.S.A. followed suit—though none of them was expected to pay so much interest.

To Europeans who felt that they had paid for victory in blood it seemed unreasonable that the U.S.A., which had prospered while they suffered, was now expecting them to pay again—this time in dollars. But to Americans the repayment of the loans seemed a straightforward business obligation. 'They hired the money, didn't they?' said President Coolidge in 1923. And it seemed particularly intolerable that the Europeans should quibble about paying their debts to the country which had won the war for them. But even as a business arrangement the repayment of war debts had disadvantages. Europe could only earn the dollars needed for paying the debts by exporting to the U.S.A.; and since the dollars earned by exports were handed to the American government in payment of war debts they could not be used to buy American goods. This had a stultifying effect not only on world trade but also on American industry, which became too dependent on its home market.

Tariff barriers and post-war loans

The situation was made worse by the high tariff barriers which Congress set up in 1922 to protect American industry from foreign competition. These made it more difficult for European countries to sell their goods to the U.S.A. and therefore more difficult to earn the dollars they needed for paying off their war debts. As a result they had even less dollars left for buying American goods.

In order to make it possible for them to buy American goods the American government arranged short-term loans for them, so that during the twenties the total European debt to the U.S.A. increased instead of being paid off. With the help of these loans Europe's economy seemed to be recovering, and the loans to Germany, which were particularly large, enabled Germany to rebuild her industry until by the thirties it was the best equipped in Europe. But Europe's prosperity in the late twenties was very precarious, for it depended on the ability of Germany to buy goods from other European countries, and Germany's ability to do that was based not on income from exports but on loans from the U.S.A. Europe's economy was likely to collapse if the loans stopped, and the loans depended on the health of the American economy.

The great slump

During the twenties America's economy had boomed, but it depended on the home market, and by 1928 too much was being produced for the home market to absorb, and prices began to drop. Despite this, confidence in growing prosperity continued, and share values on Wall Street, the American stock market, continued to rise until September 1929. But then investors began to worry, worry rapidly became panic, and soon there was such widespread anxiety to sell that during October share values dropped $40,000 million—approximately four times the total value of the Allies' war debt to the U.S.A.

This collapse of the American economy checked the flood of loans to Europe and rapidly created financial difficulties for European governments. In June 1930 President Hoover tried to alleviate these difficulties by permitting the postponement of all government debts to the U.S.A. for a year. But in the same month Congress made it even more difficult for the European countries to earn the dollars which they so desperately needed if world trade was to continue flowing, and if they were to be able to pay their debts, by raising the tariffs around the U.S.A. even higher. In June 1931, when the 'moratorium' ended and the U.S.A. began pressing for payments, most countries were quite unable to start paying again, and in the end only Finland and the Union of South Africa paid their debts in full.

Meanwhile there had been heavy withdrawals from European banks, and in May 1931 *Kredit Anstalt*, the largest bank in Austria, had failed. All over the world banks found it increasingly difficult to meet their obligations, and soon there were widespread bank failures and financial crises. In industrial areas machines stood silent and there was not enough food. In agricultural areas crops were burnt and fields left unsown, and there were insufficient manufactured goods. World trade dropped by a half, and millions of men were out of work.

The crisis brought Franklin D. Roosevelt to the American Presidency with his promise of a New Deal in domestic affairs. It also brought a further intensification of economic nationalism. In 1933 the World Economic Conference held in London broke down because the U.S.A. was determined to maintain its tariff barriers, and in 1934 Congress forbade granting credits to any nation which had failed to pay its war debts. In the economic as in the political field the U.S.A. was trying to isolate herself from the affairs of Europe.

The second World War and Lease-Lend

The second World War brought the U.S.A. back into intimate involvement in the affairs of Europe. President Roosevelt saw that America's security would be threatened by a German conquest of Europe, and he determined to give Britain every help 'short of war'. He argued that a man whose house was likely to catch fire because a neighbour's house was burning would scarcely haggle over terms for lending a hosepipe, and in line with this attitude he persuaded Congress to pass the Lease-Lend Act in March 1941. By this Act supplies could be lent or leased to any country whose defence was considered by the President to be vital to the security of the U.S.A., regardless of whether or not they could afford to pay. Britain was the only country involved at first, but in June, when the Germans invaded Russia, Lease-Lend was immediately extended to the U.S.S.R., and throughout the war the U.S.A. continued to pour out food and military equipment to her allies.

Marshall Aid and the Cold War

Once again war acted as a stimulus to the American economy. By 1945 American industry was manufacturing three times as much as before the war and the U.S.A. was by far the richest country in the world. But by this time the Americans had learned, as Roosevelt declared in 1945, 'that our well-being is dependent on the well-being of other nations far away', and although Lease-Lend came to an end immediately after the war the policy of enlightened self-interest which it represented was continued.

As the Cold War developed the U.S.A. spent heavily on military aid to non-Communist countries. Immediately after the proclamation of the Truman Doctrine (p. 291) in March 1947 Congress

granted $400 million for military aid to Greece and Turkey, in
1949 when N.A.T.O. was formed $1,000 million was spent on re-
arming Western Europe, and gradually military aid was extended
to non-Communist countries all round the world.

But economic aid was also essential. Apart from the argument
that the most prosperous nation in the world had a moral obligation
to use its resources for the relief of poverty and suffering abroad, it
was also clear that in the long run the best antidote to Communism was to destroy the poverty and suffering in which Communism would thrive. George Marshall, President Truman's Secretary of State, saw both the moral obligation and the practical
advantages of economic aid, and in June 1947 he proposed that the
U.S.A. should provide money for a programme of European economic recovery, declaring, 'Our policy is not directed against any
country or doctrine, but is directed against hunger, poverty, des-
peration, and chaos', and at the same time pointing out that one
object of the aid would be 'to permit the emergence of political and
economic conditions in which free institutions can exist'. The
Russians rejected the Marshall Plan, and exerted pressure on the
East European countries to do the same, for they were suspicious
of what the effects would be of co-ordination of economic policy
with the West. Thus when Truman presented the Plan to Congress
it embraced only Western Europe and seemed a natural and
integral part of Cold War strategy.

The Point Four Programme

In fact Marshall Aid was something more than a mere move in
the Cold War. Unlike military aid, which was no more than a
means of holding back Communism, it was a positive attempt to
demonstrate the virtues of an alternative system to Communism;
and in 1949 this attempt was continued by President Truman, who
declared, in what became known as the Point Four Programme,
that the U.S.A. should foster capital investment in areas needing
development and make technical knowledge available to 'the free
peoples of the world' in order to help them to help themselves.
The military expenditure occasioned by the Cold War tended to
retard this programme, but in the middle of the century, when
Congress was frequently tempted to cut down overseas economic
aid and concentrate on military aid, President Eisenhower, who
like Marshall had spent most of his life as a soldier, regularly emphasised that in the long run economic aid was more important,
and this policy was continued by his successors.

58 ISOLATION AND INTERVENTION

'Manifest Destiny' and the Monroe Doctrine

THE first century of the history of the U.S.A. is largely the story of how settlers pushed the frontier Westwards until in 1890 it was officially declared that the frontier no longer existed. Many Americans believed in their 'manifest destiny' to rule the whole North American continent. They acquired land from Britain, France, Spain, and Mexico, and in 1867 even bought Alaska from Russia. They killed off or drove Westwards the native Indian inhabitants of the continent.

Hand in hand with the concept of 'manifest destiny' went the Monroe Doctrine. In 1823 President Monroe in a message to Congress declared that the American continents were 'not to be considered as subjects for future colonization by any European powers.' This came to be interpreted as a declaration that the U.S.A. had no intention of interfering in the affairs of Europe and would resist by force any attempt by a European power to interfere in the affairs of the American continents; and thus the Monroe Doctrine formed the basis of the traditional American foreign policy of isolation from Europe.

Anglo-American relations

During the nineteenth century the policy of isolation depended on Great Britain, whose navy could usually be relied on to defend the American continent from any force which a continental power might wish to send. And it was impossible for the U.S.A. to maintain rigid political isolation from Britain, for Britain already had colonies in America before 1823, and also, by virtue of her navy, means of defending her interests there.

The Americans unwillingly accepted the separate existence of Canada to their North. And once the boundary had been finally settled in 1846, the only serious Anglo-American clash arose out of a long drawn-out dispute between Britain and Venezuela over Venezuela's boundary with British Guiana. In 1895, after an American syndicate had acquired a business interest in the area, President Cleveland brought the issue to a head by declaring his intention to set up a boundary commission, and by expressing his willingness to go to war with Britain to enforce its decision. Nothing came of this, for the British government led by Lord Salisbury behaved moderately and managed to have the issue referred to independent arbitrators, who in 1899 decided in Britain's favour.

The Spanish-American War, 1898–9

Far more important for the U.S.A. were the consequences of another event happening at the same time—a revolt in Cuba against Spanish rule. For years the American government had been disturbed by Spanish misrule in Cuba, and in 1898, when the U.S. warship *Maine* was blown up in harbour at Havana, the capital of Cuba, the U.S.A. took the opportunity of declaring war on Spain.

The Spanish fleets in the Caribbean and in the Philippines were rapidly destroyed, American forces invaded and conquered Cuba and then Puerto Rico, and in less than a year the war was over and Spain had lost all her Caribbean and Pacific possessions. The U.S.A. bought Puerto Rico, Guam, and the Philippines for $20 million. In theory Cuba became independent, but her foreign policy had to accord with the wishes of the U.S.A., and temporarily even her internal affairs were placed under American control. The American government also took the opportunity to annex Hawaii and part of Samoa, and in the next few years the U.S.A. extended her influence and even control over several Caribbean states.

The Spanish-American War has often been regarded as the first occasion when the U.S.A. abandoned isolation and entered into

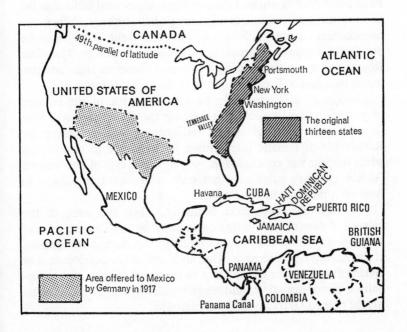

world affairs. In fact it was no such thing, for it was fought over an essentially American issue and was an assertion of the predominance of the U.S.A. in the American sphere. Admittedly the war spread across the Pacific to the Philippines, but isolationism had never involved exclusion from Pacific affairs. It had always been specifically a policy of isolation from Europe.

Naval power

But the Spanish-American War was fought at a time when one of the basic assumptions on which the Monroe doctrine rested was being challenged. As other nations developed heavy industries and built powerful navies the U.S.A. realised that she could not rely on Britain indefinitely for the protection of her interests. She needed a navy of her own, and by the beginning of the twentieth century she was, after Britain and Germany, the third naval power of the world.

The Panama Canal: Despite the Venezuela boundary dispute there was little likelihood of a clash between the U.S.A. and Great Britain, but the American government was increasingly concerned by the potential threats of German naval power in the Atlantic and Japanese naval power in the Pacific. This led to a desire to be able to transfer the American navy rapidly from the Atlantic to the Pacific and back again, and then to negotiations with Colombia for an agreement to build a canal through her territory. When the negotiations ran into difficulty in 1903 a convenient revolt broke out in the Colombian province of Panama. President Theodore Roosevelt promptly recognised Panama as a separate state, and two weeks later he acquired the right to build a canal through it.

The Treaty of Portsmouth: In 1904 the issue of the balance of power in the Pacific was raised by the Russo-Japanese War (pp. 312–13). Although it was the Japanese who had asked for Roosevelt's diplomatic intervention he took care to ensure that when the war was concluded in 1905 by the Treaty of Portsmouth (U.S.A.) Japan's gains were not such as to constitute a threat to American interests in the Pacific.

The Algeciras Conference: Similarly, when the issue of the balance of power in the Atlantic was raised by the Tangier crisis of 1905 (p. 85) Roosevelt ensured that the U.S.A. was represented at the Algeçiras Conference. On this occasion the development of German naval power had led him to intervene in what was essentially a European affair, and understandably the U.S.A. cast its weight against Germany at the conference.

The first World War

In 1917 the use made by Germany of her naval power in the Atlantic was the most important factor in causing the U.S.A. to intervene in European affairs on a large scale. At the beginning of the year public opinion had already hardened against Germany when the British government handed on to the U.S.A. a telegram intercepted by its secret service from Zimmermann, the German Foreign Minister, to Mexico, offering her Texas, Arizona, and New Mexico in return for help against the U.S.A. In February diplomatic relations with Germany were broken off as the result of Germany's proclamation of unrestricted U-boat warfare. And in March the overthrow of the Tsarist government in Russia enabled the Americans to regard the war as a struggle between democracy and autocracy. Then in April, after German U-boats had begun to sink American merchant ships, the U.S.A. declared war.

The first American troops were in the trenches in France in October, they began to arrive in large numbers during the military crisis in the spring of 1918, and from then onwards they poured into Europe until by the end of the war more than a million had been involved in the fighting. Even before the military intervention the supply of food and war materials from the U.S.A. had made it possible for the Allies to continue the war. And now the additional American manpower enabled the Allies to win before the end of 1918.

Isolationism between the wars

America's part in negotiating the post-war settlement was as important as her contribution to winning the war. President Wilson was one of the dominant figures at the Paris Conference and was the principal author of the League of Nations. But meanwhile the mass of the American people was increasingly indifferent to external affairs, and the U.S.A. swung back to isolationism. The Senate failed to ratify the peace treaties primarily in order to prevent the U.S.A. from joining the League of Nations, and the U.S.A. reverted to an isolationist foreign policy.

There was no fundamental difference between the foreign policies of the three Republican Presidents of the twenties, Harding, Coolidge, and Hoover, and that of the Democrat, Franklin D. Roosevelt, during his first Presidential term, to which he was elected in 1932.

Sea power: All of them realised that American security depended on sea power. Although Germany was no longer a threat in the

Atlantic, Japanese power was developing in the Pacific, and this caused the U.S.A. to propose the Washington Conference of 1921–2 (p. 234) and to insist that Japan's fleet should be only three-fifths the size of her own.

The 'good neighbour' policy: Meanwhile relations with the Latin American and Caribbean states were improving. In 1921 Colombia was paid $25 million compensation for the losses she had suffered as the result of the Panamanian revolution of 1903, and gradually the U.S.A. abandoned her rights and powers in the Caribbean, finally, in Roosevelt's time, dropping the last vestige of political control over Cuba—a claim that she was entitled to intervene to ensure good order.

Isolation: But the central feature of American foreign policy was isolation from Europe, and in these years isolationism was even coming to involve separation from events across the Pacific as well as across the Atlantic. The only contribution of the U.S.A. to the political problems of the world in the twenties was the Kellogg–Briand Pact of 1928 (p. 235), and when Japan seized Manchuria in 1931 (p. 230) the American government merely protested and then refused to recognise the new government of Manchukuo. The isolationist policy reached its culmination in the Neutrality Acts of 1937–8, which forbade Americans to sell arms or give credit to any nation at war and made it clear that victims of aggression should not expect help from the U.S.A.

The second World War

But by this time Roosevelt had realised that the security of the U.S.A. would be threatened by any great extension of German or Japanese power, and in November 1939, two months after the European war had begun, he was able to get the Neutrality Acts amended to allow trade with belligerents on a 'cash and carry' basis—a measure which favoured Britain, whose navy commanded the Atlantic. The German victories in 1940 and the subsequent danger that Britain would be defeated enabled Roosevelt to persuade Congress to accept a massive rearmament programme, in which the U.S.A. spent more in one year of peace than her total outlay on the first World War. And as early as September 1940 Congress even introduced peace-time conscription.

These were regarded as defensive measures, and Roosevelt, campaigning for re-election as President for the third time, declared 'Your boys are not going to be sent into any foreign wars.' But meanwhile he was preparing to supply Britain with the food and war materials she now desperately needed. In March 1941

Congress was persuaded to pass the Lease-Lend Act (p. 284), and in the same month, at a secret meeting between representatives of the British and American fighting services, the U.S.A. agreed to concentrate on the European war first 'if and when' she should be involved in war against both Germany and Japan.

In August Roosevelt joined Churchill in drawing up the Atlantic Charter, in which they reaffirmed the principle of self-determination and declared their wish to see 'freedom from fear and freedom from want' for all men in the post-war world. In September the U.S. navy was ordered to sink any U-boat in the West Atlantic; and in November the last remnants of the Neutrality Acts were repealed and armed American merchant ships began carrying supplies to Britain. War with Germany was clearly imminent. But Japan, with whom Americans had been forbidden to trade since July, attacked first, on 7th December 1941. Four days later Germany and Italy declared war, and the U.S.A. was intimately involved in developments across both the Pacific and the Atlantic.

The Truman Doctrine

When the war was over most Americans accepted the inevitability of continued involvement in the affairs of the world. The U.S.A. was the most powerful nation in the world, it was already a member of U.N.O., and its government had undertaken to participate in the occupation of Germany and Austria. It would have been pleasant to have been able to retreat again into isolation, but it was impossible to allow the Russians a free hand in spreading Communist revolution, for that would result in a vast extension of the power of the U.S.S.R., which would then become a threat to the security of the U.S.A. Also, since Americans generally regarded Communism as an evil force which suppressed individual liberty, they felt some moral obligation to defend peoples and nations threatened by Communism.

Consequently, when the British government told the American government early in 1947 that it could no longer bear the financial burden of supporting Greece and Turkey, the American President promptly asked Congress to sanction military and economic aid to those countries, and in his speech to Congress he declared the intention of the U.S.A. to 'support free peoples who are resisting attempted subjugation by armed minorities or by outside pressure'. This declaration of March 1947, known as the Truman Doctrine, marks the irrevocable abandonment of the isolationist attitude. The U.S.A. had acquired a permanent commitment which involved her in the affairs of the whole world.

59   WAR IN THE PACIFIC

FOR Europeans the second World War began in 1939. For Americans it began late in 1941. But in a sense the war which the Americans fought in the Pacific, and won in 1945, began as early as 1931 when Japan seized Manchuria from China (p. 229), or perhaps in 1937, when an unofficial clash between Chinese and Japanese soldiers was allowed by the Japanese government to develop into a full-scale invasion of China.

Soon after this the situation was complicated by Japan's relations with the U.S.S.R. In the summer of 1938 Japanese troops were in action against the Russians where Korea, Manchuria, and the U.S.S.R. meet, and from May to September 1939 their troops were engaged in an unofficial war with the Red Army in Outer Mongolia. While this was in progress Japan's leaders were shocked by the announcement at the end of August of the Russo-German non-aggression pact (p. 258). Previously some of them had been eager to transform the Anti-Comintern Pact of 1936 (p. 243) into an alliance and join Germany in attacking the U.S.S.R.; but now they determined to remain neutral in the European war.

However, the German victories in 1940 over the British, French, and Dutch provided Japan with the temptation to seize their colonial possessions in South-East Asia, and this eventually involved her in war. In July 1940, after the fall of France, she occupied the North of French Indo-China. In September, the month the Battle of Britain reached its climax, she signed a military alliance with Germany and Italy, aimed at securing herself from the possibility of an attack by the U.S.A., and in July 1941 she occupied bases in South Indo-China—a suitable spring-board for an invasion of the British and Dutch colonies of South-East Asia.

This produced a ban on trade with Japan from the governments of Great Britain, the Dominions, the Netherlands, and also the U.S.A. This meant that Japan was denied access to the oil of South-East Asia at a time when she only had sufficient oil for two years of war, and that meant that she must either withdraw or seize what she wanted by force.

Pearl Harbor

The Japanese leaders saw that Britain and the Netherlands government in exile were scarcely in a position to defend their colonies effectively, but an expansionist policy might involve Japan in war with the U.S.A. as well. However, the U.S.A. would not be able to hinder them without a navy strong enough to dominate the

Pacific, so they decided to destroy the American fleet, calculating that the U.S.A. would come to terms rather than face a long war in which she would have to build a completely new fleet.

As in 1894 (p. 312) and 1904 (p. 313) Japan commenced hostilities with a naval attack before declaring war. On 7th December 1941 planes from a Japanese carrier squadron attacked the American naval base of Pearl Harbor, destroying most of the ships and aircraft. But the American aircraft carriers were all at sea, and aircraft carriers were to be decisive in the naval battles of the Pacific, for aircraft have a longer range, greater accuracy, and heavier striking power than any battleship's guns. The raid on Pearl Harbor had brought the U.S.A. into the war angry and united, but it had failed to cripple her as a naval power, and her potential strength on land, sea, and in the air was vastly greater than Japan's.

Comparative strengths of the U.S.A. and Japan in 1941, measured by population and steel production.		
Population, in millions.	U.S.A.	0 25 50 75 100 125 150
	JAPAN	
Steel production, in millions of tons.	U.S.A.	
	JAPAN	0 10 20 30 40 50 60 70

The Coral Sea and Midway

However, Japan's successes in the early months were massive. They swept through the Philippines, Malaya, and the Dutch East Indies, they took Hong Kong and Singapore, and they advanced into Burma and New Guinea. But then, instead of consolidating their early conquests, they aimed to extend their power further by landing troops on the South coast of New Guinea at Port Moresby, where they would be an immediate threat to Australia, and by seizing Midway Island, which would give them a base within bombing range of Pearl Harbor.

The attempt on Port Moresby was frustrated by the American navy in the battle of the Coral Sea in May, and the attempt on Midway in the battle of Midway in June. These two battles, fought within a month of each other, mark the turn of the tide in the Pacific. The Japanese fleet was so much weakened by losing one carrier in the Coral Sea and four off Midway that the Americans felt able to seize the initiative, and two months later they struck at Guadalcanal in the Solomons.

From Guadalcanal to the Philippines

They were committed to an overall strategy of beating Hitler first, but at the Casablanca Conference in January 1943 they were able to get British acceptance of their assuming the offensive in the Pacific in return for accepting the British strategy in Europe of going on in 1943 to invade Sicily and Italy rather than France.

By this time their submarines were already sinking ten times as much shipping as the Japanese were building, and in February, after six months fighting, they took Guadalcanal. But for the moment they were not able to continue on the offensive, for they had only two carriers left, having lost one in the Coral Sea, one off Midway, and two in the struggle for Guadalcanal, and there was a pause in the fighting until the new fast *Essex*-class carriers came into service.

In June 1943 General MacArthur's forces in the South-West Pacific opened an offensive in the islands East of New Guinea, where they developed the strategy of leap-frogging, or island-hopping. They would by-pass strongly fortified islands, leaving them in Japanese hands, but isolated so that they were virtually useless, and would go on to establish bases in islands which were less well defended.

In November Admiral Nimitz's forces in the Central Pacific took Tarawa in the Gilberts, and in the next month the American Joint Chiefs of Staff adopted a strategy of advancing through the Pacific in two parallel lines. While MacArthur's forces worked their way round the North of New Guinea, Nimitz's forces were to leap in great stages across the Pacific. Early in February 1944 he took Kwajalein in the Marshalls, and in June his forces landed on Saipan in the Marianas, 1,400 miles from Tokyo, which was now in range of B29 bombers.

The Japanese fleet came out to try to frustrate this landing. As in the battles of the Coral Sea and Midway two years earlier no ship came in sight of an enemy vessel, for the fighting was done by aircraft, and on this occasion most of the Japanese ships got away because the American fleet broke off the action to cover the amphibious operation at Saipan. But it was still a disastrous defeat for the Japanese, whose aircraft were destroyed in what the Americans called 'the Marianas' Turkey Shoot'.

After taking Saipan the next important stage was the liberation of the Philippines to get a large firm base for the invasion of Japan. In October MacArthur and Nimitz joined forces for this. The Japanese fleet came out again in a desperate and virtually hopeless attempt to win a victory, but in the battle of Leyte Gulf it lost four more carriers, three battleships, and ten cruisers. Japan could no longer be regarded as a naval power.

The war in Burma and China

However, she still held most of the territories she had seized by the middle of 1942. Although she had been driven back by the Australians in New Guinea she held most of Burma and much of China, and in 1944 even tried to extend her conquests. In March she launched an attack on Imphal, the main British base on the Indo-Burmese border, in the hope that a break-through into India would be followed by the Indians rising against the British. But the Japanese forces suffered an overwhelming defeat at the hands of British and Indian troops, who went on from Imphal to re-conquer most of Burma by the end of the war.

A Japanese offensive in South China later in the year was far more successful, for the Chinese Nationalists were more concerned by this stage with their rivalry with the Communists, and the Japanese were able to overrun the bases in South China from which American bombers had been operating against Japan.

But these land campaigns were of secondary importance, for the American advance across the Pacific was by-passing the Japanese Empire and aiming direct at the homeland.

Iwo Jima and Okinawa

In March 1945 the Americans took the tiny island of Iwo Jima, only 750 miles from Tokyo, and as a result were able to intensify their bombing of Japan. In June they took Okinawa in the Ryukus, which was only 350 miles from Japan and was intended to be a last stepping-stone for the invasion. But Iwo Jima had cost twenty thousand casualties and Okinawa forty thousand, for on land Japanese soldiers fought until all were dead and at sea suicide pilots crashed their bomb-laden planes into enemy ships. The Joint Chiefs of Staff calculated that it would cost another million casualties to invade Japan. It was a horrifying prospect.

The atomic bombs and surrender

However, during the fighting for Okinawa Germany had surrendered. This produced a change of attitude in the Japanese government, which now asked the Russians, with whom they were not at war, to mediate for them. The British and American governments had made it clear at the Casablanca Conference that they wanted unconditional surrender, and when Stalin told them at Potsdam of the Japanese approaches President Truman of the U.S.A. and Attlee, the British Prime Minister, issued a demand that Japan should surrender her armed forces or face 'prompt and utter destruction'. Two days later, on 28th July, the Japanese government publicly rejected the Potsdam Proclamation, calculating that the Allies would suffer such heavy losses when they tried to invade that they would be driven to concede a negotiated settlement.

But by this time the final successful tests had been made in America of the atomic bomb, and on 6th August 1945 the first atomic bomb was dropped on the town of Hiroshima, killing eighty thousand people. The Japanese government still could not agree to accept defeat. But after the U.S.S.R. had declared war on 8th August and another atomic bomb had been dropped on the 9th on the port of Nagasaki, killing forty thousand people, fear of further destruction and of Communism caused the Japanese government to offer on the 10th to surrender so long as the Emperor's sovereignty was guaranteed.

On the 11th the Allies replied that the Emperor's authority would be subject to the Supreme Commander of the Allied Powers and that Japan's future constitution would be according to the 'will of the Japanese people'. The government could not agree on whether or not to hold out for better terms. But on the 14th the Emperor intervened decisively on the side of surrendering, and on the 15th he broadcast to his people asking them to join him in 'enduring the unendurable and suffering what is insufferable'. For the first time in Japan's history she had been defeated in war.

IN the years after the second World War most Americans saw Communism as a threat. In the autumn of 1949 the Russians exploded an atom bomb and the Communists came to power in China. In 1950 the Cold War turned hot when the Korean War broke out. And besides all this it seemed to many Americans as if Communists were intending to infiltrate American society and destroy all that was best in the American way of life.

McCarthyism

This fear of Communism was stimulated by the disclosure of successful espionage activity. In January 1950 a senior State Department official, Alger Hiss, was convicted of perjury after denying that he was involved in Communist plots to send American documents to the U.S.S.R. And in February the brilliant war-time atomic physicist, Klaus Fuchs, was convicted in Britain of giving atomic secrets to the Russians.

This produced an extraordinary effect in the U.S.A. Fear of an international Communist conspiracy swept the country and produced the rise of Senator McCarthy, who used a Senate sub-committee to carry out an extensive witch-hunt for Communists. Reason was displaced by passionate conviction, and just as the Russians had hunted saboteurs in the 1930s the Americans now hunted Communists. From outside it looked ludicrous. The methods McCarthy used discredited the U.S.A. in the eyes of the world and eventually discredited him in the U.S.A. In December 1954 his behaviour was condemned by more than two-thirds of the Senate, and McCarthyism was in effect over.

Dwight D. Eisenhower

Two years earlier, at the height of the McCarthy fever, Dwight D. Eisenhower had been elected President—the first Republican in the White House for twenty years. He brought the Korean War to an end in the summer of 1953, and soon things were looking better in the U.S.A. His government got down to the tasks of cutting expenditure, reconsidering the needs of defence, and rooting out government corruption. His own approach to problems was moderate and reasonable. And no-one was surprised when in 1956 he was re-elected. His second Presidential term of office began in January 1957 with the U.S.A. in a complacent mood of self-satisfaction.

But that complacency was shaken in the autumn of 1957 by two things: trouble at Little Rock and the launching of Sputnik I.

Little Rock

In September 1957 the school board at Little Rock, Arkansas, acting in accordance with a judgment of the Supreme Court in 1954 that segregated education was unconstitutional, decided to admit seventeen Negro students to the Central High School. Governor Faubus reacted by stationing the Arkansas National Guard outside. Ostensibly they were there 'to prevent racial violence'. In fact they were there to stop the Negroes entering.

Eisenhower, despite his Republican dislike of interfering in the internal affairs of a state, placed the Arkansas National Guard under his own authority and sent a thousand federal paratroopers into Little Rock to enforce the law.

The whole affair was profoundly disturbing. It revealed the passionate and bitter feelings of segregationist Southerners against 'uppity Niggers' and 'Nigger-lovers'. It also revealed the equally passionate feelings of some Negroes and white liberals against 'white racists'. Above all it revealed that the feelings on both sides were so powerful that military force was needed to control them.

The Little Rock affair was followed by similar incidents elsewhere, by a growing 'Civil Rights' movement, and eventually by a 'white backlash'.

Sputnik I

The second disturbing event of the autumn of 1957 was the launching by the Russians on 5 October of a space satellite, Sputnik I, which orbited the earth. This shocked the Americans in two ways. First, it seemed to pose a serious potential military threat. Second, it made them wonder if Russian scientific and technological education was ahead of that of the U.S.A.

The immediate result of these twin fears was the passage of a National Defence Education Act providing large sums of money for any educational project which seemed as if it might be helpful for national defence. Consequently vast sums of money were spent and a mass of skilled man-power was recruited and trained so that Americans might be the first men on the moon.

This had a number of side-effects. The expenditure of large sums of money on something as useless as getting to the moon understandably bred resentment of the government's neglect of poverty in the U.S.A. The linking of expenditure on education so closely to defence needs rather than to the pursuit of truth understandably bred resentment, disillusionment, and even revolt among American students.

John F. Kennedy

Resentment of the neglect of poverty, tension over 'Civil Rights', and student unrest all contributed to make Americans less contented by the end of Eisenhower's second term than they had been at the end of his first. Meanwhile Fidel Castro's take-over in Cuba and the development of civil war in South Vietnam, where the U.S.A. was supporting the corrupt government of Ngo Dinh Diem, made Americans less self-assured.

Then in 1960 John F. Kennedy, a rich forty-three year old Democrat, was elected President. He appealed to the frontier spirit which had won the West, and he called on Americans to conquer 'New Frontiers'. He tried to tackle poverty and cut restrictive tariffs. He tried to improve education for the masses and provide civil rights for Negroes, houses for the homeless, and medical care for the aged. He formed a Peace Corps of American youth to carry American idealism and help to foreign countries.

In the event he achieved relatively little before he was assassinated in Dallas, Texas, in November 1963. But his vision of a better society had captured the imagination of the American people, and his death turned him into a national hero. His successor, Lyndon B. Johnson, won an overwhelming victory in the presidential election of 1964 and set out to continue Kennedy's policies and transform the U.S.A. into a 'Great Society'.

Black Power

But America's problems were not easy to solve, and the 'Civil Rights' issue was particularly intractable. The Negro minority numbered twenty million—one in ten of the population. And increasingly they were moving out of the Deep South into the great industrial centres of the North. Thus the race issue came to be diffused over the U.S.A. And even though a Civil Rights Bill went through Congress in 1964 on the wave of sentiment following Kennedy's assassination and guided by the political skill of Lyndon Johnson, the problem got worse rather than better.

Increasingly Negroes became dissatisfied with the peaceful Civil Rights movement. Many of them preferred to meet white racists with language they would understand: hatred, prejudice, and violence. And in the summer of 1967, ten years after Little Rock, there were riots in 125 American cities, causing 86 deaths. Some Negroes rejected the whole idea of Negro integration into white society, and called for a Negro republic in the Deep South. They would meet white racism with black racism, white power with Black Power.

'Flower-Power'

At the same time the youth of America, whose idealism had been stirred by Kennedy, were increasingly alienated from Lyndon Johnson's government as they were conscripted in their tens of thousands for an unpopular war in Vietnam. 1967 saw the rise of 'flower-power'. Idealistic young men and women tried to break free from the corrupt materialist society in which they had grown up and build a new life in 'hippie' communes permeated with brotherly love. Meanwhile the escapist young tried to get away from their own emotional problems by taking drugs. The two threads were inextricably and tragically inter-mingled. Soon the gentle flower people were moving from soft to hard drugs. Love gave way to hatred. Gentleness gave way to violence. And the whole hippie movement degenerated into a mess of disease, violence, crime, filth, and misery.

Law and Order

The threat to the stability of American society from Black Power and 'flower-power' was made worse by the incapacity of the police to deal with the increase in crimes of violence. Each state controlled its own force. The police were often inadequate, usually poorly paid, and sometimes brutal and corrupt. Their job of maintaining law and order was made more difficult by the right of American citizens to carry fire-arms—a right guaranteed in the constitution. And increasingly Americans took to carrying guns to protect themselves against the growing number of other people carrying guns. By about 1968 a third of all Americans kept fire-arms, and killings were at the rate of over a thousand a month. Americans had good cause to be worried about what was happening in their society.

Richard M. Nixon

The issue of 'law and order' was important in the Presidential election of 1968. So was the issue of the Vietnam War. More and more Americans wanted peace and stability both at home and abroad. In the twenty years after 1932 the Democrats had given the U.S.A. Roosevelt's New Deal and involvement in the Second World War, and then Truman's Square Deal and involvement in the Korean War. But the Republican Eisenhower had extricated them from the Korean War and given them a period of stability at home. Then the Democrats gave them Kennedy's search for a 'New Frontier', Johnson's 'Great Society', and increasing involvement in the Vietnam War.

Now they wanted a return to stability. So in 1968 they elected the Republican Richard Nixon to try to extricate them from the war in Vietnam and establish law and order at home.

'Hull down over the horizon'

Nixon made a vigorous attempt to extricate the U.S.A. from the Vietnam War. He got away from the attitude that the Chinese Communists were plotting to take over all Asia and would succeed unless the U.S.A. stood firm. He tried to establish friendly relations with China, he declared his belief in 'Asia for the Asians', he began withdrawing American troops from Vietnam, and he implied that the U.S.A. would never again move in and take over another country's civil war as she had in Vietnam.

This was a deliberate retreat from the Truman Doctrine of 1947 (p. 291). But Nixon did not intend to adopt a policy of isolationism so much as one of disengagement. The U.S.A. was going to be 'hull down over the horizon' from Asia. And it seemed likely that Nixon wanted the same policy to apply to America's relations with Europe and the Middle East, for he ordered a review of all the U.S.A.'s alliances with a view to transferring more of the burden of maintaining them to other members.

The Price of War and Rocketry

Certainly there was reason to want to cut military expenditure. The space race had been expensive, and by July 1969 the U.S.A. had spent so much on it that she achieved the questionable ambition of being the first country to put a man on the moon. But the cost of the space programme was insignificant by comparison with the vast and growing expense of the Vietnam War. By 1970 the cost of a single F111 'swing-wing' strike aircraft was $5,000,000. And expenses like this diverted public funds away from many urgent needs.

Meanwhile the problem of pollution from refuse and industrial and chemical waste was growing. Poverty, sickness, racial unrest, drug addiction, violence, and crime continued. Americans were no worse than other men. But their society demonstrated more clearly than anywhere else in the world how far Man could go in solving technical and scientific problems while making very limited progress in dealing with human problems.

IN 1493, the year after Columbus discovered the West Indies, the Spanish Pope Alexander VI drew an imaginary line down the Atlantic dividing the Portuguese colonies of the East from the new Spanish lands of the West. The Portuguese persuaded the Spanish to move the line further West a year later, so that they acquired Brazil. But most of the rest of South and Central America and most of the Caribbean islands were to be ruled by the Spanish for more than three hundred years.

Their colonial government was authoritarian and meticulous. It was conducted by officials sent from Spain and gave little opportunity for participation in local government even to the Creoles (the aristocratic land-owning descendants of the Spanish settlers) and none to the native Indians and the ever-increasing number of *mestizos*, people of mixed race. Roman Catholicism became the religion of the continent, and, except in Portuguese Brazil, Spanish became the language.

In the early nineteenth century, influenced by the American War of Independence and the French Revolution, moved by the ideas of Liberty and Nationalism, the Creoles of Latin America rebelled and established a number of independent republics. There were eventually eighteen Spanish-speaking states on the mainland of America and in the Caribbean. These independent republics acquired a national consciousness, usually maintained good relations with each other, but remained an international backwater for more than a century.

They had been established by war and were usually ruled by a military strong-man, or *caudillo*. Government was authoritarian and conservative, influenced by the 'sacred triangle' of the great land-owners, the hierarchy of the Roman Catholic Church, and the army leaders. Extremes of wealth and poverty were characteristic of Latin America, and the mass of the people had no more share in political life than they had had under the old colonial government. So by the twentieth century there was much latent political unrest.

The twentieth century also revealed the weakness of the economies of most Latin American countries. The British blockade during the first World War cut them off from their traditional markets and suppliers of manufactured goods in Europe. So they were driven to develop their own industries, and this resulted, in the Argentine for example, in the rapid growth of the town-dwelling working class. Then the great depression of the thirties hit them. Many of them were dependent for prosperity on one crop—Brazil, for example, on coffee, and Cuba on sugar. So when demand from the U.S.A. slumped this brought disaster to the Latin American countries. The result was resentment of the 'dollar imperialism' of the U.S.A. and unrest which brought down almost every government in Latin America. Meanwhile improvements in communications in the World made Latin America more susceptible to outside influences. The victory of the democracies in the first World War encouraged a demand for democracy, and the success of the Bolsheviks in Russia encouraged the development of left-wing parties. Then the success of Franco in Spain gave a boost to military dictatorship, though the defeat of Hitler and Mussolini in the second World War helped to produce a demand for the ending of dictatorship in Latin America.

But it was difficult for Latin American countries to throw off dictatorship. The one really significant difference by the mid-twentieth century was that the *descamisados*, 'the shirtless ones', could no longer be ignored, and some dictators even looked to them for support. This can be seen both in the history of the Argentine and that of Cuba.

The Argentine and Perón

The Argentine was controlled in the nineteenth century by a few great landowners, and the economy depended on producing meat and grain for export. The late nineteenth and early twentieth century saw an influx of about six million immigrants from Europe, the development of industrialisation, and the growth of a commercial middle class and an industrial working class.

The economic disaster of the thirties and the continuation of corrupt government by the old ruling class led to an army coup in 1943. One army officer who soon rose to prominence was Colonel Juan Domingo Perón—a good-looking man with a very strong personality. He was married to a young, beautiful, blonde wife, Eva, who came from a working-class background, was intensely ambitious, passionately opposed to the old ruling class, and concerned about the conditions of the working class.

As Secretary of Labour and Social Security in the military government Perón was able to get the support of many of the working class by promoting a programme of social welfare. At the same time he turned the police into his own private army. And on top of this he advocated free elections. The outcome was that in 1946 he was elected President.

For the next nine years Perón ruled the Argentine as a dictator. But his social policies of high minimum wages, shorter working hours, and holidays with pay ensured him working class support. So did his economic policies, which were fiercely nationalistic, concerned with making the Argentine self-sufficient and with driving out foreign interests. It was for this reason that he nationalised the British-owned railways, and this was understandably popular with the workers.

But policies of this sort inevitably alienated many of the old ruling class and the army leaders, and the repression and corruption which permeate a dictatorial regime alienated some of his supporters. Then in 1952 his wife, who had kept him in touch with the popular feeling, and who was always immensely popular, died of leukemia while only thirty-three.

Without the support and advice of his wife Perón made some bad mistakes. In 1954 he launched a campaign against the Roman Catholic Church, imprisoned a number of priests, banned religious demonstrations, legalised divorce and prostitution, and eventually in the spring of 1955 tried to disestablish the Roman Church. It was also in 1955 that he annoyed many of his own supporters by allowing a foreign oil company, Standard Oil of California, to prospect in the Argentine. Faced with riots and trouble Perón dismissed some of his ministers, released some political prisoners, and moved towards greater political freedom. But he had offended too many people, and in September 1955 the garrison of the Catholic stronghold of Cordoba revolted under the slogan *Christus vincit*, and Perón fled to exile in Spain.

The next fifteen years saw continued economic problems and continued political instability. *Peronismo* remained the strongest single political force in the Argentine, for the workers remembered that Perón had tried to give them both material benefits and *dignidad*. But the old conservative 'sacred triangle' of army, church, and landowners remained suspicious of 'Peronist' left wing social and economic policies, and every few years (in 1962, 1966, and 1970) civilian government was interrupted and replaced for a period by military rule.

Cuba and Castro

Cuba provides a more unusual but even more striking example of the explosive nature of Latin American politics in the second half of the twentieth century. From 1933 to 1944, and again from 1952 to 1958, it was ruled by a dictator, Fulgencio Batista, and its economy was dominated by American business interests. By

Latin American standards it was a relatively rich country, with a higher average income per head than Italy. But the extremes of wealth and poverty were vast, the economy depended on sugar, which provided four-fifths of the country's exports, and foreigners owned well over half the land.

In 1956 a young Cuban called Fidel Castro led an expedition of Cuban revolutionaries back from exile in Mexico to Cuba. They were rapidly smashed by Batista's troops, but the remnant fled to the mountains, where, over the next two years, Castro organized guerrilla warfare. This provoked Batista into creating a system of indiscriminate terror which bred opposition to itself, and eventually Batista's regime fell apart.

On New Year's Day, 1959, Batista fled and Fidel Castro came to power. He came promising land reform and hinting at nationalisation, he instituted rent reductions and wage increases, and stepped up the building of houses, schools, and hospitals. He also promised free elections, free speech, freedom of the press, and and end to corruption. He seemed to be both a radical reformer and a liberal democrat.

But it became increasingly obvious that he was a Communist. During 1959 and 1960 the more moderate revolutionary leaders resigned from office or were dismissed and even imprisoned as the Communist Party took over. Hundreds of potential opponents were executed, and parliamentary elections were postponed indefinitely.

In the autumn of 1959 the land reform programme was extended to include the nationalisation of American-owned estates. In 1960 Castro began establishing contacts with the U.S.S.R., and in June 1960 he nationalised the Shell and Esso oil companies because they refused to process the crude oil which was now being imported from Russia.

A week later President Eisenhower struck at the most vulnerable part of Cuba's economy by cutting the quota of sugar which could be imported into the U.S.A. from Cuba. Castro reacted by seizing American assets in Cuba and starting to import weapons from the Soviet *bloc*. In October the American government banned the export to Cuba of most goods except medical supplies. And on 3 January 1961, just two years after Castro had come to power, the U.S.A. broke off diplomatic relations with Cuba.

By this time the U.S.A. had been giving secret military training for nearly a year to Cuban exiles—not just those who fled with Batista but also those who had become disillusioned with Castro, such as José Miro Cardona, who had been Castro's first prime minister and now led the exiles. In April 1961 an invasion force of 1,500 of these exiles sailed from Florida to the Bay of Pigs. They had been led by American intelligence to expect mass support from the people of Cuba. But the whole operation was bungled, in particular the air support was inadequate, and within a few days the invasion force had to surrender.

The Bay of Pigs incident, the continued economic boycott by the U.S.A., and Castro's own Marxist convictions resulted in Cuba drawing even closer to the U.S.S.R., and this led to the Cuban missile crisis of the autumn of 1962 (pp. 439–40).

Castro had brought Cuba out of its Caribbean backwater into the very centre of the world politics, and in doing so he established her independence from the great powers. One consequence of the missile crisis was that President Kennedy gave an undertaking not to invade Cuba. And Russia was too far away to interfere effectively in Cuba, as the missile crisis clearly demonstrated.

Castro's regime also brought social benefits to Cuba. There were improvements in health, housing, education, and social security. Above all the redistribution of wealth helped to raise the standard of living of the poor. And government was less corrupt than in the past.

But as an economic revolution Castro's revolution was far less successful. The loss of the American market was disastrous. An attempt to get a massive increase in sugar production failed and in the process harmed other aspects of the economy. In 1970 consumer goods were still rationed, and Castro admitted publicly that his economic policies had failed.

Politically the revolution was a betrayal. Many, perhaps most, Cubans did not want Batista in 1958. They wanted freedom. Instead they just got a more efficient dictator.

Latin America in 1971

What was true of Cuba and the Argentine tended with modifications to be true of many of the countries of South and Central America and the Caribbean. Latin America had emerged into the world of international politics but was still tied to the U.S.A., as to a parent, by bonds of need and resentment. There were some social reforms. But most of the old problems remained. The population was rising faster than anywhere else in the world. Attempts to industrialise or diversify the economy brought further problems, such as overcrowding and violence in the towns. Government usually remained authoritarian. And in the last resort it was those who controlled the army who made the decisions.

Section VIII   The East

62   TURKEY

A T the beginning of the nineteenth century, the Ottoman Empire of the Turks had still included almost the whole Balkan peninsula and the whole North African coast, and had stretched through Asia as far as the Persian Gulf. But by the twentieth century the collapse of this once great empire seemed imminent. Britain and France appeared to be dividing its North African territories between them, the demand for independence in what was left of the European lands was increasingly difficult to resist, and in Asia the Arabs were discontented with Turkish rule. Even in Anatolia, the homeland of the Turks, there was discontent with the autocratic nature of Sultan Abülhamid II's government, and meanwhile the Empire was coming under the economic and political influence of Germany—a development symbolised by an agreement at the end of the century to build a railway from Berlin to Baghdad.

The Young Turk movement

However, in 1889 a group of army medical students had formed a secret society called 'the Ottoman Society for Union and Progress'. They wanted to preserve and modernise the whole Empire, establish parliamentary institutions, and enable all religious and racial groups to live contentedly and in equality together. This Young Turk movement spread through the army, and nearly twenty years later, in July 1908, army leaders in Salonika took advantage of a crisis to send an ultimatum to the Sultan demanding a parliamentary constitution. Abdülhamid gave in, and in April 1909, after trying to reassert his authority, he was deposed and succeeded by his brother, Mehmed V.

In practice the Young Turks were unable to construct a stable multi-racial Empire, and their more efficient rule only stimulated nationalist risings by the subject peoples. In 1910 there were risings in Albania and the Yemen, in the first Balkan War of 1912 (p. 101) the Turks were driven out of all Europe except Eastern Thrace, and meanwhile Tripoli, Rhodes, and the Dodecanese had been lost in the Italo-Turkish War of 1911–12 (p. 94).

Enver Pasha and the first World War

The effect of all this was to stimulate Turkish nationalism, and in

308 THE EAST

January 1913 a zealous Nationalist called Enver, who was also one of the principal Young Turks, seized power and destroyed the constitution which his party had established five years earlier. Enver, who accepted the title of Pasha from the Sultan and married the Sultan's daughter, believed in maintaining the closest relations with Germany and whole-heartedly advocated fighting at Germany's side in 1914.

Defeat in the first World War destroyed his position and at the same time destroyed the Ottoman Empire. By an armistice of 30th October 1918 all Ottoman possessions in Africa and Asia, other than Anatolia itself, were handed over to the Allies, who also acquired the right to control the Straits and occupy any strategic point in case of a threat to their security. French and Italian spheres of influence in Asia Minor had previously been agreed on by the Allies, the Russians wanted Kars, and in 1919 British, French, and Italian troops arrived in the Straits zone and a Greek division landed at Smyrna. Sultan Mehmed VI, who had succeeded his brother, Mehmed V, in July 1918, was prepared to accept any terms which the Allies would offer, and in August 1920 he accepted the Treaty of Sèvres (p. 219).

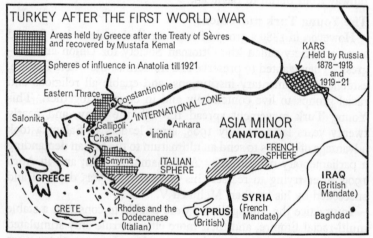

TURKEY AFTER THE FIRST WORLD WAR

Areas held by Greece after the Treaty of Sèvres and recovered by Mustafa Kemal

Spheres of influence in Anatolia till 1921

KARS
Held by Russia
1878–1918
and
1919–21

Eastern Thrace
Constantinople
INTERNATIONAL ZONE
Salonika
Gallipoli
Chanak
Ankara
İnönü
ASIA MINOR
(ANATOLIA)
Smyrna
ITALIAN
SPHERE
FRENCH
SPHERE
GREECE
IRAQ
(British
Mandate)
SYRIA
(French
Mandate)
CRETE
Rhodes and the
Dodecanese
(Italian)
CYPRUS
(British)
Baghdad

Mustafa Kemal

This was the crowning indignity, and it produced a revolutionary nationalist movement, at the head of which stood Mustafa Kemal, an army officer who had taken part in the events of 1908, but had later left the Young Turk movement because he believed that soldiers should cease to interfere in politics once the constitution had been gained. Kemal had become a national hero during the war, for in 1915 it was largely his leadership which had frustrated the Gallipoli campaign (pp. 166–7), in 1917 he had commanded the troops who drove the Russians out of Eastern Anatolia, and in 1918 he had prevented the retreat in Syria from becoming a rout.

Kemal organised a movement which demanded complete independence for the Turkish portion of the Ottoman Empire but laid no claim to the non-Turkish provinces. In April 1920 a Grand National Assembly of Turkey met at Ankara and elected him its President, and during the summer he gradually extended his control over more and more of Anatolia.

The war with Greece

But meanwhile the Greeks were advancing from Smyrna, and although İsmet, Kemal's Chief of Staff, inflicted a heavy defeat on them at İnönü early in 1921, they advanced again during the summer, and in the resulting crisis the Assembly conferred supreme power on Kemal. He held the Greeks in battle and then spent nearly a year preparing his army to drive them out of Anatolia. Meanwhile the French, Italians, and Russians withdrew their claims to Anatolian territory, and eventually in August 1922 the Turks attacked the Greek army and destroyed it. In September they sacked Smyrna, and then they advanced to Chanak where British troops were entrenched ready to defend the international zone. The French and Italians had withdrawn, but it seemed that there might be war between Britain and Turkey until in October the British government climbed down and Kemal got control of Constantinople, the Straits, and Eastern Thrace.

Negotiations for a new peace treaty began at Lausanne in Switzerland, with İsmet, now Foreign Minister, representing Turkey; and by the Treaty of Lausanne which was signed in July 1923 Turkish control over the areas regained in the previous year was confirmed.

The transformation of Turkey

Kemal's authority was now firmly established. In October a republic was established with the seat of government at Ankara, and Kemal became President with the right of presiding over meetings of both Assembly and cabinet and of appointing the Prime Minister. He appointed İsmet as his first Prime Minister, and together they approached the problem of transforming Turkey into a modern Westernised state.

The main obstacle to this was Islam, the religion of the Moslems, which influenced the whole way of life of the Turkish people. Kemal attacked this influence even to the extent of banning the practice of wearing headgear without any brim or peak so that the forehead could touch the ground in prayer. From November 1925 all Turkish men were compelled to wear hats or caps, and some religious leaders were even hanged for preaching against this new law. In 1928 Islam ceased to be the established religion of Turkey.

It was particularly difficult to break down the traditional Islamic attitude that women should occupy an inferior position in society. Although polygamy was made illegal in 1926 and women were given the right to vote in general elections in 1934, there was little improvement in their social status in most country areas. Even after the second World War the veil was still widely worn, and census figures demonstrated that polygamy was still practised in some regions.

But in many other ways Kemal was successful. In 1926 the European system of dating was adopted and he introduced a completely new legal system based on Western legal codes. In 1928 he introduced the Latin alphabet, and from the end of the year it was illegal to publish anything in Arabic type. The metric system of weights and measures was adopted at the end of 1932. And from the beginning of 1935 all Turks had to have surnames. Kemal himself became Kemal Atatürk (Father-Turk), and İsmet took the name of İnönü where he had won his victory against the Greeks. Also in 1935 the Western habit of having a weekly holiday on Saturday was adopted, and over the years community centres were set up in most towns and villages to spread the new ideas. By the end of 1938, when Kemal Atatürk died and İsmet İnönü was elected President in his place, he had done much to transform Turkey.

The Republican People's Party and opposition parties

Kemal's system of government was dictatorial and at first all members of the Assembly were in one loosely united party. But some opposed Kemal's autocratic methods, many disliked his anti-religious policy, and in October 1924 an opposition party had been formed whose attacks on İsmet in the Assembly had succeeded in the following month in getting Kemal to replace him as Prime Minister with Fethi, a more liberally minded member of the governing Republican People's Party.

Three months later a revolt of the Kurds in the Eastern provinces broke out. İsmet was brought back to suppress it, Fethi was sent off to Paris as Turkish ambassador, and in the summer the opposition party, which was accused of complicity with the Kurds, was suppressed. A year later, when a plot against Kemal's life was discovered, he took the opportunity to have all the leading opponents of his rule and policies hanged.

But Kemal was not adamantly opposed to the formation of a constructive opposition party, and indeed at a time when many European countries were turning towards dictatorship he seems to have been looking forward to a time when Turkey would grow out of dictatorship into a democratic system on the Western model. When Fethi returned from Paris in 1930 Kemal permitted him to form a new party, the Liberal Republican Party, which participated in the local elections of 1930. It was overwhelmingly defeated, apparently because many local officials falsified the election results. But this was not on government instructions but rather because many local officials felt that their own positions depended on the government's survival and at the same time regarded opposition to the government as opposition to the state. Later in the year Fethi dissolved his party and there was no organised opposition for the next fifteen years.

Constitutional government

By 1945 considerable opposition to the Republican government was building up. Pious Moslems and Liberals both disliked it, the working-class wanted the right to strike, and businessmen wanted an end to financial restrictions. Prices were high, and the Republican Party itself was beginning to split apart; so President İnönü told the Assembly that there was now room in Turkey for an opposition party.

Early in 1946 the Democratic Party was formed, and in 1950, led by Adnan Menderes, it came to power. The new government was popular in country districts, for it was tolerant of organised religion and distributed state land to the landless. But the Liberal principles which it professed at first soon wore thin. In 1953 it confiscated all the property of the Republican Party and took over its leading newspaper. And in 1954 it restricted the freedom of the press to criticise the government.

To members of the Republican Party it seemed that the new government was betraying the Kemalist revolution, especially when they saw mosques being built rather than hospitals and schools. And an army *coup* in 1960 was followed by the execution of Menderes and the re-establishment of İsmet İnönü.

Between them Menderes and the army leaders seemed to have destroyed constitutional government. But İnönü again allowed the formation of an opposition, and in 1965 the new Justice Party took office. Constitutional government was not, perhaps, very firmly rooted in Turkey, but it did seem to be surviving.

IN 1853, after two centuries in which foreigners had been rigidly excluded from Japan, a visit from four American warships commanded by Commodore Perry persuaded her to open her ports to trade. She saw the danger of colonisation by the European powers, and in order to avoid it decided to imitate them. Soon Japan was transformed. In 1871 education for all became compulsory, and in 1873 the first railway was built and conscription was introduced, providing the country with a national conscript army on the German model. The government promoted industrial development through great industrial and business combines, or *zaibatsu*. And in 1889 a new constitution was introduced, again in imitation of Germany, with power remaining in the hands of the Emperor and his ministers rather than in the hands of parliament.

The Sino-Japanese War, 1894–5

As Japan acquired Western techniques she also acquired the Western ambition to colonise China. In 1894 she seized the opportunity of a revolt in Korea, a tributary state of the Chinese Empire, to go to war with China. Her navy struck at Chinese shipping six days before war was declared, and soon her armies were threatening Peking. China quickly acknowledged defeat and in 1895 by the Treaty of Shimonoseki granted Japan trade concessions such as she had already granted to the European powers, acknowledged the independence of Korea, thus leaving it open to Japanese domination, and ceded Japan Formosa and the Liao-tung peninsula.

Russia, France, and Germany intervened at this stage to compel Japan to return the Liao-tung peninsula to China, but it was clear that Japan was emerging as a competitor with the European powers for colonial influence, and the part she now played in the scramble for concessions in China and in the suppression of the Boxer Rising (p. 318) demonstrated that she could expect to be treated as an equal by them.

The successful use of force and consequent rise in the prestige of the army and navy had an important effect on Japan's constitution: an Imperial ordinance of 1900 decreed that only a general could be Minister of War and only an admiral Navy Minister, and thus gave the army and navy power to break any government they disliked.

The Russo-Japanese War, 1904–5

Meanwhile Japan's relations with Russia were deteriorating, for their ambitions to dominate North China conflicted. In 1898

Russia had acquired a lease of the Liao-tung peninsula, which Japan had been forced to hand back to China three years earlier, and in 1900 she had taken advantage of the Boxer Rising to extend her influence in Manchuria.

The effect of this was that Japan drew closer to Britain, which was also concerned to check Russian expansion in North China, and in 1902 signed the Anglo-Japanese Alliance (p. 77), which enabled her to attack Russia without fear of French intervention.

Once again the Japanese navy struck before a declaration of war. The Russian Far East fleet in Port Arthur was strategically important because the best way to frustrate Japan's plans was to cut her sea route to the continent, so the Japanese navy attacked it in the port in February 1904, and thereafter blockaded it. This enabled the Japanese forces to cross the sea freely. They took Port Arthur on 31st December 1904 after a five-month siege, and then they destroyed the Russian ships with the shore batteries.

During February and March of 1905 the Russian armies were decisively defeated in the battle of Mukden. Then in May the forty ships of the Russian Baltic fleet arrived in the Straits of Tsushima, and in a battle which lasted two days the Russians lost all but two of their ships while the Japanese lost only three torpedo boats.

However, Japan's financial and military resources had been stretched to the limit, and immediately after the battle of Tsushima the Japanese government asked President Theodore Roosevelt of the U.S.A. to approach the Russians with peace proposals. In September the Treaty of Portsmouth (U.S.A.) was signed. Russia transferred to Japan her lease of the Liao-tung peninsula and of the South Manchuria railway, ceded to her the Southern half of Sakhalin, and accepted Japanese influence in Korea (map, p. 76).

The first World War

In the following years Japan extended her influence through South Manchuria and into Inner Mongolia, and in 1910 she actually annexed Korea. But it was the preoccupation of the European powers with the first World War which gave her an opportunity for extending her influence and even control over China.

She began in 1914 by driving the Germans from Shantung province, and then in January 1915 she presented what were called the Twenty-one Demands to China, demanding an extension of her influence in Shantung, Manchuria, and Inner Mongolia, control of the most important parts of China's coal and iron industry, and the right to impose political, military, and financial advisers on the Chinese government. Britain was able to get her to modify some of the more outrageous demands, but an ultimatum forced China to accept most of them.

In 1917 Japan was able to get British agreement, in return for naval assistance in the Mediterranean, to her taking over Germany's rights in Shantung and Germany's island colonies in the North Pacific. In 1918 she took advantage of the political confusion in Russia to send troops into Siberia and North Sakhalin.

Japan in the post-war world

The Treaty of Versailles confirmed Japan's control of Shantung and the islands of the North Pacific, and Japan's position in the Pacific was potentially even stronger than these gains implied, for the war had produced a drastic change in the balance of power in the Far East. The European powers were no longer significant in the Pacific, where the U.S.A. was now dominant in the East and Japan in the West. This Japanese dominance in the West was ensured by the Washington Naval Treaty of 1922 (p. 234), for although the British and American fleets were both to be larger than the Japanese fleet, they needed to be too widely dispersed to control the West Pacific. This effect was increased by British and American undertakings not to build naval bases or fortifications in the West Pacific, which left Britain with no base nearer than Singapore, and the U.S.A. with no base nearer than Pearl Harbor.

However, this does not mean that Japan was satisfied with her position in the post-war world. In fact she had been bitterly offended by the refusal of the peace-makers to include the principle of racial equality in the Covenant of the League of Nations, and she regarded the whole Washington Conference, with some reason, as an American device for preventing the renewal of the Anglo-Japanese Alliance which expired in 1921. Friction with the U.S.A. was increased by American legislation in 1924 prohibiting Japanese immigration. Friction with most of the Western world was increased by their imposition of tariff barriers to keep out cheap Japanese manufactured goods. And her territorial ambitions received a check when the Bolsheviks became firmly established in Russia, for she had to withdraw her troops from Siberia in 1922 and from North Sakhalin in 1925.

'The Manchurian Incident'

Internally Japan seemed to be moving tentatively in the direction of Western constitutionalism. In 1918 a commoner became Prime Minister for the first time, and in the twenties most members of the frequently changing cabinets came from the parliamentary parties. But there were widespread and often well-founded accusations of corruption in political circles, and many people disliked the close links between the parties and the *zaibatsu* and were very ready to blame them when Japan suffered in 1930 from the economic crisis which was affecting the whole world.

The army was also discontented with party rule, largely because it disliked the more conciliatory policy pursued towards China in the twenties, and on this issue the army acted on its own authority in September 1931 when the Japanese forces on the South Manchuria Railway seized Mukden and began to extend their control over Manchuria.

The government accepted a League of Nations resolution at the end of the month demanding Japan's withdrawal, but it could no longer control the situation, for the army's action was widely popular. Nationalist sentiment was strong among the Japanese people, and Manchuria had sentimental associations since the war with Russia in 1904–5 and also seemed to offer opportunities for immigration and industrial development.

Meanwhile party government became even more unpopular. In December 1931 a new government was formed by the *Seiyukai* Party, which had close associations with the Mitsui *zaibatsu*, and one of its first actions was to take Japan off the gold standard, to the great financial advantage of Mitsui. Party government was yet further discredited, and in May 1932 the Prime Minister was assassinated. After this the army always made it impossible for the leader of a political party to form a government by refusing to provide a Minister of War. The generals did not directly seize power, but they tightened their stranglehold over the country.

'The China Incident'

Military influence in politics was increasingly apparent. In 1934 Japan issued the Amau Declaration that she would not tolerate interference by any other power in China. In 1936 she rescinded the Washington Naval Treaty and signed the Anti-Comintern Pact with Germany (p. 243), and in 1937 the army leaders decided to renew the invasion of China. They had miscalculated badly, for they were not able to settle 'the China incident' in a few months. But they continued the invasion in 1938 without interference from the European powers, who were drifting towards a war of their own, and in November, shortly after one of the most extreme militarists, General Tojo, had entered the government, they proclaimed the 'New Order in East Asia'—a plan for the political and economic union of Japan, China, and Manchukuo, as Manchuria had been renamed in 1932. In August 1940, when Germany's successes in Europe indicated that Japan would have a free hand in the East for some time, the 'New Order' was extended into the 'Greater East Asia Co-prosperity Sphere', involving the political and economic subjugation of East and South-East Asia to Japan's needs under the guise of a programme of economic co-operation and deliverance from Western colonialism; and in September Japan signed the Tripartite Pact (p. 264) with Germany and Italy. After another year, in October 1941, Tojo became Prime Minister, and two months later he launched the attack on Pearl Harbor. What had begun as 'the China incident' was to end after eight years fighting in total collapse.

Post-war Japan

When the war ended in August 1945 Japan lost her vast empire and for nearly seven years was occupied by American forces. During most of this period the ruler of the country was General MacArthur, the Supreme Commander of the Allied Powers, and in the early years of his rule two hundred thousand people in positions of responsibility were dismissed, nearly a thousand war criminals were executed, the army was disbanded, the *zaibatsu* began to be broken up, and a new constitution was drawn up establishing a representative system of government and emphasising human rights.

In these early years the American occupation was widely popular, for it was unexpectedly and outstandingly humane. But after the American decision in 1948 to build up Japan as an ally against Communism there was some disillusionment, for the American administration began to emphasise economic recovery rather than human rights, the *zaibatsu* grew again, and in 1950 rearmament began. In April 1952, when the occupation ended, there was resentment that the Americans still had bases in Japan; and in 1954, when some Japanese fishermen suffered radiation sickness from an American hydrogen bomb explosion near Bikini in the Pacific, relations with the U.S.A. were severely strained.

For the moment Japan was still heavily dependent on the U.S.A. both for defence and economic growth. Her years of dominance in East Asia seemed over. But she had a vast and growing population of ninety million, her economic growth in the next twenty years was extraordinary, and by 1971 it was being predicted that by the end of the century Japan could well be the leading industrial nation of the world.

IN the middle of the nineteenth century a Chinese Empire which included Amur province in the North, Indo-China in the South, and a vast inland area of Asia, was ruled from the old capital of Peking by an Emperor of the Manchu dynasty, which had come two centuries earlier from the area known as Manchuria.

The opening up of China

For centuries the Chinese had ignored foreign countries, but now the great European colonising powers, Britain, Russia, and France, were trying to extend their trade and influence into the Far East. By 1860 Britain had forced China to cede her Hong

Kong and open sixteen ports and the Yangtse River to trade, Russia had acquired Amur province and the coastline as far South as Vladivostock; and between 1880 and 1890 France took control of Indo-China. Then in 1891 the Russians began building the Trans-Siberian railway around China's boundaries. They were plainly threatening Manchuria, Mongolia, and Korea, so at this stage the Japanese, who had recently been growing increasingly powerful, decided to forestall Russia and stake their own claim quickly to a share in the spoils of the crumbling Chinese Empire.

In 1894 Japan attacked China, and in 1895 by the Treaty of Shimonoseki China ceded Formosa and the Liao-tung peninsula to Japan and acknowledged the independence of Korea. This precipitated a scramble by the European powers to get leases of both territories and ports, and also concessions for trading and building railways. France, Russia and Germany, which was, as in Africa, a late arrival on the colonial scene, began by forcing Japan to return the Liao-tung peninsula to China. Then Russia, as a reward for her part in this, was allowed by the Manchu Emperor to build the Chinese Eastern Railway across Manchuria to Vladivostock, and while Russia sought to dominate North China by a railway network France aimed to do the same in the South. In 1898 the scramble for concessions became intense. Early in March Germany acquired extensive rights in Shantung province, including a lease of the valuable port of Kiao-chow. By the end of the month Russia had acquired a lease of Port Arthur on the Liao-tung peninsula and the right to build a railway linking it with the Chinese Eastern Railway. Two weeks later France gained further concessions in the South. And within the next three months Britain also gained several further concessions.

The Boxer Rising

This colonising activity stimulated Nationalist feeling in China, and the widespread resentment of Europeans found expression in the activities of a secret society called the Righteous Harmonious Fists, known in Britain as the Boxers, which was formed in September 1898. Rioting and the slaughter of Europeans and Christian Chinese culminated in the summer of 1900 in a siege of the European embassies in Peking.

The rising was put down by an international expedition whose cost had to be paid for by the Chinese government, and thereafter the foreign powers fortified the embassy area and stationed troops to protect their communications with the sea. The Russians seized the opportunity to occupy Manchuria, and the next few years saw an intensification of the rivalry between Russia and Japan for domination of the North of the Chinese Empire which only died down after Japan's victory against Russia in 1904-5 (p. 313).

Sun Yat-sen and revolution

The failure of the Manchu government to do anything to check foreign encroachments discredited it, and a revolutionary movement developed led by a Dr. Sun Yat-sen and inspired by the principles of 'Nationalism, Democracy, and the People's Livelihood', which he was eventually to proclaim in a series of public lectures in Canton in 1924 as the 'Three Principles of the People'. 'Nationalism' implied opposition to foreign influence, 'Democracy' implied a form of provincial self-government, but not universal suffrage, and 'the People's Livelihood' meant land reform.

Ironically it was an attempt by the Manchu government to face the dangers of foreign influence by strengthening the central government which sparked off revolution, for its decision in 1911 to take over all main railways conflicted with the demand for provincial self-government. Once the rebellion had started it spread quickly. By the end of the year the Chinese Republic had been proclaimed, with Sun Yat-sen as its first President, and in February 1912 an edict of abdication was issued on behalf of Pu-yi, the five-year-old Emperor.

The Kuomintang

However, the immediate result of the breakdown of accepted authority was that power passed to whoever had control of armed force. Sun Yat-sen did not, and in March he had to resign the Presidency. The following year saw him in the South leading another rebellion, this time against the Republican government, at the head of the newly formed Nationalist Party, the Kuomintang. The rising was swiftly put down, and Sun Yat-sen had to flee abroad. But the authority of the Republican government was weakened by its acceptance of most of Japan's Twenty-one Demands of January 1915 (p. 332), and by 1918, when Sun Yat-sen returned to South China to re-establish Kuomintang rule, there was anarchy in China, with individual military commanders ruling as large areas as they could hold. The chaos China was in was demonstrated to the rest of the world by the fact that she was represented at the Paris Peace Conference by two different sets of delegates—one from the Republican government and one from the Kuomintang.

The insistence of the colonial powers at the Paris Peace Conference of 1919 on retaining their colonial concessions in China drew Sun Yet-sen towards the Russian Bolsheviks, who were at the time fighting British, French, and Japanese armies of intervention in Russia. And soon Russian advisers were reorganising the Kuomintang: all party members were taught Marxist principles, and some of the leaders went to Russia for military training. But Sun Yet-sen and the Bolsheviks wanted different things.

Sun wanted Russian help to enable China to assert her independence. The Bolsheviks wanted control of the Kuomintang in order to spread Communist revolution in the Far East.

The rise of Chiang Kai-shek

In 1925 Sun Yat-sen died. His successor as leader of the Kuomintang was Chiang Kai-shek, who had been sent to Russia in 1923 to study the Red Army and then in 1924 had been put in command of the new Whampoa Military Academy. Chiang's first aim was to establish his control over the whole country, and in the summer of 1926, against the advice of his Russians advisers, he launched a campaign for the conquest of the North. He was rapidly and overwhelmingly successful. In the spring of 1927 he took Shanghai. By then he was virtually the ruler of all China South of the Yangtse, and later in the year he married Mai-ling Soong, the daughter of one of Shanghai's richest bankers. In June 1928 he took Peking. By then he was virtually the ruler of all China. He moved the capital to Nanking, which was more central than Peking, and he drew up a new constitution under which he was head of the government, the party, and the army. He seemed to have succeeded in reuniting China.

The fall of Chiang Kai-shek

His troubles were only just beginning. In April 1927 when he took Shanghai he had broken with the Communists, and for the next ten years he was engaged in a series of unsuccessful campaigns to destroy them. The civil war with the Communists was temporarily halted in 1937 only because of the more immediate threat from the Japanese, who had seized Manchuria in 1931 and in 1937 renewed their invasion of China. Chiang then suffered heavy defeats at the hands of the Japanese. But rather extraordinarily his prestige in the World was high when the Japanese war ended in 1945, and China became one of the five permanent members of the Security Council of the United Nations Organisation.

His prestige inside China was far lower. Soon the Kuomintang was collapsing before the forces of the Communists, and in December 1949 Chaing had to withdraw the remnant of his forces to the island of Formosa, or Taiwan. He still claimed to be legitimate ruler of all China, and strangely enough the United Nations accepted that claim for over twenty years. In 1971, when Communist China at last replaced Nationalist China in the United Nations, Chiang was still ruling Formosa.

Lenin's theory of imperialism

KARL MARX, writing in the mid-nineteenth century, believed that the middle class capitalists of Western Europe, in their lust for profits, would oppress the working class till they were driven by poverty, hunger, and misery to rebel. This did not happen. Instead the standard of living of the European working class rose. Lenin later explained this by saying that the capitalists had appeased the European working class by paying them more out of the profits made by exploiting the colonial peoples. But this, he said, could not last for ever. The imperialist powers would need more colonial territories to exploit, and one day their scramble for colonies would plunge them into imperialist wars with each other. This in turn would produce a revolutionary situation in the colonies, and the colonial peoples would rise against their oppressors. London and Paris, said Lenin, would fall on the banks of the Yangtse.

The Communists and the Kuomintang

At the Paris Peace Conference of 1919, despite talk about self-determination, the British, French, and Japanese governments insisted on retaining their trading concessions in China, and Germany's concessions were transferred to Japan. This provoked violent demonstrations in Peking against imperialism on 4 May 1919, and a May the Fourth Movement spread through China stimulating nationalist feeling. To some passionately nationalistic young men, such as Mao Tse-tung, it seemed clear that Lenin's analysis of China's troubles was correct, and that summer they formed the Chinese Communist Party.

But at this time the main revolutionary party in China was the nationalist Kuomintang, led by Sun Yat-sen, and in 1923 the Moscow Comintern decided to support the Kuomintang. The Russian Communists had decided that China needed to undergo a bourgeois revolution before she could progress to a Socialist one. So a Comintern agent, Michael Borodin, was sent to reorganise the Kuomintang and the Chinese Communists were ordered to join it and get into positions from which they would be able to work for the Socialist revolution.

The purge of the Communists

Some of the Kuomintang wanted to co-operate with the Communists and work for radical reform. Others, such as Chiang

Kai-shek, who became the leader of the party in 1925 when Sun Yat-sen died, feared that the Communists would carry the revolution too far. Chiang acted against the advice of his Russian advisers when he launched a campaign in 1926 against the war lords of the North, and in 1927 he sent the Russians home and decided to destroy the Communists.

When his victorious army reached Shanghai in the spring of 1927 the Communists inside the town, led by Chou En-lai, had seized control of the town, and the Communists in Chiang's army wanted to go in and seize the property of the rich business-men. But Chiang preferred to ally with the businessmen, and on 12 April 1927 he sent his troops into Shanghai to destroy the Communists. This was followed by a massacre of Communists and their supporters throughout the territories held by the Kuo-mintang. It seemed for a while as if Communism in China had been destroyed.

Mao Tse-tung and the peasantry

But it was at about this time that Mao Tse-tung was breaking free from the traditional Marxist theory that the workers in the towns would make the revolution. There were only two million industrial workers in China. Most of the population of 600 million were peasants. So Mao persuaded his fellow Communists to disappear into the countryside and try to win the support of the peasants before trying to extend their control over the coun-try. The peasants were the sea, said Mao, and the Communists must be like fish swimming in that sea. They concentrated on Kiangsi province in the South, and they were so successful that, despite two Kuomintang campaigns against them, they were able in November 1931 to proclaim a Soviet republic.

Chiang launched two further campaigns against them. But Mao developed an effective guerrilla strategy based on the support of the peasantry. When an enemy army advanced, the Communists retreated; when it halted, they harassed it; when it tired, they attacked; and when it retreated, they pursued it. Nevertheless, the forces of the Kuomintang were too strong for them, and at the beginning of 1934 Chiang, acting on the advice of a German mili-tary mission, adopted a new more effective strategy. He surrounded the Communists and seemed about to destroy them.

The Long March

Incredibly they broke out and fought their way westwards, be-ginning what came to be known as the Long March. One hundred and forty thousand set out. Only twenty thousand of them reached North Shensi more than a year later after marching more than 6,000 miles.

The Long March was one of the great events of Chinese history in the twentieth century. It stirred the imagination of the Chinese people, it hardened the survivors and united them as an effective political and military nucleus of the future Communist movement, and it established the undisputed leadership of Mao Tse-tung. Militarily it saved the Communists. Politically it made them.

The Japanese War

Chiang was still planning their destruction. But to many Chinese it seemed shameful that the Kuomintang and the Communists should be fighting each other when the real enemy was Japan, with which China had been at least technically at war ever since the Japanese seizure of Manchuria in 1931. So at the end of 1936, when Chiang flew North to encourage a more vigorous campaign against the Communists, the general commanding the Kuomintang forces imprisoned him and demanded the formation of a united front. Chiang was released without giving any such undertaking. But the mood of the country was clear. So in 1937, shortly before the Japanese renewed their attack on China, he reached an agreement with Mao.

Despite their agreement both Chiang and Mao knew that victory over Japan would be followed by renewed fighting between them. And to many people it seemed that the Kuomintang deliberately avoided fighting the Japanese and husbanded their resources for the future struggle with the Communists. In December 1937, when the Japanese attacked and took Nanking, Chiang withdrew South. In the autumn of 1938, when they took Canton, he withdrew inland to Chungking.

But while the Kuomintang armies gave ground the far weaker Communist forces continued to fight in the North-West, using the same strategy as they had previously used against the Kuomintang, and even extending their guerrilla activities far behind the Japanese lines. The effect of this was to make the Communists appear as the patriotic party and rally support to them. The rivalry between the Communists and the Kuomintang intensified, and in practice, though not officially, the united front broke down in 1941.

Civil War

In the summer of 1945, when the Japanese war suddenly ended, the Kuomintang, with about two million men, probably out-numbered the armed forces of the Communists by about three to one. Chiang was able, with the help of American equipment and money, to establish control over virtually all the great cities, ports, and railways of China. He also signed a treaty with Stalin by which, in return for Chiang's recognising the 'independence' of Outer Mongolia, Stalin recognised Chiang's government and promised not to support the Communists. And in the spring of 1946 the Russian troops who had liberated Manchuria from the Japanese in 1945 handed over control of all the main towns of Manchuria to the Kuomintang.

Meanwhile the Americans had given Chiang another $1,000 million to aid the recovery of China. But idleness and personal rivalries had weakened the leadership of the Kuomintang, and much of the money was squandered. The effect of all this was to make the Kuomintang leaders seem to be what the Communists said they were: the lackeys of foreign imperialism. They retained the support of the upper and middle classes in the towns. But the influence of the Communists spread rapidly among the peasants in the countryside.

During 1946 Lin Piao, the most brilliant of the Communist generals, occupied the countryside in Manchuria. Then in the spring of 1947 he attacked. His control of the countryside enabled him to cut the Kuomintang's lines of communication, and he rapidly took one isolated city after another. The morale of the Kuomintang leadership suffered a serious blow. Gradually effective government was breaking down. And inflation became so serious that between the summers of 1946 and 1947 prices increased forty-fold.

Political and economic collapse were followed by military collapse, and by the end of 1947 civil war had spread through the country. The Communists were demonstrating what Mao had long taught: that in a civil war it is not primarily superior numbers and equipment that matters; it is men, their beliefs and their morale, and the quality of their leadership.

During 1948 more and more of the country transferred its allegiance to the Communists. Whole armies, with their valuable equipment, changed sides. By the end of the year most of the countryside was in Communist hands. In January 1949 the Communists were in Peking. In May they were in Shanghai. And on 1 October 1949 Mao Tse-tung was able to proclaim the People's Republic of China.

Once the People's Republic of China was proclaimed on 1 October 1949 Mao Tse-tung and the Communist Party were faced with the task of re-establishing order after the upheaval of civil war. They were rapidly and remarkably successful. Peace brought stability to the economy. Inflation was brought under control within six months. The railways were working properly within a year. And the peasants were able to start increasing food production.

Land reform and collectivisation

Land was the basis of China's economy, and most of it was farmed by poor peasants. But great landlords, who lived on their income from rent, owned it. So in June 1950 a land reform programme was launched. Over the next three years about 12,000,000,000 acres of arable land was confiscated and redistributed to poor peasants; about 800,000 people, including many village headmen, were killed; and the old power structure in the villages was destroyed.

By 1953 Mao was ready to launch a Five Year Plan. In order to modernise and industrialise China it was necessary to stop importing food and instead grow enough to export the surplus to pay for machinery. So the Five Year Plan for 1953–7 aimed at a great increase in grain production as well as at massive industrial development. But peasants farming small plots could not produce the vast surpluses needed. So the Chinese, like the Russians thirty years earlier, introduced collectivisation in order to provide the food to make industrialisation possible. Mao made the decision in the summer of 1955, and within a year most agricultural land was collectivised. At the same time most industry and commerce was nationalised or collectivised. Inevitably there was resistance to these changes, and in 1957 Mao claimed that half a million counter-revolutionaries had been eliminated.

The 'hundred flowers'

Government in the years after the revolution was harsh. But although Mao believed in the need for discipline and complete obedience to the party, he also believed that it was necessary to involve the masses in the formulation of policy. The party should only decide its policy after careful analysis of the attitudes of the masses. So in May 1956, with the basis of a Socialist society established, Mao delivered a secret speech to the leaders of the party suggesting the need for some intellectual liberty. 'Let a hundred flowers bloom' he demanded. And in the spring of 1957 a government campaign encouraged criticism of the party and of party members.

Flowers of criticism bloomed everywhere, and some were critical of fundamental Marxist principles. This was going too far. So after only six weeks the blooms of criticism were cut down in a new campaign against 'bourgeois rightists'.

The Great Leap Forward

The episode of the 'hundred flowers' indicated to Mao that something was wrong with the revolution. The party, he felt, needed to recapture the spirit of the years when they had struggled against overwhelming difficulties in North Shensi. With that spirit they would achieve in one generation what it had taken the Western industrial nations two hundred years to accomplish. If the peasants would work hard enough they could double grain production in a year. If they would set up furnaces in their back-yards steel production could be doubled at the same time.

So in May 1958 he proclaimed the Great Leap Forward. Communes were formed from groups of about thirty co-operatives, partly as a way of making the economies which would go with large-scale production, and partly as a deliberate social and political move towards 'Communism'. A People's Militia was formed in the Communes, partly as a way of tightening up control over the people, and partly as a source of labour for road building and irrigation works.

Some steps backwards

There were some successes. But the failures were more obvious. A campaign for killing grain-eating birds, in which a billion sparrows were slaughtered, seriously upset the balance of nature. The steel produced in the backyard furnaces was of a very poor quality. And it was difficult to gather in the harvest while making steel. By the end of the year the party was driven to modify its policies.

Then 1959–61 produced perhaps the worst sequence of droughts and floods for a century, grain production fell instead of increasing, and by 1961 the Chinese had to start importing grain again. There were widespread riots and even revolts. When the second Five Year Plan ended in 1962 it was followed by three years of 'readjustment' in which the emphasis was on developing agriculture, and it took till 1965 for grain production to get back to the level of 1957.

The Cultural Revolution

Mao was dissatisfied with the progress of the revolution. He believed that revolutionary fervour was declining, and that unless something was done to stimulate it the revolution in China might degenerate into the 'bourgeois revisionism' which was, he thought, so tragically corrupting Russia. He decided that China needed a thorough cultural revolution. Decadent Communist Party officials who had turned into middle-class bureaucrats would have to be purged. And the idealistic youth of the country who had saved the nation's soul once in the May the Fourth Movement of 1919 (p. 321) could save it again.

In the summer of 1966 students were encouraged to attack university teachers and party officials. A youth organisation called the Red Guards was formed and soon numbered millions. It attacked symptoms of bourgeois decadence, such as long hair and antique furniture. It attacked 'revisionist' Communist Party officials. And eventually it attacked the organisation and administration of industry.

At the beginning of 1967 there was widespread street fighting between workers and Red Guards. China seemed to be collapsing into the sort of chaos from which the Communists had rescued her twenty years earlier. And at this point Mao had to call in the army to establish order.

Lin Piao and the army

Over the next two years many officials of the Communist Party were purged and the party organisation was destroyed—even the secretariat, which might have been able to reconstruct the party apparatus fairly quickly. Meanwhile twenty-six new Revolutionary Committees were set up to run the provinces, and most of them were headed by army officers. The army achieved a sufficiently powerful position to be able to influence policy, and in the autumn of 1968 it persuaded Mao to end Red Guard militancy. Millions of teen-agers who had been rioting with revolutionary zeal were sent off to the countryside to work in the fields and learn something about manual labour. And in April 1969 Mao announced the end of the Cultural Revolution.

One of the most interesting political developments of these years was the rise of Lin Piao, the general who had taken Manchuria from the Kuomintang twenty years earlier. He was very close to Mao, and he was intimately involved in the Cultural

Revolution. But he was also a soldier and as Minister of Defence was closely associated with the army leaders. In 1967 he rose to the second place in the party hierarchy, above the prime minister, Chou En-lai. And in 1969 he was officially designated the successor to Mao Tse-tung, who was now 75 years old.

Chinese ambitions and the U.S.A.

The importance of the army was the natural result of having such a very large army, and that in turn was largely the result of Mao's ambition to recover the lost territories of the old Chinese Empire. This ambition led Mao to send an army into Tibet to seize control of it in 1950. And the recovery of Formosa, or Taiwan, from Chiang Kai-shek remained his main ambition.

Meanwhile the determination of the U.S.A. to contain Communism meant that the U.S.A. was the natural enemy of China. American intervention first in Korea and later in Vietnam, and their use of the Seventh Fleet to defend Formosa from invasion, made the Chinese feel encircled and threatened. What seemed like reasonable defensive measures to the Americans looked to the Chinese like imperialist aggression.

The Sino-Soviet dispute

While the U.S.A. seemed China's natural enemy, the U.S.S.R. seemed her natural friend. Not surprisingly China and the U.S.S.R. signed a treaty of friendship in 1950, and the Russians sent considerable technical and material assistance to help with the first Five Year Plan of 1953–7.

But these friendly relations did not last. In the first place, Russia had herself been one of the colonising powers which had encroached on Chinese territory, and the Russo-Chinese border, stretching 4000 miles across Asia, was a potent source of trouble. Manchuria was a traditional sphere of Russian colonisation, and the U.S.S.R. only abandoned her share in the control of the industry of Manchuria in 1954–5. Outer Mongolia had actually been separated from China by Stalin in 1945 and given 'independence'. And Sinkiang, the vast undeveloped South-Western province, was also becoming a source of friction.

A second reason for trouble between China and the U.S.S.R. was that China made a clear attempt at the Bandung Conference of 1955 to put herself at the head of the Afro-Asian countries. At first the Chinese leaders had tended to regard men like Nehru of India as puppets of Western capitalism. But from 1955 she tried to align them with her against the capitalist Western World. And it was clear that she was trying to align them with herself rather than with the U.S.S.R.

A third cause of trouble between China and the U.S.S.R. came in 1956 when Khrushchev formally abandoned Lenin's doctrine of the inevitability of war between Socialist and Capitalist states and declared that he wanted 'peaceful co-existence' with the Capitalist world. Mao Tse-tung denounced him as a 'revisionist'. Khrushchev in turn criticised China's internal policies, such as the 'Great Leap Forward', withdrew 1,400 technical and other experts from China, and cancelled 600 separate aid agreements. In 1959 he decided to stop helping the Chinese make an atom bomb, and went to Peking to warn the Chinese leaders against using force over Formosa and the Indian frontier.

Sino-Soviet relations were particularly badly strained in 1962, first when Khrushchev condemned the Chinese invasion of India (p. 337), and secondly when Mao condemned Khrushchev's mis-handling of the Cuban missile crisis (pp. 439–40). Not surprisingly the Chinese, who were preparing to explode their first atom bomb in 1964, refused to sign the Partial Test Ban Treaty in 1963. In the same year they accused the Russians of trying to subvert Sinkiang. And in the late 1960s there were several frontier clashes.

The Chinese enigma

But the Chinese were so concerned with their own internal affairs during the years of the Cultural Revolution that the Sino-Soviet dispute tended to die down. And then in 1971 there was a sudden *rapprochement* with the U.S.A. In July it was announced that President Nixon would be visiting China, in the autumn the U.S.A. voted for China to join the United Nations, and in November the Chinese took their place in the Security Council.

Despite all this China remained an enigma to Western observers. Something dramatic had happened there in September 1971. But no one could be sure what it was. The most likely explanation seemed to be that Lin Piao had plotted with the army leaders to assassinate Mao Tse-tung, and had then been killed himself while attempting to escape to Russia by plane. Whether or not these events had any connection with foreign policy was uncertain. But it was clear that China's Communist leaders were engaged in a particularly bitter and bloody struggle over the leadership. And by the time President Nixon visited China in March 1972 it seemed that the most influential man in China after Mao Tse-tung was the man responsible for the visit: Chou En-lai.

AFTER the Indian Mutiny of 1857-8 the British government took control of India out of the hands of the East India Company. It vested authority in a Viceroy, and for nearly a century it retained its authority over a vast Indian Empire made up of a few large British provinces and nearly six hundred native states, and including Burma in the East, and even Aden in the West.

During this century of British rule three important problems had to be faced:

(1) India needed security from possible threats by other nations.

(2) A population approximately ten times as large as that of Great Britain needed feeding.

(3) The Indians wanted to rule themselves, but at the same time were divided among themselves.

External security

Britain looked after the security of India by acquiring extra land and by building a ring of buffer states around her.

By 1885, when Gladstone checked a Russian attempt to expand into Afghanistan by a threat of war (p. 33), Britain had already fought two Afghan wars in order to secure the North-West frontier and had occupied Baluchistan. Later in 1885, during Salisbury's first ministry, Upper Burma was annexed in order to forestall a possible French threat to the North-East frontier.

In 1904 Britain gained further security in the North-East when France agreed in the *entente cordiale* (p. 80) to leave Siam alone. And the Anglo-Russian *entente* of 1907 (p. 83) also increased India's security, for Russia agreed to keep out of Afghanistan and Tibet and to divide Persia into spheres of influence.

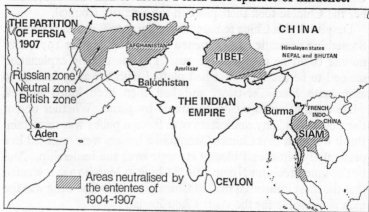

Areas neutralised by the ententes of 1904-1907

There was no serious external threat to the Indian Empire from this time until the Japanese invasion of Burma in 1941 (p. 293).

Subsistence

The question of how to feed the vast population of India was a fundamental problem which at first seemed insoluble. Most of the population were peasant farmers living permanently near starvation level and often hopelessly sunk in debt. Millions died each year from hunger and disease; and for years the problem was increased rather than solved by British rule, for peaceful conditions and improved medical care resulted in a rapid increase in population which strained the country's food resources even further.

Lord Curzon, who was Viceroy from 1899 to 1905, made an attempt to deal with the problem by planning an irrigation scheme to improve food production and by setting up co-operative societies to provide peasants with sufficient credit to improve their land or even buy it. But the problem of increasing food production faster than the rate of population growth was not solved until after the British left India.

An allied problem was that of industrial development. By the beginning of the twentieth century British investors were pouring capital into India, and by 1931 India was the eighth leading industrial country of the world. But much of the profit from this industrialisation went outside India to the British investors who had provided the capital; and although some measure of industrialisation was needed it was secondary to the need for a healthy flourishing agriculture.

The demand for self-government

A less fundamental problem in Indian life, though in some ways a more pressing one in the early twentieth century, was the question of how far the Indians should be allowed to rule themselves.

The administrative efficiency, educational advances, and economic development brought by British rule produced a politically conscious Indian middle class. In 1885 a body known as the Indian National Congress was formed with the idea of promoting greater unity among Indians, and soon it was demanding *swaraj,* or self-government. Congress increasingly influenced the attitude of Indians towards British rule, the success of the Japanese in 1905 in their war against Russia (p. 312) demonstrated that Asiatic peoples need not always be inferior to Europeans, and by the time the Liberal government came to power in Britain in December

1905 it was becoming obvious that it was time for Britain to make some concessions.

The Morley–Minto reforms of 1909

These concessions came in 1909 when John Morley, the Secretary of State for India, and Lord Minto, the Viceroy, introduced a reformed constitution. The Legislative Councils in the provinces were to have a majority of elected Indian members, and even the central Imperial Council was to have some Indian members. But these councils could do no more than offer advice to the British rulers, and Morley stressed that India was still unqualified for real self-government.

The Montagu–Chelmsford reforms of 1919

Not until the first World War did the British government accept that Indians would one day rule themselves; but in 1915 Lord Chelmsford, the Viceroy, declared that India should eventually be self-governing, and in 1917 Edwin Montagu, Secretary of State for India, announced that British policy was 'the progressive realisation of responsible government in India'.

In 1919 these two men were responsible for a Government of India Act which provided for an elected majority on the central Imperial Council as well as on the provincial Legislative Councils, and which also established that although British officials would still control such matters as finance, police, and foreign policy, the elected legislatures would have real responsibility over what were thought to be the less vital sections of government, such as health, education, and agriculture.

The Amritsar Massacre, 1919

These reforms did not satisfy the Indian National Congress, which was now dominated by those who wanted complete self-government for India, and in particular by Mohandas Karamchand Gandhi—a remarkable man who had trained as a lawyer in England and came to be regarded throughout the world as a saint and was known in India as *Mahatma* or 'great soul'.

Gandhi advocated making the new constitution unworkable by means of civil disobedience. But although he insisted that the British should be opposed only by peaceful methods, such as strikes, boycotts, and other forms of passive resistance such as lengthy fasts, there was serious rioting in many parts of India.

After some Europeans had been murdered in the town of Amritsar, General Dyer gave orders for his troops to fire on a massed crowd of Indians who refused to disperse at a prohibited meeting. They killed 379 Indians, and wounded about 1,200. Inevitably Anglo-Indian relations deteriorated, and in the following years violence and disorder became common.

Internal divisions among the Indians

Just as it had become obvious in the nineteenth century that nothing short of Home Rule would satisfy the Irish, so it was now becoming obvious that nothing short of complete independence would satisfy the Indians. But India was even more divided between Hindus and Moslems than Ireland was between Roman Catholics and Protestants, and just as the Irish Home Rule Bill of 1912 stirred the Ulstermen to action (p. 66) so the increasing prospect of independence for India stirred the Moslems to action.

The Moslem League, which had been founded as early as 1906 and was now led by Mohammed Ali Jinnah, proposed in 1928 that India should become a federation, so that the predominantly Moslem areas in the North-West and North-East would have self-government in domestic affairs. But this was unacceptable to the Congress Party, which wanted to control a unified India.

Meanwhile the rulers of the native states, whose relations with Britain were governed by treaty, and various minority groups, such as the Sikhs and the Eurasians, began to take an interest in safeguarding themselves in the event of the British leaving India.

In 1930, when the British Labour government invited representatives of all parties and interests to a Round Table Conference in London to discuss India's future, Congress, which claimed to speak for all Indians, refused to attend on the grounds that negotiations should be with Congress alone or not at all. Eventually Gandhi, who was more willing than most Hindus to compromise with the Moslems, attended a second Round Table Conference, which began in September 1931, the month after the National government came to power in Britain. But the conference soon broke down, for Congress would accept nothing less than immediate and complete self-government.

The Government of India Act of 1935

Eventually the British government decided to impose its own solution and in 1935 passed another Government of India Act, making India a federation of native states and British provinces. The eleven British provinces all had legislatures in which the representatives were chosen by the various sects and castes, and they all had a large measure of self-government; but final authority was still vested in the British provincial governors.

The head of the federal government was the Viceroy, who remained in control of defence and foreign policy, and the members of the federal legislature were partly elected by constituencies, partly chosen by the provincial legislatures, and partly appointed by the native rulers.

At the same time the British government avoided an obvious problem which would arise from independence by separating Aden and Burma from the Indian Empire. Aden became a Crown Colony, and Burma was given a system of government similar to that of India.

Towards independence and partition

Although Congress rejected the Government of India Act, it nevertheless contested the elections of 1937 under the leadership of Pandit Jawaharlal Nehru and won an overwhelming victory in the predominantly Hindu areas. But in the Moslem areas the Congress Party refused to join in coalitions with the Moslems. This made the Moslems fear for the future and Jinnah, who had previously worked for unity on a federal basis, decided that Moslem security depended on the separation of the Moslem areas from the rest of India.

When war began in 1939 Congress declared that it would only support the war effort if India were immediately granted complete independence. The Moslem League, on the other hand, declared that it would only support the war effort if the demands of Congress were rejected, and in 1940 Jinnah called for the establishment of a separate Moslem state of Pakistan.

Inevitably nothing was done for the moment, but in 1942 India was offered dominion status after the war, with a constitution drawn up by an Indian elected assembly, so long as any province which wished could secede. Gandhi, seeing British power crumbling before the onslaught of the Germans in North Africa and the Japanese in the Far East, described this offer as 'a post-dated cheque on a failing bank' and not only refused it but even launched another civil disobedience campaign, as a result of which he and other Congress leaders, including Nehru, were imprisoned.

Thus the war ended without independence, and many Indians must have felt that it was unlikely that Britain would let India go now she had won the war. But the British Labour government which came to power in 1945 was determined to grant India independence, and after an unsuccessful attempt to preserve unity decided that partition was inevitable. In August 1947 two separate states were established: India and Pakistan.

THE creation of two separate states, India and Pakistan, in August 1947 did not solve the problem of the political future of the Indian sub-continent. In a sense it re-opened it, for the British would no longer be there to restrain opposing groups.

Independence was followed by months of rioting as Hindus and Moslems fought each other. By the end of 1947 half a million people had been killed and twelve million had fled one way or the other across the border. Some Hindus regarded the creation of Pakistan as a betrayal, and in January 1948 Gandhi, the founding father of India, was assassinated by a Hindu extremist.

The situation was complicated by the existence of about 600 princely states. Most of these promptly acceded to India. But three did not. In predominantly Hindu Junagadh the ruler was a Moslem. When he tried to accede to Pakistan the Indian army marched in and held a plebiscite. In predominantly Hindu Hyderabad the Moslem Nizam tried to remain independent. Again the Indian army marched in. But in Kashmir things were the other way round. Most of the population were Moslems, and the Maharajah was a Hindu. In October 1947, when 2,000 Pathan tribesmen from Pakistan invaded Kashmir, the Maharajah acceded to India. Indian and Pakistan troops, both commanded by British officers, moved in from opposite sides. And fighting continued until January 1949, when both sides settled down along a cease-fire line which divided Kashmir in two. There was no permanent settlement, for although the Indian government agreed in principle to having a plebiscite, it persistently avoided having one, and the Kashmir issue remained a permanent source of friction between India and Pakistan.

Pakistan from Jinnah to Ayub Khan

Pakistan also suffered from being in two parts divided from each other by 1,200 miles of Indian territory. Rather more than half the ninety million Pakistanis lived in the densely-populated, poverty-stricken area of East Bengal, which now became East Pakistan. But it was the more warlike people of the West, the Punjabis and Pathans, who dominated the political life of the country. And the Bengalis of the East understandably resented their subordination to the Westerners.

Another of Pakistan's problems was that the death of Mohammed Ali Jinnah in 1948 left her without any obvious leaders. In

the decade after independence she had eight different governments, and the constitution was never clearly established. Eventually in October 1958 the Commander-in-Chief of the army,
General Mohammed Ayub Khan, seized power and tried to
establish a system of 'basic democracy', with a mixture of appointed and elected representatives controlling things at village level,
but with central control by the army of national policy.

India under Pandit Nehru

India adapted herself far more easily than Pakistan to a British
democratic system. But she also had her problems. There were
other dissatisfied minorities besides the Moslems. The Sikhs,
for example, wanted to establish a Sikh nation in the Indian part
of the Punjab. And the largely Christian Nagas of the North-
East wanted a separate Naga state.

India had the advantage of having a leader of World stature,
Pandit Jawaharlal Nehru, as prime minister from 1947 till his
death in 1964. The Congress Party provided stability in India's
political life. And Indian politics were also strongly influenced by
the Hindu tradition that no one religion, no one political system,
and no one philosophy holds a monopoly of truth. This Hindu
inheritance can be seen in the disinclination of her politicians to
go to either a Capitalist or a Socialist extreme in economic planning. Capitalist private enterprise would have taken too long to
provide India with significant material progress. Socialist planning
on the Russian model would have involved force. So India's
leaders tried to achieve increased industrialisation and production by persuasion and a combination of central planning with
local freedom of choice.

'Non-alignment'

The Hindu tradition of tolerance also seemed to influence
India's foreign policy, for Nehru adopted a policy of 'non-
alignment'. He called for 'areas of peace' in the world, and tried
to create a 'Third World' of Afro-Asian countries under Indian
leadership, committed to the idea of peaceful co-existence.

At the Bandung Conference of twenty-one Afro-Asian leaders
in 1955, Nehru argued that it would be degrading for Afro-
Asian nations to emerge from colonial status only to become
satellites of the U.S.A. or the U.S.S.R. And he led the statesmen
at Bandung to declare that 'nations should practise tolerance and
live together in peace.'

India's own policy over Kashmir scarcely lived up to these high
principles. In 1954, when Pakistan joined S.E.A.T.O. (p. 400)

and accepted American military aid, Nehru withdrew his promise of an eventual plebiscite in Kashmir. And his signing of a treaty with China in the same year on principles of co-existence looked suspiciously like a move to find a friend against Pakistan.

But from a practical point of view India's policy of non-alignment seemed a great success. She was on friendly terms with both the U.S.A. and Great Britain and was receiving economic aid from them. She was on friendly terms with China. And at the end of the year Bulganin and Khrushchev, the leaders of the U.S.S.R., paid a friendly visit to India—but not to Pakistan.

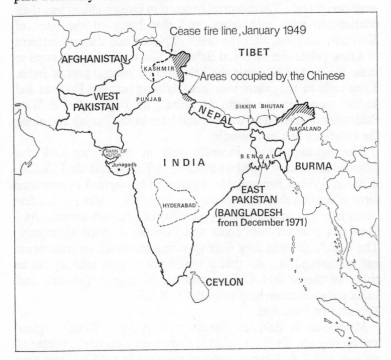

The Indo-Chinese War of 1962

The friendship with China was short-lived. A revolt in Tibet in 1959 against Chinese occupation led to the building of strategic roads by the Chinese in the mountainous North-East of India to get more rapid access to Tibet. In 1962 the Indians tried to check the Chinese encroachments. So the Chinese diverted 50,000 men from the suppression of the Tibetan revolt, advanced deep into North-East India, defeated the Indian forces, and then withdrew to the mountain territory they had taken over.

The Indians felt betrayed. Their army had planned for war against Pakistan, but not against China. So now they turned for military aid to the U.S.S.R. as well as to the U.S.A. and Britain.

Pakistan meanwhile, despite her membership of S.E.A.T.O., had been drawing closer to China. Ayub Khan had appointed as his Foreign Minister a rich, ambitious, young landowner, Zulfikar Ali Bhutto, who saw China as a potential ally against India, and in 1963 Pakistan and China reached a frontier agreement.

The Indo-Pakistan War of 1965

But for both India and Pakistan relations with the great powers were peripheral. Their central concern in foreign affairs was their relationship with each other, and that hung on the issue of Kashmir. In 1964, after the death of Nehru and the appointment of a new prime minister, Lal Bahadur Shastri, India took steps to make the part of Kashmir she held into an integral part of India. Then early in 1965 there was fierce fighting between Pakistan and Indian troops in the Rann of Kutch, on the border of West Pakistan and India near the sea, and later in the Punjab and along the cease-fire line in Kashmir.

The fighting ended inconclusively in September and was followed in January 1966 by a meeting at Tashkent in the U.S.S.R. between Ayub Khan and Mr. Shastri. They agreed to renounce force in settling their differences, but Shastri's sudden death a few hours later put an end to any possibility of a full settlement. And from this time on both India and Pakistan rearmed vigorously. The U.S.A. thought they were spending too much on armaments and announced in 1967 that it would not resume military aid to either of them. But China continued to supply Pakistan, and India got even more help from the U.S.S.R.

Trouble in Pakistan

Meanwhile in Pakistan discontent with Ayub Khan's regime was boiling up. In West Pakistan there were riots in the winter of 1968–9, and Z.A. Bhutto, who had resigned in 1966 and was now a leading left-wing opponent of the government, was arrested. In East Pakistan the people demanded home rule, and their leader, Sheik Mujib-ur-Rahman, was put on trial for treason.

Rioting continued, the release of Bhutto and Mujib in February 1969 failed to end it, and in March Ayub Khan handed over power to the Commander-in-Chief of the army, Yahya Khan. Late in 1970 Yahya Khan held a general election, Bhutto's People's Party won a majority in West Pakistan, and Mujib's followers won almost every seat in the East. But Bhutto and Mujib could not agree on a constitution and military rule continued.

The demand for home rule for the East grew stronger, and early in 1970 Pakistani troops from the West poured into the East and arrested Sheik Mujib. The Bengalis rose in revolt and proclaimed the independence of their country as Bangladesh. They were ruthlessly suppressed. Their sufferings were made worse by an appalling flood and a cholera epidemic, and by December ten million Bangladesh refugees had crossed the border into India.

The creation of Bangladesh

In India the prime minister since 1966 had been Mrs. Indira Gandhi, the daughter of Pandit Nehru (but no relation of M. K. Gandhi) and in March 1971 she had just won a large majority in an election fought largely on social and economic issues. But the great issue which now faced her was the future of East Pakistan, or Bangladesh, and as the year went on tension mounted.

At the beginning of December she sent the Indian army in. The people welcomed them as deliverers, and the Pakistan army, operating in hostile territory more than a thousand miles from its base, had to surrender after two weeks.

Bangladesh had been created out of oppression, fear, and war. It was probably the poorest and most overpopulated country in the world. Many of its leaders had been killed by the West Pakistanis, and Sheik Mujib-ur-Rahman was still in captivity.

For West Pakistanis the war meant defeat and humiliation at the hands of India, and the division of their country in two. A week after the war Yahya Khan was replaced as President by Z. A. Bhutto, who still tried to insist that West and East Pakistan were one country. But early in 1972 he released Sheik Mujib, who went home to rule Bangladesh. The tasks facing both of them were daunting.

India, on the other hand, emerged from the war exultant. She had posed successfully as the upholder of the principle of self-determination and had rescued the Bengalis from the dominance of West Pakistan—though elsewhere she ignored the same principle and kept the Moslems of Kashmir and the Nagas of Nagaland in unwilling subjection. India's image as the moral leader of the peace-loving nations of the world was somewhat tarnished. But at last she looked like a military power to be reckoned with. And Mrs. Gandhi, at the head of an India victorious in war, seemed a very different leader from her father, and even more different from her famous pacifist namesake, Mahatma Gandhi.

FOR centuries the people of Indo-China in South-East Asia were under the overlordship of the Emperors of China. Then in the late nineteenth century their Chinese overlords were replaced by French colonial administrators, and in 1940, after the defeat of France by Germany, the Japanese moved in.

During 1941 a Communist called Ho Chi Minh formed the Vietminh, or League for the Independence of Vietnam, to fight against the Japanese, and in 1945, when the French tried to re-assert their colonial authority, the Vietminh turned to fighting them. They developed an effective form of guerrilla warfare, extended their authority in the North-East, and in 1950, aided by supplies of arms and ammunition from the new Communist rulers of China, moved to co-ordinated mobile warfare.

Early in 1953 they struck Westwards. The French tried to prevent this by moving a large force into the Northern town of Dien Bien Phu. It was a strategic blunder, and was followed by military disaster. In 1954 the French garrison was surrounded and had to surrender. The French had lost the war.

The partition of Vietnam

At the Geneva Conference later in 1954 the French agreed to the division of Indo-China into four. The western territories, bordering Thailand, became the independent states of Laos and Cambodia. The long thin country of Vietnam, with mountains and a thinly populated tropical forest in the West and with a narrow coastal strip which spread out into the Red River delta in the North and the Mekong delta in the South, was partitioned at the 17th parallel. The Communists controlled the North and the French the South. It was intended that there should be free elections in both North and South by 1956, and Ho Chi Minh confidently expected to take over the whole country.

But the French withdrew more rapidly than was expected, and a Vietnamese Nationalist, Ngo Dinh Diem, soon established himself and his influential Catholic family in a dominant position in the South. By the end of 1955 he had made himself President of the Republic of Vietnam, and the U.S.A. was providing substantial aid to help him establish a stable anti-Communist state.

Meanwhile the North Vietnamese government was having internal troubles provoked by its own land reform programme and neither demanded nor wanted the free elections which were to precede reunification. In practice the division between North and South hardened during the late fifties.

The Viet Cong

It was not till 1959 that the North Vietnamese government began sending men South to infiltrate the villages and produce revolution. Southerners who had moved North in 1954 came down the Ho Chi Minh trail through the mountain jungles of Laos and entered South Vietnam from the West. And when the fighting began in September 1959 there were perhaps 50,000 of these South Vietnamese Communist, or Viet Cong, guerrillas in the South.

The government, with an army of 150,000 men trained by the Americans, seemed well able to cope with them. But it could not. The Viet Cong strategy was to assassinate as many village head-men and rural officials as possible. Soon they were killing a hundred a month. Effective government began to break down. Large areas came under Viet Cong control. Some Northerners came South to extend the scale of the guerrilla warfare. And before the end of 1960 regular troops from the North came as well.

The Domino Theory

The government of the U.S.A. was committed to supporting Ngo Dinh Diem's government in South Vietnam. When S.E.A.T.O. (p. 400) was formed in 1954 it undertook to defend not only its members' territories in South-East Asia and the South Pacific, but also South Vietnam, Laos, and Cambodia, all of which were committed to neutrality by the Geneva agreement earlier in the year.

Besides this it was arguable that the U.S.A. had a clear interest in preventing a Viet Cong victory. The Korean War had been a successful application of the lesson learnt from the history of Europe in the thirties that it was necessary to stand up to aggression by drawing a clear line and fighting any aggressor who crossed it. In Korea it was the 38th parallel of latitude. In Vietnam it was the 17th. The danger of not drawing a clear line was that aggression would spread from one country to the next, and if the U.S.A. did not stand by one country, then no other country would be able to rely on her for support. This was the so-called 'domino theory', which was sometimes put thus: if South Vietnam goes, Cambodia goes; if Cambodia goes, Thailand goes; if Thailand goes, Malaysia goes; and so on to Australia one way and India the other. It seemed plausible.

So President Eisenhower poured in military and economic aid to help the government of Ngo Dinh Diem. President Kennedy, who took office at the beginning of 1961, continued this policy, and by the time of his assassination in November 1963 the strength of the American forces in South Vietnam had risen to 25,000.

Escalation

In the same month that President Kennedy was assassinated in the U.S.A. President Ngo Dinh Diem was assassinated in Vietnam. The result was political and administrative chaos, and there was a series of political *coups d'état* which tended to bring the government into disrepute.

Meanwhile the Viet Cong grew in strength and extended its control over more villages. So during 1964 the Americans tried to cut the life-line of the Viet Cong by organising South Vietnamese raids into North Vietnam, and in August they began American air attacks on North Vietnamese naval bases. But Viet Cong successes in the South continued.

President Johnson now committed the U.S.A. to involvement in Vietnam on a large scale. He decided to put American combat troops into Vietnam, and in February 1965 he extended American bombing raids to lines of communication in North Vietnam. The number of American troops in Vietnam rose during 1965 from 25,000 to well over 150,000, and by 1968 the U.S.A. had half a million men in Vietnam and was spending $28,000,000,000 a year on the war.

'Search and destroy'

During this period of the war the strategy of the American forces under General Westmoreland was to search out the Viet Cong and destroy them. The reaction of the Viet Cong to these 'search and destroy' operations was to melt into the countryside and reappear when the Americans went away.

At the same time the Americans went on bombing the North

with the dual intention of destroying the Viet Cong's sources of supply and driving the Northern government to negotiate. At times they stopped bombing for a while and invited the North to negotiate. But this was unsuccessful. The North had no wish to negotiate while it thought it could win, and the Viet Cong seemed capable of fighting on however much the Americans bombed their supply lines and bases.

During 1965 the Viet Cong continued to increase in strength, perhaps to about 75,000, and they continued their policy of infiltration. The unstable governments of the South neglected the political aspect of the war, increasingly lost the confidence of their people, and relied on the Americans winning the war for them. Meanwhile the Viet Cong were liable to appear anywhere. In the end it was difficult to be sure which villages were held by the government and which by the Viet Cong.

The *Tet* offensive

The first significant change in the war after the American entry on a large scale came at the time of the *Tet*, or lunar New Year, truce. During this truce Viet Cong and North Vietnamese forces suddenly appeared in and around all the major cities of South Vietnam and tried to seize control of them. Hué was virtually destroyed. Saigon was badly damaged. But the Viet Cong suffered massive casualties and failed to take any important city. Yet they came so near to success that they shook the morale of the South Vietnamese and, even more important, gave the lie to American claims that victory was just around the corner.

In the U.S.A. civilian opposition to the war was building up. By 1968 the domino theory no longer looked as plausible as it had a few years earlier, and many Americans felt they were engaged in unjustified intervention in the affairs of another country. President Johnson rejected a request from the Chiefs of Staff for another 200,000 men, and in April 1968 he announced a limitation of the bombing of North Vietnam and declared that he would not be a candidate in the American Presidential elections later that year. As a direct result of this American and North Vietnamese delegates met in Paris the following month for preliminary peace talks.

'Clear and hold'

Meanwhile the fighting continued. General Westmoreland was replaced by General Abrams, who turned away from the unsuccessful offensive strategy of 'search and destroy' to the defensive strategy of 'clear and hold'. No longer were the Americans expecting complete military victory. Instead they aimed to clear the Viet Cong out of certain areas, particularly the more densely populated areas, and concentrate on holding them. In this they were more successful.

Extrication

But the time had come for the U.S.A. to try to extricate herself from the war. On 1 November 1968, just before the Americans went to the polls and chose Richard Nixon as their next President, President Johnson announced a complete stop to all bombing of North Vietnam. And in January 1969, the month Nixon took office, peace talks began in Paris involving North and South Vietnam, the U.S.A., and the Viet Cong.

The talks made little progress. The North Vietnamese and the Viet Cong felt they had won the war, and they would not agree to take part in elections in South Vietnam until after the withdrawal of all foreign troops and the formation of a coalition government from which the then leaders of South Vietnam would be excluded. The Americans felt that the acceptance of these terms would be a betrayal of their allies. So the talks dragged on. It had been easy to get into the war. Getting out was difficult.

But Nixon was determined to withdraw. The number of American troops in Vietnam, which was 550,000 when he took office in January 1969, was halved by the summer of 1971, and was cut even more during the following year. At the same time he pursued a policy of 'Vietnamization' of the war—training and equipping the South Vietnamese to defend themselves.

He was also vigorously seeking peace in secret negotiations. During 1971 he promised to withdraw all American troops within six months if the North Vietnamese would agree to a cease-fire and the release of all prisoners. But the North Vietnamese rejected the offer. It was almost as if they wanted to keep the Americans involved until they were prepared to overthrow the South Vietnamese government for them. So the war continued. But so did the negotiations. And eventually the North Vietnamese changed their mind. Encouraged by heavy bombing of the North they agreed in January 1973 to a cease-fire. All American troops were to leave in sixty days, and prisoners were to be exchanged. But all Vietnamese troops were to remain where they were. And it scarcely seemed likely that the fighting, which had now gone on intermittently for over thirty years, would come to a complete end.

THE twentieth century saw the rise of Arab Nationalism. It had two main aims: independence and unity. In achieving the first the Arabs were remarkably successful. In achieving the second they were equally unsuccessful.

In 1914 the African part of the old Ottoman Empire was controlled by European powers. France controlled Morocco, Algeria, and Tunisia, Italy controlled Libya, and Britain controlled Egypt and the Sudan.

During the first World War Britain got involved in the Arab lands further East. The Arabs had long wanted independence from the Turks, so in 1915 the British High Commissioner in Egypt, McMahon, promised them independence after the war, and from 1916 to 1918 a British officer, T. E. Lawrence, fought with the Arabs, acting as military adviser to the Hashemite Prince Feisal, who led the revolt.

In the event the British and French divided up the Northern Arab lands between them as mandated territories. France got control of Syria and Lebanon, and Britain, which had played a far larger part in the warfare in the Middle East, gained control of Iraq, Transjordan, and Palestine. Britain also established Protectorates along the South-East coast of Arabia.

The movement for independence from the Turks continued as a movement for independence from the European colonial powers. Egypt was given its independence in 1922 after forty years of British rule, though Britain insisted on retaining responsibility for the defence of Egypt and the Suez Canal. And the Kingdom of Iraq, ruled by Prince Feisal, became completely independent in 1937.

The second World War speeded up the movement towards independence. The British forced the French to withdraw from Syria and Lebanon in 1945. Transjordan, where Feisal's brother Abdullah was established as Emir, became independent in 1946 and changed its name to Jordan, implying its right to the Palestinian lands on the West bank of the Jordan. U.N.O., which was given the task of deciding the future of the Italian colonies, decided in 1949 that Libya should be independent. And in 1956 Morocco and Tunisia gained their independence from France, the Sudan was freed from Anglo-Egyptian control, and the British withdrew their troops from the Suez Canal zone.

By the summer of 1956 the last remaining vestiges of colonialism in the Arab world were the British Protectorates along the Arabian coast, Algeria, and, in a sense, Israel.

The creation of Israel

The problem of Israel was a particularly difficult one. Ever since the first Zionist Congress in Switzerland in 1897 many Jews had hoped for the eventual establishment of a Jewish state in Palestine. So in November 1917 A. J. Balfour, the British Foreign Secretary, tried to get support for the Allied cause from Jews throughout the world by promising that Britain would try to make possible 'the establishment in Palestine of a national home for the Jewish people'.

This conflicted with the promises made to the Arabs by T. E. Lawrence, but for twenty years it caused relatively little difficulty. At the end of the first World War less than a tenth of the population of Palestine was Jewish, and few European Jews wanted to emigrate to this little area between the Mediterranean and the River Jordan. But the Nazi persecution of the Jews stimulated such an exodus from Europe that by the end of the second World War a third of the population was Jewish.

Tension between Arab and Jew increased, and each side suspected the British of favouring the other side. The *Haganah*, the Jewish National Army, prepared to seize power, and in 1948 Britain, finding herself unable to cope with the terrorism of Jewish extremist organizations such as the *Irgun Zvai Leumi* and the Stern Gang, handed the problem over to the United Nations Organization and relinquished the mandate.

An Arab-Jewish War settled the future of Palestine. The *Haganah*, with 10,000 riflemen and four tanks, defeated the forces of the Arab states opposing them, which had 90,000 men and 200 tanks at their disposal. When the cease-fire came in the summer of 1949 Palestine was partitioned: part went to Jordan, a small coastal strip around Gaza went to Egypt, but most became the independent Jewish state of Israel.

Tension in the Middle East

By this time the Middle East had acquired a new importance in international affairs. It was the major source of oil in the world. Both strategically and politically it formed a buffer between the U.S.S.R. and the emerging continent of Africa. And the Suez Canal remained an important route to the Far East.

The British tried to transform the Arab League, which had existed since 1945 and which all the independent Arab states

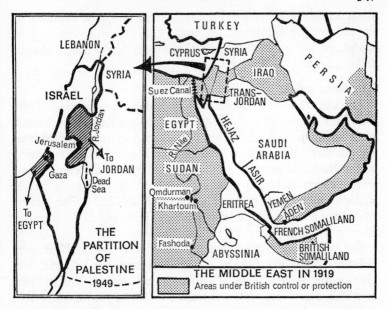

THE
PARTITION
OF
PALESTINE
--1949---

THE MIDDLE EAST IN 1919
Areas under British control or protection

joined, into a defence pact directed against Communist aggression.
But they were unsuccessful. The Arabs saw the Jews as their real
enemy, and many regarded Britain as more of a threat than the
U.S.S.R.

Gamal Abdul Nasser, who became President of Egypt in 1954,
particularly felt this, and one of his first actions on becoming
President was to get the British to agree to withdraw from the
Suez Canal zone in 1956. Then in September 1955 he signed an
arms deal with Czechoslovakia, and in October 1955 he formed
an anti-Iraqi alliance with Syria and Saudi-Arabia because Iraq
joined a new British-inspired defence organisation known as the
Baghdad Pact.

Meanwhile the war between Israel and her Arab neighbours
still technically continued, and by the end of 1955 the situation was
explosive. Israelis resented the fact that the Egyptians would not
allow Israeli ships to use the Suez Canal, and France was supplying Israel with arms, including aircraft.

One of the few hopeful signs in the Middle East was an agreement in December by the U.S.A. and Britain to finance the
Aswan High Dam project to help Egypt make better use of the
waters of the Nile. But during 1956 Nasser entered into an arms
deal with the U.S.S.R., tried to exploit his position to get the
U.S.A. and the U.S.S.R. to outbid each other with offers of

financial aid, and finally, in June 1956, bitterly offended the U.S.A. by recognising Communist China. On 19th July the U.S.A. withdrew her offer to finance the Aswan High Dam. Britain followed suit.

The Suez crisis

President Nasser then decided to finance the building of the dam from the profits of the Suez Canal Company, and a week later, on 26 July, he nationalised the canal. In August the British and French strengthened their forces in the Mediterranean and tried to get Nasser to agree to international control of the canal. Both were economically dependent on the Middle East oil which tankers brought to Europe through the Suez Canal. But Nasser would not accept 'collective colonialism', and early in October the dispute was referred to the United Nations.

But on 23 October M. Pineau, the French Foreign Minister, Selwyn Lloyd, the British Foreign Secretary, and David Ben Gurion, the Israeli Prime Minister, had a secret meeting in Paris at which, said Pineau later, the main moves of the next ten days were planned.

On 25th the Israelis began to mobilise secretly, on 27th British forces in Malta set sail for Egypt, on 28th several French *Mystère* squadrons landed in Israel, and on 29th Israeli forces with French air and sea support attacked Egypt. Both the British and French governments pretended that they were in no way involved, professed their anxiety to maintain peace in the Middle East, and at 4.15 p.m. on 30 October issued a joint ultimatum to both Egypt and Israel calling on them to withdraw their forces to ten miles either side of the Suez Canal and allow a temporary Anglo-French occupation of Suez to separate the combatants. In practice this involved an Israeli advance of over a hundred miles into Egypt and Anglo-French control of the canal. Not surprisingly Egypt refused. So when the ultimatum expired at 4.14 a.m. on 31st British bombers began attacking Egyptian airfields.

If the British and French were to achieve their real aim of re-establishing their control over the canal they needed a swift and skilful military operation which would be over before the opposition to their action could make itself felt. Instead the first British and French paratroopers did not land in Egypt until 5 November, after the Egyptians and Israelis had stopped fighting. And when the sea-borne commandos landed at Port Said the next day the crisis was virtually over.

The pressure of world opinion, financial pressure from the U.S.A., the threat of a rocket attack from the U.S.S.R., and the bitter division of British public opinion resulted in the British government deciding on 6 November to bring the operation to an end. The French unwillingly followed.

The aftermath of Suez

The Suez crisis weakened the influence of Britain and France among the Arab states and also effectively brought the Middle East into the area of the Cold War. The revolutionary Arab states now looked for help to the U.S.S.R., though they all banned the Communist Party, while Israel, the one Middle East country which tolerated Communism, looked for aid to the U.S.A.

Another effect of the crisis was to make Nasser a popular hero of Arab Nationalism right up to his death in September 1970. And in the short term it brought about in February 1958 the union of the two revolutionary republics of Egypt and Syria as the United Arab Republic.

The Six-Day War

Another result of the Suez crisis was the establishment of a United Nations peace-keeping force in Sinai along the border from Gaza to Eilat and at Sharm-al-Shaik on the Straits of Tiran so that Israel could use the port of Eilat.

This provided ten years of uneasy peace. But there were still perpetual guerrilla raids across the border. Meanwhile intense rivalry developed between Egypt and Syria, and in 1961 it resulted in the break-up of the U.A.R. Eventually Syria made a bid for the leadership of the Arab world by intensifying guerrilla raids against Israel and shelling Israel from the Golan Heights on her North-East border.

In May 1967 Israel threatened Syria with reprisals, and Nasser felt obliged to do something. At the beginning of June he moved troops into the Sinai peninsula, demanded and got the withdrawal of the U.N. peace-keeping force, and closed the Straits of Tiran to Israeli shipping.

The Israelis decided to strike first. On 5 June 1967 their aircraft swept in over the sea and destroyed three hundred Egyptian aircraft on the ground in less than five hours. Their troops swept through Sinai up to the Suez Canal. Other Israeli forces in the East drove the Jordanians across the River Jordan. And in the North they seized the Golan Heights from Syria.

Immediately after the war, which only lasted six days, Levi Eshkol, the Israeli prime minister, declared that Israel was willing to hand back the conquered territories in return for recognition and a guarantee of peace. But the Arabs failed to take swift advantage of this offer and with time the Israeli position hardened. By taking the Golan Heights and advancing up to the Suez Canal and the River Jordan Israel had acquired a more defensible frontier, and most Israelis preferred that to promises—whether the promises came from the Arab states, whom they did not trust, or the United Nations, which had removed its peace-keeping force just when it was needed in 1967, or the U.S.A., which might one day change its policies.

Arab disunity

The Arabs, meanwhile, remained bitterly divided, and the humiliation of yet another defeat at the hands of Israel produced political unrest in the Arab states. There had been a military *coup* in Iraq in 1958 after the Suez crisis. There was now another in 1968. And this was followed by *coups* in Libya and the Sudan in 1969 and in Syria in 1970.

Another effect of the Six Day War was to swell the number of Arab refugees to about 1,500,000, so that a Palestine Liberation Organization led by Yasser Arafat became virtually a state within the state of Jordan and formed such a threat to the authority of King Hussein that in September 1970 he launched his essentially Bedouin army against them and crushed them in ten days of bitter fighting. It was a striking example of Arab disunity.

So long as the Arab world remained as divided as this Israel could hope to survive. The parallel with the medieval Kingdom of Jerusalem was striking. That had been created at a time of bitter disunity in the Moslem world, but it was destroyed when a great military leader, Saladin, united the Moslems. Despite Israel's extraordinary military successes against the Arabs in 1948-9, 1956, and 1967, she remained in danger not just of defeat but of utter destruction if a new Saladin should ever accomplish the long-proclaimed ideal of Arab unity.

Section IX   Great Britain, 1939–1970

71   BRITAIN AT WAR, 1939–1945

The early months

THE second World War, unlike the first, began for Britain with several months of comparative inactivity or 'phoney war'.

On land: As in 1914 Britain sent an expeditionary force to the Continent. But this time there was no German attack to face, for the German armies were concentrated in Poland; and since the British and French armies were not strong enough to attack Germany's rear, the British force, which was at first even smaller than the B.E.F. in 1914, spent the winter training and building fortifications along the French border with Belgium, where there was no Maginot Line.

At sea: The Royal Navy played an important role even during these early months. As in 1914 it established a blockade of Germany by closing the English Channel and the sea passage between Scotland and Norway, and it also had the task of protecting British merchant shipping. The small German fleet was not a serious threat, but the Germans hoped to be able to destroy merchant shipping with fast, elusive, heavily-armed surface raiders and with U-boats. After December 1939, when the pocket battleship *Admiral Graf Spee* scuttled herself after being badly damaged by three far more lightly armed British cruisers, the German surface raiders seldom ventured out of port, but for years U-boats remained a very serious threat.

In the air: Since the first World War a new factor had transformed strategy and tactics. Aircraft could now dominate land and sea as far as they could fly, and therefore armies, navies, and lines of communication depended on air power. Air superiority had become vital for effective attack and defence. This had been demonstrated by the German campaign in Poland, and it was brought home to the British in the brief Norwegian campaign (p. 261) which brought the 'phoney war' to an end. The German forces were strongly supported by fighters and dive-bombers, and the British troops, who landed in mid-April 1940, had to withdraw from everywhere except Narvik after a fortnight, and from Narvik early in June.

Dunkirk and the Battle of Britain

The failure of the Norwegian campaign precipitated the fall of

Neville Chamberlain's government, and on 10th May Winston Churchill became the British Prime Minister. On the same day the Germans attacked in the West and ten days later reached the coast, trapping the British Expeditionary Force and part of the French army against the sea at Dunkirk in perhaps the greatest military disaster in British history. Astonishingly the Royal Navy, with air support from fighter planes and with the assistance of hundreds of small civilian craft, managed to evacuate most of the soldiers at Dunkirk—335,000 in all.

It was at this point that air power became supremely important, for there was imminent danger of a German invasion if the Germans could establish permanent air superiority over the English Channel and the South coast of Britain. Consequently Fighter Command of the Royal Air Force fought the German *Luftwaffe* for air supremacy in the skies over South-East England during August, September, and October 1940, and victory in this Battle of Britain played the same part as the naval victory at Trafalgar in 1805 in ensuring that a continental enemy would not be able to cross the sea to Britain.

The war at sea

As winter came in 1940 it was clear that Britain had survived the immediate danger of a German invasion, but she was still in danger of being starved out unless the Atlantic supply route could be kept open for her merchant shipping. Although the British fleet rapidly hunted down and destroyed the exceptionally powerful German battleship *Bismarck* when it came out in May 1941, it could not deal so swiftly with the U-boat menace. During 1941 U-boats sank more than four million tons of merchant shipping, and there seemed a serious danger of losing the battle of the Atlantic.

The Royal Navy also had to try to keep the Mediterranean open for British shipping. An air strike from the carrier *Illustrious* at the Italian naval base of Taranto in November 1940, followed by a battle off Cape Matapan in Greece in March 1941, virtually put the Italian fleet out of action. But this did not solve the problem of protecting shipping from U-boats, and the Mediterranean was an even greater problem than the Atlantic, because in certain areas shipping was vulnerable to air attack from shore-based aircraft. So for much of the war Britain had to send the supplies for her troops in the Middle East round Africa and up the Red Sea.

The Middle East

The defence of the Middle East, which was made the responsibility of General Wavell, was vital to Britain because it was the source of oil, which she needed herself and which would be valuable to the enemy if he captured it. The first threat to this area was the Italian invasion of Egypt in September 1940, and early in 1941 the British had their first military success of the war when the 7th Armoured Division, under General O'Connor, drove back ten Italian divisions 500 miles in ten weeks, capturing 130,000 prisoners and 400 tanks for a loss of less than 500 British lives. But instead of continuing the advance to Tripoli and driving the Italians out of North Africa the British force was then weakened in order to provide troops to help defend Greece from invasion, and the German *Afrikakorps* which arrived at Tripoli at about the same time, drove the British back to Egypt by the end of April. The British were also driven from Greece by the end of April and from Crete by the end of May.

Meanwhile they had been more successful in East Africa, where a campaign begun in February culminated in May in the complete conquest of Italy's East African Empire. But earlier in May a pro-German revolution in Iraq had made intervention there necessary, and fear of German influence in the Vichy-French territories caused Wavell to launch an invasion of Syria and Lebanon early in June. In the Middle East, as at sea, Britain was surviving, but her commitments were stretching her resources dangerously, and she was desperately in need of a powerful ally.

The extension of the conflict

On 22nd June 1941, exactly a year after the fall of France, the Germans invaded the U.S.S.R. At first this stretched Britain's resources even more desperately, for Churchill immediately declared that 'any man or state who fights against Nazidom will have our aid', and it became vitally important to maintain enough merchant shipping to supply the Russians with war materials by the Arctic sea route and by the route round Africa and then across Persia. But as the result of the aid received from Britain and the U.S.A. Russia was able to absorb the main impact of the German military effort, and throughout the rest of the war at least two-thirds of the German forces were engaged on the Eastern front.

The entry of the U.S.A. into the war in December 1941 was even more important, for the U.S.A. was incomparably the strongest industrial power in the world, and the mere existence of an alliance of the U.S.A., the U.S.S.R., and the British Commonwealth made eventual victory seem probable. But the immediate sequel of the extension of the war into the Pacific was a series of further disasters. On 10th December, two days after the British declaration of war on Japan, the battleships *Prince of Wales* and *Repulse*, which lacked air cover, were sunk by Japanese aircraft, and then Hong Kong, Malaya, Singapore, and most of Burma fell in rapid succession.

Japan's successes affected the war with Germany. The Japanese naval threat in the Pacific was so great that the Americans could not patrol their side of the Atlantic effectively, and the resources of the Royal Navy were stretched to the limit. The threat of a Japanese invasion of Australia was so great that the Australian troops in the Middle East were withdrawn, thus weakening the Commonwealth forces there, which were driven back to El Alamein by Rommel's *Afrikakorps* in June 1942.

The defeat of Germany

On land: However, the 8th Army under General Auchinleck held the *Afrikakorps* in the first battle of El Alamein in July, and in October, still at El Alamein but under a new commander, General Montgomery, it won the first major victory of the war over any German army. But from now onwards the part played by the British army was increasingly subordinate to that played by the Americans. The Anglo-American forces which landed in North-West Africa at the beginning of November were under the operational command of a British general, Alexander, but an American, General Eisenhower, was Supreme Commander. And although Alexander commanded the forces which invaded Sicily and Italy in 1943, the Italian front declined in importance during 1944, for the American Chiefs of Staff had never been enthusiastic about an Italian campaign, preferring a direct assault on France. When the Allied troops landed on the Normandy coast at the beginning of June 1944 the majority of them were American, most of their equipment had been constructed by American industry, and the Supreme Commander was again General Eisenhower, though Montgomery ran the operation for the first three months. Moreover, when Eisenhower took over the operational command on 1st September, he rejected Montgomery's plan for a swift direct thrust at the Ruhr in favour of his own strategy of a steady advance on a broad front.

At sea: The U.S.A. also played an important part in winning the battle of the Atlantic. From January 1943 the American ship-building programme gave top priority to escort ships for anti-submarine warfare, and by May 1944 the battle had been won to the extent that in that month U-boats only sank four ships while forty-one U-boats were destroyed.

In the air: From the summer of 1943 intensive strategic bombing aimed at the destruction of the German economy was made possible by the build-up of a massive American air force in Britain. The Americans concentrated on precision bombing from high altitudes by day and the British on saturation bombing—the wholesale destruction of German towns—by night. The only aspect of this which had any significant effect on the German capacity to wage war was the American bombing of fuel installations and of the German railway system.

Britain's contribution to victory

Britain's main contribution to victory was that she managed to survive during the first half of the war. She defeated the *Luftwaffe* in the Battle of Britain, survived the U-boat blockade in the Battle of the Atlantic, and held the *Afrikakorps'* thrust to the Middle East in the first, and often forgotten, battle of El Alamein in July 1942—the half-way point in the war. The second and victorious half of the war began with the British victory in the second battle of El Alamein in October, but it was followed closely by the more important Russian victory at Stalingrad and by the arrival in Africa of American troops, and from then onwards American and Russian power was more important than that of Great Britain in crushing Germany.

In the war against Japan Britain also played a subordinate part to the U.S.A. Unlike the German war, which had already run half its course before American troops were actively engaged, the Americans were in the war with Japan from the start, and the American campaigns in the Pacific (pp. 293–6) were more important than the British campaigns in Burma (p. 295).

The U.S.A. and the U.S.S.R. contributed far more manpower to victory than Britain, and the U.S.A. contributed far more in industrial output and technical achievements. But in the sphere of scientific achievement Britain's contribution was supremely important. The development of radar made possible the detection of enemy aircraft and ships at a distance and at night, and also resulted in more accurate gunfire. The progress made by British scientists towards an understanding of the nature of the atom helped to make possible the construction of the atom bombs dropped on Japan in 1945.

His career

WINSTON CHURCHILL, a grandson of the seventh Duke of Marlborough, lived his whole life within the century from 1871 to 1971. He was born in 1874 and died at the age of ninety in 1965. He first entered Parliament in 1900 as a youthful hero who had just escaped from captivity in the Boer War, and as a Tory. His active political career ended in 1955 when, as an established national hero, he retired from his position as a Tory prime minister. But the fifty-five years in between was no smooth ascent to eminence. Three times his political career seemed at an end.

Although he entered Parliament as a Tory Churchill found himself increasingly at odds with the leaders of his own party, and in particular he disagreed with the Protection policy advocated by Joseph Chamberlain (p. 52). On this issue he left the Conservatives and joined the Liberals in 1904.

When the Liberals came to power in 1905 Churchill began a period of ten years in office—as Under-Secretary at the Colonial Office till 1908, and then in the cabinet as President of the Board of Trade till 1910, as Home Secretary till 1911, and next as First Lord of the Admiralty, devoting himself to the task of modernising the Royal Navy.

But the war rapidly brought political disaster to Churchill. He was blamed for the failure of the Gallipoli campaign in 1915 (pp. 166–7), and the Conservatives successfully clamoured for his eviction from the Admiralty. After a brief frustrating period as Chancellor of the Duchy of Lancaster he resigned from the government in November 1915. He was forty, and his brilliant future lay in ruins behind him.

Lloyd George gave Churchill a second chance. He was unable to bring him into his coalition government for some months because of the Conservatives. Their leader, Bonar Law, thought Churchill had 'an entirely unbalanced mind'. But in July 1917 Lloyd George made him Minister of Munitions. Ironically he became Secretary for War when the war came to an end. And from February 1921 till the collapse of the coalition in October 1922 he was Colonial Secretary, playing a leading part both in the negotiations which produced the Irish Treaty of December 1921 (p. 68) and in the Middle East settlement (p. 345).

In 1922 he was the only leading member of the coalition other than Lloyd George who was a Liberal, and the collapse of the coalition deprived him of his parliamentary seat as well as of office. He shared in the general rout of the Liberals in November 1922, and he was defeated again in December 1923. In both these elections the Liberals won less seats than either of the other parties, and there seemed little chance of a Liberal government for many years. Churchill's political career was again finished. He seemed unlikely to join the Conservatives, for Baldwin had just fought the election of December 1923 on the very issue, Protection, over which Churchill, as a passionate Free Trader, had left the Conservative Party in 1904. And soon Churchill was also at odds with his own party over its support for the first Labour government. So he fought and narrowly lost a by-election in 1924 as an 'independent anti-Socialist'. He was a brilliant individual, but he was politically stranded between two great parties and had failed to get into Parliament in three elections in a row.

Baldwin gave Churchill his third chance. In the general election of October 1924, standing as a 'Constitutionalist' but without a Conservative opponent, Churchill was at last returned to Parliament. Baldwin offered him the Chancellorship of the Exchequer, partly in order to demonstrate clearly that the unpopular Protection policy had been abandoned, and partly as a way of silencing a potentially dangerous back-bench critic.

Thus began the least successful period of Churchill's political career. He was a disastrous Chancellor of the Exchequer. His return to the gold standard and over-valuing of the pound in 1925 made British exports ten per cent more expensive and produced the general strike (p. 184), and his attitude during and after the strike helped to exacerbate ill-feeling. When Baldwin's second government was ousted by the electorate in 1929 Churchill was probably the most unpopular of its ministers.

Soon he was again quarrelling with the Conservative party. He disagreed with Baldwin's support for Labour's proposals to give increased self-government to India. To Churchill Gandhi was a 'naked fakir' and Nehru a 'man of straw', while India was 'the brightest jewel in the crown of the King-Emperor'. So early in 1931 he resigned from the Conservative shadow cabinet.

He was not offered a post in the National government which was formed later in the year, and soon he was criticising not only the government's imperial policy but also its foreign and defence policies. He warned of the developing military threat from Nazi Germany and Fascist Italy and demanded increased expenditure on armaments. But by now he was not a sufficient threat to need to be included in the government. When the National government won its second general election in 1935 Churchill was sixty—an elderly and out-dated reactionary and war-monger. The chances of his ever holding office again seemed slight. He had had three chances of building a successful political career. Now his brilliant future seemed to lie behind him.

In fact it was a short way ahead. Hitler gave Churchill a fourth chance and turned him into a great man. After eight months back at the Admiralty when the second World War began Churchill became prime minister in May of 1940. He offered the nation 'blood, sweat, toil, and tears' and led it to victory. When he was removed from office by the general election of 1945 it was not Churchill whom the electorate rejected but the Conservative Party—the party of appeasement abroad and unemployment at home. Churchill then led the Conservatives in opposition for six years, while they built themselves a new image as a party of forward-looking, undoctrinaire, capable, practical men, and then he was prime minister again for three and a half years at a time of increasing prosperity until his retirement in April 1955 at the age of eighty. He had been a successful prime minister both in war and peace. He died ten years later.

His importance

As a young man Churchill was bursting with energy and ambition for fame. He sought action wherever he could find it: the Cuban revolution in 1895, the North-West Frontier of India in 1897, the battle of Omdurman in 1898, and the Boer War in 1899. He combined journalism with soldiering, and despatches and books flowed from his pen. He was an exceptionally gifted man quite apart from his statesmanship. He could always have been a successful journalist, and he eventually became both a talented painter and a considerable historian. He retained his love of action, and after his resignation from the government in 1915 spent a year in the trenches as a battalion commander.

He was always an individualist with a passionate belief in individual liberty. His devotion to the idea of freedom, in 'particular Free Trade, naturally led him into the Liberal Party in 1904. And as a Conservative leader in the mid-twentieth century he made the essentially Liberal notion of 'private enterprise' the political ideal of the Conservatives.

But his Liberalism did not extend to 'laissez-faire'. He was, with Lloyd George, one of the founders of the Welfare State. 'The rich must contribute in money and the poor in service' he wrote in 1908, and he proclaimed his belief in 'the just precedence of public interests over private interests'. As President of the Board of Trade he was responsible in 1909 for the establishment of Trade Boards and Labour Exchanges. And when he became a Conservative peace-time prime minister in 1951 his aim was to run the welfare services efficiently and maintain full employment.

With such an attitude to social welfare one might have expected that with the collapse of the Liberal Party he would have turned to Socialism. But the Bolshevik Revolution made that impossible. He saw the Labour Party as a revolutionary threat to England's traditions of constitutional government and individual liberty, and turned instead to the Conservative Party and the political philosophy of pragmatism as the best way of maintaining those traditions.

It was in his pragmatism, his practical undoctrinaire approach to problems, that Churchill was most essentially a Conservative. It enabled him to co-operate successfully with the English Labour leaders in the second World War and even with the Russian Bolsheviks. As soon as Germany attacked Russia in June 1941 he declared that 'any man or state who fights against Nazidom will have our aid'.

It was as a war leader in the year following Dunkirk in June 1940, when the British Empire stood alone, that Churchill was at his greatest. He had to make decisions on the use of resources, on strategy, and on the appointment of commanders. In August 1940, for example, he decided to send tanks to North Africa. In April 1941 he decided to fight in Greece. In June 1941 he replaced Wavell with Auchinleck in the Middle East. Such decisions were crucial. Each of them can also be regarded as a mistake. But all war leaders make mistakes. The great ones merely make less disastrous ones than the enemy.

And wars are not won by materials and strategic decisions alone. They are also won by the emotions stirring in the breasts of men. And Churchill stirred men's emotions to good effect. Nazism threatened to bring 'a new Dark Age', and like Alfred a thousand years earlier, he believed that 'the future of Christian civilisation' would depend on the struggle for England. 'Let us therefore brace ourselves to our duties', he said, 'and so bear ourselves that, if the British Empire and Commonwealth last for a thousand years, men will still say, "This was their finest hour".'

IN the first half of the nineteenth century the inequalities of life in England were wide and the restrictions on individual liberty numerous. In this situation some men appealed to the ideals of Liberty and Equality; but while the ideal of Liberty fired men's imaginations and dominated political thought and action in the mid-nineteenth century, the ideal of Equality tended by comparison to be neglected. It came into its own in the twentieth century, and after the second World War Englishmen were less free than they had been fifty years earlier but more equal.

Political equality

In so far as there was any vigorous demand for equality in the first half of the century it was a demand for political equality, which was seen as the key to future reform. As early as 1838 a group known as the London Working Men's Association had drawn up a charter demanding annual parliaments, secret voting, equal electoral districts, the abolition of the property qualification for M.P.s, payment of M.P.s, and universal manhood suffrage.

Annual parliaments, which would obviously have resulted in political instability, have never been introduced, but all the other aims of this Chartist Movement had been fulfilled by the end of the first World War. In 1872 the Ballot Act made voting secret, thus making it possible for the poor to vote as they wished without fear of being penalised by a landlord or employer. The property qualification for M.P.s was abolished in 1858, and the payment of M.P.s was introduced in 1911; and between them these measures opened up to a far wider range of people the possibility of becoming an M.P. A Redistribution Act of 1885 rearranged the constituencies of Britain approximately according to the numbers living in them and also did away with many of the two-member constituencies and raised the total number of seats in the House of Commons from 658 to 670. Subsequent Acts made further alterations as they became necessary.

Universal manhood suffrage, towards which Britain had begun to move with the passage of the Great Reform Act of 1832, was achieved by the end of the first World War in three more stages. The Great Reform Act, which had enfranchised the upper middle class, had still only given the vote to 4 per cent of the total population. But Disraeli's Second Reform Act of 1867 enfranchised most working-class men in towns, and Gladstone's Franchise Act of 1884 gave the right to vote to the agricultural workers. Between them these two Acts gave the vote to most men over twenty-one, and then in 1918 virtually all men over twenty-one were enfranchised by the Representation of the People Act. This Act's main importance, however, was that it went beyond the principle of universal manhood suffrage by giving the right to vote to women over thirty; and the principle of universal adult suffrage, towards which it was moving, was finally accepted in 1928 when the Equal Franchise Act gave the vote to women at twenty-one on equal terms with men. By then the total electorate, some 28,500,000, was approximately ten times larger than it had been fifty years earlier, shortly before the Franchise Act of 1884.

In 1944 a Redistribution Act finally abolished all two-member constituencies, and in 1948 two minor changes were made to establish the principle that each person should have only one vote: university seats and plural voting, the right of some businessmen to vote where they worked as well as where they lived, were both abolished. By this time the only group with any obvious cause for complaint was those under twenty-one. So the minimum voting age was reduced to eighteen in time for the election of 1970.

Equality of the sexes

The enfranchisement of women was accompanied by a change in their social status. Three Married Women's Property Acts, passed by Liberal governments in 1870, 1882, and 1893, gave women the full legal right to their own property, and during the same period greater opportunities for education were extended to girls. The Girls' Public Day School Trust, founded in 1871, was beginning to establish girls' schools comparable academically with many of the best boys' schools, and colleges for girls were established at both Oxford and Cambridge. While these changes affected the middle class, a new range of employment was opened up to working-class girls, who had previously found employment mainly in domestic service and factories, by the introduction of the typewriter in 1880 and by the increasing number of shops. During the twentieth century women were increasingly accepted in jobs which had once been done only by men, and there came to be women doctors, barristers, and M.P.s. The proportion of women in these jobs continued to be small, for most women still got married and devoted a large part of their lives to bringing up a family. But at least the principle of equality had been established.

The first important step in the direction of women being allowed to vote was the Local Government Act of 1888 (p. 48), which permitted them to vote in local elections. Once it was established that women could influence local affairs it seemed somewhat illogical to exclude them from any influence in national affairs, and in 1903 Mrs. Emmeline Pankhurst founded the Women's Social and Political Union, which had women's suffrage as one of its main objectives. Its members, who were known as suffragettes, tried to promote their cause by conventional methods, such as heckling politicians at public meetings, and in 1907 a further concession was made when it became possible for a woman to become a county or county borough councillor, or even a mayor.

But women seemed no nearer to being allowed to vote in national elections, so in 1908 a splinter group led by Mrs. Pankhurst's daughter Christabel formed the Women's Freedom League, which took the view that since women were without constitutional representation in parliament they were entitled to use unconstitutional methods to achieve their ends. Originally their actions took the form of irritants: they smashed windows, for example, and chained themselves to railings. But their actions were sufficiently illegal to ensure that many of them were sent to prison, and when in prison they refused to eat. This caused considerable sympathy for them, especially when they were forcibly fed. But the Liberal government refused to give in to the threat of force, and a Bill introduced in 1910 to extend the franchise to women was dropped.

The extremist group became increasingly active. Christabel Pankhurst had to live abroad in Paris, and in 1912 her followers turned to crime on a large scale. They burnt down buildings, cut telephone wires, poured acid in letter boxes, threw bombs, and slashed pictures in public galleries, such as Velasquez's Rokeby Venus, which seemed to symbolise an aspect of femininity to which they objected. Violence on this scale did their cause great harm and produced a considerable revulsion of feeling. On the other hand, many people disliked the 'Cat and Mouse Act' of 1913, which was an attempt to solve the problem of hunger-striking by enabling the government to release hunger-strikers from prison and re-arrest them later.

One hopeful development in 1913 was the formation of the National Union of Women's Suffrage Societies, which was dedicated to getting women's suffrage by peaceful and constitutional means, but when the first World War began in 1914 women still did not have the right to vote. However, the changed circumstances of the war, during which many women took over the jobs of men who had joined the army, were more effective than the suffragette movement in producing a change of public opinion. By the end of the war most women were already able to vote under the Representation of the People Act of 1918, and ten years later the Equal Franchise Act finally established the political equality of women.

The expansion of education

Towards the end of the nineteenth century there also developed a demand for equality of opportunity, and a significant move in that direction was made by W. E. Forster's Education Act of 1870, which provided for the election of local School Boards which were able to establish and supervise elementary schools in those parts of the country which did not already have Church schools. It was the first step towards a state system of education providing, as far as possible, equal educational opportunities for all. Forster's Act had given School Boards the power to insist on attendance in their areas, and in 1880 schooling was made compulsory for all children from the age of five till ten. An Act passed in 1891 made all elementary education free. In 1899 the minimum school-leaving age was raised to twelve. And by 1918, when another Education Act sponsored by H. A. L. Fisher fixed the school-leaving age at fourteen, it was already usual to leave at that age.

While the Forster Act laid the foundations of a state system of elementary education, the Balfour Education Act of 1902 laid the foundations of a state system of secondary education and placed both elementary and secondary education under the control of local education authorities. The next forty years saw a great expansion of grammar school and university education for those whose parents could afford to contribute to the cost, together with the practice of the Ministry of Education and local authorities giving grants to university students whose parents could not afford to pay. Meanwhile the Workers' Education Association, founded in 1903, was providing education courses, particularly in night schools, for adults. However, an attempt in the Fisher Education Act of 1918 to arrange a great increase in the number of free places in grammar schools was virtually destroyed by the 'Geddes Axe' (p. 194), and in 1939 the proportion of children receiving free secondary education was still only 1 per cent.

In the light of this the Education Act of 1944 introduced by R. A. Butler, Minister of Education in the war-time coalition, was a major educational reform, for it provided that primary education should be followed for all by secondary education in grammar, technical, or 'secondary modern' schools according to ability, and that the school-leaving age should be raised first to fifteen, which was done in 1947, and then to sixteen as soon as possible, which was not done until 1973.

The expansion of secondary education involved extending the practice which many education authorities had already adopted of dividing children up at eleven according to their performance in an examination; and by the middle of the century there was widespread opposition to the 'eleven-plus' examination on the grounds that it was both inefficient and unfair. Another objection to the nation's educational system was a social one. Many of the middle class could still afford to buy their children an education outside the state system in schools which were often better than state schools and usually had greater social prestige. Moreover, the state system itself seemed to many people to intensify class division by its separation of children into different types of school at the age of eleven, and in the 1960s there was a strong movement towards 'comprehensive' education. Nevertheless, the Butler Act had clearly meant a vast extension of educational opportunities for many children and a fuller life for them in the future, and it inevitably resulted in the 1960s in a vast expansion of universities and technical colleges.

Equality and liberty

This educational advance came at a time when the development of the Welfare State and a rise in the standard of living of the poor enabled more and more people to benefit from it. A century earlier all but a small minority would have been prevented by poverty from taking advantage even of free education, for in the Age of Liberalism the inequalities in society were so wide that for many people freedom merely meant freedom to be poor. But in the twentieth century the state increasingly intervened both to reduce the material inequalities in society, and also to extend the principle of 'equality of opportunity'. These two developments operate against each other. The first genuinely makes for greater equality. The second, since men are not equal in ability, provides the opportunity for men to get unequal again and thus makes the application of the first principle all the more necessary. But both are necessary if men are to be free in a fuller sense than they were in the nineteenth century. The extension of material equality can help to free men from the bondage of hunger, poverty, and sickness. The extension of equality of opportunity can free men to live full and fruitful lives.

IN the quarter of a century from 1945 to 1970 Great Britain was ruled for six years by a Labour government led by Clement Attlee, then for thirteen years by Conservative governments under Winston Churchill, Sir Anthony Eden, Harold Macmillan, and Sir Alec Douglas-Home, and then for another six years by a Labour government under Harold Wilson. The Labour Party won four elections (in 1945, 1950, 1964, and 1966), and the Conservatives won four (in 1951, 1955, 1959, and 1970).

The 1945 election

The election of July 1945 was fought when the war with Germany was just over. The war had helped to stimulate a desire for greater equality, and many people felt that there was now an opportunity to make a fresh start. From this point of view the Conservatives were clearly at a disadvantage, for they were associated in the public mind with the National government and with the unemployment and appeasement of the thirties. Their one great electoral advantage was that they were led by Winston Churchill, but they relied too much on his prestige and on the presumption that they were better suited than the Labour leaders to rule, and they failed to produce a clear programme for dealing with post-war problems.

Even Churchill was not so great an electoral asset to the Conservatives as was widely assumed, for many people who admired him as a war leader were sceptical about whether he would make a good peace-time Prime Minister, and his prestige suffered from the accusation he made that the Labour leaders, who only a few weeks earlier had been in his own government, would try to establish Socialism with 'some sort of *Gestapo*'.

The Labour Party on the other hand had a clear programme set out in its policy statement 'Let us Face the Future', and in particular it intended to nationalise several basic industries and provide a National Health Service. Moreover, the Labour leaders had demonstrated their capacity to rule during the war. While Churchill and several other Conservative ministers were occupied with running the war, domestic affairs were very largely in the hands of Labour ministers. Attlee as Deputy Prime Minister frequently presided over Cabinet meetings, Herbert Morrison was Home Secretary, and Ernest Bevin was Minister of Labour.

In the event more than twelve million votes were cast for

Labour candidates and less than ten million for the Conservatives, and the Labour Party won an overall majority of 146.

The decline and fall of the Labour Party

The government which Attlee led after the second World War was one of the great progressive ministries of English history. But its work was done against a background of 'austerity', which inevitably caused discontent, and in the next election, in February 1950, Labour's majority was cut to six.

Then in June 1950 the Korean War (p. 407) broke out. So the period of National Service was extended from eighteen months to two years, and in January 1951 Attlee announced a large increase in defence spending. This produced an open split in the government, for the new Chancellor of the Exchequer, Hugh Gaitskell, decided to find some of the money needed by imposing charges on the Health Service, and on 3 April Aneurin Bevan, the architect of the National Health Service who was now Minister of Labour, announced publicly 'I will never be a member of a government which makes charges on the National Health Service for the patient.' A week later, when the budget was introduced, he resigned, together with the President of the Board of Trade, Harold Wilson.

This split weakened the authority of the government, which was anyway being worn down by the strain of governing with a small majority. In October 1951 Attlee decided to try to gain a workable majority by fighting a general election. He failed, and Labour went into opposition for thirteen years.

Churchill and Eden, 1951–57

Winston Churchill now returned to office at the age of 77. He was an old man, and did little more than preside over a government which merely administered the country efficiently. After he had a stroke in 1953 he was even less important, and at last in April 1955 ill health caused him to retire.

Although Churchill's government had done little, the country had meanwhile prospered, and when his successor, Sir Anthony Eden, fought a general election in May, a month after taking office, the Conservatives were returned with an increased majority.

In the event Eden was prime minister for less than two years. The Suez Crisis (pp. 379–80), into which he plunged Great Britain in October 1956, imposed a terrible nervous strain on him, his health collapsed under the pressure, and in January 1957 he resigned.

Macmillan in the ascendant, 1957–59

Eden's resignation was unexpected, and there were two possible successors: R. A. Butler and Harold Macmillan. Macmillan got the job, and he settled down to the task of recreating both the party and national unity after the strains of Suez.

He acquired a reputation as 'unflappable Super-Mac' from such incidents as his casual reference in the spring of 1958 to the resignation of his Chancellor of the Exchequer as 'a little domestic difficulty.' The economy boomed. And the Conservatives won an overall majority of a hundred in the general election of October 1959. This was the high water mark of Macmillan's government. The Conservatives had increased their share of the vote in four successive general elections. The Labour Party had lost its third general election in a row.

Macmillan in decline, 1959–63

But soon afterwards economic difficulties became increasingly apparent, and many people began to see a connection between the government's financial and economic policies and the timing of general elections. The general election of May 1955 had come only a month after R. A. Butler had cut income tax by 6d., and it was followed in October by a supplementary and restrictive budget. The 1959 election was also preceded by a generous budget indicating prosperity, but it was followed by continuing economic difficulties until in June 1961 the Bank rate, the rate at which banks lend money, went up to the unprecedented figure of 7 per cent, and a pay pause was imposed on everyone in the public sector of the economy. Some indication of the extent of discontent among traditionally Tory voters was given by the success of the Liberals in a by-election in the London suburb of Orpington in March 1962.

In July Macmillan, who was acquiring a reputation for doing the opposite of what he was saying, also acquired a reputation for ruthlessness when he sacked seven cabinet ministers in an afternoon in a major re-shuffle of his government which came to be spoken of as 'the night of the long knives'. Economic problems continued, and in 1963 the number of unemployed reached 800,000 the highest figure since the war.

Then during 1963 there was a series of revelations which indicated serious security risks. These culminated in the Secretary for War, John Profumo, lying to the House of Commons about his relationship with a prostitute, Christine Keeler, who also had a sexual relationship with the Russian naval attaché.

The prime minister was widely thought to be personally responsible for the security services, though in fact security was the responsibility of the Home Secretary, and there was strong pressure on Macmillan to resign. Many Conservatives thought the party needed a new leader before the next election.

But Macmillan made it clear that he intended to go on. Then in October 1963, in the middle of the Conserative Party Conference, he was suddenly ill, and equally suddenly he resigned.

Sir Alec Douglas-Home, October '63–October '64

The scramble for the leadership was frantic. There were several possible successors, including R. A. Butler again. But in the event the man asked to form a government was the Foreign Secretary, the fourteenth Earl of Home, a relatively little-known figure, who now resigned his peerage in accordance with the Peerage Act passed earlier in the year and became prime minister as Sir Alec Douglas-Home.

He had a year in which to re-build the fortunes of the Conservative Party and create confidence in himself, for there had to be a general election before the end of October 1964.

It was not long enough.

Harold Wilson, 1964–70

The Labour Party had acquired a new confidence under Harold Wilson, who had succeeded to the leadership earlier in 1963 on the death of Hugh Gaitskell, and when the election of October 1964 came one of the deciding factors which gave Labour its narrow majority of four was probably that Harold Wilson was so much more plausible on television than Sir Alec Douglas-Home.

The Labour government inherited huge international debts and a massive balance of payments deficit from their Tory predecessors, and almost at once it had its majority cut to two by a by-election defeat. Wilson carried on like this for a year and a half. Then another election in March 1966 confirmed him in office with a comfortable majority, and the country waited to have its economic problems solved by the expert 'professional' government which Labour promised after the 'thirteen wasted years' of Tory 'shamateurism'.

But the problems continued. Enthusiasm for a government which promised much and achieved little waned. And when the next general election was fought in 1970 public opinion had swung enough to bring back the Conservatives, who were now led by Edward Heath.

A T the end of July 1945, with the German war over and two weeks before the Japanese war ended, a Labour government led by Clement Attlee took office in Great Britain and prepared to tackle the problems of post-war reconstruction and try to build a better future.

Financial and economic problems

At once it had to face serious financial and economic problems. Between 1939 and 1945 Britain had mortgaged her future to pay for the war, and whereas in 1939 she had £4,000 million more overseas assets than liabilities, by the end of the war her liabilities were £1,000 million more than her assets. Meanwhile her industries had been organised for war, and heavy reorganisation was needed before they could be turned effectively to the problems of peace-time production for export, which was essential if Britain was to be able to pay for her vital imports.

Then at the beginning of September President Truman of the U.S.A. announced the immediate ending of Lease-Lend (p. 284), which had always been intended as a purely war-time arrangement. This would have meant severe hardship and an intensification of rationing without a large-scale dollar loan, so Lord Keynes, who had described the ending of Lease-Lend as 'a financial Dunkirk', was sent to America to negotiate a loan, and he arranged for Britain to borrow $3,750 million from the U.S.A. and $1,250 million from Canada.

This prevented serious hardship but did not solve Britain's economic problems, for borrowing money merely enabled her to pay for imports she could not really afford. In the long run Britain would have to pay for her imports with exports. So the government kept imports down by continuing and in some cases even extending rationing, and it maintained a close control over industry in order to stimulate production for export. By the early months of 1949 the volume of exports had reached 150 per cent of the figure for 1938. But even this measure of success did not solve Britain's financial difficulties. To some extent the American and Canadian loans, which were both swallowed up by the end of 1947, had merely postponed the need for the mass of the country to face those difficulties, and in November 1947, when Sir Stafford Cripps became Chancellor of the Exchequer, a rigid policy of 'austerity' was imposed under which there was for a while no foreign currency for tourists and no petrol for private motoring.

The combination of 'austerity' and Marshall Aid (p. 285) produced some improvement in 1948, but in the long run the only real solution was for Britain's exports to become more competitive in the markets of the world, and in the meantime Britain's financial position remained so vulnerable to external events that in 1949 a mild recession in the U.S.A. drove Cripps to devalue the pound from $4.03 to $2.80.

Nationalisation

A fundamental aspect of the Labour government's economic policy was its intention to bring basic industries under public ownership, and the first stages of this Socialist revolution, which had been dreaded by so many for so long, were accomplished with surprisingly little opposition.

The Bank of England, which had already for some years acted in accordance with government policy, was nationalised in 1945.

The coal industry, which had an enduring legacy of bitterness from the inter-war period and had seemed almost impossible to run at a profit, was taken over by the National Coal Board at the beginning of 1947, and many mine-owners were pleased to be rid of their mines and get compensation instead.

Electricity, gas, the air lines, and part of the cable and wireless industry were already under some measure of municipal or state control, and the extension of public ownership in 1946–8 merely tidied up the control of these industries.

Transport: It was only when the government introduced a Bill to nationalise transport that it encountered stiff opposition. If it had proposed only to take over the railways it might have encountered little more opposition than it met over the mines, and for similar reasons. But the British Transport Commission, which was established in 1947, was also given control over passenger transport by road and over long distance road haulage, and it was intended that the whole transport system of the country should be integrated instead of rail and road competing with each other. The Conservatives opposed this strenuously and announced their intention to denationalise road transport as soon as possible.

Iron and steel: Even greater party strife was stirred by the government's intention to nationalise iron and steel. Memories of the early thirties, when a third of the country's unemployed had been in the iron and steel industries, had produced a strong demand in the Labour movement for nationalisation. On the other hand under pressure of war-time needs the industry had been modernised and had become far more efficient, and Conservatives objected to the nationalisation of a flourishing industry. The Iron and Steel Bill, which was introduced in 1949, was passed by the Lords after the government had agreed to put off the take-over until February 1951, and the take-over was still far from completed when the Conservatives, who were pledged to repeal the Act, returned to office in October 1951.

The Welfare State

The Labour government expanded greatly the system of social services known as the Welfare State. It extended to everyone the principle of compulsory insurance which the Liberals had introduced before the first World War, and in 1946 a National Insurance Act provided standard pensions for sickness, unemployment, and old age for the whole population, together with maternity grants, widows' pensions, family allowances, and funeral expenses grants. Also in 1946 a National Health Service Act provided for free medical, dental, and ophthalmic treatment for all, and created a national hospital service in which hospitals were financed by the state instead of out of voluntary subscriptions, and the effect of these measures was a great improvement in the health of the country. In 1948 the National Assistance Act set up boards to give financial assistance to those in need who applied for help. And in 1949 a Legal Aid and Advice Act made it possible for a poor man who had a 'sound case for litigation' to go to law by enabling him to get financial help from the state.

Failures

But the merits of these important reforms were offset in people's minds by immediate grievances arising out of shortages of the necessities of life.

Housing: An immense housing problem had been created as a result of bombing, the pause in the building and repair of houses during the war, and the rapid growth of the population. The shortage and cost of building materials frustrated any adequate solution, the position was made worse by the decision of Aneurin Bevan, who as Minister of Health was also responsible for housing, to allow private builders to put up no more than one house for every four put up by local authorities, and the target of 200,000 houses a year was not reached.

Fuel: In the winter of 1946-7 there was a serious crisis when the severe weather and a lack of co-operation among the ministers responsible resulted in transport difficulties as a result of which there was insufficient coal where it was needed. The gas and electricity industries were affected, and in February 1947 there were long reductions of gas pressure and long electricity power cuts which both caused widespread personal hardship and resulted in a loss of export sales amounting possibly to £200 million.

Food: There was also a serious food shortage in 1947, partly as the result of the bitter winter and partly because conditions abroad were causing the price of imported foodstuffs to rise. Bread had already been rationed in 1946, and in November 1947 potatoes were rationed as well. Although they were both taken off the ration in 1948, many other items remained in short supply, and sugar, tea, bacon, meat, butter and other fats were all still rationed when the Labour government eventually fell in October 1951.

Decline and fall

The early years of the Labour government had seen a flood of important legislation. In 1946, for example, when several measures of nationalisation were presented to Parliament and when the National Insurance and National Health Service Acts were passed, time was also found to pass an Act arranging for the development of peaceful uses of atomic energy, another to make possible the development of the New Towns, such as Crawley and Harlow, which were then built around London, and another to repeal the Trade Union and Trade Disputes Act of 1927 (p. 184).

But by 1950 this early legislative vigour was dying, and popular support for the government was declining. To many people nationalisation seemed to have brought few obvious benefits, there was little enthusiasm for the proposal to nationalise the sugar and cement industries, and there was widespread discontent with 'austerity'. So in February 1950, when Attlee decided to fight another general election, Labour's majority in the Commons was reduced to six.

The resignations of Cripps in October 1950 and Ernest Bevin, the Foreign Secretary, in March 1951, both due to ill health, were followed in April by the resignation of Aneurin Bevan in protest against the imposition of National Health Service charges. This open split seriously weakened the authority of the government, and Attlee found it increasingly difficult to rule effectively with his small majority. In October he decided to ask for a dissolution and hold another general election. Public opinion had continued to swing against the Labour Party, and the swing was sufficient to give the Conservatives a majority of sixteen. The Labour Party went into opposition and remained there for thirteen years.

IN 1871 the British were ruling the largest Empire the world had ever known. And during the next quarter of a century it grew rapidly larger. Before about 1885 most of the territories of the British Empire were colonies—possessions of the British Crown whose people were British subjects. But after 1885, when Lord Salisbury became Prime Minister for the first time, Britain tended to avoid annexing further territory and instead merely extended protection over those areas where her influence developed. Politically backward areas were known as Protectorates and were ruled as if they were colonies, although their people were technically not British subjects. Politically more advanced areas were known as Protected States and were governed by the native rulers, advised by British officials.

The Chartered Companies and 'indirect rule'

Part of the reason for this extension of British protection was that Africa was being opened up by a number of chartered companies. In 1886 the Royal Niger Company was formed to develop trade in the area of the Niger delta, in 1888 the British East Africa Company was formed to develop trade in Kenya and Uganda, and in 1889 Cecil Rhodes founded the British South Africa Company to exploit the mineral resources of the area later named after him. In most of these areas the native people benefited from the trade which the companies brought, from the political stability which British protection brought, and from British engineering and medical skill and education. But as British rule made it possible for the life of some of them to be something other than a mere struggle for existence it was inevitable that they should also be influenced by British ideas about Liberty and Nationalism and should eventually aim to rule themselves.

Government was at first in the hands of the chartered companies, but after Protectorates were established it was transferred to officials appointed by the Colonial office. In practice it proved too expensive, both in men and money, to provide direct British rule, and this resulted in the system of 'indirect rule' developed by Sir Frederick Lugard in Northern Nigeria, whereby British officials merely supervised the social, political, and economic institutions already in existence. This was a system which had great merits in the early years, for it meant that Britain was not imposing an alien system but merely providing political stability. But in the long run it meant that Britain found herself maintaining a peasant economy and a tribal system of government in areas where educated natives were thinking in terms of Socialism and democratic government.

British imperialism

The British were slow to take seriously the demands for political liberty which they unintentionally stimulated. This was largely because they retained the sense of superiority over other peoples of the world which they had developed in the heyday of British imperialism at the end of the nineteenth century, when Joseph Chamberlain, Colonial Secretary from 1896 to 1903, thought of the British as a 'governing race', and when Cecil Rhodes looked forward to 'bringing the whole world under British rule'. But this arrogant racialism was accompanied by a sense of obligation towards the native peoples. Chamberlain believed that British colonial rule could only be justified 'if we can show that it adds to the happiness and prosperity of the people', and Rhodes was not being entirely cynical when he spoke of imperialism as 'philanthropy plus five per cent'.

Thus long before the first World War Britain was already attempting to rule in the interest of the native peoples. She never took a levy from her colonies, so colonial revenues were always spent in the colonies themselves, and she also, unlike other colonising nations, maintained a policy of Free Trade throughout her Empire, thus allowing the rest of the world to share in the benefits of trade with the areas she administered.

The decline of imperialism

The period of vigorous extension of the British Empire came to an end with the annexation of the Orange Free State and the Transvaal in 1900 (p. 269), and although after the first World War Britain undertook mandates from the League of Nations to administer some of Germany's and Turkey's pre-war possessions, there was no further extension of the British Empire. This was because of drastic changes in the circumstances which had produced British imperialism in the previous century.

Overpopulation: In the nineteenth century Britain had been an overpopulated country from which large numbers of people had been prepared to emigrate and settle in other parts of the world. But by 1929 the rate of emigration from Britain was lower than the rate of immigration.

Trade: The development of British industry in the nineteenth century had meant that Britons were perpetually seeking new markets for their goods and new sources of raw material; but the end of Britain's industrial pre-eminence and the high prices of her exports in the late twenties meant that by then trade was no longer stimulating Imperial expansion.

Capitalism: The development of British industry in the nineteenth century had also been accompanied by the development of capitalism; and the colonies had seemed to many Britons seeking new fields of investment to promise high profits. But after the financial crisis of 1930-1 (p. 205) the British could no longer conveniently pour capital into underdeveloped countries, and indeed investment abroad was restricted by government policy (p. 212).

Force: The strength of Britain in the nineteenth century not only enabled her to subdue those native peoples who resisted the extension of her influence, but also enabled her to extend her influence further than any other nation. But by the end of the first World War Britain was no longer the greatest world power, and even at sea she was no longer supreme. Moreover, by joining the League of Nations Britain accepted a policy of opposition to aggression, and thus the idea of attempting to extend her Empire further by means of force was out of the question.

Ideas of Service: Another factor which promoted the extension of the British Empire in the nineteenth century was the sense of duty felt by many Britons towards the underprivileged peoples of the world. This resulted in many of them going abroad to preach Christianity, to provide medical services, education, justice, and efficient administration, and to work as engineers. Thus the peoples of India and Africa were brought into contact with British ways of life and thought, and consequently adopted British ideas about Liberty and Nationalism and adapted them to their own circumstances in the twentieth century.

During the twentieth century all these factors combined to prevent further Imperial expansion by Britain and even to cause the Empire to break up. The great days of an expansionist Empire were already over by the end of the nineteenth century; and their passing is marked by the Boer War of 1899-1902 (pp. 268-9), which was fought in a last dying burst of imperialist fervour.

Imperial withdrawal

If the Boer War marks the end of the great age of imperial expansion, the second World War marks the beginning of the age of imperial withdrawal. In the years after 1945 British control was being thrown off even more rapidly than it had been imposed in the second half of the nineteenth century. But it was not a straightforward matter. Independence was most urgently needed in the Indian Empire. But the existence of a large Moslem minority in the predominantly Hindu sub-continent resulted in its partition into India and Pakistan, and this was followed by widespread rioting and bloodshed. The situation in the Middle East was even worse. The Jews and Arabs living in Palestine could not agree with each other, the British, or with a United Nations committee which investigated their country's problems. So Ernest Bevin, the Foreign Secretary, announced that the British would leave Palestine in May 1948, and when the British forces left the Jews and Arabs fought it out between themselves.

There were years of fighting against Chinese Communists in the jungle before Malaya became independent in 1957. There were years of fighting in Cyprus as well, where a Greek terrorist organisation, EOKA, fought for the union of Cyprus with Greece. And it was not until 1959 that Cyprus became an independent republic within the Commonwealth.

By now even the African colonies wanted freedom. The Gold Coast had already acquired its independence as Ghana in 1957, and from 1960, when Harold Macmillan on a visit to South Africa spoke of the 'wind of change' blowing through Africa, Britain's African colonies gained their independence in rapid succession: Nigeria in 1960, Tanganyika and Sierra Leone in 1961, Uganda in 1962, Kenya and Zanzibar in 1963, Nyasaland and Northern Rhodesia in 1964, and Gambia in 1965.

Federalism

One of the ways in which Great Britain tried to deal with the problems of decolonisation was by creating federations. Federations were created in South Arabia, Malaysia, the Caribbean, Nigeria, and Central Africa. None of them was successful, and the African ones were particularly unhappy. The Nigerian federation survived, but only after a bitter and bloody civil war in 1967-70 (pp. 273-5). The Central African Federation, which the British government had created in 1953 to weld Rhodesia and Nyasaland together into a multi-racial society and an economic unit, disintegrated. The economic advantages of federation were considerable. But it was difficult to create a multi-racial society while political power was in the hands of a European minority who numbered about one in twenty of the population of Southern Rhodesia and only one in nearly seventy in Northern Rhodesia and Nyasaland.

Understandably the African leaders were suspicious of the

federation from the start, and the electoral victory in Southern Rhodesia in 1962 of an extremist white supremacist party, the Rhodesian Front, heralded the end of the federation. It was dissolved in 1963, and in 1964 Nyasaland and Northern Rhodesia both became independent states with African governments, the former as Malawi, the latter as Zambia.

U.D.I.

There were also negotiations over independence for Southern Rhodesia, now known as Rhodesia, and in 1964 Ian Smith became leader of the Rhodesian Front and prime minister of Rhodesia, while Harold Wilson became prime minister in the United Kingdom. The negotiations broke down over the issue of the rate of progress towards majority rule, Wilson made the foolish mistake of assuring Smith that Great Britain would not use force to assert her authority there, and on 11 November 1965 Smith issued a unilateral declaration of the independence of Rhodesia.

The British government indicated its disapproval by imposing economic sanctions, but convinced few people other than itself that they were likely to be effective. In 1970, after four years of sanctions, Rhodesia's imports and exports reached record figures, and the 6,000 white immigrants into Rhodesia in 1970 was the largest number for ten years. Great Britain, which had been the greatest power in the world a century earlier now lacked either the strength or the will or both to impose her authority over a rebellious white population of 220,000 in the middle of Africa.

The future of the Commonwealth

The Rhodesian issue shook the foundations of the Commonwealth. But in any case the Commonwealth lacked the cohesion of the old Empire. It had no political unity, being merely a multiracial collection of states of various constitutional complexions, including a military dictatorship. As a system of defence the Empire was being replaced by American-dominated alliances, and anyway some Commonwealth countries preferred to be nonaligned. Even the economic ties which first brought the Empire into existence were getting looser: many Commonwealth countries were finding markets other than Great Britain, and an increasing proportion of Britain's trade was with Europe.

Somehow the Commonwealth still survived. But in January 1971, when thirty-one leaders of Commonwealth countries attended the Commonwealth Conference in Singapore, it was difficult to see it as a significant occasion.

77 LITTLE ENGLAND, 1945–1971

Withdrawal

THE second World War was won by an alliance led by three great powers: Great Britain, the U.S.A., and the U.S.S.R. Great Britain, unlike her allies, was in the war from the start, and she had been an influential world power longer than either of them. But after the war the world was dominated by the U.S.A. and the U.S.S.R., Britain's strength was not comparable with theirs, and the history of British foreign policy over the next quarter of a century is the story of her withdrawal from the posture of a dominant world power into unwilling acceptance of her position as an island off the coast of Europe—no longer Great Britain, but Little England.

Ernest Bevin, who was Foreign Secretary in the post-war Labour government, faced realistically the division between the U.S.A. and the U.S.S.R., decided that Britain must commit herself to a close relationship with the U.S.A., and in 1949 helped to create N.A.T.O. (p. 431). The left wing of the Labour Party and the right wing of the Conservative Party both disliked this approach. They felt that Britain was becoming too dependent, diplomatically, economically, and strategically, on the U.S.A. But Bevin was right. The aggressive nature of Russian foreign policy and Britain's relative weakness made his policy necessary.

Meanwhile financial pressures caused Britain to hand over her traditional role as policeman of the world to the U.S.A. Her decision early in 1947 that she could no longer bear the financial burden of supporting Greece and Turkey led to the Truman Doctrine (p. 291). Withdrawal from India in 1947 and Palestine in 1948 both significantly reduced Britain's military commitment. And the government managed to reduce defence expenditure every year until the Korean War broke out in 1950.

Overcommitment

All the same there were still several heavy military expenses. The numerous garrisons throughout the Empire, the force which was engaged from 1948 in fighting Chinese Communists in Malaya, the army of occupation in Germany, and the atomic research programme which led to the explosion of Britain's first atom bomb in 1952, all imposed a heavy burden on the economy. Then in 1950, when the Korean War began, Britain sent the next largest contingent after the U.S.A. to serve in the United Nations

force, and defence costs soared. The effect on Britain's financial
and economic position was serious. It would scarcely be possible
to cope with any extra problems.

But in 1951 the government of Iran, or Persia, nationalised the
Anglo-Iranian Oil Company and ordered the British staff out of
the country. The new Foreign Secretary, Herbert Morrison, had
to consider military action. In the end, however, he did nothing,
for he realised that Britain lacked the resources for swift and effective action. Instead the British withdrew and Iran had to suffer
the consequences of her oil industry coming to a standstill until an
agreement was reached in 1953.

The Suez crisis

The Anglo-Iranian Oil Company affair raised two important
questions: the importance to Britain of the oil of the Middle East,
and how far she had the strength or the will to defend her interests.
Both of these questions were raised again in an acute form in
July 1956 when President Nasser of Egypt nationalized the Suez
Canal, the route by which tankers brought the oil of the Middle
East to Britain.

Sir Anthony Eden, who was then prime minister, saw Nasser
as a similar figure to Hitler and was against appeasement. Nasser
had 'his thumb on our windpipe', declared Sir Anthony, and he
prepared to ensure that Britain would be able to breathe freely
again. After three months of negotiation and preparation the
British and French governments took advantage of an Israeli
attack on Egypt to issue a twelve-hour ultimatum at 4.15 p.m. on
30 October demanding a temporary Anglo-French occupation
of the canal zone as a means of separating the combatants—though
the combatants were in fact many miles to the East. And early
the next morning British bombers began attacking Egyptian airfields.

From the start the country was bitterly divided. The Labour
opposition put down a motion of censure; Anthony Nutting, the
Minister of State for Foreign Affairs, and Sir Edward Boyle,
the Economic Secretary to the Treasury, both resigned; *The Times*,
the *Manchester Guardian*, and the *Observer* were all against the
government; and there were protest meetings throughout the
country demanding 'Eden must go'. But about half the country
and most of the popular press supported him enthusiastically.
Few people were indifferent.

World opinion was indicated when a resolution of the General

Assembly calling for an immediate cease-fire was carried by 64 votes to five. There was a run on the pound, the Americans refused a loan to help Britain over the crisis, and on 5 November, as the first paratroopers landed, Harold Macmillan, the Chancellor of the Exchequer, was telling the government that the continuation of the operation would mean the devaluation of the pound. That night Bulganin, the Russian prime minister, threatened a rocket attack from the U.S.S.R. And on 6 November, as the commandos at last arrived at Port Said by sea, the government agreed to end the operation.

The whole affair was humiliating, both for those who opposed the government and were ashamed that Britain had launched a war of aggression disguised as a 'police action', and for those who supported the government and were ashamed at the mismanagement and failure.

The failure was total. The operation cost Britain £250,000,000, British property in Egypt was seized, 13,000 British subjects were expelled, and British pipe-lines in the Middle East were blown up. Britain's reputation, both moral and military, suffered, and her influence in the Middle East was seriously weakened. It was an additional irony that the whole operation was demonstrably unnecessary. One of its objects had been to ensure that the Suez Canal stayed open. In the event the canal was blocked for six months, and it mattered relatively little, for soon it was cheaper to ship oil to England round Africa in super-tankers which were too big to go through the Canal.

In retrospect the Suez crisis seems out of keeping with the inevitable trend in British foreign and colonial policy towards withdrawal from great power status. It was a last, out-dated attempt at what was often called 'gun-boat diplomacy.' And it was unsuccessful because in the last resort Britain had neither the will nor the economic strength to see it through.

The nuclear argument

But the Suez crisis did not persuade the Conservative government to give up its attempt to maintain great power status for Britain. On the contrary, it seemed to emphasise the need for Britain to be able to act independently, for the U.S.A. had failed to support Britain over Suez when the British government thought a vital British interest was at stake.

The argument for independence involved the idea that Britain needed her own nuclear armoury. Russia had overwhelming conventional forces, only the nuclear threat could deter her from aggression, and it was dangerous to rely entirely on the U.S.A. What is more, it was argued, the capacity to deliver a nuclear strike conferred prestige on a country and strengthened her position at the conference table.

For the moment Britain had a bomber force which could deliver an atom bomb or two to Russia, and from 1957 she had the hydrogen bomb too. But this was the time when the super-powers were developing ballistic missiles armed with nuclear war-heads. So in 1957 Macmillan's government decided that Britain would develop her own *Blue Streak* missile.

Meanwhile the development of ballistic missiles had made this a peculiarly dangerous time in nuclear strategy (p. 438), and this produced in 1958 the Campaign for Nuclear Disarmament, or C.N.D., with its popular and pessimistic slogan 'Better Red than dead.' Its aim was for Britain to get out of the nuclear club by disarming unilaterally, and out of N.A.T.O. away from the danger of involvement in nuclear war. C.N.D. had a wide appeal, and its greatest success was at the Labour Party conference in 1960 when a resolution calling for unilateral nuclear disarmament was passed against the wishes of the leadership of the party.

Anti-Americanism

There was a strong flavour of anti-Americanism about the more passionate advocates of unilateralism, and this was strikingly illustrated by the inconsistent C.N.D. campaign against President Kennedy in 1962 because he would not tolerate Russian nuclear weapons in Cuba. But by this time the strategic situation in the world was becoming more stable (pp. 439-40), C.N.D. had passed its peak, and it no longer had the powerful emotional appeal of two years earlier.

There was also an anti-American flavour about the attitude of those right-wing Conservatives who wanted to go to the other extreme and break away from N.A.T.O. not in order to disarm unilaterally, but in order to rely for defence on Britain's own independent nuclear deterrent.

The right-wing advocates of a completely independent nuclear deterrent and the left-wing advocates of unilateral disarmament were united in their dislike of the U.S.A. and N.A.T.O. But both seemed to miss the point that the prohibitive cost of an independent deterrent on the one hand and the danger of being defenceless on the other made it inevitable that any British government would rely on the N.A.T.O. alliance and in particular on the U.S.A.

Blue Streak, Skybolt, and Polaris

In practice *Blue Streak*, which had already cost £100,000,000, had to be abandoned in 1960 because it was so expensive. And the government decided to buy American *Skybolt* missiles instead. But in 1962 the Americans abandoned *Skybolt* in favour of the *Polaris* missile, which could be launched from a submarine. So in December 1962 Harold Macmillan met President Kennedy at Nassau in the Bahamas, and they agreed that the U.S.A. would provide Britain with *Polaris* missiles for which Britain would provide her own nuclear warheads and her own submarines.

Macmillan claimed that Britain still had an independent nuclear deterrent, because at least in theory she could make her own *Polaris* missiles. It was not an entirely plausible argument. And it certainly did not convince President de Gaulle. He reacted to the Nassau agreement by vetoing Britain's entry into the European Economic Community on the grounds that she was too closely tied to the U.S.A., both diplomatically and strategically.

The end of world power status

By this time Britain's influence in World affairs was clearly declining. Conscription had ended in 1960, and Britain was now relying for her military operations on small mobile forces of regulars. As colony after colony gained its independence her military commitments declined even more, and the Labour government which took office in 1964 decided to complete the withdrawal of all British forces East of Suez by the end of 1971. Although the Conservatives who returned to office in 1970, decided to keep 20,000 men in the East, this could not obscure the fact that Britain was no longer a significant world power.

For a century the Empire had turned Britain's eyes away from Europe, and in 1950 Sir Stafford Cripps had declared that 'British participation in a political federation limited to Western Europe is not compatible either with our Commonwealth ties, or obligations as a member of the wider Atlantic community, or as a world power.' The idea of Great Britain as a world power, leading the Commonwealth, and having a special relationship with the U.S.A., was natural at the time and prevented Britain from going into Europe. Twenty years later British forces had been withdrawn from most of the world, the Commonwealth scarcely seemed an important force in the world, the special relationship with the U.S.A. no longer seemed very special, and Britain was trying rather belatedly to join a European Community which was getting on very well without her.

THE Conservative government which took office under Winston Churchill in 1951 differed little from the previous Labour government in its imperial, defence, and foreign policies. It continued to prepare colonial territories for independence, it continued to maintain conventional forces while also developing atomic weapons, and it accepted the idea of the Western Alliance and retained close political and strategic ties with the U.S.A.

The Welfare State

The main differences between the Conservative and Labour parties lay in their attitudes towards domestic affairs, and even in this area they seemed to have drawn closer together. The Conservatives had accepted the principles of the Welfare State, and in the election of 1951, instead of suggesting cutting welfare services, they promised to run them more efficiently than Labour and even expand them. Churchill could point to the fact that he had been a pioneer of the Welfare State in the years before the first World War, that the Beveridge Report of 1942, with its plan for destroying Want, Disease, Ignorance, Squalor, and Idleness by means of social insurance, had been drawn up and published during his war-time coalition, and that the Butler Education Act of 1944 (p. 363) had been passed under the same government.

The Welfare State was the natural outcome of industrialisation and technical progress. In the mid-nineteenth century nearly a half of the population had lived in the country. But the development of industry had the effect that a century later four-fifths of the population lived in towns. This urbanisation produced a need for improved housing, sanitation, and water supply, for means of lighting, for police protection from crime, and for welfare facilities, such as libraries, parks, public baths, schools, hospitals and public transport. And this in turn made necessary a system of local government to supervise these developments.

Meanwhile, as the result of medical advances, better housing and sanitation, and the rising standard of living, the death rate declined and the proportion of old people in the community increased. This resulted in the introduction of Old Age Pensions, and that meant that more people past working age were being supported by the community as a whole.

At the same time the extension of compulsory education meant that children who would previously have gone out to work remained at school, where the cost of their education was a charge on the community. All this had helped to move Great Britain in the direction of becoming a Welfare State.

Private enterprise

Socialists saw the Welfare State as a noble ideal and looked forward to the time when the state would provide the best and even the only services to be had. Conservatives merely accepted it as an unfortunate necessity and looked forward to extending affluence so that more and more people might live in their own houses rather than 'council houses', consult private doctors instead of relying on the National Health Service, send their children to independent schools instead of those provided by local education authorities, and pay for their own lawyer instead of relying on legal aid.

They saw themselves as the party of political progress, promoting prosperity based on private enterprise, and they felt that the electorate had a choice between the efficiency which results from free competition and the inefficiency which Labour's controls had brought. They wanted to keep government control of industry to a minimum, and they particularly disliked nationalisation, which they believed would bring with it a massive bureaucracy which would produce economic stagnation and crush individual liberty. So when they came to power in 1951 they began denationalising iron and steel, and in 1952 they passed a Bill which, while keeping British Road Services, gave considerable scope to private road haulage firms.

The price of affluence

In the fifties the electorate increasingly inclined towards the Conservative point of view. And the Conservatives won the elections of 1955 and 1959 because the electorate accepted what the Tories proudly proclaimed in 1959: 'You've Never Had It So Good'. The change from 'austerity' under Labour to affluence under the Tories seemed to speak for itself. Rationing came to an end in 1954. Between 1950 and 1959 the average wage and the number of private cars on the roads both nearly doubled, the amount of personal savings quadrupled, the number of television sets increased thirty times until there were more than ten million sets in use. Few people lacked the necessities of life—adequate food, clothing, heating, and housing. Indeed far more ill-health resulted from over-eating than under-nourishment. Vast sums were spent on liquor, tobacco, and gambling, and it became increasingly usual to go abroad for a holiday. Britain had become an affluent society. It was not just that the standard of living was rising. For many people their whole style of life changed.

But the price of affluence in the fifties was high. In the long run the nation's standard of living depended on the extent to which productivity increased and on the extent to which Britain could sell her goods abroad. The Tories believed that high productivity and high export figures could best be achieved by 'private enterprise', and they scorned planning. But during the period of Churchill's government from 1951 to 1955 the prices of British exports rose faster than those of any other leading manufacturing country, so that Britain's share of world trade declined. Meanwhile her rate of investment in export industries was the lowest of the leading manufacturing countries, so that she had the lowest rise in productivity and thus an even smaller share of world trade. And throughout the fifties not one hospital nor prison was built. The country's resources were devoted overwhelmingly to the production of consumer goods. The British were living beyond their means, and moving towards what an American economist, J. K. Galbraith, called 'private affluence and public squalor'.

'Stop-go' economics

The government was only prepared to take action to deal with immediate economic problems. One of these was inflation: wages and prices were both going up fast, so that money was worth less. The other was the balance of payments deficit: Britain was importing more than she was exporting.

Tory Chancellors tried to deal with these problems by deflating the economy. They increased taxes and imposed restrictions on the borrowing of money. Then, when the economy slowed down too much, they tried to stimulate it by cutting the taxes and restrictions. The result was that more was spent, more was imported, and more was produced. Soon there was renewed inflation and another balance of payments deficit. And the whole 'stop-go' process started again.

Long-term planning

It was not till the early 1960s that the Tories led by Harold Macmillan began to show that they were aware of the problems developing in society and abandoned *laissez-faire* in favour of long-term development programmes. In 1961 Lord Robens was put in charge of the National Coal Board, with the task of closing down the non-productive pits and modernising the rest of the industry. Professor Buchanan investigated the problem of what roads the country would need in the future, and in 1962 plans were made for spending £1,000,000,000 on building motorways.

In 1963 Dr. Beeching, who had been given the task of reorganising British Railways produced a report indicating that a third of the track was carrying only one per cent of the pay-load. He proposed to close 5,000 miles of route and more than half the stations in the country, and modernise what was left of the railways so that they would make a profit.

Plans were also introduced for developing the neglected hospital service by building ninety new hospitals over a period of ten years. There was a whole series of committees investigating education and the youth services, and in 1963 the government accepted the recommendation of the Robbins Committee on Higher Education that the number of universities should be increased from thirty-two to eighty by 1980. Royal Commissions studied the police and the problems of London local government, and in 1963 the London Government Act ended the L.C.C. and created the Greater London Council.

The government even made some gestures in the direction of economic planning by appointing a National Economic Development Council and a National Incomes Commission. But in practice these bodies did little other than talk. And perhaps the main reason the Conservatives lost the election of 1964 was that an increasing number of voters was inclined to accept Labour's demand that 'stop-go' economics should be replaced by steady controlled expansion.

The changing nature of Conservatism

By 1964 the Conservatives had been the predominant party in British politics for nearly eighty years. This was largely because they had continued in the steps of Disraeli, combining an appeal to Nationalist emotion with a practical approach to government. The one consistent element in British Conservatism as a political philosophy was opposition to all ideologies. In the nineteenth century, believing that the stability of society was threatened by an excess of Liberty, they had opposed doctrinaire Liberalism. By the mid-twentieth century circumstances had changed round them. By then they believed that individual liberty was threatened by an excess of state control, so they opposed doctrinaire Socialism and found themselves conserving a moderate form of Liberalism. Circumstances were still changing round them. By 1970 the Conservative Party led by Edward Heath was successfully presenting itself to the voters as a radical alternative to the Labour Party. It seemed quite possible that by the year 2000 Conservatives would find themselves conserving a moderate form of Socialism.

In the wilderness, 1951-64

THE Labour Party spent thirteen years in opposition from 1951 to 1964, and during much of this time was torn apart by bitter divisions. In the early years the trouble centred round Aneurin Bevan, and it reached a peak in 1955 when fifty-seven 'Bevanites' refused to give their support in the Commons to Labour's defence policy of relying on nuclear weapons. Bevan was expelled from the parliamentary party, and in this divided state the Labour Party went into the election of 1955 and lost it.

Shortly afterwards Attlee, who was now 72, had a mild stroke, and in December he resigned the leadership. Herbert Morrison, who was 67, seemed likely to be over 70 by the next election. Bevan, who was 58, was a suitable age, but only a minority would follow him. So the leadership went to Hugh Gaitskell, who was 49.

After this Bevan was usually on the side of the leadership until his early death in 1960. But the divisions in the party continued and reached a new bitterness in the period after the party's third successive defeat in the election of 1959. One divisive issue concerned nationalisation. In 1952 an official party statement had refuted the idea that one distinct social-economic system known as Capitalism would be replaced by another known as Socialism, saying 'There are no distinct and opposing systems, only an infinite series of gradations.' And Gaitskell now proposed to cut out of the party constitution the fourth clause, which proclaimed the Socialist ideal of 'common ownership of the means of production, distribution, and exchange.' This aroused passionate opposition. Harold Wilson likened it to 'cutting Genesis out of the Bible'. And soon there was even more passionate opposition over the issue of nuclear disarmament. In 1960 the leadership was defeated at the party conference when a resolution was passed calling for unilateral British nuclear disarmament.

Harold Wilson now challenged Gaitskell for the leadership of the party, both because Gaitskell refused to accept the conference decision and also on the clause 4 issue. But Gaitskell defeated him, got the decision on unilateralism reversed in 1961, modified his policy to indicate a willingness to negotiate towards nuclear disarmament, and did much to re-unite the party. Then in 1963 he suddenly died, just in time for Harold Wilson, as the party's new leader, to reap the harvest of the Profumo scandal (pp. 368-9) and win the election of 1964.

Plans and Problems, 1964–66

Labour won the election of 1964 promising to take advantage of the opportunities of the new scientific and technological age after the 'thirteen wasted years' of Tory rule. The Labour leaders offered a 'professional' approach to the problems of long-term economic development after the 'shamateurism' of Tory 'stop-go' economics. They still maintained their traditional demand for the re-nationalisation of iron and steel. But this, they insisted, was not for doctrinaire reasons but for the practical reason that the government needed to control the 'commanding heights' of industry in order to be able to intervene directly in the economy and control its development.

Unfortunately when the new Labour government took office it was faced with a massive balance of payments deficit and had to put off its plans for long-term development to concentrate on the immediate problem, which it tried to solve by restricting the flow of imports with a 15 per cent surcharge on all imported goods, and by encouraging British industry to export more.

But it was also faced with the allied problem of rapid inflation. The traditional Tory answer to this was to deflate the economy by increasing taxes and imposing financial restrictions. But Labour had condemned this aspect of 'stop-go' economics for so long that it was unwilling to resort to the same expedients, especially when it wanted to encourage exports. The result was that foreign financiers who held large sums of money in pounds sterling grew increasingly worried that sterling was going to lose its value rapidly. They saw no likelihood of the British government taking the necessary steps to solve its problems. So they began to exchange sterling for other currencies and for gold. The only way of preventing sterling losing its value was for the Bank of England to buy up all the sterling that anyone wanted to sell, and eventually borrow large sums of foreign currencies from the International Monetary Fund and from other countries in order to be able to go on buying the sterling that no-one else wanted. Thus at a time when the country needed to earn foreign currencies to pay for imports, the government was accumulating such vast debts that much of the earnings from future exports would have to go on repaying debts. Labour had inherited a terrible problem from the Tories. Its handling of it made it worse.

At home the government tried to deal with the problem of inflation by setting up a Prices and Incomes Board to investigate increases both in prices and pay awards. But the Board had no power and little influence, and in the eighteen months between Labour coming to power in October 1964 and the next election in March 1966 wages and prices rose three times as fast as industrial production. Instead of the steady controlled expansion Labour had promised, inflation was even worse than under the Tories.

Further financial crises, 1966, 1967, 1968

After increasing its majority the government adopted a tougher approach to the problem of inflation. It acquired from parliament the power to enforce a freeze of wages, prices, and dividends, and almost at once another financial crisis caused it both to use this power and also to engage in another spate of borrowing from foreign banks.

But none of this solved Britain's fundamental economic problems. So there was another crisis in the autumn of 1967, and this time the government was driven to devalue the pound 14 per cent and make massive cuts in expenditure on defence, education, and the social services.

Even devaluation did not make the pound secure. In 1968, when there was a World currency crisis caused by the weakness of the franc, the pound was affected too, and the government imposed restrictions on private spending. There had now been financial crises in 1964, 1966, 1967 and 1968. People were getting used to them. They seemed an integral part of life under Labour.

Ulster

Meanwhile trouble was brewing in Northern Ireland. For half a century, ever since Ulster was given Home Rule by the Government of Ireland Act of 1920, the Protestant Unionist majority, fearful of an eventual take-over by the South, had discriminated against the Catholic minority. In 1967 a Catholic Civil Rights movement was formed. It wanted 'one man, one vote' in local elections, fair electoral boundaries, fair allocation of council houses, and the disbandment of the 'B' Specials—the Protestant-dominated armed volunteer reserve. In 1968 it held its first protest march, and the Irish Republican Army, or I.R.A., which wanted the reunification of Ireland, took advantage of the situation to launch a campaign of violence. There was increasing trouble in Belfast and Londonderry, and by August 1969 conditions were bad enough for the Labour government at Westminster to send troops in to try to maintain order.

At about this stage an extremist group of the I.R.A., the Provisionals, broke away from the main body. They aimed to use urban guerrilla warfare to create a sufficient break-down of law and order to force the British government to impose direct rule in Ulster. Once this happened it would look, they believed, like a simple matter of the British occupying Ireland, and the next stage would be British withdrawal and reunification of Ireland. They were sufficiently successful to create a situation in which they dominated most Catholic areas of Belfast and Londonderry. And the British troops, who had been welcomed by the Catholics in 1969, came to be regarded by them as the enemy and as a prop for the detested Unionist government.

This was the situation when the Labour government in England fell in June 1970. Most of the original demands of the Civil Rights Movement had been met. But it was too late. Rioting and violence were getting worse. Bomb explosions and shootings were daily occurrences. The Catholics had learnt the lesson that violence could achieve things which parliamentary democracy had denied them for fifty years. The future was to be grim.

Immigration and race relations

Ulster was an old sore re-opened. At the same time a new problem was developing in England. During the 1950s large numbers of immigrants had arrived from Commonwealth countries—first of all from the West Indies, and then from India and Pakistan. As the numbers of immigrants rose they tended to concentrate in particular areas, such as Notting Hill, Brixton, and Smethwick. They were usually poor. They did the jobs no-one else wanted, and they were more likely than white men to find it difficult to get jobs. The social problems from which the country suffered, such as poor and inadequate housing and schools, were particularly acute in the areas where the immigrants lived.

The Labour government continued the Conservatives' policy of trying to limit the problem by restricting immigration, and they also passed a Race Relations Act, making discrimination against anyone on grounds of race or colour illegal. It was a reasonable attempt to cope with one of the consequences of the problem. But the problem itself continued.

Failure and inadequacy

So did many other problems. And most of them proved too great for the government to cope with. Attlee's post-war Labour government had eventually run out of steam. Wilson's government never raised enough steam to get moving. It did carry out its intention to nationalise steel. But that had little effect on fundamental economic problems. It faced the problem of deteriorating industrial relations by introducing legislation to regulate the conduct of industrial disputes. But then it withdrew it when faced with Trade Union opposition. Too few houses were built. The proposed raising of the school leaving age to sixteen was postponed to save money. The one really important piece of legislation which the government was preparing, a Pensions Bill which would have related pensions to earned incomes, failed to get passed by the time the government fell.

One small reform which was accomplished was the appointment of a Parliamentary Commissioner to whom appeals could be made against administrative injustice. But apart from this and some legal reforms the Labour government of 1964–70 achieved little. Its application in 1967 for membership of the European Economic Community was rejected (pp. 435–6). It grossly mishandled the problem of Rhodesia (p. 377). It had no solution to the problem of Ulster. And almost everything was overshadowed by the continuing economic problems and the recurrent financial crises. Even the foreign policy decision which Wilson announced in January 1968 that Britain would withdraw all her troops East of Suez by the end of 1971 was the direct consequence of the financial crisis of November 1967 which had also produced the devaluation of the pound.

Electoral defeat, 1970

Labour's electoral defeat in 1970 had little to do with Europe, Rhodesia, Ulster, or withdrawal East of Suez. It was due to rising prices. During the six years of Labour rule real wages, or what a person can buy with his pay, had on average not risen at all. All that had happened was inflation. Things cost more, and pay generally went up by about the same amount.

Labour had hoped to achieve rapid economic growth. It had failed. The gross national product was increasing only by 2 per cent per annum. Meanwhile government spending, which was rather more than half the gross national product, was increasing at about 4 per cent per annum. So there was nothing left for an increase in real wages.

Labour had promised much and achieved little. But the swing against it in the election was not great. When the Tories came back to office in 1970 promising 'Action, not Words' few of the electors who returned them expected a dramatic improvement.

Section X   The Modern World, 1945–1971

80   THE DIVISION OF THE WORLD

As the second World War drew towards its end it already seemed as if the whole world might soon be divided into two opposed spheres of influence—one dominated by the U.S.S.R., and the other dominated by the U.S.A. and her allies. President Roosevelt of the U.S.A. would not accept that this was likely and hoped for friendly co-operation after the war between the U.S.A. and the U.S.S.R. But Winston Churchill had no such illusion, and one of his aims was to ensure that the Russian sphere of influence after the war should be as small as possible.

The most immediate problem was the future of Europe, where the Russian and Anglo-American forces were advancing towards each other, and the most important aspect of this problem was the question of the future of Germany and Austria. In February 1945 Roosevelt, Churchill, and Stalin met at Yalta in the Crimea and agreed to divide Germany and Austria into zones of occupation. But two months later, despite this agreement, Churchill, who distrusted Stalin and wanted to bargain from a position of strength, tried to get the Anglo-American forces to withdraw to the agreed occupation zones until after a fair settlement had been made for the whole of Europe.

The position of General Eisenhower, who was commanding the Anglo-American forces, was made particularly difficult by the sudden death of President Roosevelt. But since he could see no specifically military need to press on, he held his forces back and the Russians were allowed to liberate Vienna, Berlin, and even Prague, where the resistance had invited the Americans in. Although the Americans were unable to avoid advancing into Turingia and Saxony, they withdrew to their own previously agreed zone before the Potsdam Conference of June–July 1945.

Russian expansion

Thus by the Potsdam Conference the Russian armies held Eastern Europe as far as half-way across Germany and Austria and up to the borders of Jugoslavia and Greece. Under these circumstances the Russians could settle the affairs of Eastern Europe without interference from the West.

The first effect of this was that the boundary of the U.S.S.R. was pushed much farther West than it had been at the outbreak of the second World War. Finland again lost the territory which she had been forced to cede to the U.S.S.R. at the end of the winter war of 1939–40. Estonia, Latvia, and Lithuania were completely swallowed up, together with the Northern part of East Prussia.

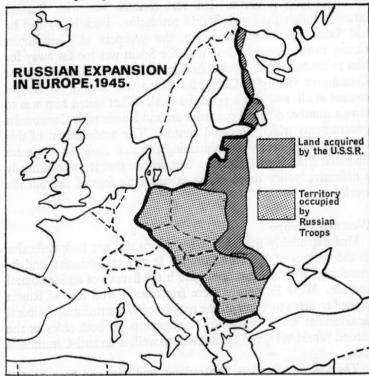

RUSSIAN EXPANSION IN EUROPE, 1945.

Land acquired by the U.S.S.R.

Territory occupied by Russian Troops

Poland lost approximately the area she had seized from Russia and Lithuania in 1920–1. Roumania lost Bessarabia and Bukovina. And Ruthenia, which had been transferred from Czechoslovakia to Hungary in March 1939, also went to the U.S.S.R.

The second effect was that the countries of Eastern Europe which were occupied by Russian troops (Poland, Czecholsovakia, Hungary, Roumania, and Bulgaria) had to have governments acceptable to the U.S.S.R.

In the Far East Stalin acquired the Kurile Islands and South Sakhalin, which had been lost to Japan in 1905, and pushed Russian influence into Outer Mongolia, Manchuria, and the North of Korea.

The reason for this expansionist foreign policy was the traditional Tsarist reason: to cushion the heartland of Russia from external attack by acquiring as much territory as possible. Stalin was not primarily interested in the spread of Communism. He preferred a Communist to a parliamentary system in, for example, Czechoslovakia or Outer Mongolia. But this was mainly because he understood it better. His real concern was with Russian interests rather than with World revolution. Back in 1936–9 he had been unenthusiastic about the prospect of Communist victory in the Spanish Civil War, for Spain was too far away for him to control it effectively. And in 1949 he was horrified by the Communist victory in China, for China was too big for him to control at all, and also a potential rival. What suited him was to have a number of small countries around Russia with Communist governments which he could control. The achievement of this aim inevitably involved maintaining the Red Army in the areas liberated from Nazi Germany. But despite that it was essentially a defensive policy based on an unreasoning fear of the outside world.

Western Europe

Understandably Stalin's foreign policy did not look defensive to the nations of Western Europe. It was expansionist, and its association with Communism gave it the flavour of an ideological crusade. West Europeans were frightened. And fear of Russia tended to drive together all the nations of Western Europe, liberal democracies and dictatorships, belligerents on both sides in the second World War, and the neutrals as well, in an anti-Communist bloc.

The neutrals: Sweden, Switzerland, and Eire had been neutral in the second World War, and they continued to keep free from any alliances, but as they were parliamentary democracies their relations with the U.S.S.R. were inevitably rather distant. Spain and Portugal had also been neutral. Their governments' sympathies had been with the Axis powers, and the Spanish government had even sent a volunteer division to join in the invasion of the U.S.S.R. After the war their detestation of Communism ensured their alignment with the West.

The allied belligerents: Britain, like the neutral countries, was able to maintain her pre-war system of government without interruption, for she did not suffer a German occupation. But the continental countries which went to war were all occupied by

German troops. Norway, Denmark, the Netherlands, and Belgium quickly resumed their pre-war constitutions after the war, and in 1946 France adopted a new constitution very similar to that of the old Third Republic. They all joined N.A.T.O. (p. 431) in 1949.

Italy: Apart from Germany and Austria, the two countries occupied by the Allies, Italy was the only West European country whose constitution was drastically changed after the war. The Italians were allowed to settle their own future. In June 1946 there was a referendum which resulted in the abolition of the monarchy, and at the same time an Assembly was elected to draw up a new constitution. It produced one similar to that which had been in force before the Fascist era, and the Italians once again set out to try to make parliamentary democracy work. They also joined N.A.T.O.

The area of uncertainty

A few European countries were neither occupied by Russian troops nor clearly aligned with the anti-Communist West.

Finland: Although the Finns had fought the U.S.S.R. in 1939–40, and again as the ally of Germany in 1941–4, and although they had been recognised at Yalta as within the Russian sphere of influence, the Russians did not swallow Finland up. Instead they allowed the Finns political independence, but compelled them in a peace treaty to provide the U.S.S.R. with specified manufactured goods as reparations payments, thus ensuring that Finland built up industries which made her economically dependent on Russia. But the Finns were able to retain their political independence, and in foreign policy they trod carefully between East and West, trying to offend no-one.

Jugoslavia: While Finland was a non-Communist country which was in some ways dependent on the U.S.S.R., Jugoslavia was a Communist country which was independent of the U.S.S.R. In April 1941 Jugoslavia had been conquered by Germany, but a Serb officer, Colonel Draža Mihailović, had continued the struggle in the mountains, where he organised bands of resistance fighters known as *Chetniks*. Unfortunately the traditional division between the Serbs and the other peoples of Jugoslavia was perpetuated by Mihailović, who seemed to be fighting as much to establish Serb supremacy over the Croats and Slovenes as to drive out the Germans, and Hitler was able to establish a separate state of Croatia under a Croat named Ante Pavelić in which Croats slaughtered Serbs in tens of thousands.

However, in November 1942 another Croat, a Communist

called Josip Broz who is better known as Tito formed a resistance movement aimed at uniting all Jugoslavs against the Germans. It soon became apparent that his *Partisans* were a more effective opposition to the Germans than the *Chetniks*, and in 1943 the Western Allies transferred their support from Mihailović to Tito. During 1944 the *Partisans* drove Pavelić out of Croatia, captured Mihailović, and took Belgrade from the Germans. They had liberated their country without direct intervention from the Russian army, and although Tito established a Communist government he had no inclination to let Jugoslavia become a Russian satellite. This resulted in a breach between Stalin and Tito which became so wide that in June 1948 Jugoslavia was expelled from the Cominform (p. 422).

Albania had been a Jugoslav satellite since the Germans had been driven out in 1944. But the Albanians disliked their subordinate position, and when Jugoslavia was expelled from the Cominform they took the opportunity of throwing off Jugoslav control by declaring their allegiance to Moscow.

Greece was the only other Balkan country which was not occupied by Russian troops, and it was to be the only Balkan country without a Communist government, for during the war the British had restored the monarchy, established a system of parliamentary government, and put down a Communist rising. But in September 1946 the Communists rose again and this time got assistance from the three Communist countries on the Northern border— Albania, Jugoslavia, and Bulgaria. The outcome of this in March 1947 was the Truman Doctrine (p. 291) and American aid to Greece. The civil war continued until nearly the end of 1948, but the expulsion of Jugoslavia from the Cominform had the effect that the Greek Communists lost their main source of supply, and that, combined with American help to the Greek government, ensured that Greece remained aligned with the West.

The 'iron curtain'

As early as March 1946 Winston Churchill had spoken at Fulton, Missouri, of the 'iron curtain' which had come down over Europe. It had come down along the line reached by the Red Army in its victorious advance against Nazi Germany. And much the same applied in the Far East. Korea, like Germany and Austria, was divided along the line reached by the Russian forces. Over the next few years the division hardened, and in about 1948 it became clear that East and West were not just divided. They were in a state of 'Cold War'.

The origins of the Cold War

THE Cold War of the mid-twentieth century had its origins in the hostility between Russia and the outside world after the Bolshevik Revolution of 1917. The great powers feared Bolshevism, with its threat of World revolution, so Great Britain, France, the U.S.A., and Japan all sent armies into Russia to fight against the Bolsheviks. The Bolsheviks drove out the armies of intervention, but the experience left them with the fear of an alliance of the capitalist nations of the world against them.

Mutual suspicions continued. At the time of the Munich Conference of September 1938 (p. 245) Stalin feared that Britain and France were trying to turn Nazi Germany against the U.S.S.R. So in August 1939 he agreed to a non-aggression pact with Germany and set Nazi Germany against Britain and France.

When Germany attacked Russia in June 1941 and Britain and Russia became allies Stalin wanted British troops to land in Western Europe and turn the German pressure away from Russia. But the Anglo-American invasion did not come until June 1944, three years later. So throughout the war, while Russia bore the brunt of Germany's armed might, Stalin wondered if the British and Americans were now trying to use Nazi Germany against him, and even in the last weeks of the war he accused the Western allies of intending to make a separate peace with Germany in order to be able to advance Eastwards and check the Red Army. There were no grounds for Stalin's fear. But certainly Churchill was suspicious of Stalin's expansionist intention, and he was only prevented by the Americans from launching a secondary invasion in 1944 North from the Adriatic against the German forces, with the aim of cutting across the Red Army's advance into Central Europe and thus keeping Russia's sphere of influence in Europe as small as possible.

But despite their mutual suspicions the allied leaders generally co-operated well during the war, and the split between East and West only opened up seriously as victory approached and they had to face the difficult problems of peace instead of the relatively simple problem of winning a war. When the new leaders of Britain and the U.S.A., Attlee and Truman, met Stalin in Potsdam in June and July of 1945, after the German war was over, the strains in the Grand Alliance were apparent. They particularly disagreed over Stalin's plans for Poland and the German lands East of the rivers Oder and Neisse (p. 412). And towards the end of the conference things were made worse by the revelation by the Western allies of their secret development of the atom bomb.

Russian expansion

The demonstration of the destructive power of the atom bomb at Hiroshima and Nagasaki intensified Stalin's obsessive concern over the security and the power of Russia and helped to produce two responses, both in line with the traditional Tsarist approach to international affairs.

First Stalin was determined that Russian heavy industry and armaments should catch up with the West. She must develop the atom bomb and at the same time maintain massive conventional forces. To achieve this the Fourth Five Year Plan was introduced in 1946, and the political police, whose control over the people had been relaxed during the war, tightened their grip again. To the same end Stalin stripped Manchuria of machinery, exacted massive reparations from Germany, and subordinated the economies of the East European countries to the needs of Russia.

Secondly Stalin continued the centuries-old Tsarist policy of pushing out Russia's boundaries and influence as far as possible. In the East he pushed Russian influence into Outer Mongolia, Manchuria, and North Korea, and he acquired South Sakhalin and the Kurile Islands. In the West he moved Russia's frontier far enough to add 21,000,000 people to the pre-1939 population of Russia, and he kept the Red Army in control of all the countries it had liberated from Nazi Germany. He delayed for some months withdrawing Russia's war-time garrison from Iran. He demanded the cession of territory from Turkey, and also that she should allow Russian bases in the Straits. He supported the Communist guerrillas in Greece in the hope of extending Russian influence to the Mediterranean.

Cold War in the West

President Truman reacted to the Russian threats to Greece and Turkey with the Truman Doctrine (p. 291) of March 1947. And tension between the former allies increased. Relations between them deteriorated all the faster because what was really a conflict over power and security came to look like an ideological conflict and took on the highly-charged emotional quality of a war of religion. Stalin proclaimed his devotion to world revolution, when he was really concerned about Russian power. Americans looked for Communist conspiracies at home and abroad, when the real threat was from the Red Army.

Stalin suspected the Americans' intentions as much as they suspected his. He reacted to the Marshall Aid proposals of June 1947 (pp. 284–5), which he saw as an American bid for capitalist domination of Europe, by establishing the Cominform (p. 422) in September 1947. And he went on pushing out Russia's power. In February 1948, at his instigation, the Communist Party seized power in Czechoslovakia, and in June Jugoslavia, which had never been occupied by the Red Army and was insisting on its independence, was expelled from the Cominform. In the same month Stalin tried to drive the Western allies out of Berlin by imposing a blockade. And the direct result of the prolonged crisis over Berlin was to drive the countries of Western Europe and North America so close together that in April 1949 they formed the North Atlantic Treaty Organization (p. 431).

Hot war in the East

Up till 1949 the Cold War centred on Russia. Russia and Communism were virtually synonymous. But then on 1 October 1949 the Chinese People's Republic was proclaimed, and suddenly the whole Asian continent seemed to be under Communist control. The U.S.A. was faced with the formidable task of containing China as well as Russia.

In the autumn of 1950 the Chinese invaded Tibet. Meanwhile the Communist government of North Korea had invaded the South, and by the end of the year Chinese and American forces were fighting each other in the North of Korea. The Cold War had not only spread to the Far East. It had turned hot.

The Russian 'peace offensive'

The end of the fighting in Korea in July 1953 and the death of Stalin in the previous March marked the end of a stage in the Cold War. The change in the East is obvious. It was a switch from war to peace. The change in the West was less obvious but equally significant, for Russia's new leaders wanted to improve relations with the West and launched a 'peace offensive'. In May 1955 they agreed to a peace treaty with Austria under which their troops withdrew and Austria became independent in return for a guarantee that she would remain neutral. And in July there was an apparently cordial 'Summit Meeting' at Geneva between the leaders of the U.S.S.R., the U.S.A., Great Britain, and France.

The alliance systems

But just before Stalin died Eisenhower had become President of the U.S.A., and John Foster Dulles had taken office as Secretary of State. Dulles was determined to prevent any extension of Communist control in the World. He spoke of going to the 'brink of war' in response to Russian threats, and he declared that 'massive retaliation' would follow any Communist aggression. His declared aim was to 'roll back Communism' both in Europe and the Far East. So just as the Russian leaders were starting to talk of 'peaceful co-existence' Dulles was constructing a system of alliances all round the Communist bloc.

In the Far East a bi-lateral defence treaty with Japan of 1952 was followed by a treaty with South Korea in 1953 and another with Formosa at the end of 1954. The North Atlantic Treaty Organization, or N.A.T.O., formed in 1949, was expanded in 1954 to include West Germany. And in the same year the U.S.A. signed a Mutual Aid Agreement with Spain, which was not a member of N.A.T.O., acquiring the right to establish naval and air bases there. It was also in 1954 that the Balkan Pact and the South-east Asia Treaty Organization, or S.E.A.T.O., were formed. Finally in 1955 a mutual defence organisation known as the Baghdad Pact was established in the Middle East. And ever since 1947 there had existed an Inter-American Treaty of Reciprocal Assistance.

The Russian reaction to this encirclement was to form the satellite countries of Eastern Europe in 1955 into a mutual defence organisation known as the Warsaw Pact. China, which had had a bilateral treaty with the U.S.S.R. since February 1950, emphasised the solidarity of the Communist bloc by declaring that she was willing to assist the Warsaw Pact countries against aggression. And both China and Russia promised economic and technical aid to North Vietnam and, by implication, help against aggression.

Thus paradoxically just as the Russians began to talk of 'peaceful co-existence' the Communist and anti-Communist nations of the world came to be aligned more clearly than ever before in opposing alliances. But even the alliances helped to maintain peace. In the first place they gave a measure of stability to international relations. In the second place they tended to give the two super-powers considerable control over conflicts between their allies, and they were in practice able to prevent war in the areas they dominated.

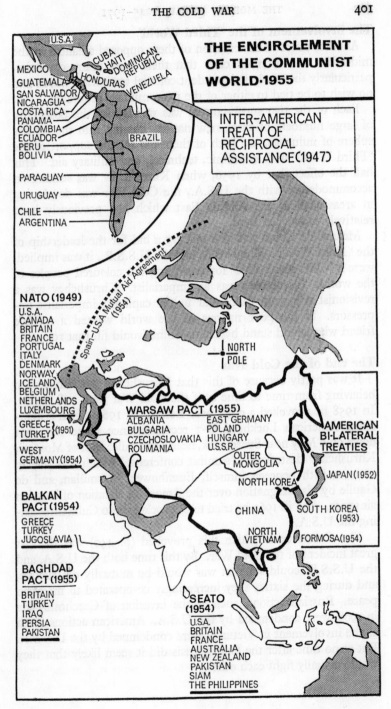

THE ENCIRCLEMENT OF THE COMMUNIST WORLD·1955

INTER-AMERICAN TREATY OF RECIPROCAL ASSISTANCE (1947)

U.S.A.
MEXICO
GUATEMALA
SAN SALVADOR
NICARAGUA
COSTA RICA
PANAMA
COLOMBIA
ECUADOR
PERU
BOLIVIA
PARAGUAY
URUGUAY
CHILE
ARGENTINA

CUBA
HAITI
DOMINICAN REPUBLIC
HONDURAS
VENEZUELA
BRAZIL

NATO (1949)
U.S.A.
CANADA
BRITAIN
FRANCE
PORTUGAL
ITALY
DENMARK
NORWAY
ICELAND
BELGIUM
NETHERLANDS
LUXEMBOURG
GREECE
TURKEY } (1951)
WEST GERMANY (1954)

Spain-USA Mutual Aid Agreement (1954)

NORTH POLE

WARSAW PACT (1955)
ALBANIA
BULGARIA
CZECHOSLOVAKIA
ROUMANIA
EAST GERMANY
POLAND
HUNGARY
U.S.S.R.

BALKAN PACT (1954)
GREECE
TURKEY
JUGOSLAVIA

BAGHDAD PACT (1955)
BRITAIN
TURKEY
IRAQ
PERSIA
PAKISTAN

OUTER MONGOLIA
NORTH KOREA
CHINA
NORTH VIETNAM

AMERICAN BI-LATERAL TREATIES
JAPAN (1952)
SOUTH KOREA (1953)
FORMOSA (1954)

SEATO (1954)
U.S.A.
BRITAIN
FRANCE
AUSTRALIA
NEW ZEALAND
PAKISTAN
SIAM
THE PHILIPPINES

The involvement of the 'Third World'

Another effect of the creation of these opposed alliances in the mid-fifties was to make clear that there were many countries, particularly the newly independent colonial territories, which had no wish to be tied to either of the main military groupings.

Each of the two super-powers was worried by the possibility of large numbers of these new nations coming into the other's sphere of influence. So both of them bid for the support of the 'Third World' with economic, technical, and military aid. This had the effect that by 1956, when Khrushchev was seeking an accommodation with the U.S.A., the Cold War was developing in areas such as the Middle East which had previously been relatively untouched by it.

Meanwhile China was also making a bid for the leadership of the 'Third World'. The U.S.A. and the U.S.S.R., it was implied, were a 'white man's club' for exploiting the coloured peoples of the world. Eisenhower was an imperialist. Khrushchev was a revisionist who was selling out to the capitalist imperialist oppressors. If the poor nations of the world wanted a reliable friend who would stand by them, China would fill that role.

The end of the Cold War

It was partly because of this that Khrushchev was driven into behaving from time to time as if the Cold War were still raging. In 1958 he provoked a crisis over Berlin. In 1960, when a high-flying American Lockheed U-2 reconnaissance plane was shot down on 6 May near Sverdlovsk, nearly 900 miles East of Moscow, Khrushchev destroyed a 'summit conference' which was due to start on 16th between himself, Eisenhower, Macmillan, and de Gaulle by his indignation over the American violation of Russian air space. And in 1962 he tried to put rockets onto Cuba threatening the U.S.A.

The Cuban crisis which this provoked (p. 440) was the last great incident of the Cold War. By this time both the U.S.A. and the U.S.S.R. could see that war would be mutually destructive, and during the sixties they increasingly co-operated to maintain peace. Russian actions, such as the invasion of Czechoslovakia in 1968, were condemned by the U.S.A. American actions, such as the involvement in Vietnam, were condemned by the U.S.S.R. But at no time after the Cuban crisis did it seem likely that they would actually fight each other.

THE UNITED NATIONS ORGANIZATION

Origins

AT a meeting in Moscow in 1943 the foreign ministers of the U.S.A., the U.S.S.R., and Great Britain agreed on the need for 'a general international organization, based on the principle of sovereign equality of all peace-loving nations, open to membership by all such states, large and small', and Roosevelt, Stalin, and Churchill endorsed this declaration when they met at Teheran in November. Roosevelt, remembering the fate of the League of Nations in the U.S.A., was anxious that the organisation should be established before the war ended. So in August 1944 a conference was held at Dumbarton Oaks near Washington, attended by representatives of the U.S.A., the U.S.S.R., Great Britain, and China, to reach agreement on the organisation and functions of the proposed organisation. At Yalta in February 1945 Roosevelt, Stalin, and Churchill agreed on the important issues which had not yet been settled. And in a conference at San Francisco from April to June the constitution was settled and fifty nations signed the Charter of the United Nations Organization.

Aims

The primary aim of U.N.O., as of the League of Nations, was the preservation of peace and security. There was less emphasis on disarmament, though an Atomic Energy Commission was established at the first meeting of the Assembly in January 1946 to consider arrangements for the international control and development of atomic energy. But it was intended to provide U.N.O. with a peace-keeping force of its own and to ensure adequate facilities for the open investigation and discussion of disputes and their peaceful and just settlement. It was regarded as particularly important to encourage international social and economic co-operation as a means of eliminating potential sources of trouble.

Organisation

The League of Nations had failed partly because its constitution did not accord with the realities of power politics (p. 140). The Assembly of the League, in which each member had one vote, had sometimes been able to make decisions which a great power disliked, but it had not been able to enforce them. The Council of the League had been able to do no more than offer advice to the Assembly, and even in the Council the great powers were never a majority. The founders of U.N.O. learnt from these failings and exalted the position of the great powers as against the weaker members, and of the Council as against the Assembly.

The Security Council consisted of both permanent and non-permanent members. The permanent members were the U.S.A., the U.S.S.R., Great Britain, France, and China, and six non-permanent members were elected for two years at a time by the Assembly. It was to remain in permanent session, its decisions were binding on all members, and it decided on whether or not to accept any application for membership. The small nations were generally prepared to accept the limitations on their national sovereignty implied by the fact that they were bound to accept any decision of the Security Council, for it was a worthwhile concession in return for the measure of security and the economic and other aid which many of them got from U.N.O. One of the most important features of the Security Council was that each of the five permanent members had the right of veto. Roosevelt had suggested this at Yalta, for he knew it would be unrealistic to expect the U.S.A. to accept a majority decision to which it strongly objected, and Stalin and Churchill had agreed, for they knew that the same applied to their own countries. Roosevelt assumed, of course, that the great powers would usually co-operate. He was mistaken, and the work of the Security Council was frustrated because the Russians used the veto regularly. But even this was better than a situation in which the Security Council would have been able to reach majority decisions which could then only have been carried into effect by war against the U.S.S.R.

The General Assembly consisted of representatives of all member states, each state having one vote regardless of its size. It met every September and could easily be summoned for special sessions. Its usual function was to discuss international co-operation, such things as 'the principles governing disarmament', and 'any questions relating to the maintenance of international peace and security'. It could make recommendations about these matters, but it could not do anything about them. And this meant that the mass of small nations had no powers under the Charter to take any action. Once again they were generally prepared to accept this, for it accorded with the realities of power politics. Moreover, the General Assembly was far from valueless. It provided a useful platform for the expression of opinion. Its resolutions, which were reached by a two-thirds majority, could be influential in the world. And it had the important function of electing the non-permanent members of the Security Council and the representatives of the United Nations on the various subsidiary organisations.

The Secretariat of U.N.O., like that of the League, was a permanent Civil Service headed by a Secretary-General and made up of as broad a cross-section of nationalities as possible.

The International Court of Justice at the Hague continued to function, but although all members of U.N.O. recognised its jurisdiction, the submission of disputes to it remained voluntary.

The Trusteeship Council took the place of the Mandates Commission in supervising the administration of mandated territories, which were now known as Trust Territories, and it was elevated to the position of one of the principal organs of U.N.O. It had more extensive powers of investigation than the Mandates Commission had had, but it had no power to take action.

The Economic and Social Council, or ECOSOC, was the only other primary organ of U.N.O. It consisted of eighteen members, each elected for a three-year period, and it had the task of promoting economic and social progress in the world. Again it had no power to take action, but could only try to encourage co-operation.

The subsidiary organisations of U.N.O. were even more numerous than those of the League. Some, like the I.L.O., were inherited from the League. Some, like the Universal Postal Union, were even older. Others, such as the International Monetary Fund, the World Health Organization (W.H.O.), and the United Nations Educational, Scientific, and Cultural Organization (U.N.E.S.C.O.), were formed by U.N.O. In their various ways these organisations, like those of the League, did much of the most valuable work of U.N.O., relieving suffering, giving advice and assistance, and building a great network of international co-operation.

Membership

From the beginning U.N.O. was a world-wide organisation. Its membership always included most of the independent countries of every continent, and by 1955, when sixteen new members were admitted at once, including five Asian and one African country, making the total membership up to seventy-six, it was becoming apparent that the Asian and African countries, so many of which were becoming independent, were soon going to be a dominant influence in the General Assembly.

One unsatisfactory aspect of the structure of U.N.O. was that it was impossible to change the permanent members of the Security Council so as to reflect more accurately the changing balance of power in the world. When the Kuomintang government of China was overthrown in 1949 by the Communists the U.S.A. refused to accept the Russian demand that China should be represented at U.N.O. by Communist rather than Kuomintang representatives. As a result the Russians walked out of the Security Council in January 1950, so that when the Korean War (p. 407) broke out in June the Security Council was able to take advantage of Russia's absence to condemn North Korea's action. The Russians then appreciated that they had made a tactical mistake and returned to the Security Council. But the deadlock over China remained, and China was still represented on the Security Council by the Kuomintang until the rapprochement between Communist China and the U.S.A. in 1971.

Constitutional development

The likelihood of the Security Council being ineffective in the event of future dangers to peace because of the use of the veto led in 1950 to an attempt by the Assembly to assume greater power than it possessed under the Charter. It passed a resolution that if the use of the veto in the Security Council resulted in no decision being reached about a threat to peace, then the Assembly could itself consider the issue, and if a resolution were reached by a two-thirds majority those states which voted for it should act in accordance with it.

The right to do so was questionable, for this 'uniting for peace resolution' conflicted with the Charter of the United Nations, which could not be amended because an amendment could be prevented by veto in the Security Council. It was, therefore, to be anticipated that the U.S.S.R., against whom the resolution was clearly directed, would object with some justification if an attempt were made to act on it. Ironically the first time the General Assembly acted on it was not against the U.S.S.R. but against Britain and France, when they used force against Egypt in the Suez crisis of 1956 (p. 348), and while they protested against this procedure the U.S.S.R. seemed tacitly to accept it.

In a sense U.N.O. had found a way of ensuring that if the U.S.A. and the U.S.S.R. agreed with each other on any issue they could find a way round the veto of the other permanent members. But no resolution of the General Assembly could detract from the force of the American or Russian power of veto, for in their cases that power was backed by overwhelming military strength. And when the U.S.A. and the U.S.S.R. confronted each other, as they did during the Cuban missile crisis of 1962 (p. 440), the United Nations could do little other than stand and wait.

WHEN the United Nations Organization was formed in 1945 it was intended that there should be an international peace-keeping force under the control of the Security Council. But the permanent members of the Security Council were unable to reach agreement about this force, and in 1948, when it became obvious that co-operation between them was impossible, the negotiations were abandoned.

Without a military force of its own U.N.O. was likely to be as ineffective as the League of Nations in dealing with outbreaks of fighting, and this ineffectiveness was demonstrated when the British abandoned their Palestine mandate in May 1948 and handed the problem over to the United Nations. The solution favoured by U.N.O. was partition. But neither the Arabs nor the Jews wanted partition, and they began fighting each other. The Swedish Count Bernadotte, who was sent out by the United Nations to mediate, was promptly assassinated by a Jewish terrorist, and the Jews set up the state of Israel by force. The United Nations could only accept what had been accomplished, and in 1949 Israel was admitted to membership of U.N.O.

The Korean War

Rather surprisingly the United Nations was able to take prompt and effective action when North Korean forces invaded the South in June 1950. But this was only because the U.S.A. was willing and able to act vigorously. And it was only possible for it to be regarded as a United Nations action because the Russians were absent from the Security Council as the result of their walk out in January 1950 (p. 406) and thus could not use their veto.

The situation in Korea after the second World War was in some ways parallel to that in Germany. The Russians had come in from one side and the Americans from the other. They agreed that Korea should eventually be independent. But in 1947 a Commu-nist government was established in the area occupied by the Russians, to the North of the 38th parallel, in 1948 the Republic of South Korea also came into existence, and both governments claimed the right to rule the whole country. The Russian and American occupation forces were both withdrawn during 1949, and then on 25 June 1950 the North Korean army invaded the South and within a month nearly completed the conquest of the whole country. But President Truman of the U.S.A. acted swiftly. He put General MacArthur, who was then controlling

Japan, in charge of the operation, and poured American troops from Japan into Korea. But the North Korean troops continued to advance, and by August the United Nations forces had almost been driven into the sea. They were holding an area in the South-Eastern tip of Korea which came to be known as the Pusan box and was only about seventy miles square.

Then in September MacArthur launched an amphibious attack by the 10th Corps half-way up the West coast and took Seoul. This force and 8th Army in the Pusan box trapped the North Korean army between them. It fell apart. By the end of October 135,000 North Korean prisoners had been taken—more than the total size of the North Korean army at the beginning of the war.

The success of this operation resulted in the passing of a United Nations resolution calling for the unification of all Korea. The United Nations forces, which included troops from sixteen nations, swept across the 38th parallel and North towards the Yalu River, the border with China. And late in October the 10th Corps made another amphibious landing—this time on the East coast of North Korea.

But as the United Nations forces advanced North they over-extended their lines of communication, and they were advancing on such a broad front that the 10th Corps in the North-East lost contact with the main army. Then the bitter November winds, for which they were quite unprepared, struck the United Nations troops and lowered both their efficiency and their morale.

Meanwhile 150,000 Chinese 'volunteers' had crossed the Yalu. Late in November they suddenly struck at the U.N. centre and tore such a hole in it that the troops on the flanks had to withdraw rapidly to avoid complete defeat. Soon it looked as if the Chinese were going to advance South through Korea as rapidly as the U.N. forces had advanced North, and in December the Chinese rejected a United Nations cease-fire proposal.

In the early months of 1951 the U.N. forces laboriously fought their way back to the 38th parallel. MacArthur came to the conclusion that the war could only be won by bombing of bases and lines of communication inside China, and he wrote a letter on these lines to the leader of the Republican minority in the American House of Representatives. The letter was read out. President Truman, who was not going to have political decisions dictated to him by the commander in the field, dismissed MacArthur on 11 April 1951 and appointed General Ridgway, the commander of the 8th Army, in his place.

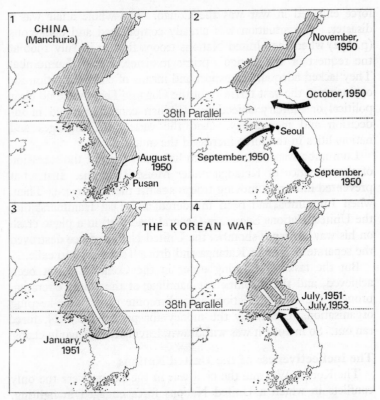

For the next few weeks fighting flowed backwards and forwards across the 38th parallel, and in July 1951, when the war had lasted just over a year, negotiations for peace began. The negotiations and the fighting dragged on for two years, and when a truce was eventually signed in July 1953 it was accepted that North and South Korea should at least temporarily remain separate, with the boundary along the line where the fighting finished.

The Korean War seemed to illustrate the political wisdom of the principle which the events of the thirties had taught so effectively: one should draw a clear line and attack any enemy who crosses it. The United Nations applied the principle when the North Koreans crossed the 38th parallel in June 1950. The Chinese applied it when the United Nations crossed the same line in October. And in the end, three years and five million casualties later, the boundary was much where it had been at the start.

The Congo

The only country other than Korea where a United Nations

force engaged in war was the Congo. The whole affair was a disaster. The situation was already complicated and dangerous (p. 272) when the United Nations troops flew in in July 1960 at the request of the Congo's prime minister, Patrice Lumumba. They lacked adequate transport and means of communication for operating in the vast territory of the Congo. There were no clear political or military objectives. Civilian control resulted in indecision and inefficiency. And the variety of languages and nationalities in the force increased the muddle.

Lumumba wanted the force to help him prevent the secession of the province of Katanga under Moise Tshombe. Instead it prevented him from moving troops against the Katangese. Then, when Lumumba had been murdered and Dag Hammarskjöld, the United Nations Secretary-General, had died in a plane crash on his way to visit Tshombe, the United Nations force destroyed the separate regime in Katanga and drove Tshombe into exile.

But the task of restoring order in the Congo had not been achieved, and the incompetent handling of the whole operation brought the United Nations into disrepute as a peace-keeping organisation. Eventually the money for paying the U.N. force ran out. So in 1964 it was withdrawn, leaving the Congo in chaos.

The ineffectiveness of the United Nations

The Korean War and the civil war in the Congo were the only conflicts in which a United Nations force engaged in fighting. But there were many other conflicts in the world. China, for example, seized Tibet in 1950 and invaded North-East India in 1962. The U.S.S.R. invaded Hungary in 1956 and Czechoslovakia in 1968. And India and Pakistan fought each other both in 1965 and 1971. In none of these nor the many other conflicts of these years was U.N.O. able to do anything.

Nor could U.N.O. do anything when nations flouted specific resolutions. India avoided having a plebiscite in Kashmir. Egypt refused to allow Israeli ships through the Suez Canal. And South Africa refused to accept United Nations authority in South-West Africa.

The main reason for this ineffectiveness of U.N.O. was its lack of armed force. And that in turn was partly due to lack of money. Her only income was subscriptions from members, and she had no way of collecting income from members who defaulted. The U.S.S.R. and all the other Communist countries, France, Belgium, and South Africa all refused to pay their contributions towards the

Congo operation, and there was nothing the United Nations could do about it.

Peace-keeping forces

All the same the United Nations did raise a number of peace-keeping forces for specific purposes.

Kashmir: The first of these was a small force which was stationed along the cease-fire line in Kashmir after the Indians and Pakistanis stopped shooting in January 1949. It achieved little. It could do nothing to implement the United Nations policy of settling the future of Kashmir by a plebiscite, and in the event it could do nothing to prevent another Indo-Pakistan War in 1965 and yet another in 1971.

Sinai: Near the end of the Suez crisis in 1956 (p. 348) another United Nations force was formed. It started as a temporary means of keeping the peace between the Egyptians and the Israelis. But it remained in Sinai for more than ten years. Strangely enough it was withdrawn in the summer of 1967 when President Nasser of Egypt decided to attack Israel (p. 349). He demanded that it should go, and it promptly went—apparently so as not to impede the outbreak of another war.

Cyprus: Yet another U.N. force was formed in March 1964 to separate the hostile Greeks and Turks in Cyprus. It seemed to have some success in calming the situation down, and this was all a U.N. force could be expected to do. The main reason the U.N. peace-keeping forces in Kashmir and Sinai had failed was that the opposing nations had failed to take advantage of the opportunity provided by temporary peace for them to reach a just and lasting settlement. And if the Greeks and Turks in Cyprus ever wanted to start killing each other again, the U.N. was scarcely going to be able to prevent them.

No-one expected more of the United Nations than this. Its function was to provide opportunities for nations to express their views, discuss international problems, and learn to co-operate peacefully with one another. It was the task of the great powers to maintain peace. But even the great powers could not do that. They could not prevent the Six-Days War of 1967 (p. 349) or the Indo-Pakistan War of 1971 (p. 339) any more than the United Nations could. Nations which wanted peace had to continue seeking it by diplomacy and by following the ancient principles that he who wants peace should prepare for war.

THE approaching end of the second World War raised in an acute form what may be called the German Question—the question of what to do about Germany. The American Secretary of the Treasury, Henry Morgenthau Jnr., put forward a plan for destroying Germany as an industrial state: she was to be stripped of her movable machinery, and her towns and factories were to be ploughed into the ground. In September 1944 Roosevelt and Churchill agreed to this.

But it was entirely impractical to expect an agricultural economy to support Germany's vast population. So the Morgenthau Plan was soon dropped. Instead the allied leaders, Roosevelt, Churchill, and Stalin, agreed when they met at Yalta in the Crimea in February 1945 to establish a united 'democratic' post-war Germany, in which Nazis would be purged away and war criminals tried and punished, and which would be divided temporarily into zones of occupation.

The post-war settlement

The details of the settlement were left till the Potsdam Conference in June and July 1945, after Germany's surrender, when Stalin negotiated with the new leaders of the U.S.A. and Great Britain—Truman and Attlee.

One of the most important issues at Potsdam was the future of the Eastern areas of Germany. Stalin insisted that the Northern part of East Prussia should be taken over by the U.S.S.R., and he wanted the rest of the area East of the rivers Oder and Neisse to be incorporated in Poland. In practice he was moving Poland Westwards. The U.S.S.R. had annexed a large part of the East of Poland and the Poles were to be compensated in the West with a large part of Germany.

Truman and Attlee objected. But the Red Army was actually occupying the area, and nothing could be done without fighting the Russians. So they accepted that the lands East of the Oder–Neisse line should be administered by Poland until a final decision should be reached in a German peace treaty. In the event this area became an integral part of Poland, and five million Germans were forcibly expelled. The Western allies and the Germans remained dissatisfied with this situation, and the question of the lands to the East of the Oder–Neisse line formed an obstacle in the way of a German peace treaty.

The rest of Germany was divided into four occupation zones,

administered by the Americans, Russians, British, and French, with Berlin, which was in the middle of the Russian zone, also divided into four sectors. The occupation was intended as a temporary arrangement until Germany should become a sovereign state again after signing a peace treaty. The Allies agreed that democratic institutions should be established, and that Germany should be treated as one economic unit. They set up a joint Allied Control Council to supervise the military administration of Germany.

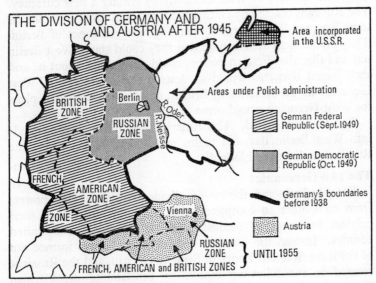

THE DIVISION OF GERMANY AND AND AUSTRIA AFTER 1945

Area incorporated in the U.S.S.R.

Areas under Polish administration

BRITISH ZONE   Berlin

RUSSIAN ZONE

R. Oder   R. Neisse

German Federal Republic (Sept. 1949)

German Democratic Republic (Oct. 1949)

FRENCH ZONE

AMERICAN ZONE

Vienna

Germany's boundaries before 1938

Austria

RUSSIAN ZONE   } UNTIL 1955

FRENCH, AMERICAN and BRITISH ZONES

The allies drift apart

But the members of the Allied Control Council found it impossible to act together. There was a fundamental disagreement over what was meant by 'democratic institutions'. The Russians did not mean the same as the Western powers by 'democracy' and refused to accept the Western demand for free elections. There was an equally fundamental disagreement over economic policy. The Russians wanted to extract heavy reparations from Germany and keep Germany weak, while the Americans and the British, now they had put the Morgenthau Plan behind them, were concerned with German reconstruction. In the event American aid poured into Germany from one side and out the other side as reparations to the Russians, who now ran their zone separately.

In May 1946 the Americans declared that no more reparations would be sent East from the Western zones unless the Russians would co-operate. But this had no effect. The division between the Russian zone and the other three became rigid, and at last in March 1948 the Russian representative on the Allied Control Council walked out.

The Berlin Blockade

This brought matters to a head. The Western powers decided to go ahead with plans for reconstruction in the three Western zones, and in June 1948 they took an important step towards the economic recovery of West Germany by issuing a new currency. The Russians reacted by cutting road, rail, and canal communications between West Germany and the Western zones of Berlin. They intended to demonstrate that they could starve West Berlin out and that the Western powers could do nothing about it; and they hoped that this would so destroy the confidence of West Germans in the Americans, British, and French that their plans for West Germany would come to nothing.

The Russians failed. The Americans and British flew goods into West Berlin day and night, and at last in May 1949 the Russians ended their blockade.

The two Germanies

The blockade and the air-lift divided the occupying powers from each other so completely that they now abandoned their original intention of reconstructing Germany as one united country. Instead the German Federal Republic was formed out of the three Western Zones in September 1949, and the Russians reacted in the following month by proclaiming the German Democratic Republic in their zone. Thus there came into existence one country of West Germany, with a population of over fifty million, plus another two million West Berliners, and the far smaller country of East Germany with a population of only about seventeen million. But the mass of Germans would not accept that this division should be permanent, and one declared aim of West German foreign policy through the fifties and sixties was the reunification of Germany.

The problem of reunification

The main obstacle to reunification was perhaps a military one. One effect of the prolonged crisis over Berlin had been to provoke in West Europe fear of Russian aggression, and in April 1949 most of the countries of Western Europe had joined with the U.S.A. and Canada in the North Atlantic Treaty Organization. The Russians feared that the reunification of Germany would enable

N.A.T.O. to advance up to the Oder–Neisse line. So they demanded the demilitarisation of Germany as an essential condition of reunification. The Western allies, on the other hand, feared that demilitarisation would leave West Germany open to Russian invasion and instead demanded that a united Germany should be free to decide its own military policy.

The Germans themselves scarcely helped. The West German government continued to claim that the land East of the Oder–Neisse line was still part of Germany. And in 1952, when the Russians proposed that Germany should be united, with its own army, but committed to neutrality, the Communist government of East Germany refused to allow a United Nations committee in to establish conditions for free elections.

All this made the prospect of reunification very unlikely. But few people other than the Germans were sorry. Most Englishmen and Frenchmen, with their memories of two World wars, probably agreed with the Russians in not wanting to see a united and powerful Germany in the middle of Europe.

West Germany

Meanwhile economic developments were tying West Germany ever more closely to the West. The German *Wirtschaftswunder*, or 'economic miracle', began in 1948 with the influx of American Marshall Aid (pp. 284–5), the establishment of the new currency, and the appointment of Dr. Erhard to preside over economic affairs in the three Western zones. By 1950 production was back to the 1938 level, over the next twenty years West German industrial production multiplied more than four times, and West Germany became one of the leading members of the thriving European Economic Community (pp. 433–6).

The German Chancellor through most of this time was the Christian Democrat leader, Konrad Adenauer, who seemed to have three main aims in his foreign policy:

(i) to establish the sovereignty of West Germany,
(ii) to establish friendly relations with the nations of Western Europe, and especially France,
(iii) to achieve the re-unification of Germany.

He achieved the first of these aims in 1954 when it was agreed that the occupation of West Germany should end and that West Germany should join N.A.T.O. His success in achieving the second aim is indicated by the creation of the European Economic Community in 1957 and by the signing in 1963 of a Franco-German treaty of friendship and co-operation. But the inevitable price of these successes was failure to achieve reunification. The closer West Germany came to Western Europe, the more she was cut off from East Germany.

East Germany

While West Germany flourished East Germany faced serious political and economic difficulties. The Communist government was unpopular, and the East Germans voted against Communism with their feet. In the sixteen years after the war they crossed the border at an average rate of over five hundred a day—a total of over three million persons. Many of those who left were young adults, and their mass exodus had a serious effect on the East German economy. This produced a tightening of security on the border in 1952. But the refugees now fled West through Berlin, where there was no obstacle to crossing between the sectors.

In 1961 the government decided it could no longer tolerate this drain on its labour force, and in August it built a wall enclosing West Berlin. The Berlin Wall was not there to keep anyone out of East Germany. It was there to keep the East Germans in, and it stood as a permanent reminder that the democracy of East Germany was suspiciously close to what West Europeans would call slavery. It was also a symbol of the division of Germany, and after it was built it became increasingly difficult for anyone to believe that reunification could happen in the forseeable future.

Brandt's *Ostpolitik*

Even Germans came to accept the division as permanent. And in 1969 Willy Brandt, the leader of the Social Democrats, who believed in a new Eastern policy, or *Ostpolitik*, of establishing better relations with the Communist countries of Eastern Europe, took office as Chancellor. In August 1970 a non-aggression treaty was signed between West Germany and the U.S.S.R., and Brandt went on to reach an agreement with Poland by which West Germany recognised the Oder–Neisse line as Poland's Western frontier.

In theory the German question remained unsolved. The war-time allies were still unable to agree on a peace treaty, and the occupation of West Berlin continued as the only practical way of preventing its annexation by the East. But in practice the area East of the Oder–Neisse line was no longer in question, and the existence of two separate Germanies was generally accepted. Even the extraordinary situation in Berlin had now gone on for so long that it no longer seemed a potential flashpoint for a third World war.

The legacy of Stalin

WHEN Stalin died in March 1953 he left behind him a constitutional system through which he had operated perhaps the most thorough and effective dictatorship the world had ever known. Theoretically power in the U.S.S.R. was in the hands of the *soviets*, or committees, which existed even at village level. In fact it was in the hands of a small disciplined body of Communists led by Stalin, who controlled the only political party in the country and also the government, which acted as a form of civil service, carrying out the orders of the party. Opinions and pressure could filter up through the party apparatus. But power was at the top, and Stalin could always switch off any influences from below which he disliked. His successors were faced with the double problem of how far the party ought to control or be controlled by its leader, and how far freedom of expression could be allowed to those who disagreed with the government.

Stalin also left behind him a centralised economy in which production of consumer goods had increased only one and a half times since 1940 and agricultural production scarcely at all, while production of capital goods had increased two and a half times. Stalin's successors were faced with the problems of how far they should develop industry rather than agriculture, and how far they should continue to insist on the production of capital goods rather than consumer goods.

The long-term aim of Stalin's foreign policy had been the extension of revolutionary Socialism through the World. His successors were faced with the problems of how to conduct their relations with capitalist societies at a time when military conflict seemed likely to produce nuclear catastrophe, and at the same time how to maintain their influence and even control over Socialist revolutionary movements throughout the world if they took a less tough line towards capitalist societies.

'Collective leadership'

At first the government of Russia after Stalin was through a five-man 'collective leadership' in which Malenkov, who had been General Secretary of the Communist Party, became Prime Minister. The others were Molotov, in charge of foreign affairs, Bulganin, in control of the armed forces, Beria, the chief of the security police, and Khrushchev, who took over from Malenkov as General Secretary of the Communist Party.

An immediate relaxation of the Stalinist terror was, rather surprisingly, advocated by Beria, and this resulted in greater freedom for writers in Russia and better treatment of the satellite countries. This 'thaw' had the effect of letting loose resentments, and in June workers rose in revolt in East Berlin and numerous other towns of East Germany. The risings were put down by military force, and then Malenkov, Molotov, Bulganin, and Khrushchev turned on Beria, who was dangerous to them partly because of the popularity he hoped to get from a relaxation of the terror and partly because of his control of the secret police. Later in June he disappeared, and in December 1953 his execution was publicly announced.

'The Anti-Party Group'

By this time it was clear that a struggle for power was going on in the Russian 'collective leadership', and it seemed that the dominant figure was the prime minister, Malenkov, who extended the policy of the 'thaw' to economic affairs and began to divert resources to the production of consumer goods. But the Secretary of the Party, Khrushchev, disagreed with him over this. Khrushchev thought that agricultural expansion should come first, and he wanted capital goods, in the form of agricultural machinery. to achieve this. So in December 1954 he attacked Malenkov's economic policies in *Pravda*, the party newspaper.

Bulganin, who controlled the army, agreed with Khrushchev, He wanted to restore the emphasis on heavy industry and war materials. This combination of the party and the army proved decisive. In February 1955 Malenkov was forced to resign and accept the post of Minister of Electric Power Stations, Bulganin succeeded him as Prime Minister, Marshal Zhukov, Russia's most distinguished general of the second World War, became Minister of Defence, and economic emphasis was shifted back to heavy industry.

Khrushchev also disagreed with Molotov. In May 1955 he headed a delegation to Jugoslavia and publicly acknowledged the right of Socialist states to follow their own paths to Socialism. Molotov, who opposed this change of policy, confessed in October that he was mistaken.

But early in 1957 Molotov combined with Malenkov to attack the plans which Khrushchev introduced for the decentralisation of economic administration. Khrushchev was able to rely both on the Central Committee of the Party and on Bulganin and Zhukov against them. So Malenkov and Molotov and their fellow members of what was called 'the Anti-Party Group' were expelled from the top leadership.

The establishment of Khrushchev

The final stages in the rise of Khrushchev came a few months later when he used his dominance in the party to have Zhukov dismissed in October 1957 and to take over from Bulganin as prime minister in March 1958. Like Stalin Khrushchev had risen by controlling the party machine. Using the party as his base of power he had defeated first Beria, whose power depended on control of the security forces, then men like Malenkov and Molotov who controlled the apparatus of government, and finally Bulganin and Zhukov, whose power and influence rested on the armed forces.

But Khrushchev was a very different man from Stalin. In February 1956, in the middle of his rise to supreme power, he had attacked Stalin and Stalinism in a secret session of the Twentieth Congress of the Communist Party. He rejected both the idea of the tyranny of an individual and also the subordination of the Communist Party to its Secretary. Thus the rise of Khrushchev involved the rise of the party to a prominence it had never had under Stalin, and Khrushchev's continuation in power was to depend not, like Stalin's, primarily on a rule of terror, but rather on his retaining the confidence of the Central Committee of the party.

De-Stalinisation

Khrushchev's denunciation of Stalinism and 'the cult of personality' had a dramatic impact both inside and outside Russia when it leaked out. But it was essentially an attack on Stalin's personal failings rather than on the system in which Stalinist tyranny was possible. Khrushchev called for more influence by the party, not less. And the difference between his rule and Stalin's was essentially that he tried to operate the system in a less tyrannical fashion. In October 1956 control of labour camps was taken out of the hands of the security services and transferred to the Ministry of the Interior. And by May 1957 two-thirds of the labour camps in Siberia had been dissolved.

All the same Russia remained a country in which any political opposition was a crime, with the law deliberately left vague so that it was always possible to condemn anyone who incurred the disfavour of the authorities. And Russia continued to control the East European countries by force. It was Khrushchev who suppressed the Hungarian rising in 1956 (pp. 423-4).

Decentralisation

Perhaps the most important change in economic policy under Khrushchev was his attempt to get away from the traditional centralisation of economic affairs. The system which had operated throughout the period of Stalin's Five Year Plans involved having one ministry in Moscow responsible for all steel production in the U.S.S.R. and another responsible for all soap production in the U.S.S.R. Khrushchev replaced this with regional economic administrations, each responsible for the affairs of its own area.

He also arranged for more decentralisation of agriculture. Collective farms were allowed more control over their own affairs and were, for example, allowed their own machinery instead of having to depend on Machine Tractor Stations.

Once the production of more agricultural machinery which Khrushchev had demanded in 1954 had been achieved, the 'thaw' was extended to economic affairs. In 1959 a programme of expansion of consumer goods was announced. And in 1960 changes were made in the trading system to help the consumer get what he wanted rather than just what the government had decided to produce.

Peaceful co-existence

The reduction of tyranny and the decentralisation of economic affairs were both important in the internal affairs of Russia. But in the context of world history Khrushchev's greatest achievement was probably his recognition of the strategic revolution produced by nuclear weapons and his consequent fundamental change of official Communist doctrine. At the Twentieth Congress of the Communist Party in 1956, the same congress at which he launched his denunciation of Stalin, Khrushchev formally abandoned Lenin's doctrine of the inevitability of war between Socialist and Capitalist states. He still asserted that the spread of Socialism was inevitable. But he suggested that it might be possible for some countries to achieve it by non-violent parliamentary means rather than by violent revolution. And in the meantime he wanted 'peaceful co-existence' with the Capitalist world rather than a nuclear holocaust.

This resulted in better relations between the U.S.S.R. and the non-Communist world, and in worse relations between the U.S.S.R. and China, where the pure Leninist dogma was still accepted. The Chinese leaders denounced Khrushchev as a 'revisionist', and in 1960 he described them as 'madmen' determined on nuclear war.

The fall of Khrushchev

The Sino-Soviet quarrel affected the whole Communist world, and by 1964 Khrushchev seemed determined to make the split formal and insist that the Communist parties of the world should choose between Russia and China. Some of his colleagues were worried that by pushing the quarrel with China too far Russia would lose control of the world Communist movement.

Meanwhile his influence with Russia's military leaders, which had been weakened by the Cuban crisis of 1962 (p. 420), had been further weakened by his acceptance of the Partial Test Ban Treaty in 1963. The men in charge of agriculture were worried by the consequences of his policies. His schemes for the development of agriculture had not been entirely successful, and grain had to be imported, even from the U.S.A. The men in charge of industry were worried too. Some decentralisation of the economy had been needed. But it was taking the U.S.S.R. a long while to adjust to anything other than massive centralised Five Year Plans. Flexible planning was also needed. But Khrushchev seemed to be switching backwards and forwards between concentration on capital goods and consumer goods.

Besides all this his cheerful, earthy, roly-poly peasant personality, which gave him some popularity outside the U.S.S.R., did not seem sufficiently impressive inside Russia. A more sober, solid figure, it was felt, would be better suited to Russia's prominent position in the world. But more important was the feeling among his colleagues that he was becoming intolerably inconsistent and unpredictable. There was no way of knowing what he would do next, whether over industry, agriculture, defence, or even over China. New ideas and new policies had been needed to cope with the problems facing Russia after the death of Stalin, and Khrushchev had provided them. But by October 1964 he had lost the confidence of the Central Committee of the party. So he fell from power, asking to be allowed to retire because of 'advanced age and deterioration of health'.

His fall indicates his success in making the party more influential in Russian political life. Stalin had ignored the Central Committee. Khrushchev revived it, dominated it for a decade, and then was brought down by it. His retirement indicates his success in achieving some liberalisation of Russian political life. Stalin had ruled through the Security Police. Khrushchev ruled through the party, and after his fall he lived peacefully in Moscow until his death in 1971.

As the Red Army drove the German armies back through Eastern Europe during 1944 it drove out the influence of the Nazi government of Germany and brought in the influence of the Communist government of Russia. Over the next few years Communist governments which would obey Stalin's wishes were established in Poland, Roumania, Bulgaria, Hungary, Czechoslovakia, and, finally, in the Russian occupation zone of Germany. This happened in three main stages.

(1) *The People's Republics:* The political climate in Eastern Europe after the second World War was suited to left-wing revolution, for the propertied classes had on the whole co-operated with the Nazis, and the natural inclination of the peasant masses once the war was over was towards parliamentary government and land reform. So the first stage after liberation by the Red Army saw the establishment of People's Republics ruled by left-wing coalitions, usually with a large measure of popular support. Stalin was prepared to allow this so long as the key ministries, controlling, for example, the police and the army, were in Communist hands, and so long as it remained possible for him to change the government if and when he should think a change desirable.

(2) *Local Communists take over:* During the second stage the local Communists took over, with Russian pressure if necessary. At the end of 1946 Georgi Dimitrov, the Bulgarian Communist leader, returned after many years in the U.S.S.R. to head the Bulgarian government. In 1947 the peasant leaders in Poland and Hungary, Mikołajczyk and Ferenc Nagy, were forced to resign and were replaced by Communists. And at the end of the same year King Michael of Roumania was forced to abdicate when the Communists took complete control. In February 1948 the Czechoslovak Communists, who had been the main party in a coalition government, established one-party rule.

(3) *Russian control:* While this process of transfer of power to the Communist Party was going on throughout Eastern Europe there was formed in September 1947 the Communist Information Bureau, or Cominform, to assist in 'the co-ordination of activities' of Communist parties. In practice it was an organisation for the transmission of Stalin's orders to the governments of Eastern Europe. He insisted on the subordination of the governments of the People's Democracies to himself, and soon decided that many of the local Communist leaders were unreliable. Thus the

third stage in the history of these countries was the destruction of those local Communist leaders on whom Stalin felt he could not rely. In 1949, Gomułka, the First Secretary of the Polish Communist Party, was dismissed, and a Russian general, Marshal Rokossovsky, was brought into the government as Minister of Defence. In the same year a leading Hungarian Communist, Rajk, was hanged. And Dimitrov, the Bulgarian Prime Minister, who had offended Stalin by advocating a federation of East European states, died while on a visit to Russia.

Unrest in Eastern Europe

This purge of local Communist leaders naturally provoked ill-feeling in Eastern Europe. Further ill-feeling was caused in 1949 by the decision to impose the collectivisation of agriculture and by the persecution of the Roman Catholic Church which followed Pope Pius XII's excommunication of all Communists—also in 1949. All this, together with the continued presence of the Red Army, the many restrictions on individual liberty, and the low standard of living, produced a permanent state of unrest in Eastern Europe. The people disliked their Communist governments. The Communist governments disliked Russian control.

Stalin's death in 1953 was followed by a political 'thaw', and the consequent hopes of release from Russian oppression led to a number of risings in East Germany and Czechoslovakia. They were put down by military force, and hopes for independence from Russia faded.

But these hopes revived again as the result of Khrushchev's speech in 1956 attacking Stalinism. In Poland this resulted in the summer in strikes and demonstrations. It also resulted in the rehabilitation of Gomułka, who led the movement for a national approach to Communism free from Russian control, and to the dismissal of Marshal Rokossovsky. The Russian leaders were alarmed, and some of them, including Khrushchev, flew to Warsaw in October to deal with the situation themselves. In the event they accepted an agreement by which the Poles could run their own internal affairs so long as they followed Russia's foreign policy. And on 19 October 1956 Gomułka was re-instated as First Secretary of the Communist Party.

The Hungarian Uprising

Four days later there was a mass demonstration in Budapest, the capital of Hungary. The mood of protest had been growing for months, and some concessions had been made. Imre Nagy, a moderate Communist who had been dismissed both from the premiership and the party in 1955, was re-admitted to the party. The body of Rajk, who had been hanged in 1949, was given a state funeral. The mood of protest had grown even stronger, and a series of public rallies had culminated on 23 October in the great demonstration in Budapest.

It turned into an armed national rebellion against Russian occupation and control. The protestors saw themselves as part of a wide anti-Russian movement. They wanted solidarity with Poland, by which they meant national Communism instead of dictation from Russia. They wanted an end to collectivisation, a policy which had been imposed by the Russians. They wanted the establishment of the rule of law and an end to arbitrary tyranny. In short, they wanted independence from Russia.

At first the Russians seemed to give way, and on 26 October they accepted Imre Nagy as prime minister. Nagy allowed the formation of other political parties and formed a coalition government. There was public freedom of expression never before known in a Communist country. The tide of revolt and of liberty was flowing strongly. And on the 30th the Red Army began to leave.

Understandably the Russian leaders were worried, for if they lost control of Hungary other satellite states would seek their independence also, and eventually they might lose their whole empire. The turning point came on 31 October, the day on which the attention of the World was focused on Suez as the British began bombing Egyptian airfields (p. 348). That day Nagy denounced the Warsaw Pact, the alliance of Communist states which had been formed the previous year, and proclaimed Hungary's neutrality. This was the crucial issue on which the Russian leaders felt they could not give in, and that evening Russian troops began to move back into Hungary.

On 4 November the Russians set up a new government under Janos Kadar, the Secretary of the Hungarian Communist Party, who was prepared to co-operate with them. And on the same day they launched an attack in force on Budapest. The Hungarian freedom fighters were ruthlessly suppressed. Within a few days three thousand of them had been killed and the Red Army was in effective control of all Hungary.

Russian economic imperialism

By the time of the Hungarian uprising of 1956 Russia's control of the East European countries was increasingly being extended to economic as well as political affairs. Stalin had had little interest in the economic development of East Europe. But after Stalin's death in 1953 the new Russian leaders tried to develop an overall economic plan for East Europe. And this meant that they were trying to impose greater economic control over the satellite countries at just the same time as they were easing political control. And this had helped to cause the Hungarian uprising.

The Russian leaders wanted to develop heavy industry in Eastern Europe. Human and material resources were directed into heavy industry, and the development of light industries and agriculture was deliberately held back. Poland, Hungary, and Czechoslovakia, for example, all had to build huge steel-works and make steel from iron-ore brought hundreds of miles by train from Russia. This meant that the production of consumer goods and food suffered, and the standard of living remained low while the Russian military-economic monster was fed with steel.

Centralised planning and centralised party control was an effective means for achieving this. But when the time came to attempt the expansion of light industry and the production of more and better quality consumer goods central planning proved peculiarly ineffective. The mistakes of the central planners, inefficiencies of administration, transport, and marketing led to perpetual shortages and surpluses. Various attempts were made to solve the problem. They all involved the reduction of central control, and this led to trouble in Czechoslovakia.

The rape of Czechoslovakia

In Czechoslovakia the liberalization of economic life was attempted by Alexander Dubcek, who was elected First Secretary of the Czechoslovak Communist Party in January 1968. Dubcek allowed competition between different factories in an industry, proposed to increase trade with the West, and even to raise loans in the U.S.A. and Western Europe in order to re-equip Czechoslovak industry for this trade.

This liberalisation of economic life led on to liberalisation of political life. Dubcek believed in what came to be called 'Socialism with a human face'. He argued that a free press, freedom to travel abroad, and even some electoral freedom, ought to be possible in a Socialist society. And he introduced free elections to positions within the Communist Party instead of nominating all officials from above.

The Russian leaders were worried at what this might lead to. It seemed that Dubcek might soon allow the formation of other political parties, and there was also the danger that Czechoslovakia might decide to withdraw from the Warsaw Pact. But they were also worried by the effect that use of force would have on World opinion and on opinion in the other Communist countries. So they tried to get Dubcek to withdraw his reforms by using diplomatic pressure and threats.

Dubcek refused to be bullied. The support for him inside Czechoslovakia was overwhelming. And in the middle of August it seemed to many people that the Czechoslovaks had won their bid for freedom.

Then on 21 August 1968 400,000 Warsaw Pact troops, of which 300,000 were Russian, suddenly invaded Czechoslovakia. Dubcek and other Communist leaders were taken to Moscow manacled, and an unsuccessful attempt was made to intimidate them. Meanwhile back in Czechoslovakia the Russians tried to form a puppet government. They failed. So in the end they allowed Dubcek to carry on for a while, but kept their troops there to ensure the destruction of Czechoslovakia's new-found freedoms.

The Russians at first justified their invasion by claiming that Czechoslovakia was too weak to defend her Western border, so that the whole Warsaw Pact was in danger from N.A.T.O. Later Brezhnev, the General Secretary of the Russian Communist Party, formulated what came to be known as 'the Brezhnev Doctrine': that Socialist countries have a duty to intervene in others threatened by counter-revolution. Whatever the justification it was clear that the Russians had the military strength to insist on having their own way.

In April 1969 Dubcek was replaced as First Secretary, and in June 1970, after six months as ambassador to Turkey, he was expelled from the Communist Party. Several hundreds of men who had supported him were still in prison. Far more had lost their jobs. And many others had fled abroad.

The hard-line Communists were back in control. And the men of the Party apparatus were re-imposing discipline. The effect on economic affairs was tragic. The country went back to the sort of central planning which had worked so badly before.

And as for political affairs, the lesson seemed obvious. Russia's Communist leaders might tolerate some measure of slow political evolution. The one thing they would not tolerate was anything that smacked of revolution.

De Gaulle and the Free French

IN 1934 a forty-three year old French professional soldier,
Charles de Gaulle, published a book, 'The Army of the Future',
in which he argued that future wars would be won by mobile
armoured forces supported by aircraft and infantry. His superior
officers did not believe him. The Germans did. And in May 1940
their armoured forces smashed into France. On 6 June, as the
armies of the Third Republic collapsed under the German onslaught, de Gaulle was summoned to Paris by the prime minister,
Paul Reynaud, and appointed Under-Secretary of State for War.
He was to be the one really great figure in French history for the
next thirty years.

When Reynaud resigned ten days later and a new government
was formed by Marshal Pétain with the clear intention of surrendering to the Germans, de Gaulle flew to London to form a
Free French force and broadcast to Frenchmen to join him and
carry on the struggle.

At first very few joined him, and he was condemned to death
in his absence by a military court. France was now officially
neutral. Pétain was President, and the government, which moved
South to Vichy, was soon dominated by Pierre Laval who believed
in collaboration with the Germans. But after the German attack
on the U.S.S.R. in 1941, on the anniversary of the fall of France,
a powerful underground resistance movement developed among
the French Left, and support for de Gaulle also grew. In 1944
Free French troops took part in the invasion of Normandy, and
in August de Gaulle entered Paris claiming to be the President of
a republic which had never ceased to exist, and was able to form a
provisional government which included some of the Communist
leaders of the resistance.

Post-war reconstruction

Many Frenchmen felt that de Gaulle had saved France's
honour in 1940. Now he had to build a new France and re-
establish her in the World. First the collaborators were purged.
Thousands were executed, including Laval, and even Pétain was
sentenced to death, though this sentence was commuted to life
imprisonment. Then the government tackled the problem of reconstruction, extending state control over the economy and

planning the rebuilding of roads, railways, bridges, and factories Meanwhile de Gaulle also managed to get France a permanent seat on the Security Council of the United Nations and a share in the occupation of Germany.

But neither abroad nor at home did things go smoothly. Abroad he found it impossible to play an influential part in relations between the U.S.A. and the U.S.S.R. At home his financial policy resulted in rapid inflation and widespread racketeering, and he found it increasingly difficult to work with the Communists in his government. By January 1946 he felt his position was impossible, and quite suddenly he resigned.

The Fourth Republic and Algeria

During 1946 a Fourth Republic was established with a constitution very similar to that of the Third Republic. It proved as difficult as ever to form a stable government, and in the twelve years from 1946 to 1958 France was ruled by twenty-four different coalition governments.

By the mid-1950s the main problems facing French governments arose out of the demand by the Arabs of Algeria for independence. Algeria had been French for over a century, and one tenth of the population was of European descent. It was administered as part of metropolitan France, and it had thirty deputies in the Assembly. But in 1954 a small group of militant Algerians formed the *Front de Liberation Nationale*, or F.L.N., and by the end of 1956 20,000 F.L.N. guerrillas were keeping a French army of 400,000 occupied in Algeria.

The leaders of the French army in Algeria, Generals Salan and Massu, were determined not to let Algeria go. After the military disaster at Dien Bien Phu (p. 340) in 1954 and the Suez fiasco (p. 348) in 1956, this was one war they were not going to lose. So they used torture on a large scale against F.L.N. suspects, defied their orders and bombed a Tunisian village which they believed to be an F.L.N. base, and eventually in May 1958, seized political power in Algeria.

It looked as if they might seize power in France as well. Any day General Massu's *paras* might land near Paris. And in this situation de Gaulle was recalled to office to save France a second time. He had never withdrawn completely from politics. Indeed, in 1947 he had formed a Gaullist Party which had won more votes in the municipal elections than any other party. But then its support had declined until it was merely one more right-wing party and de Gaulle looked like another Boulanger (p. 26) who had missed his chance. In 1958, however, he was the only man with sufficient personal authority to be generally acceptable at a time when civil war seemed imminent. The army leaders in Algeria thought he would save Algeria for France. The politicians thought he would save France from the army. So the Assembly handed him full power for six months.

The Fifth Republic

In the event he disappointed both the generals and the politicians.

By the end of 1960 he had granted independence to almost all of France's African Empire and was preparing to grant independence to Algeria. The army leaders felt betrayed. A secret terrorist organisation, '*l'Organisation de l'Armée Secrète*', or O.A.S., developed with the aim of using violence to keep Algeria French. And in January 1961 there was another army revolt in Algeria led by the commander of the French army, General Salan, who, it later appeared, was also the head of the illegal O.A.S. But this time de Gaulle broadcast to the troops telling them not to obey their rebellious officers. They obeyed him and the revolt collapsed. Early in 1962 Salan was caught and imprisoned. Later in 1962 Algeria became independent.

Meanwhile de Gaulle had brought the Fourth Republic to an end and replaced it with a new system of government in which very considerable power was in the hands of the President, who was elected for a seven year term. And de Gaulle was himself the President of this Fifth Republic.

Now that he was President, and a President with real power, he felt that he again had a chance of restoring France to her rightful place in Europe and the World. 'France cannot be France without greatness' he had written at the beginning of his memoirs. And he had a vision of France at the head of a 'Third Force' in the World separate from the U.S.A. and the U.S.S.R. He kept close links with France's former African colonies and made them large grants of economic aid, and he tried to establish similar links with Latin America. In Europe he established very close relations with Germany and in 1963 reached agreement with Adenauer on a Franco-German treaty of co-operation and friendship.

Above all he wanted to keep Europe European and free from American influence. This explains why he vetoed British entry into the European Common Market in 1962: the British were too closely tied, both economically and strategically, to the U.S.A. De Gaulle's desire for strategic independence led him to refuse to sign the Partial Test Ban Treaty of 1963 (p. 440) and even to withdraw the French forces from N.A.T.O. command in 1966. And he further asserted French independence from the U.S.A. by recognising Communist China in 1965 and attacking American policy in Vietnam, and by going to Moscow in 1966 to try to establish closer relations with the U.S.S.R.

The fall of de Gaulle

By the end of 1966 de Gaulle's prestige was very high in France. He had solved the Algerian problem. He had given independence to most of France's colonies and kept on good terms with them. He had established close relations with West Germany and had improved relations with the U.S.S.R. He had asserted France's independence from the U.S.A. and had exalted her prestige in the World. Above all he had given France a new stable system of government. And in 1965 the French people elected de Gaulle for another seven-year term as President.

In 1968 things began to go wrong. A widespread student revolt in May was followed by a series of strikes which paralysed the country. Student demonstrations got out of hand, workers took over factories, and there were widespread riots in the streets. De Gaulle dissolved the National Assembly, promised reforms, warned that he would use force to ensure public order, and brought the unrest to an end. To some Frenchmen it seemed that de Gaulle had saved France for a third time: 1940, 1958, and now 1968. And in the election of June 1968 the Gaullists won an overall majority in the National Assembly for the first time.

But the troubles of May had brought France near to chaos and had cost £400 million in gold reserves. In November there was a European currency crisis caused by the weakness of the French franc, and de Gaulle had to borrow heavily and make drastic economies to avoid devaluation.

Unrest continued. In April 1969 de Gaulle, who was now 78 and had been in power for nearly eleven years, put some constitutional changes to the country in a referendum which he announced he would treat as a vote of confidence. He won only 48 per cent of the vote, so he promptly resigned. But his constitution survived him. In June M. Pompidou, who had been de Gaulle's prime minister from 1962 till 1968, won the next Presidential election to become the second President of the Fifth Republic.

AFTER the second World War the dominant powers in Europe were the U.S.A. and the U.S.S.R. The Russians were no longer building 'Socialism in one country'. They were using the Red Army to enforce Socialism throughout Eastern Europe. The Americans were no longer in isolation. Instead the Truman Doctrine of March 1947 committed them to 'support free peoples' against aggression throughout the World.

The military and political threat from the U.S.S.R. drove the nations of Western Europe to seek closer co-operation with each other militarily, politically, and economically. And they were able to stand up to the Russian threat because of the willingness of the U.S.A. to provide military and economic support. During the quarter century after the second World War the nations of Western Europe gradually drew closer. The movement for European unity was encouraged by the U.S.A., and was stimulated by the threat from the U.S.S.R.

The movement for military integration

N.A.T.O.: As the Cold War developed the U.S.S.R. came to be regarded as a possible enemy, and the direct result of the Berlin blockade (p. 414) which began in June 1948, was that in December Great Britain, France, the Benelux countries, the U.S.A., and Canada began negotiations which culminated in April 1949 in the establishment by those countries, together with Norway, Denmark, Iceland, Italy, and Portugal, of the North Atlantic Treaty Organization. The members agreed that 'an armed attack against one or more of them . . . shall be considered an attack against them all.' They also agreed that plans should be co-ordinated and equipment standardised, and that a Supreme Command should be established headed by an American.

E.D.C.: After the outbreak in 1950 of the Korean War, which committed a large part of America's military resources in the Far East, the Americans wanted to strengthen the N.A.T.O. forces in Western Europe by re-arming the West Germans. The French particularly disliked this and suggested an alternative. They proposed the establishment of a European Defence Community, within which there should be a European army under international command, with units of different nationalities intermingled, and all wearing the same uniform. All members other than Germany would also retain other forces of their own. But the British, with heavy military commitments outside Europe, declined to surrender any of their forces to a supra-national authority. And in August 1954 the French, who saw that German forces would form the dominant part of the European army if Britain did not join, backed out.

W.E.U.: Instead Great Britain, France, Germany, Italy, and the Benelux countries agreed at the end of 1954 to commit part of their forces for fifty years to a Western European Union. Britain, for example, agreed to maintain four divisions and a tactical air force on the continent. At the same time the occupation of Germany came officially to an end and the German Federal Republic became a fully sovereign state and joined N.A.T.O.

The movement for political integration

Meanwhile there was a growing recognition that a united Western Europe, with its large population and its great natural resources, might one day be as powerful politically, economically, and militarily as the two super powers. As early as 1946 Winston Churchill had spoken at the University of Zurich of the need for some sort of 'United States of Europe'. A number of other distinguished European statesmen, such as Konrad Adenauer of West Germany, Robert Schuman of France, Alcide de Gasperi of Italy, and Paul-Henri Spaak of Belgium, also spoke in favour of European unity. And in May 1949 fourteen European states agreed to establish a 'Council of Europe'.

This Council of Europe consisted of two bodies: a Committee of Ministers, and a parliament, or Consultative Assembly, which first met at Strasbourg in 1949. But in practice any proposals involving the transfer of aspects of national sovereignty to these supra-national bodies were rejected. Decisions of the Committee of Ministers, which consisted of the Foreign Ministers of all the member countries, were only binding if all members ratified them. And the Consultative Assembly could only talk and make recommendations to the Council of Ministers.

As far as the achievement of European unity was concerned, the Council of Europe was a failure. Political and constitutional discussions could not create unity. European unity, like national unity, depended on emotions. It needed to exist as a widespread emotional reality before there was any point in providing it with a constitutional framework. And the way to create that reality was not by talking but by the practical experience of working together and solving common problems together.

The movement for economic integration

In the economic sphere considerable progress had already been made. In July 1947 an agreement to form a customs union was reached by Belgium, the Netherlands, and Luxembourg, which now came to be known as the Benelux countries, and the success of this Benelux venture encouraged further co-operation. So in May 1950 Robert Schuman, the French Foreign Minister, proposed a 'European Coal and Steel Community' within which there would be no tariffs on coal and steel. Although Britain refused to join, France, Italy, West Germany, and the Benelux countries accepted the Schuman Plan and in 1951 signed an agreement by which E.C.S.C. gradually came into existence over five years.

The establishment of a supra-national authority controlling the coal and steel industries of West Europe was clearly an effective answer to the problem of freeing those industries from the restrictions imposed by tariff barriers. It was also an answer to the political problem of how to prevent the development of Germany yet again as an aggressive power with military strength based on a flourishing steel industry. And it had political as well as economic consequences. It demonstrated that the 'Six' could put their joint interests before their particular interests, and it demonstrated that a supra-national solution could work.

The leaders of the 'Six' decided to create a customs union which would lead on to political union, and with this in mind they signed the Treaty of Rome in March 1957. The intention was that tariffs between member states should be reduced over a period of twelve years, so that by 1970 there would be no tariff barriers restricting trade between members, but there would be a common tariff against the rest of the world. At the same time they pooled their nuclear resources in Euratom.

British insularity

Western Europe was still a long way from unity, and so far the main obstacle to closer integration, whether military, political, or economic, had been Britain. It was the British who had prevented the Council of Europe from becoming a genuinely representative body in 1949 by insisting on the right of each government to decide its own method of selecting its delegation, and then by making the British delegation an all-party group chosen by parliament. Then in 1951 the British declined to put any British forces under a supra-national authority in the E.D.C., and in the same year declined to place Britain's coal and steel industries under the supra-national authority of the E.C.S.C.

The main reason for this was that the British were unwilling to forgo any part of their national sovereignty. England's geographical position, cut off from the continent by water, had kept the English safe from invasion for nearly a thousand years, and had encouraged insularity and self-confident nationalism. The second World War had brought the humiliation of defeat and military occupation to all of the 'Six'. This had delivered a blow to nationalist attitudes and encouraged them to accept some abandonment of national sovereignty. But the English had neither been defeated nor occupied. They could and did look back on both their recent and their more distant History with pride. And most Englishmen felt that England neither was nor wanted to be a part of Europe.

In 1956 the British suggested an alternative to the proposed European Economic Community: a free trade area with no common external tariffs and no reduction of national sovereignty. This was unacceptable to the 'Six', who went ahead with forming the E.E.C. But the British also went ahead with their proposal, and together with Denmark, Sweden, Norway, Austria, Switzerland, and Portugal set up a European Free Trade Area, or E.F.T.A.

E.F.T.A. was not a move in the direction of European unity. On the contrary, it was an attempt to get some of the economic benefits of unity while maintaining national sovereignty. And it was still possible that the European movement might founder against the rock of British insularity. It was also possible that the European movement would develop without the British, who might be left uncomfortably isolated.

The European Community

In practice the European Economic Community drew the 'Six' even closer together. There was a common agricultural policy, with one price structure throughout the 'Six'. There was free movement of labour and of capital, so that a man from one E.E.C. country could go freely to another with his savings, buy a house, and get a job there. The close integration of the Six made it necessary to develop common policies on, for example, social welfare and transport, and even to attempt to establish common standards in the professions so that a doctor or surveyor could move from one country to another. Dealings on matters of tariffs with countries other than the 'Six' were conducted jointly. Investment, production, and trade increased. The 'Six' prospered.

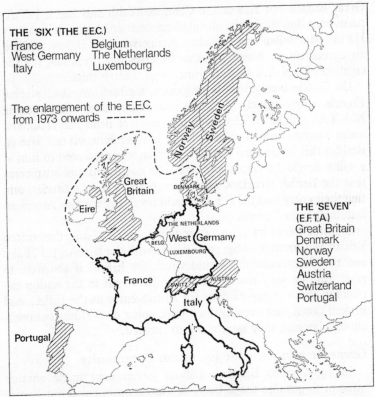

THE 'SIX' (THE E.E.C.)

France   Belgium
West Germany   The Netherlands
Italy   Luxembourg

The enlargement of the E.E.C.
from 1973 onwards – – – – –

Great
Britain

Eire

THE 'SEVEN'
(E.F.T.A.)
Great Britain
Denmark
Norway
Sweden
Austria
Switzerland
Portugal

But two quite different views of the future of Europe emerged:
1. M. Jean Monnet, the founding father of the E.E.C. and the
first President of the High Authority of the E.C.S.C., envisaged a
federal Europe with an elected parliament and its own central
government. He also expected Europe to act as a partner with the
U.S.A. in the Atlantic Alliance.
2. General de Gaulle, on the other hand, who became President
of France in 1958, wanted a *Europe des patries*—a Europe of
strong, independent nation–states which would be bound together by economic interests and would in practice ally under the
leadership of France to form a third force in international affairs
and act independently of the U.S.A.

The exclusion of Great Britain

It was because of this that de Gaulle eventually vetoed British
entry into the E.E.C. In 1961 the British government, led by
Harold Macmillan, applied for entry into the E.E.C. so long as
arrangements could be made to safeguard the interests not only of

Great Britain but also of the Commonwealth and her E.F.T.A. partners. But while the detailed negotiations were in progress Harold Macmillan and President Kennedy of the U.S.A. reached an agreement at Nassau in the Bahamas on proposals for the creation of a N.A.T.O. fleet armed with *Polaris* missiles.

De Gaulle disliked these proposals, for they involved placing French ships under N.A.T.O. command and strengthening N.A.T.O. just when he wanted to break free from N.A.T.O. and make Europe into a World force independent of the U.S.A. Besides this he disliked the way the plan was presented to him as a joint Anglo-American proposal. It confirmed his suspicions that the British were not really European in their attitudes, and that their entry into the E.E.C. would result in excessive American interference in Europe.

So three weeks later, on 14 January 1963, de Gaulle denounced Britain as a country whose special links with the U.S.A., E.F.T.A., and the Commonwealth would wreck the E.E.C. if she were to join. And on 30 January Macmillan broadcast to the nation explaining that the negotiations for British entry to the E.E.C. had broken down 'not because they were going to fail, but curiously enough because they were going to succeed.'

Great Britain joins the European Community

In 1967, when Britain's Labour government made another attempt to get into the E.E.C., de Gaulle again ruled out British entry. He wanted a 'European' Europe dominated by France, while Britain seemed to offer the prospect of an 'Atlantic' Europe dominated by Britain and the U.S.A. What is more, the E.E.C. had now had ten years of vigorous economic growth, and Britain was in serious economic difficulty.

But in April 1969 de Gaulle resigned, and six months later the 'Six' agreed to re-open negotiations with four applicants for membership of the E.E.C.: Britain, Eire, Denmark, and Norway. The talks began in June 1970, the month in which a Conservative government took over in England, and a year's negotiating culminated in agreement in principle on British entry.

The British were themselves still very much divided on the issue, and both the main political parties were split over it. But in October 1971 the Conservative government got a majority of 112 in favour of entry, and at 11.00 p.m. on the last day of 1972 Great Britain ended her centuries-old isolationism and, together with Eire and Denmark, became an integral part of Europe.

IN the quarter of a century after the second World War the U.S.A. and the U.S.S.R. were in an overwhelming dominant position in relation to the rest of the world. Their relations with each other and other nations were strongly affected by the existence of nuclear weapons. And the strategic situation was perpetually being changed by developments in nuclear weaponry.

American monopoly, 1945-49

In the years immediately after the war the U.S.A. rapidly reduced her conventional forces. In the first year they were cut from 12,000,000 to 3,000,000, and then in the next year they were nearly halved. The U.S.S.R., on the other hand, still maintained a vast army in Eastern Europe. In 1948-49 at the time of the Berlin blockade (p. 414) she still had 4,500,000 men in arms— more than sufficient to defeat the conventional forces of the U.S.A. and her allies in Western Europe.

But the U.S.A. was known to have the monopoly of the atom bomb, and in 1945 she had used it. She also had air bases in Europe and the Middle and Far East. There was no balance of power in the world, but the threat of the atom bomb deterred further Russian expansion.

Proliferation, 1949-53

The next stage involved the spread of atom bombs and the building of bigger ones. The Russians exploded an atomic device in 1949, and the British exploded one in 1952. It was also in 1952 that the U.S.A. produced a far more powerful weapon. Up till now atom bombs had worked by splitting the uranium atom— i.e. by nuclear fission. Now the U.S.A. exploded a device which worked by nuclear fusion, the fusing together of hydrogen nuclei, and had far more destructive power. And in 1953 the Russians followed suit.

To many West Europeans this explosion of a hydrogen device by the Russians in 1953, the era of 'brinkmanship' (pp. 399-400), was comforting rather than frightening. Russia's possession of a hydrogen bomb, they felt, ought to deter the Americans from going over the brink.

Bombers and stability, 1954-57

The effectiveness of the Russian deterrent depended on having bombers capable of delivering nuclear bombs as far as the U.S.A. The Americans had long had a strategic nuclear bomber force.

By 1954 the Russians had one too.

Meanwhile, partly because of the cost of maintaining conventional forces while developing nuclear ones, and partly as the result of the end of the Korean War, both the U.S.A. and the U.S.S.R. began reducing their conventional forces. So the maintenance of peace was increasingly coming to depend on the fear that each side had of the other's nuclear-armed bombers. There had developed a balance of terror.

Missiles and instability, 1957-61

The era of strategic balance based on nuclear-armed bomber forces did not last long. It was upset because both sides were developing rockets, or ballistic missiles, armed with nuclear warheads. In October 1957 the Russians demonstrated the power of their rocketry by putting an artificial satellite, Sputnik I, into orbit in space around the Earth. Three months later in January 1958, the U.S.A. also launched a satellite, Explorer I. And by this time both could launch ballistic missiles with a range of 5,000 miles—i.e. more than the distance from Moscow to New York.

The speed of these ballistic missiles made them impossible to destroy in flight. So a peculiarly dangerous situation was created. The advantage in a nuclear war would be with the power that got in the first shots and destroyed the other side's missiles before they could be launched. This made it far more likely that a war would be started by one side in order to forestall an attack by the other. It also meant that it was essential to hit back immediately in order to avoid being totally disarmed. And this in turn increased the danger of accidental war—of launching a retaliatory nuclear attack in response to a false alarm.

Thus the strategic situation in the early years of ballistic missiles was frighteningly dangerous. Fortunately the leaders of the great powers understood the danger, and this was why Khrushchev as early as 1956 abandoned the Leninist doctrine of the inevitability of war in favour of 'peaceful co-existence'.

The incredibility of the nuclear threat, 1961

In 1961 the situation changed again. Both the U.S.A. and the U.S.S.R. 'hardened' their launching sites: they installed their missiles in deep concrete emplacements so that even a direct attack was unlikely to destroy completely their capacity for hitting back. This would allow them to react less hastily in a crisis. It was no longer essential to get in the first blow. Nor was it necessary to retaliate before making absolutely sure that there was something to retaliate against. So nuclear war seemed less likely.

Meanwhile the destructive power of nuclear weapons was increasing, and this also made nuclear war seem less likely. In 1961, when Russia exploded a nuclear device with an explosive power nearly three thousand times as great as the bomb dropped on Hiroshima, it scarcely seemed credible that either the U.S.A. or the U.S.S.R. would commit national suicide by fighting a war with such weapons.

But the very incredibility of nuclear war created another problem. The U.S.S.R. still had a massive superiority in conventional forces in Europe, and West European governments began to wonder if the American nuclear threat was any longer a deterrent to the U.S.S.R. If it was not, West Europe was very vulnerable.

Credibility, 1962

But the U.S.A. had three great strategic advantages over the U.S.S.R.

(1) She had numerous bases in Western Europe and Turkey from which she could threaten the U.S.S.R. with medium range ballistic missiles, and the U.S.S.R. had no such bases from which she could threaten the U.S.A.

(2) In order to be able to strike effectively at the N.A.T.O. bases in Europe the U.S.S.R. was in 1961 investing a very high proportion of her rocket resources in medium range missiles, while the U.S.A. was building up a substantial lead in long range intercontinental ballistic missiles, or ICBMs.

(3) It was also in 1961 that the U.S.A. began to be able to locate the larger Russian missile sites accurately by reconaissance from space satellites.

In June 1962 Robert Macnamara, the American Defence Secretary, tried to make it clear to America's N.A.T.O. allies that the U.S.A. would resort to nuclear war if necessary, and that she calculated that she could now fight a nuclear war not by indiscriminate destruction but by destruction of Russian nuclear capacity. The U.S.A. now had some two hundred ICBMs and was getting more. The U.S.S.R. had far less, the U.S.A. knew where they were, and they were easier to destroy. If it came to fighting a nuclear war the U.S.A. stood to win. Europe and Russia would suffer terrible destruction. The U.S.A. might well survive.

The Cuban crisis, 1962

The Americans convinced their allies that they were in a dominant strategic position and were prepared to use nuclear weapons. They also convinced the Russians. And the understandable Russian reaction, especially in view of taunts from Peking that they were going soft on capitalism, was to find a way of increasing the number of missiles they had trained directly on the U.S.A.

On 14 October 1962 an American Lockheed U-2 reconnaissance plane flew over Cuba and brought back evidence of Russian missile installations and the presence of *Ilyushin 28* light bombers. On 22 October President Kennedy announced a naval blockade to check the build-up and remove the 'offensive' weapons. And he warned the U.S.S.R. of massive retaliation against her if any Russian missile were fired at a target in the Western hemisphere. Twenty-five Russian ships continued to approach Cuba. But at the last moment they turned away—except for one tanker which was allowed through. Then an agreement was reached between Kennedy and Khrushchev. The U.S.S.R. agreed to withdraw her weapons. The U.S.A. gave an assurance that she would not invade Cuba. And on 21 November the blockade was lifted.

American superiority in ICBMs had helped to produce the Cuban missile crisis. Her superiority in naval power meant that she was able to control events in the waters round Cuba. But the U.S.S.R. could only influence those events by precipitating a nuclear war which would destroy her. So it was sensible of Khrushchev to climb down.

The re-establishment of stability, 1963-68

The two super-powers had possibly come closer to nuclear war than at any other time. And both were anxious to avoid a similar crisis. One consequence of this was that a permanent communications link, the 'hot-line', was established between Moscow and Washington in June 1963. Another was that in August 1963 they signed a Partial Test Ban Treaty agreeing not to test nuclear weapons in the atmosphere.

Over the next few years a position of stability was re-established. By 1968 the U.S.A. and the U.S.S.R. each had more than 750 ICBMs, mostly in strongly 'hardened' positions. They also had heavy bombers armed with nuclear warheads and, even more important, ballistic missile submarines, which were far more difficult to locate. Thus neither side was in a position to wipe out the other's capability. This meant that either side would be able to survive a nuclear attack sufficiently to be able to destroy the other's cities.

So long as this balance of terror lasted there seemed a relatively good chance of avoiding a nuclear war. And it also made for stability in relations between the two super-powers. Neither could interfere in the other's sphere of influence without challenging the other to nuclear war. Thus just as the U.S.S.R. had to climb down in 1962 over the Cuban crisis, so the U.S.A. could not take action over Czechoslovakia (p. 425) in 1968.

Developing dangers

Unfortunately this stability was being upset almost before it was established. In the first place other nations were developing nuclear weapons. After Great Britain in 1952 had come France in 1960 and China in 1964. In the second place the U.S.A. and the U.S.S.R. were now developing Anti-Ballistic Missiles, or ABMs, to shoot down in-coming missiles. Both of these developments were dangerous. The danger of the proliferation of nuclear weapons is obvious. The danger of ABMs is that a really effective ABM system would put a nuclear power in the position of being able to attack without fear of retaliation.

Some limitation was placed on both these developments in 1968. It was in that year that the Eighteen Nation Disarmament Conference produced a Treaty on the Non-Proliferation of Nuclear Weapons. And it was also in 1968 that the U.S.A. and the U.S.S.R. indicated that they were willing to discuss restraint in developing ABM defences. Although the Russians had begun building ABM defences in 1966, and the Americans had begun to construct the *Sentinel* ABM system in 1967, the cost of developing them had fortunately proved to be too vast.

But the dangers remained. Relatively few potential nuclear powers had signed the non-proliferation treaty, and there was no easy way of enforcing it. So an irresponsible government in any country which built nuclear weapons might plunge the world into nuclear conflict. It was also quite possible that either the U.S.A. or the U.S.S.R. would one day feel able to spend its resources on an effective ABM system or some other even more sophisticated nuclear development which would upset the delicate balance of terror.

For a quarter of a century a nuclear balance of terror had in one way or another managed to prevent a nuclear war. It might continue to do so for another hundred years. But it was difficult to feel confident that it would continue to keep the peace for five hundred or a thousand years.

90   EPILOGUE—1971

A LL history is a story of conflict between human beings, for human beings naturally tend to live in communities and are also self-centred. These two aspects of human nature create tensions since the satisfactory running of any community involves some limitation of the interests of each individual. Similarly the peaceful and contented co-existence of groups of human beings, whether families or nations, involves some limitation of the interests of each group.

The struggle for power

The century from 1871 to 1971 saw a particularly violent power struggle between groups of human beings who failed to accommodate their own interests to the interests of others. Ideological issues and issues of principles were frequently involved. Men fought for Liberty and for Social Justice as well as to extend or defend the power of their own group. But power was the central feature of the struggle and ideological issues were usually subordinate to the issue of power. In the late nineteenth century, when the main ideological division among European nations was between liberal democracy and authoritarian monarchy, the French Third Republic was allied with Tsarist Russia. In 1939 Nazi Germany and Communist Russia, which for years had publicly condemned each other's political ideology, found it convenient to reach an agreement for dividing Eastern Europe between them. In 1941, after the German attack on the U.S.S.R., the liberal democracy of Great Britain was allied with Communist Russia because both were threatened by the strength of Nazi Germany. And the ideologically isolationist U.S.A. became involved in the conflict as the result of its hostile reaction to the threat of increased Japanese power across the Pacific and increased German power across the Atlantic.

The U.S.A. and the U.S.S.R.

At the end of the second World War the U.S.A. and the U.S.S.R. were the two greatest world powers, and since the expansionist nature of Russian policy constituted a potential threat to American security the U.S.A. adopted a policy of keeping Russian expansion in check. Thus the dominant feature of international affairs in the post-war decade was a struggle for power between the U.S.A. and the U.S.S.R. Most Americans saw this as an ideological conflict between Liberty and Communism, for the contrast between the American and Russian solutions to the problems of the world had been made clear a generation earlier. In 1917 President Wilson had brought the U.S.A. into the European war promising to make the world safe for democracy and offering a new era of international relations based on co-operation through the League of Nations. In the same year the Bolsheviks seized power in Russia and offered the prospect of a world transformed by the revolution of the international working class.

When the U.S.A. and the U.S.S.R. became the dominant world powers in the years after the second World War nations tended to align themselves with one or the other. But neither the U.S.A. nor the U.S.S.R. was successful in producing the millennium. The Communist ideal looked suspiciously like Russian military domination, and many nations turned for protection to the U.S.A. But these included right-wing dictatorships. And the American ideal of making the world safe for democracy came to look like making the world safe for any nation which would support the U.S.A. against the U.S.S.R. In practice the Americans were defending not so much the principle of Liberty as the principle of non-intervention by Russia in the affairs of any country which she did not already dominate. Both the Americans and the Russians tried to pretend that the Cold War was an ideological struggle. But it was in reality a continuation of the age-old struggle for power between one group of humans and another. The main difference in this case was that the groups involved were very big.

By 1971 both the U.S.A. and the U.S.S.R. were faced at home with a demand for a higher standard of living and with some measure of disenchantment with the merits of the societies they so proudly proclaimed. Abroad they had both met difficulties in persuading peoples of different historical and cultural traditions of the benefits of what they had to offer. And both had used force to impose their will.

The decline of Europe

It is of some significance that the two great powers of the post-war years were not European. Both the U.S.A. and the U.S.S.R. had grown out of Europe. But they had also outgrown Europe. And Europe was no longer the dominant area of the world. Indeed, after the second World War, Europe had virtually been partitioned, like Korea, into a Russian and an American sphere of influence. And countries such as China and India were growing in importance while Europe's importance declined.

It was possible that a united Western Europe might one day be a world power comparable with the U.S.A. and the U.S.S.R., and the Treaty of Rome (p. 433) pointed in the direction of political unity. But the chances of Eastern and Western Europe coming together seemed negligible. And even the nations of Western Europe were still not naturally cohesive. They had no common language, no commonly accepted ideology or economic system, and no common political system. In 1971 parliamentary democracy was the predominant political system, but Spain, Portugal, and Greece were ruled by dictators. Capitalism was the predominant economic system, but many West Europeans, and even some governments, were trying to replace Capitalism with Socialism. Christianity was the predominant religion, but the proportion of Christians in the population was probably no higher than in the East European Communist countries.

The Christian tradition

But for all its diversity Western Europe did share a common history, and also a tradition of what may be called Western Christian civilisation. Christian beliefs and attitudes permeated the political thought and policies of many people who rejected the Christian faith. It is not difficult to see the influence of centuries of Christian tradition in the great French Revolutionary slogan 'Liberté, Egalité, Fraternité'. And even Marxism, which explicitly denied Christianity, stood very clearly in the prophetic Judaeo-Christian tradition.

The power of the ideas which burst out of Europe, and the energy generated in Europe, transformed the world in the nineteenth century and during the first half of the twentieth century. Europe herself declined in importance. But the history of any part of the world in the second half of the twentieth century was inevitably in very large measure a continuation of the European history which had gone before it.

Problems and perspectives

By 1955, when the American system of alliances was completed and the Warsaw Pact (p. 400) was formed, most of the world was grouped into one or other of the two great power blocs, and mankind was faced with the problem of whether or not full-scale conflict could be avoided. The destructive power possessed by both the U.S.A. and the U.S.S.R. made this a question of whether or not the world was going to destroy itself. Both had the prospect of a greatly improved standard of living if peace could be maintained, and both faced the probability of utter destruction in the event of war.

The issue of whether or not the world was going to destroy itself in nuclear war became even more crucial a few years later, with the development of nuclear ballistic missiles. But that is not to say that viewed from the perspective of the future it would always seem the most important issue which then faced the world. That which is feared but does not happen seldom seems as important later as it did at the time. And by the 1970s a number of other world problems had become objects of wide concern. The break-up of the European colonial empires had laid bare the twin problems of poverty and colour. Three-quarters of the world's resources were in the hands of a quarter of the world's population, and that quarter was the population of the predominantly white Capitalist and Communist countries. The poverty of black men in Africa was in striking contrast to the wealth of white men in the U.S.A., or England, or the U.S.S.R., and the relationship between white skins and affluence on the one hand and black skins and poverty on the other exacerbated racial tensions in the world. The former colonial peoples did not just want independence. They wanted equality, including equality of esteem, which would scarcely be possible so long as almost anyone with a dark skin was poorer than almost anyone with a pale skin. By 1971 it was possible to regard the problems of poverty and race as far more dangerous for the future of the world than the threat of nuclear warfare.

But it was also possible to regard other problems, such as over-population, or the pollution of the environment, as more critical. And it was impossible to tell at the time which of them would seem in another ten or a hundred years time to have been most important.

Past, present, and future

In the same way it is impossible looking back over the century from 1871 to 1971 to be sure which aspects of it will seem most significant in the future. One function of the historian is to discern what seemed important in the period about which he is writing. Another function is to discern what has significance for his own time. But he cannot predict the future. Eventually the rise and fall of Germany may seem insignificant in relation to the decline of Europe's importance in the world, and the rise and fall of Japan during the same period may similarly seem an insignificant interruption in centuries of Chinese predominance in the Far East. But none of this is certain: Europe may recover her importance; Japan may again become the predominant power in the Far East.

Depending on the time and place from which one views the years 1871–1971 they may appear primarily as a time when European imperialism stimulated the emergence of the Afro-Asian peoples, as a time when revolutionary Socialism began to transform the world, as a time of immense technological advance, or as a time when aggressive Nationalism began to give place to internationalism.

These viewpoints are not mutually exclusive. On the contrary, they are closely interrelated, but it is impossible to know which theme will seem the most significant in a hundred years time and which will seem relatively unimportant. For the future depends on the complicated interrelationship of unforeseeable events, and in particular it depends on both practical and moral decisions made by men. Men have to make decisions not only about what the most convenient course of action is in a particular situation but also about, for example, how far the end justifies the means, how far the present should be sacrificed for the future, how far the interests of the individual should be subordinated to the interests of society, and how far any one society should sacrifice its interests to the wider interests of all mankind.

In making such decisions a man's motives are likely to be mixed. He may be torn between self-interest and altruism. He may find it difficult to choose between what seems ideal and what seem possible. It is not the function of the historian to make moral judgments on the way such decisions were made in the past, but rather to seek some understanding of how they came to be made. And even in this task he cannot expect complete success, for human motives are deeply hidden as well as inextricably mixed. But the historian can at least grope towards an understanding of the past, and he can show something of the way in which history is moulded by human decisions. Men themselves are moulded by circumstances, but by their reactions to circumstances men make history.

Appendix A
Heads of State, 1871-1971

1   THE UNITED STATES OF AMERICA

(Italics indicate the succession of a Vice-President on the death of a President)

	Republicans	Democrats
1869–1873	Ulysses S. Grant	
1873–1877	Ulysses S. Grant	
1877–1881	Rutherford B. Hayes	
1881	James A. Garfield	
1881–1885	*Chester A. Arthur*	
1885–1889		Grover Cleveland
1889–1893	Benjamin Harrison	
1893–1897		Grover Cleveland
1897–1901	William McKinley	
1901	William McKinley	
1901–1905	*Theodore Roosevelt*	
1905–1909	Theodore Roosevelt	
1909–1913	William H. Taft	
1913–1917		Woodrow Wilson
1917–1921		Woodrow Wilson
1921–1923	Warren G. Harding	
1923–1925	*Calvin Coolidge*	
1925–1929	Calvin Coolidge	
1929–1933	Herbert Hoover	
1933–1937		Franklin D. Roosevelt
1937–1941		Franklin D. Roosevelt
1941–1945		Franklin D. Roosevelt
1945		Franklin D. Roosevelt
1945–1949		*Harry S. Truman*
1949–1953		Harry S. Truman
1953–1957	Dwight D. Eisenhower	
1957–1961	Dwight D. Eisenhower	
1961–1963		John F. Kennedy
1963–1965		*Lyndon B. Johnson*
1965–1969		Lyndon B. Johnson
1969–1973	Richard M. Nixon	
1973–	Richard M. Nixon	

447

2 CHINA

The Chinese Empire, –1912.

The last Emperor of the Manchu dynasty, Pu-yi, was forced to abdicate in 1912 (p. 319).

The Chinese Republic, 1912–1949.

The first President of the republic was Dr. Sun Yat-sen. The last was Chiang Kai-shek. But neither of them was technically President for more than a few years, and neither ever effectively controlled the whole of China. Numerous generals who controlled part of the country held office as President for short periods.

The Chinese People's Republic, 1949–

The first Chairman of the Chinese People's Republic, from 1949 to 1959, was Mao Tse-tung. But his importance was as Chairman of the Communist Party — a position he retained when he resigned from the chairmanship of the republic in 1959. Subsequent chairmen of the republic were relatively insignificant.

3 RUSSIA

(from 1923 known as the Union of Soviet Socialist Republics)

Tsar:

1855–1881	Alexander II
1881–1894	Alexander III (son of Alexander II)
1894–1917	Nicholas II (son of Alexander III)

Head of the provisional government:

March–July, 1917	Prince Georgi Evgenievich Lvov
July–November, 1917	Alexander Kerensky

After the Bolshevik Revolution the head of state was the Chairman of the Central Executive Committee, and from 1936 Chairman of the Presidium of the Supreme Soviet. Each of these posts was primarily ceremonial. It was unusual for the holder to wield political power.

4 AUSTRIA-HUNGARY

Emperor:

1848–1916	Franz Josef
1916–1918	Karl (grand-nephew of Franz Josef)

5 GERMANY

German Emperor:

1871–1888	Wilhelm I
1888	Friedrich III (son of Wilhelm I)
1888–1918	Wilhelm II (son of Friedrich III)

Head of the provisional government:

November, 1918–August, 1919   Friedrich Ebert

President:

1919–1925	Friedrich Ebert
1925–1932	Field-Marshal Paul von Hindenburg
1932–1934	Field-Marshal Paul von Hindenburg
1934–1945	Adolf Hitler

6 GREAT BRITAIN

Monarch:

1837–1901	Victoria
1901–1910	Edward VII (son of Victoria)
1910–1936	George V (son of Edward VII)
1936	Edward VIII (son of George V)
1936–1952	George VI (brother of Edward VIII)
1952–	Elizabeth II (daughter of George VI)

7 JAPAN

Emperor:

	Reign name	*Personal name*
1867–1912	Meiji	Mutsuhito
1912–1926	Taisho	Yoshihito (son of Mutsuhito)
1926–	Showa	Hirohito (son of Yoshihito)

8 FRANCE

The Presidents of the Third Republic (1871–1940) were generally men of the utmost insignificance. The only one mentioned in the text is Raymond Poincaré (President 1913–1920), who was more important when he was Prime Minister (1911–13, 1922–24, and 1926–29).

The head of state during the period of German occupation from 1940 to 1944 was Marshal Pétain.

The head of the provisional government from September 1944 until his resignation in January 1946 was General Charles de Gaulle. The two other heads of the provisional government before the constitution of the Fourth Republic was accepted at the end of 1946, and the two Presidents of the Fourth Republic before its collapse and de Gaulle's return in 1958, were just as insignificant as the Presidents of the Third Republic.

Presidents of the Fifth Republic:

1959–1965	General Charles de Gaulle
1965–1969	General Charles de Gaulle
1969–	M. Georges Pompidou

9   ITALY

King:

1861–1878	Vittorio Emanuele II
1878–1900	Umberto I (son of Vittorio Emanuele II)
1900–1946	Vittorio Emanuele III (son of Umberto I)
May–June, 1946	Umberto II (son of Vittorio Emanuele III)

The Presidents of the Italian Republic, which was proclaimed in June 1946, were as insignificant as the Presidents of the third and fourth French republics.

10   POPES

1846–1878	Pius IX	(Giovanni Mastai-Ferretti)
1878–1903	Leo XIII	(Joachim Pecci)
1903–1914	Pius X	(Giuseppe Sarto)
1914–1922	Benedict XV	(Giacomo della Chiesa)
1922–1939	Pius XI	(Achille Ratti)
1939–1958	Pius XII	(Eugenio Pacelli)
1958–1963	John XXIII	(Angelo Roncalli)
1963–	Paul VI	(Giovanni Batista Montini)

11   THE UNITED NATIONS ORGANIZATION

Secretary-General:

1946–1953	Trygve Lie	(Norwegian)
1953–1961	Dag Hammarskjöld	(Swedish)
1961–1971	U Thant	(Burmese)
1977–	Kurt Waldheim	(Austrian)

Appendix B
British Governments, 1868–1971

(* *indicates that the government took office just after a general election*)

Date of formation	Name of the Prime Minister	Nature of the government	Approx. duration
February 1868	Benjamin Disraeli	Conservative	10 months
December 1868	*W. E. Gladstone	Liberal	5 years
February 1874	*Benjamin Disraeli	Conservative	6 years
April 1880	*W. E. Gladstone	Liberal	5 years
June 1885	Marquess of Salisbury	Conservative	8 months
February 1886	W. E. Gladstone	Liberal	6 months
August 1886	*Marquess of Salisbury	Conservative	6 years
August 1892	*W. E. Gladstone	Liberal	1½ years
March 1894	Earl of Rosebery	Liberal	1¼ years
June 1895	Marquess of Salisbury	Unionist	7 years
July 1902	A. J. Balfour	Unionist	2½ years
December 1905	Sir Henry Campbell-Bannerman	Liberal	2¼ years
April 1908	H. H. Asquith	Liberal	7 years
May 1915	H. H. Asquith	Coalition	1½ years
December 1916	David Lloyd George	Coalition	6 years
October 1922	A. Bonar Law	Conservative	6 months
May 1923	Stanley Baldwin	Conservative	8 months
January 1924	*J. Ramsay MacDonald	Labour	10 months
November 1924	*Stanley Baldwin	Conservative	4½ years
June 1929	*J. Ramsay MacDonald	Labour	2 years
August 1931	J. Ramsay MacDonald	National	4 years
June 1935	Stanley Baldwin	National	2 years
May 1937	Neville Chamberlain	National	3 years
May 1940	Winston Churchill	Coalition	5 years
May 1945	Winston Churchill	Conservative	2 months
July 1945	*Clement Attlee	Labour	6½ years
October 1951	*Winston Churchill	Conservative	3½ years
April 1955	Sir Anthony Eden	Conservative	1¾ years
January 1957	Harold Macmillan	Conservative	6¾ years
October 1963	Sir Alec Douglas-Home	Conservative	1 year
October 1964	*Harold Wilson	Labour	5¾ years
June 1970	*Edward Heath	Conservative	

Appendix C
British General Election Results, 1868-1970

The party whose leaders formed the government after a general election is indicated in bold type.

Those who generally supported the government while not joining it are indicated in italics.

The election results for 1868 are so inaccurate as to be quite misleading. This is because many members, and in particular members sitting for Irish constituencies, were not committed to either the Liberal or Conservative side. But the Liberal government usually had a majority of about 112. After the formation of the Irish Nationalist Party in 1870 it gradually becomes easier to assess how many members adhered to any party. But even up to the second World War party allegiance was less clearly defined than is usually assumed.

Date	Government and support		Opposition		Total membership of the House of Commons
December 1868	**Liberal**	385	Conservative	273	658
February 1874	**Conservative**	353	Liberal Irish Nationalist	246 59	658
April 1880	**Liberal**	365	Conservative Irish Nationalist	228 65	658
December 1885	**Conservative** *Irish Nationalist*	249 86	Liberal	335	670
July 1886	**Conservative** *Liberal Unionist*	316 78	Liberal Irish Nationalist	191 85	670
July 1892	**Liberal** *Irish Nationalist* *Labour*	273 81 1	Conservative Liberal Unionist	269 46	670
July 1895	**Conservative** **Liberal Unionist**	340 71	Liberal Irish Nationalist	177 82	670
October 1900	**Conservative** **Liberal Unionist**	334 68	Liberal Irish Nationalist Labour	184 82 2	670
January 1906	**Liberal** *Irish Nationalist* *Labour*	377 83 53	Conservative Liberal Unionist	132 25	670
January 1910	**Liberal** *Irish Nationalist* *Labour*	275 82 40	Conservative and Unionist	} 273	670
December 1910	**Liberal** *Irish Nationalist* *Labour*	272 84 42	Conservative and Unionist	} 272	670

Date	Government and support		Opposition		Total membership of the House of Commons
December 1918	**Cons. and Unionist**	338	Labour	63	
	Cons. and Unionist	48	Liberal (Asquith)	28	
	Liberal (Lloyd George)	136	Irish Nationalist	7	
			Independent	3	
	Labour	11	*Sinn Fein	73	707
November 1922	**Conservative**	347	Labour	142	
			Liberal (Asquith)	59	
			Liberal (Lloyd George)	59	
			Irish Nationalist	3	
			Communist	1	
			Independent	4	615
December 1923	**Labour**	191	Conservative	258	
	Liberal	159	Irish Nationalist	3	
			Independent	4	615
October 1924	**Conservative**	419	Labour	151	
			Liberal	40	
			Irish Nationalist	1	
			Communist	1	
			Independent	3	615
May 1929	**Labour**	288	Conservative	260	
	Liberal	59	Irish Nationalist	3	
			Independent	5	615
October 1931	**Conservative**	471	Labour	47	
	Liberal (Simon)	35	I.L.P.	5	
	Liberal (Samuel)	33	Liberal (Lloyd George)	4	
	Labour	13	Irish Nationalist	2	
	Independent	3	Independent	2	615
November 1935	**Conservative**	387	Labour	154	
	Liberal	33	Liberal (Sinclair)	17	
	Labour	8	Liberal (Lloyd George)	4	
	Independent	3	I.L.P.	4	
			Irish Nationalist	2	
			Communist	1	
			Independent	2	615
July 1945	**Labour**	393	Conservative	213	
	I.L.P.	3	Liberal	12	
	Commonwealth	1	Irish Nationalist	2	
			Communist	2	
			Independent	14	640
February 1950	**Labour**	315	Conservative	299	
			Liberal	9	
			Irish Nationalist	2	625
October 1951	**Conservative**	321	Labour	295	
			Liberal	6	
			Irish Nationalist	2	
			Independent	1	625
May 1955	**Conservative**	345	Labour	277	
			Liberal	6	
			Irish Nationalist	2	630
October 1959	**Conservative**	366	Labour	258	
			Liberal	6	630
October 1964	**Labour**	317	Conservative	304	
			Liberal	9	630
March 1966	**Labour**	364	Conservative	253	
			Liberal	12	
			N. Irish Independent	1	630
June 1970	**Conservative**	330	Labour	289	
			Liberal	6	
			Scottish Nationalists	1	
			N. Irish Independents	4	630

Never took their seats.

Feb. 1974   Labour   301

Oct 1974   Labour   320

Index of persons

b. = born; *d.* = died; *m.* = married.

Abdülhamid II, *b.* 1842; sultan of Turkey, 1876; deposed and exiled, 1909; *d.* 1918; 307.

Abdullah, *b.* 1882; ruler of Transjordan, 1921; king of Jordan, 1946; assassinated, 1951; 345.

Abrams, General Creighton Williams; commander of U.S. forces in Vietnam, 1968–   ; 343.

Adenauer, Dr. Konrad (1876–1967), lord mayor of Cologne, 1917–33; dismissed by the Nazis, 1933; imprisoned, 1934 and 1944; founded Christian Democratic Union, 1945; chancellor of German Federal Republic, 1949–63; 415, 432.

Alexander VI, *b.* Rodrigo Borgia, 1431; elected pope 1492; *d.* 1503; 302.

Alexander II, *b.* 1818; tsar of Russia, 1855; assassinated, 1881; 7, 20, 448.

Alexander III, *b.* 1845; tsar of Russia, 1881; *d.* 1894; 20, 448.

Alexander, General Sir Harold (1891–1969); field marshal, 1944; viscount, 1946; earl, 1952; minister of defence, 1952–54; 354.

Alexander, *b.* 1888; king of Jugoslavia, 1921; assassinated by Croat gunmen in the pay of Mussolini, 1934; 121.

Alexei, only son of tsar Nicholas II; *b.* 1904; shot by the Bolsheviks, 1918; 24.

Alfonso XIII, *b.* 1886; king of Spain from birth; deposed, 1931; *d.* in exile, 1941; 151.

Alfred, *b.* 849; king of the West Saxons, 871; *d.* 899; 359.

Amery, Leopold (1873–1955), cabinet minister, 1924–29 and 1940–45; 215.

Arthur, Chester A. (1830–86), 447.

Asquith, Herbert Henry (1858–1928), earl, 1925; 40, 44, 58–61, 66–7, 72–3, 171–3, 188–91, 198, 206, 451.

Atatürk, Mustafa Kemal (approx. 1880–1938); 308–11.

Attlee, Clement (1883–1967), earl, 1955; 175, 185, 200, 296, 365–6, 369, 372, 387, 390, 397, 412, 451.

Auchinleck, General Sir Claude, *b.* 1884; field marshal, 1946; 354, 359.

Ayub Khan, *b.* 1907; c.-in-c. Pakistan army, 1951–66; president of Pakistan, 1958–69; 335–38.

Baden, Prince Max von (1867–1929), 15.

Baldwin, Stanley (1867–1947), earl, 1937; 42, 69, 173–5, 178, 188, 195, 201–3, 206–14, 252–4, 282, 357, 451.

Balewa, Sir Abubakar Tafawa, *b.* 1912; prime minister of Nigeria, 1957; knighted when Nigeria became independent, 1960; assassinated, 1966; 274.

Balfour, Arthur James (1848–1930), earl, 1922; 40, 45–53, 56, 65, 71–2, 172, 191, 206–10, 346, 363, 451.

Balfour, Gerald (1853–1945), 2nd earl of Balfour, 1930; 50.

Baring, Sir Evelyn (1841–1917), lord Cromer, 1892; 47.

Barnes, George (1859–1940), 198–9.

Batista y Zaldivar, Fulgencia, *b.* 1901; fled from Cuba to the Dominican Republic, 1959; 304–6.

Baudouin I, *b.* 1930; king of the Belgians, 1951; 163.

Beaverbrook, Lord, *b.* William Maxwell Aitken in Canada, 1879; lord Beaverbrook, 1917; member of Lloyd George's government, 1918; bought *Daily Express*, 1919; member of Churchill's government, 1940–45; *d.* 1964; 162.

Beeching, Dr. Richard, *b.* 1913; chairman of British Railway, 1963–65; life peer, 1965; 386.

Béla Kun, see Kun, Béla.

Benedict XV, *b.* 1854; elected pope, 1914; *d.* 1922; 450.

Beria, Lavrenti Pavlovich, *b.* 1899; executed, 1953; 417–19.

Bernadotte, Count Folke, *b.* 1895; assassinated, 1948; 407.

Bethmann-Hollweg, Theobald von (1856–1921), 14, 15, 107–8.

Bevan, Aneurin (1897–1960), 185, 366, 371–2, 387.

General index